THE BEST OF
JAZZ

To Steve and Jenny Voce,
under whose hospitable roof the best of jazz
constantly resounds.

THE BEST OF JAZZ

Humphrey Lyttelton

 Robson Books

Published in Great Britain in 1998 by Robson Books
Ltd, Bolsover House, 5-6 Clipstone Street, London
W1P 8LE

Grateful acknowledgement is made to Jazz Music
Books for the photographs which appear in this book.

British Library Cataloguing in Publication Data
A catalogue record for this title is available from the
British Library

ISBN 1 86105 187 5

Printed in Finland by W.S.O.Y.

Contents

Introduction

THIS PAPERBACK brings together two books which were published in hardback in 1978 and 1984 respectively. In the introduction to the first, *Basin Street to Harlem*, I wrote 'This book sprang from a single thought'. Having outlined that thought, I spent the rest of the introduction explaining how the very act of expanding it on paper produced a different sort of book altogether.

Let me explain again, briefly. By 1977 my weekly BBC radio programme *The Best of Jazz* had been running for ten years. The letters it attracted often complained of the difficulties confronting anyone wanting to build a sensible record collection. Vinyl LPs were then coming on to the market in great profusion, many of them bearing the names of those musicians who, according to the pundits, were 'musts' in any self-respecting library of records. But there was no guarantee to the layman that an album compilation would offer essential, important or even worthwhile examples of an artist's work.

The thought that occurred to me then was that those of us who cultivated an interest in jazz during the pre-micro-groove era of 'seventy-eights' were particularly lucky, though we were far from thinking it at the time. In Britain in the late thirties, the monthly ration of jazz consisted of a handful of 'singles' in a Jazz and Swing corner of the big-label catalogues. How we grumbled when, out of perhaps eight or nine offerings, only two or three conformed to our then rather strict notions of The Real Thing! But the upshot was that, taking new and reissued recordings into account, the products of the very greatest sessions in jazz to that date – those by King Oliver's Creole Jazz Band, Jelly Roll Morton's Red Hot Peppers, Louis Armstrong's Hot Five as well as the more contemporary Muggsy Spanier Ragtimers and Bob Crosby Bobcats – were fed to us two titles at a time, like some life-giving saline drip. In the musical papers and magazines, each coupling would be reviewed and dissected in about the same space and detail as would later be devoted to a complete LP or CD album.

Pursuing the thought, I originally intended to produce a handbook, listing with brief reviews all those 78 rpm recordings which I and my contemporaries came to regard as 'classics'. Having worked on it for a month or two, I found that I had researched and written five thousand words on the Original Dixieland Jazz Band's 'Tiger Rag' alone. It became apparent that my original master plan had come seriously unstuck. My research was assembling a great mass of material – historical details, anecdotes, quotations, musical analogies and so on – which drew me far deeper into the subject than I originally intended. Many of the facts and the thoughts which they prompted were new to me. I pursued them enthusiastically as much for my own interest and enjoyment as for the information of potential readers, ending up with a limited number of essays covering little more the first decade of jazz recording, from 1917 to 1930.

The book still focused on classic seventy-eights of the period discussed under the chapter headings of the key musicians who made them. But having reduced the area of subject matter to be tackled, I had more space to take a look at the background of the recordings and the artists who made them, and probe into the jazz life of the cities in which those artists worked. It could be said that these jigsaw fragments interlocked into an informal, rough-and-ready history of jazz in the twenties. But it did not pretend to be a comprehensive history. As I confessed at the time, some important musicians were mentioned only fleetingly, and some not at all. But a line had to be drawn somewhere.

Things were more complicated still when I came to write a second collection of essays – and I stress again that this is what both books turned out to be. 'Enter the Giants' seemed at the outset to be a simple matter of extending the same mixture of selection, analysis and historical background into the period from 1931 onwards. But once again I had underestimated the task. The title of the book reflected a change in the way in which, during the second jazz decade, the music was perceived and discussed. Towering figures did emerge during the twenties, but there was a tendency for them to be discussed in the context of equally important ensembles – the Creole Jazz Band, the Hot Fives, the Red Hot Peppers and so on. In the Thirties, with a huge growth in published and widely disseminated jazz criticism, it became more usual for jazz to be observed in terms of the great individuals, sooner or later to be dubbed 'jazz giants'.

Since most of these giants first made their mark in the twenties, the lines between the decades are blurred, one further reason for not regarding these books as a comprehensive history. It will be seen, all the more easily since the two volumes are brought together here, that in the second I made frequent back references to the first. And indeed, since the notion of a master plan incorporating a third book still lingered in my mind, there were promises that some glaring omissions would be rectified at a future date. Rash promises, as it has turned out!

As it is, the two books now reappear unrevised. I repeat my indebtedness at the time to the books by Leonard Feather and John Chilton which were constantly at my elbow. Other books which helped me are listed in the bibliography. The discographies are combined, to give the reader help in tracking down the recordings which I selected, a task much easier today when reissues and compilations abound. As I wrote at the time, my aim was to initiate, rather than impose, critical thoughts, to which end kites were flown, hobby horses were mounted and bees were given untrammelled access to bonnets without too much concern for any controversy they might arouse. That aim still holds good, as does the hope that newcomers to jazz as well as old hands will find both enjoyment and food for thought herein. *Bon appetit!*

Basin Street
to Harlem

The Original Dixieland Jazz Band

THE ORIGINAL DIXIELAND JAZZ BAND—hereinafter referred to frequently as the ODJB—has turned out to be something of a scapegoat in modern jazz history. Its fall from grace was all the bumpier because jazz historians of the Thirties, working on the slender evidence then available from gramophone recordings, raised the Dixielanders so far above their station. It is true that the ODJB was the first jazz band, recognisable as such in hindsight, to make records. I am not going to dwell here on inconclusive speculation about the origins of the word 'jazz'. But I will include, for its entertainment value, the information given by the band's biographer, H. O. Brunn, that the original spelling, 'jass', was changed by the band 'because children, as well as a few impish adults, could not resist the temptation to obliterate the letter "j" from their posters'.

It is also true that the ODJB was the first New Orleans Band to cause a worldwide sensation—it overwhelmed New York in 1917, London in 1919—and start a craze that was to be the hallmark of a decade. The similarity between what would nowadays be dubbed 'ODJB-mania' and contemporary pop crazes emerges from H. O. Brunn's sentence, 'Night-clubbers flocked to Reisenweber's to be frightened by this compact little group of rebel musicians.'

Like most crazes, the Dixieland Band quite quickly found itself out of fashion. For one thing, the Eastern musicians, as those working in and around New York were known, prided themselves on a certain musical sophistication and had a tendency (which died hard in the course of the Twenties) to look down on the rough and rugged music coming from what they termed 'the West', which meant anything from the direction of New Orleans or Chicago. In 1924, Paul Whiteman, the massive leader of an increasingly massive band whose self-appointed mission it became to make an honest woman out of the wayward hussy from the New Orleans whore-houses, started an important concert at New York's Aeolian Hall with a note-for-note take-off of the ODJB's first hit record of seven years earlier, the 'Livery Stable Blues'. The stunt nearly backfired, as Whiteman himself recalled later: 'When they laughed and seemed pleased with "Livery Stable Blues", the crude jazz of the past, I had for a moment the panicky feeling that they hadn't realised the attempt at burlesque —that they were ignorantly applauding the thing on its merits.' Dignity was restored, however, when the elephantine Whiteman band went on to waddle through 'symphonic jazz' versions of 'Yes, We Have No Bananas' and the like, hitting the heights of respectability with an inaugural performance of George Gershwin's 'Rhapsody in Blue' with the composer at the piano.

History revels in irony. Whiteman's often over-dressed arrangements of popular songs have long been buried among the ephemeral bric-à-brac of the Twenties, surfacing only briefly during spasmodic epidemics of nostalgia. 'Rhapsody in Blue' survives where it belonged in the first place, in the lower reaches of the orchestral concert repertoire. The only element in that 1924 concert that had vitality and durability in the jazz context was 'Livery Stable Blues', Dixieland versions of which still delight audiences today.

For another truth about the ODJB is that it had a profound influence on the young white musicians who bought its records avidly when they first came out. The Wolverine Orchestra, with twenty-one-year-old Bix Beiderbecke on cornet, shared none of Paul Whiteman's condescension in 1924. Making their recording debut in that year, they took many of the tunes from the ODJB's repertoire. The same tunes reappeared in 1928 when a more mature and established Bix made informal jazz with his 'Gang'. In the late Thirties, as a revival of interest in New Orleans jazz began to stir, out came the sturdy old war-horses again, in bright new harness furnished by Bob Crosby's Bobcats and Muggsy Spanier's Ragtime Band. A decade later, every capital city in the western world resounded to 'Fidgety Feet', 'At the Jazz Band Ball' and 'Tiger Rag' as jazz spread worldwide. And it is a lucky purveyor of traditional jazz whose public appearances, even now, are not dogged by stentorian cries of 'Play "Tiger Rag"!', almost fifty years after the tune made its muffled debut on record.

And here is irony again. The very movement back to the New Orleans roots of jazz which rejuvenated the ODJB's tunes in the Forties and Fifties led to the devaluation of the band's historic reputation. In magazine articles, recorded interviews and auto-biographies, veteran jazzmen queued up to give their recollections of what really happened in those early days. And the notion that the ODJB gave birth to jazz single-handed in the studios of the Victor Talking Machine Company in 1917 suffered lethal damage.

What emerged from many ear-witness accounts was that the Original Dixieland Jazz Band was by no means original. It must always be borne in mind that black musicians who watched white contemporaries collect the richest rewards from the music to which they themselves had made the major contribution (and it is a recurring theme throughout jazz and pop music history) are not exactly disinterested witnesses. On the other hand, jazz musicians are usually men of staunch independence, not much given to conspiracy. And the verdicts of, for example, Sidney Bechet, Bunk Johnson and Jelly Roll Morton on the ODJB match each other so closely that they must either be true or the result of close collusion.

In his autobiography, *Treat It Gentle*, Bechet said: 'All these Dixielanders could do was play what they learned from us . . . take a number like "Livery Stable Blues", we'd played that before they could remember; it was something we knew about a long way back.'

Jelly Roll Morton told his story for the archives of the American Library of Congress in 1938, shortly before his death. In it, he calmly appropriated the ODJB's most famous composition. 'The "Tiger Rag", for an instance, I happened to transform from an old quadrille, which was originally in many different tempos. First there was an introduction, "Everybody get your partners!", and the people would be rushing around the hall getting their partners. After a five-minute lapse of time, the next strain would be the waltz strain . . . then another strain that comes right beside the waltz strain in mazooka time . . . we had two other strains in two-four time. Then I transformed these strains into the "Tiger Rag", which I also named, from the way I made the tiger roar with my elbow. A person said once, "That sounds like a tiger hollering." I said to myself, "That's the name." All this happened back in the early days before the Dixieland Band was ever heard of.'

We must not be elbowed into disbelief by the alacrity with which Jelly Roll laid claim to any common musical property which happened to be lying about. Bunk Johnson was not a close associate of Morton's at any time, and his account of the origins of 'Tiger Rag' puts the authorship elsewhere. Otherwise, it is remarkably close. 'This quadrille, the first eight bars of what the bands are usin' today, "Tiger Rag", that's King Bolden's first eight bars we would play to get your partner ready for the quadrille. And, in later years, t'was taken and turned into "Tiger Rag" by musicians that could read. Had Bolden knew music, probably Bolden would have made "Tiger Rag". So we had "Tiger Rag" before we had any Dixieland Jazz Band.'

Where does this leave the poor old ODJB? Well, it certainly showed up as glib all those jazz 'histories' which assumed that the ODJB was first in the field simply because it beat all comers to the recording studios. On the other hand, there was at first some over-reaction when the comments I have quoted, and others like them, came out. The New Orleans Revival—the great exploration to the source of jazz—was under way, working up a fine head of romantic steam about those black pioneers of the music whose work, and indeed existence, had up till then been ignored. It was one thing to say that the Original Dixieland Jazz Band was not particularly original. It was quite another to claim, as some commentators did, that it was simply a white 'ragtime' band whose style, greatly inferior to that of contemporary black bands, can only grudgingly be accepted as 'a form of jazz'. If the New Orleans Revival discovered anything, it was that in New Orleans in the first two decades of the century, embryonic forms of jazz were played by both black and white bands, the common denominator being a position near the bottom of the social and cultural scale.

It took all sorts to make the musical world from which jazz emanated. A good picture of this world can be found in Alan Lomax's book, *Mister Jelly Roll*, which was written around Jelly Roll Morton's Library of Congress reminiscences. From the testimony of one old-timer after another it emerges that not every black musician was a jazzman born and bred. Some were 'hot' players, some were 'sweet', some were readers, some were 'fakers' who played by ear, some produced refined music, others specialised in the rugged blues. One of them, the clarinettist Alphonse Picou, whose claim to jazz immortality lies in the traditional—and unimprovised—clarinet solo in the piece 'High Society', had some difficulty in mastering the improvised style of the rough street bands. He was himself a Creole and had received formal musical training. 'One day Bouboul Augustat, the trombone player, heard me practising in the house and ask me if I want to come to one of his rehearsals. I say, "You got any music?" "You don't need no music," say Bouboul. "That's impossible. What I'm gonna play? Just sit there and hold my instrument?" "Don't worry. You'll know." That's what Bouboul tell *me*. So I went. They were playing some good jazz that I didn't know nothing about . . .'

In this context, the Original Dixieland Jazz Band was undoubtedly a 'hot' band—the trombonist Eddie 'Daddy' Edwards was the only member who could read music, and it was he who would play over new numbers from the published sheet music until the other members of the band had learned the tune. Jelly Roll Morton alleged that the band's style came very close to that of the Original Creole Band, led by cornetist Freddy Keppard. It was this band, in fact, which preceded the ODJB on the grand tour out of New Orleans, causing quite a sensation in its own right in both Chicago and New York two years before the ODJB arrived. Indeed, had Freddie Keppard not declined a recording offer (to prevent other bands stealing his stuff, says the popular legend, but it's just as likely that he didn't take the new 'toy' seriously enough to bother), we might have been spared this lengthy explanation of the ODJB's true role!

Jelly Roll's comparison between the Original Creole Orchestra and the ODJB is corroborated to a large extent if we listen to the only comparable record which Keppard ever made. 'Stockyard Strut', by Freddie Keppard's Jazz Cardinals, was recorded in 1926, nine years after the first ODJB recordings. Keppard, like Nick LaRocca, was born in 1889, and both men lead their bands in a similar rhythmic style which derives directly from the even eight-notes-to-a-bar rhythm of ragtime. To get an idea of this basic rhythm, just repeat 'one-and-two-and-three-and-four-and' evenly and rapidly, and the result will be the machine-gun *rat-tat-tat-tat* which characterised this 'old' style. In the chapters that follow there will be frequent references to the gradual change from this 'ragtime' rhythmic feeling to the looser four-four rhythm that was introduced in the playing of Sidney Bechet and Louis Armstrong in the early Twenties and which became the basis of jazz phrasing throughout the changing fashions of the next five decades. So let us leave it now and go on to look in greater detail at the ODJB's most famous showpiece, 'Tiger Rag'.

In referring to other recordings in this collection which were recorded in more than one version within a short period of time— King Oliver's 'Dippermouth Blues', for instance, or Duke Ellington's 'Black and Tan Fantasy'—I have been careful to specify one particular version as being, by general consensus or in my own view, the best one. The ODJB's 'Tiger Rag' does not demand any such scrupulous selection, except perhaps on the grounds of audibility. For the several versions which they recorded between 1917 and 1919 are alike in practically every detail. This is one reason for the band's rejection in later years by critics who set greater store by improvisation than did many of the musicians themselves. The theory that all the great players since the birth of jazz lived by the dictum that 'we never play a tune the same way twice' doesn't stand up to even cursory examination, and would certainly disqualify more than one of the great recorded classics cited in this book.

But to work out a solo in advance or repeat a 'head' or memorised arrangement is not quite the same thing as making each performance a replica of the last in every detail. Even a written score is open to a wide range of interpretation. The funny thing is

that 'Tiger Rag' has, over the years, been played in more
ways than, perhaps, any theme in jazz history, and yet the five
men who claimed authorship of it through their leader, Nick La
Rocca, could only keep trotting it out with the jerky predictability
of a player-piano.

However it came about, the old New Orleans quadrille, with
its waltz and 'mazooka' sections, is transformed here beyond
recognition. The first B flat 'get your partners' theme is, according
to Jelly Roll Morton's analysis, quite close to the original, though
taken here at breakneck speed. With its bugle-call theme over
the two basic chords of B flat and F, it has something of a rallying
cry about it. One interesting aspect of the New Orleans style is
high-lighted in this opening section, and it is the tendency among
trumpet-players to phrase across the beat rather than squarely
on it. It was the primary function of the trumpet to 'carry the
melody' in the ensemble, and with all but he improvising to their
heart's content, rhythmic variation was about all that was left to
him. (When I first joined a Dixieland band in 1947, I was denied
even this freedom—the band had a second cornet-player who
intimated the rhythmic accents with a very sharp elbow in my
ribs!) A more serious explanation for this rhythmic flexibility
no doubt lies in the African origins of jazz. In his book, *Early
Jazz*, the musicologist and musician Gunther Schuller goes into
this at great length. It will suffice me to say that one finds the same
freedom in the melody line of a *genuine* Cuban rhumba or Trini-
dadian calypso. It has to be added that Nick LaRocca does not
do it in a very subtle way—the anticipation of the last phrase in
the opening four bars is so exaggerated each time that it simply
sounds as if he has raced ahead of his colleagues.

We are told that the original quadrille, once the partners
were settled, began with a stately waltz in the key of F major.
In 'Tiger Rag', this theme is relegated to what is called a 'bridge
passage', a short relief from the opening B flat theme which
modulates back into it by way of an F dominant seventh. In this
short section we have a foretaste of the clarinet 'breaks' by
Larry Shields which were such a feature of the ODJB's version.
It has become the accepted belief that 'breaks'—that is, short
passages in which one instrument is left on his own to fill a gap—

were the first manifestation of the jazz solo and that, as musicians became more proficient, they were able to spread these ad lib excursions over a full chorus and beyond. It's a theory that might look all right on the blackboard of a lecture-room, but does not appeal to me. I have never understood why a musician capable of improvising his way through countless ensemble choruses should be suddenly struck dumb when left on his own. Recordings made in more recent years of primitive New Orleans bands offer at least one more down-to-earth explanation—that the jazz solo originated in human frailty, one instrumentalist being left on his own when the others got tired. It is no coincidence that most of the solo work in early New Orleans jazz was undertaken by the clarinettist, whose instrument is less punishing to lip and lungs than either trumpet or trombone.

If we look to Larry Shields for a demonstration of wit and inventiveness in his solo 'breaks', we are surely doomed to disappointment. Sidney Bechet claimed that Shields once took lessons from him. Certainly no one can deny that the clarinet in 'Tiger Rag' is accomplished—the pitching is accurate, the tone, so far as one can discern it, is rounded, and the piercing high notes that must have caused seizures in the control room reveal a sound technique. But there, alas, it ends. In the E flat section that follows a reprise of the opening theme, the clarinet 'breaks' could hardly be more dull or obvious. If we listen for what the New York jazz critic Whitney Balliett has called 'the sound of surprise', we listen in vain. These interpolations by Larry Shields are clearly worked out in advance and most of them sound uncomfortably like 'novelty' effects. We know from what other musicians have said that New Orleans music had its jokey side—'New Orleans hokum' is what they called it, and it incorporated all sorts of extracurricular noises such as horse-whinnying from the clarinet and macabre laughter from the muted cornet. In the best jazz, the jokes were offset by the music's more profound qualities. In 'Tiger Rag', they just sound like jokes, and repetitive jokes at that. Later chapters will dwell on the sobering influence of the blues on jazz through the ages. We shall try and define, as we go, the 'blues feeling' which gives passionate and melancholy undertones to the jauntiest of tempos. The blues did not feature in the musical heritage of the white musicians in New Orleans, although some of them—for example, the cornetist Wingy Manone and the clarinettist Leon Rappolo—were sensitive enough to receive the message. Despite the fact that several of their early titles incorporated the word 'Blues', the ODJB were almost totally devoid of blues feeling. In later years, exponents of 'Dixieland' jazz, delving with furrowed brow into the profundities of the blues, have often been riled by having their music labelled 'jolly jazz', 'good time music' and even 'funny hat stuff' by their antagonists. If any bands deserve such dismissal, it is those who interpret not only the music, but the spirit of the ODJB too closely.

The final section of 'Tiger Rag' moves into A flat and consists of four variations on a theme. First comes a free-for-all ensemble on what can be described as a standard harmonic sequence over thirty-two bars. Mr H. O. Brunn has it that the sequence was deliberately borrowed from the trio section of the 'National Emblem March'—which, incidentally, Louis Armstrong always used to quote in his many versions of the tune. Be that as it may, it is the part of 'Tiger Rag' which, over the years, has given the greatest scope for improvisation, consisting of long expanses of unchanging harmony over which new melody can be imposed. The ODJB start with a demonstration of the classic Dixieland ensemble style—the cornet stabbing out a leading melody in the instrument's middle register, the clarinet weaving a descant or counter-melody all around it, and the trombone playing a bass-part that conforms quite closely to the role of the trombones in a military band. (The New Orleans trombonist made freer use of the instrument's slide mechanism than was accepted in 'straight' bands, and the name 'tailgate', given to their sliding and slithering style derived from the need for the trombonist, on wagon-borne outings in the cause of advertising, to give himself elbow-room by sitting on the back end, or tailgate, of the wagon.)

After this spirited ensemble comes a chorus which, with justice, was dropped from most subsequent versions of the tune. According again to H. O. Brunn, this unsyncopated, thudding passage in straightforward 2/4 time began as a humorous imitation of the alto part in a German band. Jelly Roll Morton, on the other hand, includes it as one of the original quadrille themes. Either way, it proved to be invincibly jazz-proof material and vanished.

What remained instead as 'Tiger Rag's' primary theme was the ODJB's third variation, similar to the preceding one but this time syncopated across the beat and with the trombone making the 'tiger roar' which Jelly Roll Morton claimed to be the inspiration of his left elbow. Somewhere along the way, novelty versions of 'Tiger Rag' appended the words 'Hold that tiger!' to this theme, but this is irrelevant to the jazz history of the tune. After this straightforward variation, the band returns to a final ensemble —and offers a carbon copy of variation No. 1, though with another of Shields's standard 'breaks' substituted.

Here lies, surely, the greatest flaw in the ODJB's general performance. Sidney Bechet put his finger on it when he said, apropos the band's sudden decline in the early Twenties, 'Those Dixielanders had played all that they had learned and the thing just dropped.' We can argue ad infinitum about whether the ODJB did or did not play 'jazz', whether they should be disqualified for memorising rather than improvising their music, whether they stole all of their stuff, or only some of it, from other more talented musicians, and whether they were in any way representative of New Orleans music. What is fact, and not conjecture, is that, once they had made their initial impact on the world, 'the thing just dropped'. Of the musicians in the band who survived into the Twenties and Thirties, not one went on after their fall from grace to expand and develop his talent in other surroundings. When, in 1936, they came together again to enjoy a brief Indian summer, it was as if they had been pickled in soundproof aspic during the intervening years. 'Tiger Rag' had lost some of the explosive vigour that 'frightened' the avid customers at Reisenweber's Restaurant nineteen years earlier, and had gained nothing.

Why, you might have begun to ask yourself several pages ago, have I chosen a band so low in creativity and inspiration to launch this anthology of jazz on record? There are several reasons. For all the band's shortcomings and eventual eclipse, it did, by virtue of those first recordings, have a pervasive in-

fluence on the jazz which came afterwards. However suspect their
'compositions' may have been, they certainly collated, in neatly
packaged form, many of the themes and musical ideas which were
bandied about in New Orleans before gramophone recording
came on the scene, and a striking number of the resulting pieces
found a permanent place in the jazz repertoire. Again, by the very
meticulousness with which they worked out and memorised their
style they provided a sort of blue-print of how the line-up of
trumpet-clarinet-trombone could be organised, and from that
blueprint a lot of more creative jazz in what has come to be called
the Dixieland style has stemmed. In considering their place in the
early scheme of things we have revealed quite a lot about the
beginnings of jazz in New Orleans, albeit negatively. And we
have ensured that any reader unlucky enough to find himself at
a jazz concert sitting next to one of the stentorian 'Play "Tiger
Rag"!' brotherhood will at least know what the fool is on about.

James P. Johnson

THE MEMBERS OF THE ODJB were still scattered among diverse bands in New Orleans and Louis Armstrong, at twelve years old, was yet to experience his first cornet lessons in a New Orleans Waifs' Home when James Price Johnson, known to jazz historians and discographers as James P. Johnson and to friends such as Duke Ellington as 'just James', undertook his first professional engagement at Coney Island in 1912. For some time before that he had worked sporadically as a piano-player or 'tickler', a young recruit in a huge army of such entertainers who had developed ragtime along the Eastern seaboard of the United States from Washington to New York.

And yet we do not speak of James P. Johnson as a ragtime pianist but claim him as one of the founding fathers of a jazz piano style which, with benefit of hindsight, we can trace through Fats Waller, Duke Ellington, Count Basie and Thelonius Monk to the present day, when it still manifests itself in all sorts of surprising places. When is a ragtime player not a ragtime player? What was the ingredient, or recipe of ingredients, that converted music clearly descended from the rags of Scott Joplin and his contemporaries into jazz?

The answer has been given in many thousands of weighty words on the subject. Even in the somewhat cursory explanation for which I have time and space here, it is necessary to set the scene. In an interview with Tom Davin (quoted at length in a book called *Jazz Panorama*, edited by Martin Williams), James himself does this succinctly. 'In the years before World War I, there was a piano in almost every home. The piano makers had a slogan: "What Is Home Without A Piano?" It was like having a radio or TV today. Phonographs were feeble and scratchy. Most people who had pianos couldn't play them, so a piano-player was important socially. There were so many of them visiting and socialising that some people would have their pianos going day and night all week long.' In his autobiography *Music Is My Mistress*, Duke Ellington brings to life graphically a ritual which still persisted when he arrived in Harlem in the early Twenties: 'Other times, Lippy [a piano-playing colleague] and the bunch would get together, get James cornered, find a taxi, of maybe walk over to someone's house, and ring the bell. This would be 3 or 4 am. People stuck their heads out of windows, ready to throw a pot (flowerpot, maybe).

"Who's that down there?" they'd growl.

"This is Lippy," the answer would be. "I got James with me." Those doors flew open. Lights switched on. Cupboards emptied, and everybody took a little taste. Then it was me, or maybe Fats [Waller] who sat down to warm up the piano. After that, James took over. Then you got the real invention—magic, sheer magic.'

As this story implies, these piano-ticklers with an entrée into every home at whatever hour were a very special breed. Happily, their lives and times are well chronicled. Accounts such as James P. Johnson's interview or the autobiography (*Music On My Mind*) which Willie 'The Lion' Smith wrote, contain a litany of formidable and colourful names—Walter 'One Leg Shadow' Gould, 'No Legs' Cagey, Jack the Bear, Stephen 'The Beetle' Henderson, Richard 'Abba Labba' McLean, not to mention more conventionally named but no less talented players such as Luckey Roberts, Willie Gant and Eubie Blake. Rather like tennis-players in the modern international circuits, these men were, at their various times, friends *and* keen competitors, vying for the most important and lucrative jobs. Since they worked as both soloists and accompanists, the technical demands on them were high. As Willie The Lion said: 'One of the many important things you had to be able to do when playing piano in the saloons back in those days was to accompany the singer-entertainers. Some of the larger concert saloons and cabarets had as many as ten male and female singers around the joint regularly. You had to be a fast thinker to handle them. First, it was necessary to be able to play in any key, run the chords as we call it, because the entertainers worked in them all. A singer might change into any key on the piano at any time. They themselves didn't know half the time what key they worked in.' In the early days, when James P. Johnson began to earn his living at the keyboard, the required repertoire had little of the easy-going, pick-and-choose informality of later jazz. 'I played "That Barbershop Chord" . . . "Lazy Moon" . . . Berlin's "Alexander's Ragtime Band". Some rags, too, my own and others. . . . Joplin's "Maple Leaf Rag" (everybody knew that by then) . . . his "Sunflower Rag" . . . "Maori", by Will Tyers . . . "The Peculiar Rag" and "The Dream" by Jack the Bear. Then there were "instrumentals"; piano arrangements of medleys of Herbert and Friml, popular novelties and music-hall hits—many by Negro composers . . . Blues had not come into popularity then, they weren't known or sung by New York entertainers.'

It was the stress of competition from their peers, rather than any highbrow demands from employers or audiences in the often down-at-heel places where they played, that encouraged the ticklers to include several classical selections in their repertoires. James P. Johnson did rag variations on the William Tell Overture, the Peer Gynt Suite and even the relatively modern Prelude in C Sharp Minor by Rachmaninoff. The 'Polonaise Militaire' and the 'Miserere' from *Il Trovatore* (also favoured in a far distant context by Jelly Roll Morton) were two of The Lion's specialities. Anyone who can trace and hear some of the recordings made in this genre by the little-known and highly underrated pianist, Don Lambert, will know that such performances were no mere 'jazzing' of the classics in frivolous vein, but adhered conscientiously to the originals in all but their rhythmic aspect, and demanded a concert-pianist's technique and discipline.

If technical prowess was all-important to these piano 'professors', 'attitude' was not far behind. This was their word for what we would now call 'showmanship', the difference being that showmanship is dictated by the employers and enterpreneurs of the entertainment world while attitude was self-imposed. As

Willie The Lion recalled, 'It didn't take me long to notice that everybody in the entertainment business made it a point to dress sharp. It behooved us to look spectacular, not only to get and hold a gal, but to make a good impression all round.' The impression one gets from the reminiscences of The Lion and James P. is that they resembled in their way the flamboyant actor-managers of the old London theatre. 'Every move we made was studied, practiced, and developed just like it was a complicated piano piece,' said James P. Johnson. A 'real smart tickler' would wear a military or coachman's overcoat, double-breasted, full-skirted and in blue, grey or brown according to taste. This would be complemented by a distinguished hat—a Homburg with three buttons on the side or, with The Lion, a Derby worn at a jaunty angle. Having made a theatrical entrance, the great man would refrain from removing hat and coat until he reached the piano, when he would go into a highly stylized and personal routine. If he was carrying a gold- or silver-headed cane he would lay it with great deliberation on the music rack of the piano. The prized overcoat would be removed and laid along the top of the piano, folded to show off the expensive lining. Then, according to James P., 'you took off your hat before the audience. Each tickler had his own gesture for removing his hat with a little flourish; that was part of his attitude, too. You took out your silk handkerchief, shook it and dusted off the piano stool.' It's not hard to see where Duke Ellington's predilection for the flamboyant gesture was nurtured!

We have arrived, then, at a picture of a breed—a guild, almost —of highly-skilled and intensely professional freelance piano-players who, largely through their own pride in their calling, had mastered an enormous repertoire of works, both popular and classical. We still have to explain how the men of James P. Johnson's generation, who reached their prime in the post-war period when the recording-machine was on hand to commit their work to posterity, made the transition from a style based on ragtime to one that was recognisably jazz. The answer is embedded in black American history from the Civil War onwards. Anyone wishing to go into the question in some depth would do well to get hold of a book called *They All Played Ragtime* by Rudi Blesh and Harriet Janis, which tells the detailed story. I shall be content here to lay a trail of clues.

A comment by Willie 'The Lion' Smith starts us off on the scent. 'This story wouldn't be complete if I didn't mention one of the most fabulous piano men of them all—Walter (One Leg Shadow) Gould. He came from Philadelphia and he must have been over a hundred years old when he died in Albany, New York, in 1959. The Shadow was one of the first to start sprucing up the quadrilles and schottisches that were popular around the time of the Civil War.' The Shadow was in fact a modest eighty-four when he died, but he lived long enough to take us back even further via the researches of Blesh and Janis. 'Old Man Sam Moore was ragging the quadrilles and schottisches before I was born.' Here, then were the seeds of the tradition in which young Jimmy Johnson would interpret the popular songs of the day— the 'sprucing up' of European-style dances in a manner derived, but distinct, from the composed and formal ragtime.

But there was another, equally important influence. In *They All Played Ragtime*, James is quoted, apropos his early childhood, as saying: 'The Northern towns had a hold-over of the old Southern customs. I'd wake up as a child and hear an old-fashioned ring-shout going on downstairs. Somebody would be playing a guitar or jew's-harp or maybe a mandolin, and the dancing went to "The Spider and the Bed-Bug Had a Good Time" or "Susie, Susie". They danced around in a shuffle and then they would shove a man or woman out into the centre and clap hands. This would go on all night and I would fall asleep sitting at the top of the stairs.'

The ring-shout was a hold-over from African culture, and it has survived in the United States in both religious and secular form. In the black Baptist churches, the shout (which, having little to do with shouting, is better understood by substituting the word 'dance') has long been used to generate a state of trance-like ecstasy. Forming a circle, the congregation shuffle round with the feet barely leaving the floor and the body jerking rhythmically in a hitching motion, chanting a chorus response to the words of a spiritual uttered by the preacher or one or more lead singers. We shall come across this 'call and response' formula in subsequent chapters, but suffice it to say now that, clearly, the rhythm generated by the ring-shout was hypnotically insistent and compelling. Willie The Lion put it this way: 'Shouts are stride piano— when James P. and Fats and I would get a romp-down shout going, that was playing rocky, just like the Baptist people sing. You don't just play a chord to that—you got to move it and the piano-players do the same thing in the churches, and there's ragtime in the preaching.'

One further element must now be brought in to complete the picture. The metamorphosis of Harlem from a small Dutch village far from the centre of New York to a city suburb and then a densely populated black ghetto was a gradual one. Black communities, which had previously clustered together in many different districts, began at the start of the century to converge upon the northern part of Manhattan Island. First stop was the area of San Juan Hill, on the northern boundary of the tenderloin district known as Hell's Kitchen. The black section of Hell's Kitchen was known as The Jungles, and it was here that the 'ticklers', of the generation that preceded James P. Johnson, found their most regular haunts.

In the early years of the century the population of the San Juan Hill area was boosted by an influx of migrants from the South, some from Alabama, some from the part of South Carolina and Georgia that centred around Charleston. From the testimony of both The Lion and James P., it is clear that these latter people, known as Gullahs or Geechies, had a powerful effect on the style of the local piano men. First Willie The Lion: 'Our soft, slow, four-o'clock-in-the-morning music got to those folks from the South. They danced cakewalks and cotillions; by this time we had learned to play the natural twelve-bar blues that evolved from the spirituals . . . the Gullahs would start out early in the evening dancing two-steps, waltzes, schottisches; but as the night wore on and the liquor began to work, they would start improvising their own steps and that was when they wanted us to get-in-the-alley, real lowdown . . . it was from the improvised steps that the Charleston dance originated.' James P. Johnson, one of whose Charleston-style compositions, 'The Charleston' itself, launched a worldwide dance craze a decade later, has similar recollections.

'The dances they did at the Jungles Casino were wild and comical —the more pose and the more breaks the better. These Charleston people and the other Southerners had just come to New York. They were country people and they felt homesick. When they got tired of two-steps and schottisches . . . they'd yell: "Let's go back home!" . . . "Let's do a set!" . . . or, "Now, put us in the alley!" . . . Breakdown music was the best for such sets, the more solid and groovy the better. They'd dance, hollerin' and screaming until they were cooked.'

It was the big influx of these country people which drove the long-established black population of New York (many of whom were well acclimatised to the habits of the North and more interested in emulating the white people than in preserving their Southern culture) further north into the then quieter avenues of Harlem. We shall see, in the later chapter on Fletcher Henderson's Orchestra, how their staid and sober tastes kept the jazz influence at bay until a further massive migration from the South in World War I and afterwards broke down the defences. Their relevance here is that they provide us with a situation which is uncannily close to the manner in which jazz was procreated in New Orleans at about the same time. There a once free and proud half-caste or Creole population with a strong European cultural tradition lost status and privileges through the general emancipation of Negroes after the Civil War, and, in their decline, met the descendants of freed slaves on the way up. The fusion of the European traditions of the Creoles and the African traditions of country people who came in from the plantations resulted in jazz.

If we substitute for the Southern creoles the long-established Negro families around New York, some of whose forebears had come there as Negro freemen before the Civil War, we find a parallel situation. Consider the influences which came to bear upon young Jimmy Johnson once he started as a professional piano-player. The ethos of the black New York establishment in which he was brought up was modelled on that of 'respectable' white society, from whom a knowledge of, and respect for, the European popular classics derived. The musicians of his immediate experience were not concert pianists but friends of his older brothers: 'They were the real ticklers—cabaret and sporting house players. They were my heroes and led what I felt was a glamorous life—welcome everywhere because of their talent.' From these men he learnt the Eastern style of ragtime, less formal and rhythmically more 'spruced up' than the parent style that had emanated from Missouri in the Mid-West. As with jazz itself, much of the rhythmic impetus of this Eastern ragtime derived from the African dance, probably more varied than the single term 'ring-shout' implies, which survived in the black Baptist church ritual and spilled over from there into Negro social life. As Willie The Lion said, when playing for 'shouts', you had to move it. The Gullahs or Geechies who had come up from the South put further demands on the piano-tickler. When they shouted 'Let's go back home' they wanted lowdown music, tinged with the blues, to match their improvised steps until such time as they or the piano-player dropped.

It would be surprising if a musician whose formative years were assailed by such diverse influences emerged at the other end as a mere backroom piano-tickler. In the course of a long career, which ended in his death in 1955, James P. Johnson wrote several symphonic works, a one-act opera, some Broadway shows and popular songs (of which the best-known today are 'The Charleston', 'If I Could Be With You' and 'Old Fashioned Love'), at least one classic piano blues ('Snowy Morning Blues') and a large number of rags and 'shouts'. As an executant he also appears in the discographies as a prolific blues accompanist—of Bessie Smith among others—and as the pianist in all kinds of jazz bands. But out of all this widely-spread endeavour, it is as the Father of Harlem Stride Piano that James P. Johnson will always be best known.

I have no idea when, and by whom, the term Harlem Stride Piano was coined, nor do any of us know, other than by hearsay and deduction, whether Johnson was indeed the father of the style or simply one of several equally impressive uncles. Willie The Lion was vague on the subject. 'The writers who make up titles for the ways of playing music have called our piano style here on the eastern seaboard Harlem Stride Piano. I'm not very sure I know what they are talking about.' It has to be said that, having coined the term, the writers themselves have not been very sure what they were talking about. For example, in one of George Hoefer's 'interludes' in Willie The Lion's book, John S. Wilson of the *New York Times* is quoted as giving the popular definition of the term 'stride': 'The stride effect is produced by the left hand hitting a single note on the first and third beats and a chord of three or four notes on the second and fourth beats.' On the other hand, Whitney Balliett of the *New Yorker* brings the right hand into account, too. 'Stride piano is characterised chiefly by an oompah left hand (a two-beat seesaw, whose ends are a powerful mid-keyboard chord and a weaker single note played an octave or a tenth below) and by an arabesque of right-hand chords and arpeggios, fashioned in counter-rhythms.' Apart from seemingly reversing the bass figure to provide a pah-oom bass, Balliett's is an accurate picture of the sound of stride piano. But James P. Johnson himself adds to the confusion by saying that 'the characteristic strides were performed by the *right hand*' (my italics). It seems as if, like the word 'shout' in the same context, 'stride' simply exists to confuse the layman. Happily, the phonograph developed in time to give us audible examples of a style that came to be most widely known through the work of Johnson's protégé, Thomas 'Fats' Waller. Furthermore, the style has shown remarkable powers of survival. While ragtime long since died, to be resurrected only during bouts of nostalgia, stride piano goes on and on. It lay at the heart of the piano styles of Duke Ellington, Count Basie and Art Tatum, who carried it into the Swing music of the Thirties. In the Forties, as an off-shoot of the retrospective New Orleans Revival, it was itself revived in its basic form by a generation of young musicians which included Ralph Sutton, Don Ewell and Dick Wellstood in the States, Dill Jones, Dick Katz and Lennie Felix in Britain, Eddie Bernard and, for a while, Bernard Peiffer in France and Henri Chaix in Switzerland. Even when modern jazz seemed intent upon erasing all evidence of earlier jazz conventions, there was Thelonius Monk building his sparse and harmonically austere music on at least a scaffolding of earlier stride. Since then, any number of modern jazz performers —one thinks of Roger Kellaway, Jaki Byard, Nat Pierce, Britain's Mick Pyne and, of course, Oscar Peterson—have taken trouble to assimilate stride piano into their technical armoury.

I would guess that all of them have, in private, had a tilt at James P. Johnson's 'Carolina Shout'.

'My first encounter with James,' wrote Duke Ellington, 'was through the piano rolls, the QRS rolls. Percy Johnson, a drummer in Washington who told me about them, took me home with him, and played me "Carolina Shout". He said I ought to learn it. So how was I going to do it, I wanted to know. He showed me the way. We slowed the machine and then I could follow the keys going down. I learned it!' It was when James P. went to Washington in person a short time afterwards that Duke, by playing 'Carolina Shout' back at him at his own supporters' insistence, earned his respect and friendship. It was not the first, or the last time that 'Carolina Shout' was used as a piano test-piece. Indeed, so obligatory did it become for aspiring stride-men to master it that I was once able, for my own amusement, to compile from recordings a 'cutting contest' consisting of versions by Johnson himself, Willie The Lion, Don Lambert, Fats Waller, Dick Wellstood, Cliff Jackson and Henri Chaix. With unscrupulous use of a portable tape-recorder I could have captured a Duke Ellington version at one of his latter-day concerts when he was apt to trot it out, albeit a trifle creakily, as an encore.

James P. Johnson, playing the piano for dancing in a 'dancing school' called the Jungles Casino (it was easier for Negroes to get a licence for a dancing school than a dance-hall), liked to inject a little ring-shout fervour into the music. The 'pupils' danced two-steps, waltzes, schottisches and a new step called the 'Metropolitan Glide'. 'I played for these regulation dances, but instead of playing straight, I'd break into a rag in certain places. The older ones didn't care too much for this, but the younger ones would scream when I got good to them with a bit of rag in the dance music now and then ... The Charleston, which became a popular dance step on its own, was just a regulation cotillion step without a name ... My "Carolina Shout" was another type of ragtime arrangement of a set dance of this period.'

Even in its earliest version, recorded by James P. in 1921, 'Carolina Shout' reveals those qualities of swing and fervour which made the younger dancers at the Jungles Casino scream in ecstasy. We have all been well-enough acquainted, through Scott

Joplin's rag 'The Entertainer', with the stately rhythms of formal
Mid-Western ragtime to know at once that this is something quite
different. From the introduction onwards, the music rolls forwards
in an even four-beats to the bar. The bass rhythm is anything but
the limited oom-chah that some of the definitions suggest. In the
first chorus the single notes on the first and third beats, played in
broken octaves, often take over all four beats in the bar to define
a counter-melody to the romping right hand. In the second
chorus, a left-hand device that was a favourite of James P., if not
his actual creation, makes its appearance. It is just the kind of
invention, technically tricky and at the same time musically
dazzling, with which the combatant ticklers would challenge
their opponents. It involves a sporadic reversing of the oom-chah
bass figure—in parade-ground terms, a 'change step'—by playing,
for example, a passage that goes *oom-chah-oom-chah-chah-oom-
chah-chah*, weaving an intriguing rhythmic pattern out of the
strong and weak beats. The variation of the cascading opening
theme that the right hand plays over this shifting rhythm is the
very epitome of stride piano. Keeping to the broad shape of the
original, it skips and dodges and pirouettes on its way, managing
to impart a sense of exhilaration even through the dulling mists
of antiquated recording.

Had 'Carolina Shout' been a conventional rag in the Mid-
Western style, the tuneful opening strain would have given way to
another equally melodic, perhaps reverting to the first theme
before moving on to a trio section in a contrasting key. But it was
not for nothing that James P. Johnson called his piece a shout.
The prime function of the pianist in this circumstance is not to
weave elegant melodic variations but to 'move it' according to
Willie The Lion's prescription. So we shall see that, in each
successive variation from now on, Johnson feeds the dancers'
feet with a fresh rhythmic idea. Having moved on to a simpler
theme in the third chorus, he first of all establishes a rolling,
hand-to-hand rhythm which, appropriately enough, came to be
known in later jazz as a 'shuffle rhythm'. Then, on the same
harmonic theme, he moves into a 'call and response' pattern in
which we see the origins of the repeated figures or 'riffs' of
which later jazz, especially in the big band field, made effective

and sometimes excessive use. For two choruses running he matches riffs in the right hand with answering figures in the left, pushing ahead of the beat to build a powerful momentum. This leads to a change of theme with an equally simple harmonic pattern over which, with the pumping left hand working up a fierce head of steam in the stride manner, his repeated phrases in the right hand are strikingly similar to those used by Morton in the final section of his 'King Porter Stomp'. This is neither coincidence nor plagiarism. Johnson records in the Davin interview that Morton once told him that 'King Porter Stomp' was, like 'Carolina Shout', taken from cotillion music.

At this point the reader can be left to marvel at the way in which, reverting to the call and response pattern, James P. Johnson varies and breaks up the left hand figures while maintaining the momentum with his right hand. We get three variations here, and, in each successive one, more is made of the halting, almost hiccuping bass response, until in the final chorus it rumbles prodigiously. In the second variation, the right hand reminds us of much of Duke Ellington's piano-playing in this idiom. It has another of the stride men's favourite effects, an octave struck at the beginning of the phrase and given an added fillip by the addition of a grace note half a tone below the upper note. Try it on the piano by striking a G octave with thumb and little finger of the right hand and just flipping the F sharp with the fourth finger (counting the thumb as 1) a fraction of a second before the octave is sounded. It gives a very spritely attack.

One can see how 'Carolina Shout' came to be the test-piece for all aspiring pianists in Harlem in the early Twenties. It incorporates all the elements of a style which has to be assiduously learnt—even today there are technically advanced pianists who would hesitate to tackle it for the first time without some diligent practice. Every one of James P. Johnson's variations presents a challenge which cannot be shirked. And yet it is in the nature of the shout idiom that it should be capable of almost limitless extension to keep up with the dancers' enthusiasm. And so we find in some subsequent versions—Fats Waller's is a good example —that having got their fingers around James P. Johnson's variations, the players went on to add some of their own. There was nothing to hinder them. The smooth, four-beat foundation was in keeping with, not to say ahead of, the modern rhythms of the emerging jazz music (in this respect James P. offered a better example than Jelly Roll Morton, whose own extension of ragtime into jazz, influenced by the contrapuntal style of New Orleans band music, retained more of the somewhat sedate rhythms of ragtime). And Johnson's themes, being more rhythmic than melodic, gave the same scope for improvisation as the chord sequences of popular tunes to which jazz musicians have long been indebted.

In short, from its jaunty introduction to its witty and ingenious coda, 'Carolina Shout' is jazz. What's more, the style which it epitomises—Harlem Stride Piano—has proved to be one of the most durably satisfying of jazz forms. To hear Dick Wellstood, one of the younger ticklers, applying its principles to the harmonically-complex John Coltrane composition, 'Giant Steps', is to marvel at its infinite adaptability. At the Montreux Festival in 1977, Count Basie was playing a stalking, middle tempo blues with a trio when he suddenly doubled the tempo and went into some time-honoured stride piano in the manner of James P. Johnson. Both the huge audience and the all-star band onstage broke into spontaneous cries of delight, as if an old and valued friend had unexpectedly walked through the door.

King Oliver

BY 1923, JOE OLIVER was past his prime, according to ear-witnesses. Born in 1885 not far from New Orleans, he had been proclaimed 'King' in his early twenties when the connoisseurs who crowded round the stand at the Abadie Cabaret at the corner of Marais and Bienville Streets concluded that he had outplayed the reigning monarch, Freddie Keppard. (Joe must have been a slow starter, for Keppard was four years his junior.)

Joe Oliver was playing at the time in a quartet led by the pianist Richard M. Jones, and one of the more fanciful legends in jazz mythology tells of one night when, provoked by hearing other musicians speaking well of his rivals, he growled 'Beat it out in B flat, Jones!' and walked out on to the sidewalk to unleash a few challenging blues choruses in the direction of Pete Lala's Cabaret a block away, where Freddie Keppard held sway. The legend goes on predictably to record that the customers streamed out of Pete Lala's and followed Oliver like the children of Hamelin back into the Abadie. It doesn't tell us if Jones was still patiently beating it out in B flat.

Shortly after this incident, Keppard left New Orleans at the head of the Original Creole Orchestra, the band which preceded the Original Dixieland Jazz Band in blazing the trail for the new ragtime style from New Orleans northwards to Chicago and New York. The story of how the fruits of their pioneering tours were reaped by the ODJB has been told in a previous chapter. But Keppard and his men did have their own successes, and, in the years between 1911 and 1917, they opened up the market in

Chicago for New Orleans musicians.

Again, legend has put the gloss of romanticism on the move of jazz musicians away from New Orleans up to Chicago, suggesting a mass exodus following the closing down by City ordnance of the Storyville brothel and entertainment district of New Orleans which had been the nursery of jazz. (In the ludicrous but enjoyable film *New Orleans*, made in 1947, this exodus was actually depicted, with Louis Armstrong and his 'girl-friend', Billie Holiday, leading the throng!) No doubt the Storyville episode did act as a spur, but the migratory movement had been under way for some time. As Alan Lomax wrote in his study of Jelly Roll Morton, *Mister Jelly Roll*: 'The shift of New Orleans musicians to Chicago was only a grace-note in a big movement. The factories and mills of wartime America needed fresh supplies of labour and for the first time they were hiring great numbers of Negroes . . . in five years a half-a-million Negroes moved North, one tenth of them settling in Chicago's South Side.'

This was the new audience of which Keppard and his musicians spoke with enthusiasm whenever they communicated with friends and colleagues in New Orleans. And it was inevitable that the ambitious and skilled musicians would flock to where the action was. Joe Oliver travelled to Chicago in 1918 and soon formed a band of his own. In June 1922, King Oliver's Creole Jazz Band, returning from a stint on the West Coast, was offered a residency at a big dance-hall on Chicago's South Side called the Lincoln Gardens (formerly the Royal Gardens immortalised in the 'Royal Garden Blues', a favourite old jazz standard by the unrelated Spencer and Clarence Williams). The line-up of the band which opened at the Lincoln Gardens is as listed, with the exception of Louis Armstrong, who came North to join Oliver a few weeks after the opening.

Various guesses, informed and otherwise, have been made as to why Joe Oliver, established in Chicago with a band of conventional line-up and apparently set fair for a great popular success, sent off a telegram in the summer of 1922 to Louis in New Orleans inviting him, in the tones of a Royal Command, to join his band. In New Orleans, when Joe was unchallenged king, the teenaged Louis had become his protégé, to the extent that Louis, whose childhood had involved a dimly-remembered father and a procession of 'stepfathers', accepted Oliver in loco parentis and called him 'Papa Joe'.

Paternal feelings, then, may have come into Joe Oliver's reckoning, although the fierce and ruthless competitiveness that went into the making and breaking of trumpet 'Kings' in New Orleans can have left little room for sentiment. Louis had already shown prodigious talent back home and, after Oliver headed North, stepped effortlessly into his jobs, establishing a reputation which must have reached the older man's ears on his travels. There may, then, have been truth in Lil Hardin Armstrong's assertion years later that King Oliver said to her one night that Louis could play better than he could. 'He says, "But as long as I keep him with me he won't be able to get ahead of me. I'll still be the King!" '

Whatever the reason for Oliver's decision, it transformed his Creole Jazz Band into the most creative and influential jazz unit of its time, whose thirty-seven recordings, made between April and December 1923, provide us with the audible source of the jazz 'mainstream'.

'Dippermouth Blues' (the title was a stock nickname for anyone with a capacious mouth in general, and for Louis Armstrong in particular) was King Oliver's speciality, the piece for which his audiences on the Chicago South Side clamoured nightly. It is a loosely-constructed blues which the Creole Band recorded twice. In contrast to the ODJB's rigid treatment of 'Tiger Rag', Oliver's two versions of 'Dippermouth Blues', made for the Gennett and Okeh labels respectively, vary considerably in detail while conforming to the same overall pattern.

I have chosen for special consideration the earlier Gennett version, recorded at the band's first session. Even by pre-electric standards, Gennett seem to have been less well-equipped for sound than the Chicago studios of Okeh. Listeners brought up, not to say spoon-fed, on hi-fi might wonder why I do not go at once for the version that is considerably easier on the ear. I had to ask myself whether it was not pure sentiment and nostalgia that made me choose the recording which I first bought some time in the late Thirties on a Brunswick '78' and to which jazz-loving friends and I listened in a posture not unfamiliar to junior jazz buffs of any era—namely, kneeling round a gramophone on the floor with our ears pressed to the speaker, looking like ostriches in search of concealment.

Having given both versions the same sort of concentrated attention over and over again, I am convinced that, sound quality apart, the Gennett version is in most other respects the better performance. The tempo is gloriously relaxed, a consistently-neglected object lesson to the traditional jazz barrds (not excluding the otherwise exemplary Muggsy Spanier Ragtime Band of 1939) who have since spurred the tune into a brisk canter. Through the mists of time, it is just possible to hear the interplay between the two cornetists in the opening choruses. In the 1940s, several 'revivalists' bands—Lu Watters and his Yerba Buena Band in America, George Webb's Dixielanders in Britain, Claude Luter's early band in France—adopted the two-cornet line-up, allegedly under the influence of recordings by King Oliver's Band. But they all used the two instruments in a different and more obvious way, coupling them together closely in parallel harmony like musical Siamese twins. In effect, theirs were conventional three-part front-lines of cornet, clarinet and trombone with the cornet line 'thickened' by an additional harmony.

The Oliver band's two cornets were separated in the recording studio in more senses than one. Lil Hardin, the pianist with the band who, a year later, became the second Mrs Louis Armstrong recalled their first recording session in 1923. 'At the first session . . . the band was around the horn, and Louis was there, as he always was, right next to Joe . . . it didn't work out. Couldn't hear a note Joe was playing. So they moved Louis way over in the corner away from the band. Louis was standin' there looking so lonesome—he thought it was bad for him to have to be away from the band . . . and that's the only way we could get the balance—Louis was at least fifteen feet from us, on the whole session.'

Apart from this physical separation, the two cornets in Oliver's front-line operated, except in their co-ordinated breaks, as separate voices in the ensemble. Other more clearly-recorded performances reveal young Louis playing a free harmonic role in mid-ensemble, aided by the unconventional role which the trombonist Honoré Dutrey adopted. One hardy jazz legend attributes Dutrey's curious, wandering ensemble style to the fact, reported by his contemporary and fellow-trombonist Preston Jackson, that he learned new tunes from the cello parts. 'I used to sit behind Dutrey every night and watch him play cello parts because cello parts were easier to get than trombone parts.' Apart from the formally-trained Lil Hardin, Dutrey was probably the only member of Oliver's band who could read music at all in those days. It is hardly conceivable that any cello part ever found its way into the preparation of 'Dippermouth Blues', but it is true that Dutrey's carefully worked-out trombone part, almost identical in each version of the tune and sounding rather more like a euphonium than a cello, has little to do with the conventional 'tailgate' role of the New Orleans trombone. That role, as exemplified by 'Daddy' Edwards in the Original Dixieland Jazz Band and, in later recordings, by Kid Ory, derived from the military band trombone part with its insistence on the root harmonies in the ensemble. Dutrey's mournful moo-ing in the Oliver band was altogether less rigid and dictatorial, and it allowed Louis quite a lot of scope among the harmonies left unattended. Glimpses of the way in which he moved among those harmonies with great sensitivity show through the murk of 'Dippermouth's' opening chorus, although it is better heard on later recordings such as the Okeh versions of 'High Society', 'Riverside Blues' and the superb 'Mabel's Dream'.

Another reason for my preference for the earlier version of 'Dippermouth Blues' lies in the clarinet solo by Johnny Dodds, played against interrupted 'stop-chords' from the rest of the band. This solo, like that taken by Oliver himself later on, exemplifies the 'set pieces' which were an accepted feature of New Orleans jazz—the pinch of salt, if you like, with which the theory of constant improvisation must be taken. In this first recording, Dodds plays two twelve-bar choruses. The first descends from an upper keynote in a mournful phrase that is redolent of the blues, as was Dodds's playing at all times. The second starts an octave lower and wanders upwards to provide a nicely balanced contrast. This solo, which successive clarinettists have always reproduced in essence as being an indispensable part of 'Dipper-mouth Blues', was clearly worked out in advance. It is there again in the later recording, but this time Dodds omits the second, contrasting twelve-bar variation and simply repeats the first—a victory, perhaps, of improvisation over concentration!

After the Dodds solo it is Louis Armstrong who takes over the cornet lead in a reprise of the opening theme. Although differences in the cornet styles of Oliver and Armstrong are blurred by the recording requirement that the horns should be muted (and for the same reason the ebullient drumming of Baby Dodds was restricted to deathwatch beetle caperings on the woodblock and some indistinct thumping on a muffled tom-tom), it is still possible to hear two strongly contrasted styles. Oliver's sound on the 1923 recordings—and I am talking now of the straight-forward muted sound and not the 'wa-wa' effects—is vigorous, attacking and almost sternly commanding. His cornet lead bears down on the melody in an inexorable way which is often emotion-ally moving through its very lack of overt sentiment. Some of the notes end with a rapid 'shake' but otherwise the tone has very little vibrato to soften it.

Louis Armstrong's style is draped all over with ostensible Oliver influences. The downward leap of an octave on the dominant note (from G to lower G in the key of C) at the end of a chorus was one trade mark which he took over from Oliver for a while, and there were several other turns of phrase which he inherited. But his musical approach was fundamentally different. If, as a reflection of the human personality, music can be said to have masculine and feminine elements, then Louis' style, though palpably virile, showed from the start a generous endowment of the latter. There was a softness, an absence of aggression, manifested in the way the tone was ameliorated by a pulsating vibrato, the angular corners of the phrases were rounded off and the most functional cadences were imbued with a caressing warmth far beyond their purely structural requirements. In interviews throughout his life Louis always laid great stress on his over-riding belief that music should be 'pretty'. When in later years angry and aggressive modern sounds erupted all around him, he growled his disapproval of musicians who paid little heed to the melody and trumpet-players who sacrificed tone and accuracy for speed and a stratospheric range. 'We always used to make sure that our notes were *covered*!' he used to say, by which I take it to mean that they were hit bang in the middle and surrounded by a comfortable cushion of tone. Fortunately, Louis Armstrong's remarkably consistent and reliable musical taste almost invariably offset the 'prettiness' by a strong instinct for construction and a feeling for the noble phrase. As a result, what he intended as 'pretty' reached the listener as sheer beauty. In later examples of Louis Armstrong's work we shall appreciate this more clearly. The rather busy and angular theme of 'Dippermouth Blues' offers him little scope to do other than demonstrate the leaping energy which set all who heard him at that time back on their heels.

But this is, after all, Joe Oliver's record. There is a practical reason for his absence from the ensemble that follows Dodds. He is preparing himself for a dramatic entry into his own set piece. The inaccurate balance of this early recording has led us into the habit of referring to Joe Oliver's three declamatory muted choruses as a 'solo', but Armstrong, Dodds and Dutrey can be heard maintaining the ensemble behind, simply standing back a little to give him air. Another common assumption about these three choruses is that they were played with a 'plunger' mute. I do not agree. The plunger mute is in fact usually a combination of two mutes—a small metal or fibre mute that fits flush into the cornet or trumpet bell, and an ordinary rubber sink-cup or plunger that is waggled in front of the bell to make a 'wa-wa' sound.

It is difficult to find any eye-witness evidence that King Oliver used this sort of mute at the time of the Creole Band recordings. Fellow-trumpeter Mutt Carey, who emulated Oliver's muted style, recalled many years later: 'He was the greatest freak trumpet-player I ever knew. He did most of his playing with cups, glasses, buckets and mutes.' Trombonist Preston Jackson, who followed the Oliver band closely during the Chicago period, was more specific: 'He used a half-cocked mute, and how he could make it talk.' Buster Bailey, who joined Oliver's band for a short while at the end of 1923, adds a further clue: 'King Oliver was a great musician with a mute. With an ordinary tin mute, he could make the horn talk.' Most conclusive of all is Garvin Bushell's recollection, quoted more fully in the chapter on 'Black and Tan Fantasy', of Bubber Miley copying Oliver by 'using his hand over the tin mute that used to come with all cornets'.

One would have thought that, if Oliver used a plunger in the period under discussion, someone would have mentioned it. Danny Barker, the veteran New Orleans-born guitarist and jazz archivist, goes so far as to say, apropos a primitive New Orleans trumpeter called Chris Kelly, 'He was the first one I saw play with a plunger. Although New Orleans never featured it, he could play with it.' One last bit of circumstantial evidence—examination of all the available photographs of King Oliver's Creole Jazz Band shows no sign of a rubber plunger although in most of them the band's instruments and accoutrements are laid out like exhibits at the musicians' feet. On the other hand, several of the pictures show Oliver using the small tin mute (of the pear-shaped variety that is little used today) at half-cock—in other words, half out of the bell and cupped in the hand. I hesitate to be didactic about a sound which reaches us through such a fog of low-fidelity sound, but having experimented with a similar mute, I think it probable that this was the method that Joe Oliver used to make the peculiarly plaintive, softly articulated 'wa-wa' sound that distinguished his 'Dippermouth Blues' choruses.

Several highly distinguished trumpet-players—among them Louis Armstrong (several times), Rex Stewart, Harry James, Yank Lawson and Muggsy Spanier—have reproduced Oliver's variations, using a selection of mutes or, as in some of Armstrong's versions, no mute at all. They have made them jaunty, fervent, imperious, savage, blue. None has even tried to match the peculiar eerie, nocturnal sound that Oliver imparts to them in this first recording. But it is not only the sound which they have found elusive. Joe Oliver's phrasing, too, has a subtlety which which later versions miss. For a chorus which is alleged to have stirred the audiences at the Lincoln Gardens to a frenzy, it is remarkably restrained in its construction. The first chorus hangs on the blue-est of blue notes, not a straightforward minor third as most subsequent interpreters have assumed, but a marginally flattened third which establishes the eerily plaintive sound straight away. This is about the earliest manifestation we have on record of 'preaching' trumpet, a jazz device which derived immediately from black American sources—the call and response of preacher and congregation, of work-leader and railroad gang, of blues singer and accompanist—and beyond that, from African song forms. It is no mere flight of fancy to think of Joe Oliver here in the role of orator haranguing a responsive audience.

The three choruses build in declamatory fervour by the most economical means. The second chorus raises its point of focus from the 'blue' third to the fifth note, then the third chorus hammers away at the sixth note in rousing exhortation. All this fervour and exultation take place virtually within a range of six notes, building to a climax which leads quite naturally, if faintly absurdly, to the cry of 'Oh, play that thing!' that is as much a traditional ingredient of 'Dippermouth Blues' as the clarinet and trumpet sections. (Since the spread of the New Orleans Revival and the subsequent 'Trad boom' in the late Fifties, there is hardly an accent, from true-blue British to rugged Glaswegian, from guttural Teutonic to sing-song Oriental, which has not been heard mangling the ritualistic incantation 'Oh, play that thing!')

The final chorus of 'Dippermouth Blues' canters proudly up the home straight, the epitome of Joe Oliver's forthright and positive ensemble style. The form of it is exactly right, neither straining to improve on the climax already reached nor reverting tamely to the opening theme. Careful listening to some of the later 1923 recordings made for the Okeh company in which the two cornets are well-favoured will show Oliver's same unfailing sense of structure in what we know, from comparing alternative versions where they exist, to be largely improvisation. Two examples which I warmly recommend are the Okeh recording of 'Snake Rag' and the overwhelming, all-ensemble performance of 'I Ain't Gonna Tell Nobody' which under Oliver's inspired direction achieves the momentum of an express train. For years I was rather puzzled by Louis Armstrong's often reiterated statement that 'When you hear them four or five trumpets cut loose in the swing bands, what you're hearing is Joe Oliver.' Louis seldom if ever talked idle nonsense on the subject of music, but this did seem to carry homage to his former mentor too far. But having listened again extensively to the Creole Band recordings, I see the point. In the full fervour of the Swing Era, few arrangers, bent on building a stirring climax with full benefit of eight brass and five reeds, improved on King Oliver and his imperious cornet. Today, it is usual to take for granted this instinct for structure—'chorus-building', it is sometimes called—in good jazz ensembles or solos. It is nevertheless impressive to hear it so fully-fledged in Joe Oliver's playing in 1923, especially when fellow-musicians have testified that he was past his prime.

This alone would have justified me in referring earlier to King Oliver's Creole Jazz Band as the primary source of the jazz mainstream. But so many other things were going on within this musical power-house. In Joe Oliver and Johnny Dodds it had two men thoroughly steeped in the blues. We shall be dealing later in more detail with the relationship of the vocal tradition of the blues with instrumental jazz. It is enough to say here that what jazz writers have rather vaguely called 'blues feeling' is a quality, only partially explicable in purely musical terms, which throughout jazz history has given to the most superficially light-hearted performance a backbone of what I can only call *seriousness*. In analysing the jazz tone, Leonard Bernstein once used the admirable phrase 'the hint of pain', and I would extend that to the jazz performance as a whole. Certainly there was in the Oliver band's most jaunty pieces a power to stir the listener's emotions which the Original Dixieland Jazz Band lacked entirely.

Just as importantly, the King Oliver Creole Band in its rhythmic 'feel' stood on the threshold of a new era. In discussing the ODJB, I noted that it played in the two-beat rhythmic style of piano ragtime, an even 'One-and-two-and-three-and-four-and' rhythm which, in the conventional 4/4 notation in which jazz is usually set down, would appear as eight even quavers or eighth notes to the bar. This was the rhythm which, in recordings as late as 1926, Freddie Keppard's Band still used. It is the basic rhythm also of another black band from New Orleans, Kid Ory's Sunshine Orchestra, which recorded a few sides in 1922. Like me, the New Orleans bassist George 'Pops' Foster favoured an

onomatopoeic description when he spoke of Keppard playing
'what I called walkin' trumpet—it was Ta-ta-ta-ta-ta. They
were straight, clear notes.' This was not the only rhythm prevalent in the dance music of the early Twenties. Listen to early
recordings by bands as diverse as the Wolverine Orchestra and
Fletcher Henderson's Orchestra and you will hear what is in
effect a variation on the even-quaver two-beat rhythm. In his
contentious book *Shining Trumpets*—the most thorough exposition
of the 'purist' philosophy underlying the New Orleans revival—
the American writer Rudi Blesh brings in onomatopoeia to help
him give an accurate picture of this rhythm. Discussing the
Wolverine Orchestra, he says, 'Their rhythm is deformed by the
peculiar, jumpy pattern often called *vo-de-o-do*. Say *do-do-vo-de-o-
do* aloud and you have the pattern as it was derived . . .' Blesh's
book was a fine piece of special pleading for the supremacy of
Negro musical concepts, hence his use of the pejorative word
'deformed'. I don't know any evidence that suggests that this
rhythm (which would be set out in 4/4 time with the eight even
quavers of our 'ragtime' example altered to combinations of
dotted quavers and semi-quavers to give a jerky 'one a-two a-three
a-four' effect) derived 'probably from attempts of white singers of
popular tunes to imitate the rhythmic Negro scat song and the
stomp rhythms of the band'. It seems to have been the fashionable
rhythm of much American dance music, black or white, from the
war years onwards.

We shall see that both the 'ragtime' and the 'vo-de-o-do'
rhythms with their underlying two-beat feeling died hard during
the Twenties and were still perceptible in recordings made near
the end of the decade. Inside the Oliver band, a new rhythmic
concept was stirring. For one thing, the rhythm section, in which
the most consistent components were piano, banjo and drums,
did not lean heavily on the first and third beats of the bar but
gave all four beats an equal value. The banjoists in particular
eschewed the plinky-plonky upstrokes that the dance bands of the
period favoured, and instead kept a steady and uncluttered four-
in-a-bar going which was complemented by the 'walking' left-
hand arpeggios of pianist Lil Hardin.

Over this even, and utterly relaxed, rhythm a different and

more subtle rhythmic concept was beginning to emerge. And the
man who felt it most clearly and decisively was the young Louis
Armstrong. In this respect he was ahead of his colleagues—and
indeed, of practically every other musician currently appearing
on record. The performance which best summarises the difference
between the new and the old concepts of rhythm is the Okeh
version of 'Riverside Blues' by King Oliver's Band, recorded not
long after 'Dippermouth Blues'. This number incorporates solo
'breaks' by, in turn, Johnny Dodds, Honoré Dutrey and Louis.
Both Dodds and Dutrey phrase, as does Joe Oliver in the opening
chorus, in the 'one-and-two-and-three-and-four' ragtime manner,
albeit in a much less rigid way then either the ODJB or Keppard.
When they come to their short unaccompanied passages, this
phrasing lands them in what, to modern ears, sounds like rhythmic
trouble. The best way I can describe it without elaborate notation
is to say that they are like explorers trying to cross a yawning
chasm by means of a rope-ladder with its rungs too widely spaced.
They get to the other side of the 'break' somehow, but it is not
an elegant crossing. Now, throughout this whole recording we
hear Louis Armstrong's second cornet part predominating, and,
lo and behold, he is up to something quite different. There is
no 'one-and-two-and' feeling here, but a loping stride which
formal notation would describe as in 12/8 time and which can be
demonstrated phonetically as 'one-and-a-two-and-a-three-and-a-
four'. (In conventional 4/4 notation, this would be written as four
sets of quaver triplets to the bar.)

When Louis stalks out of the ensemble with measured tread to
play his own solo chorus at the end of the piece (I once described
this ascending phrase in a broadcast as 'the sound of genius
emerging' and was inordinately pleased with the notion), it is
clear that he has the answer to the rhythmic problem posed by
that high-wire break at the end, and, sure enough, he plays it
with enormous poise. To revert to the rope-ladder analogy, his
12/8 rhythmic conception gives him rungs which are more
frequent and more closely-spaced, and he can plant his feet more
accurately.

The notion of subdividing the four beats in a bar, not into
eight quavers as in 'ragtime' and 'vo-de-o-do', but into twelve

quavers arranged in triplets, was no doubt instinctive to Louis, who was no musical theoretician. It would be rash to say that Louis was the only musician around to feel his music in this way—when Sidney Bechet first appeared on record a few months later, he seemed to have a pretty good grasp of it, as did Bessie Smith in her earlier work. We *can* say that no musician whose work is available to us on early jazz recordings showed such assurance in what was clearly a new concept. It would, I think, have been this quality in his playing which led Tommy Brookins, a youthful eye-witness to the King Oliver Band in Chicago, to say: 'Opposite the young Louis, who was already prodigious, Oliver's style rapidly appeared to date a little and it was frequent to hear musicians talk among themselves of the "old style".'

I am no believer in the theory of immaculate conception with regard to musical innovations. All sorts of influences, some quite unknown to us, must have gone into the formation of Louis Armstrong's style. We should not discount Joe Oliver among them. He may have played in an old style, but within that style his rhythmic subtlety and sure-footedness were masterly, and there is nowhere any sign of the stiff-necked rigidity that later came to be called 'corny'. I have no doubt that the rhythmic assurance of Oliver within what, for convenience, I have called the 'ragtime' framework, was father to his protégé's discovery of a freer rhythmic form.

It was, as I have said, to be another decade or so before jazz improvisation became completely at home with the 'new' 12/8 feeling that stirred within the 1923 King Oliver Band. For this reason alone, it is permissible to think of the Oliver Band as the first jazz band in the modern sense. If you doubt this, go back to 'Dippermouth Blues' and consider, when comparing it with later Dixieland and Swing versions of the same tune, how little had to be altered to keep up with the times. Most of it was there in the first place.

Sidney Bechet

'WILD CAT BLUES', once an extreme rarity, serves here as an introduction to Sidney Bechet. Today's newcomer to jazz has the advantage over those patient and painstaking enthusiasts of the Thirties whose quota of jazz '78's, mostly geared to popular taste, emerged in monthly rations of two or three. We used to read occasionally about Bechet in *Melody Maker* or *Rhythm*, but the fact that he was usually called 'the legendary Sidney Bechet' speaks for itself. The first time the legend became a fact of any real substance was towards the end of the Thirties when recordings by his own New Orleans Feetwarmers began to join Benny Goodman, Tommy Dorsey and Fats Waller in the catalogues.

By this time, Bechet was approaching his fifties and already showed a fair crop of those prematurely white hairs which made him in journalistic eyes a Grand Old Man before his time. In the reference books, Bechet's date of birth is tentatively put forward as 1897, although some musicians who remember him in New Orleans suggest that it was earlier. In his autobiography (*Satchmo: My Life in New Orleans*), Louis Armstrong spoke of Bechet as a 'youngster from the Creole quarter', but went on to describe him in such reverential terms that it is not improbable that Bechet was a little more than three years older: 'The first time I heard Bechet play that clarinet he stood me on my ear . . . My [next] great thrill was when I played with Bechet to advertise a prize fight. I have forgotten who was fighting, but I will never forget that I played with the great Bechet.' Sidney Bechet recollected what must have been the same incident in his own memoirs, though the details are slightly different. 'I had a little job for an advertisement that I was doing twice a week for a picture theatre . . . so I hired Louis to come with me on this advertising and, you know, it was wonderful . . . That was the first time I ever heard Louis play cornet.' But elsewhere, Bechet recalls that, when he was working with Bunk Johnson in the Eagle Orchestra, he was urged by Bunk to 'go hear a little quartet, how they sing and harmonize'. This was the juvenile quartet with which Louis earned a few nickels on the streets before he ever took up cornet. He cannot have been more than twelve years old then. 'I went many a time to hear this quartet sing,' Bechet goes on, 'and I got to like Louis a whole lot, he was damn' nice. I was a little older than him. At that time he sort of looked up to me, me playing in bands and being with the big men.' If we believe Bechet when he says 'I was about seventeen when I first started playing with the Eagle Orchestra', then he was five years older than Louis.

What is more interesting than speculation about dates is the insight which these recollections provide into the hierarchical nature of the New Orleans jazz fraternity. Both men were well advanced into middle age when they produced their memoirs, and yet, as if through total recall, Bechet assumes a note of condescension, Louis one of boyish hero-worship, in their memories of each other. This is all the more strange in the light of what happened later. In 1925, Louis and Bechet met in the recording studios in New York. Louis was then with Fletcher Henderson's Orchestra, Bechet was moving through a succession of jobs which included a short stint with Duke Ellington's new band. The records which the two young men from New Orleans made together under the direction of Clarence Williams survived into the Thirties as much sought-after collector's items. It was inevitable that, when each of them had attained a certain eminence, a move would be made to reunite them. It happened in 1940, the occasion being an album devoted to New Orleans music. Louis Armstrong was at this time rather more famous than Bechet and this, coupled with the feeling of seniority which Bechet appears to have retained from those youthful New Orleans encounters, may account for the stern and rather sour strictures which he passed on Louis' contribution to the recordings. In short, he accused him of ignoring the prearranged routines and hogging the limelight to the detriment of the ensemble.

The idea of Sidney Bechet being challenged, let alone over-whelmed, by any trumpet-player from the Archangel Gabriel downwards will no doubt seem richly entertaining to anyone well-enough acquainted with his imperious style. Certainly there is no evidence on the recordings themselves that Louis was in-temperate or Bechet subdued. So far as I know, Louis didn't enter into this particular controversy, but, apart from the strictly retrospective admiration to which I have referred, he was markedly cool about his boyhood hero in later life. To understand this, we have to dispel a popular myth which New Orleans musicians themselves have propagated through their gushing reminiscences of the good old New Orleans days. From references in potted jazz histories to the music 'moving up-river to Chicago' in 1917, we gather the impression of a concerted exodus, a sort of school-leaving ceremony with all the young musicians setting out arm-in-arm and glowing with camaraderie to face a new life in the big outside world. As the short biographies in this book reveal, things happened very differently. Several of the New Orleans men, Bechet included, were born 'loners' who were up and away while the New Orleans era was still in full swing. Others stayed together for a while in the intensely competitive atmosphere of Chicago in the Twenties, but sooner or later adopted the philosophy of 'each man for himself'. Indeed, many musicians born and bred elsewhere than New Orleans have remarked at one time or another upon the jealousy bordering on violent detestation with which New Orleans musicians appeared to view each other while at the same time generalising ecstatically about the great times they all had years ago.

Several explanations present themselves. Lone wolves in pursuit of the same elusive prey cannot be expected to assume the team spirit just because they were reared in the same lair. Furthermore, the sense of an unchanging hierarchy, based on age and length of experience, has always been very real among New Orleans men and, as jazz historians fumbled to unravel the tangled threads of early jazz history, it was more and more frequently offended. 'The critics and guys who write about jazz think they know more about what went on in New Orleans than the guys that were there,' roared Pops Foster, the doyen of New Orleans bass-players, in a taped autobiography. 'They don't know nothing . . . We had a whole lot of trumpet-players around New Orleans besides Oliver and Armstrong.' Pops Foster played with all of the lone wolves at one time or another, and from his vantage point at the rear of the bandstand he took a poor view of them as colleagues. Bechet—'the most selfish, hard to get along with guy I ever worked with—a tough baby and all for himself.' Louis— 'real jealous of other players who put out . . . he works too hard because he don't want nobody to do nothing but him.' Albert Nicholas, the New Orleans clarinettist with whom Foster played for some years in the Luis Russell Band—'very hard to get along with, he had his own ways and he didn't want nobody to tell him nothing.'

This assessment will come as little surprise to jazz fans who visited the Parisian jazz scene in the Fifties when both Bechet and Nicholas were resident in different parts of the city. Albert Nicholas was the same age as Louis Armstrong and, as Bechet himself recalled, 'Albert was younger than me, and afternoons we'd sit together on the back steps and we'd play along together and I'd kind of advise him.' Thirty-odd years later, this cosy comradeship had evaporated. Ingenuous jazz buffs meeting either of the men in Paris would invariably ask after the other. The best they would receive was a monosyllabic reply and a blank, un-compromising look. I should perhaps inject the comment here that I worked alongside the admittedly formidable trio of Louis Armstrong, Sidney Bechet and Albert Nicholas at different times, and I do not believe that the sensitive, courteous and indeed, kindly side of each man that I saw was entirely due to the 3,000-mile gap between New Orleans and Windsor, England where I was born! But on one occasion when I was touring in his company and talking long into the night, Albert Nicholas unburdened himself of his own unashamedly jealous grievance against Sidney Bechet. 'Everybody talks about Bechet did this and Bechet did that. Listen, when we were making all that jazz history, Bechet wasn't even there.'

I know what he meant, and it explains why any recording of

Bechet's from the few that he made in the Twenties will serve more as an introduction of his name into this survey than an account of his impact upon jazz in that decade.

.It was in 1914, not long after his encounters with young Louis, that Sidney Bechet left New Orleans on his travels. Thenceforward, he was to return to the city only for intermittent visits which covered a few months in all between 1914 and 1917, when the break became permanent. There was a brief spell in Chicago, but Bechet was not a man to settle down even in the conducive ambience that Chicago offered to musicians at the end of World War I. With Will Marion Cook's Southern Syncopated Orchestra he came to Europe in 1919, playing in London (on one occasion before King George V) and moving on later to Paris. This phase of his travels ended when, back in Britain, he fell foul of the law (in a fight with a prostitute) and, though acquitted, was ordered to be deported back to America. It was in the short period between 1923 and 1925 that he made the New York recordings which are his sole legacy from the Twenties. In September 1925 he was off again to Europe, popping up in Paris, Russia and all stations between in groups that ranged from big stage orchestras to small jazz bands. And by the time he returned to America the Roaring Twenties had roared their last.

During Sidney Bechet's first trip to Europe, in 1919, the Swiss orchestral conductor, Ernest Ansermet, made some remarkably perceptive and prophetic comments on the music of the Southern Syncopated Orchestra. He reported: 'There is in the Southern Syncopated Orchestra an extraordinary clarinet virtuoso who is, so it seems, the first of his race to have composed perfectly formed blues on the clarinet . . . I wish to set down the name of this artist of genius, as for myself, I shall never forget it—it is Sidney Bechet.' Later, he went on, 'What a moving thing it is to meet this very black, fat boy with white teeth and that narrow forehead, who is very glad one likes what he does, but who can say nothing of his art, save that he follows his "own way", and when one thinks that his "own way" is perhaps the highway the whole world will swing along tomorrow.'

In the light of what was known about jazz in Europe, or indeed America, in 1919, Ansermet's remarks were almost clairvoyant.

The word 'blues', for example, was then known to the world at
large only through published songs from Tin Pan Alley which
carried the word, or from recordings by the Original Dixieland
Band and others in which tunes labelled as 'Blues' were very often
nothing of the kind. It is probable that Ansermet likewise used
the term as a generalisation for jazzy, syncopated music. And
yet, in the recordings that he made twenty or more years later,
Bechet was to show that he was, indeed, a master of the perfectly
composed blues. What else are masterpieces such as 'Really the
Blues', 'Out of the Gallion' or, the greatest of all, 'Blue Horizon'?
It is uncanny, too, that Ernest Ansermet should have hit intuitively
upon the word 'swing' which was, in 1919, more than a decade
away from acquiring a special significance in the jazz vocabulary.

In order to lead the reader back to a point as near as possible
to that from which Ernest Ansermet made his observations, I have
chosen the earliest Bechet recording hitherto issued. In July,
1923—a magical year, as it will transpire—Bechet was booked
for a recording session by a New Orleans compatriot, Clarence
Williams. Williams, a rather indifferent pianist, had emerged ten
years earlier as New Orleans music's first entrepreneur. It would
not be unfair to say that his music publishing business was
founded on the rubble of unclaimed, unattributable material that
the city's prolific but feckless music-makers scattered around. In
those days, and for some years to come, jazz musicians were more
interested in cash-in-hand than pie-in-the-sky, so original
melodies would often change hands across the table in exchange
for the price of a week's rent. If the publisher—and, as a result of
the transaction, 'composer'—happened also to be a musician and a
man in good standing with a recording company, a recording of
the tune would result and royalties beyond the original composer's
wildest dream would accrue. Bitter would be the cries of 'Horse-
thief!!' when this was discovered! Even when the real composers
themselves began to get their due acknowledgement, it was a long-
standing custom for publishers and/or bandleaders who recorded
a tune to add their names to the composer credits. In most cases
there was a certain rough justice in this, since much of the
material would never have earned a penny without entrepreneural
assistance. 'You write it, I'll sell it' was undoubtedly the principle

of many of the collaborations in which Clarence Williams's name appeared.

'Wild Cat Blues' was brought to Williams by a twenty-year-old pianist called Thomas Waller (nicknamed 'Fats' for visibly obvious reasons) who frequented the Harlem saloons and dives where good piano-players were at a premium, and whose habit of throwing off brilliant keyboard compositions without a thought for their future had been the despair of the businesslike Mr Williams. Having acquired the composition—Fats's first to be published— Clarence Williams quickly assembled one of his studio bands to record it.

The tune—or, more accurately, series of themes—suited Bechet perfectly. While he had been in Europe with Will Marion Cook, he had been attracted to the sound of the soprano saxophone, experimenting first with a standard curved model and eventually purchasing in London the straight model with which he became permanently associated. This instrument, which handled like the clarinet on which he was already a virtuoso and which jutted and flared aggressively like a trumpet, was custom-built for Bechet's personality. Louis Armstrong recalls having heard him in New Orleans playing cornet at the head of a parade, and it is true that his style, as revealed on this earliest record, combined the fluency of the New Orleans clarinet style with the strutting, rallying, domineering voice of the parade trumpet. It has become a cliché in jazz commentary to speak of Bechet overwhelming all but the most assertive trumpet players in the ensemble. The fact is that Sidney Bechet was not particularly interested in just transferring the decorative role of the New Orleans clarinet to the stronger instrument. Had that been his intention, it's difficult to see why he was drawn so compulsively to the soprano saxophone. He intended to dominate the ensemble, and expected trumpet players to find a satisfactory role in support. As one who played and recorded with Bechet, I can testify that this was not easy. 'Don't be afraid to play that lead,' he told me after our concert together in 1949. By 'lead' he meant the clear statement of the melody which is the function of trumpet or cornet in a New Orleans or Dixieland ensemble. Flanked by gruff trombone or shrill clarinet, the trumpet usually assumes, through its central role and tonal strength, absolute leadership of the ensemble. I doubt if I was the first or last trumpet-player to find, with Bechet at his elbow, that the ability to command was sapped!

In the long-defunct magazine *Jazz Music*, the French critic Hugues Panassié drew attention in 1948 to 'Wild Cat Blues' and its coupling, which were then extreme rarities in Britain: 'A remarkable thing about these two sides is that Bechet assumes the lead from the first bar to the last; the rest of the band is there merely to support him. These are really two great soprano saxophone solos. In them Bechet shows himself in his grandest manner and I doubt if he has ever played better than on this record.'

It is unlikely that the cornetist Thomas Morris minded taking a supporting role in 'Wild Cat Blues'. Fats Waller's piece is essentially a piano composition, clearly derivative of ragtime in its series of well-balance themes but with the overriding four-in-a-bar momentum which characterised the Harlem 'stride' piano of Waller's teacher and mentor, James P. Johnson. Indeed, there is a strong family likeness between this first published composition of Fats Waller's and the classic 'Carolina Shout' by Johnson. With the added mobility afforded by the soprano sax, Bechet found he could get around these fluent melodies more easily than a trumpet-player, and he loved them. All through his recording career, similar pieces crop up—'Polka Dot Rag', 'Temptation Rag', 'Coffee-grinder' and so on. In the same issue of *Jazz Music* from which Hugues Panassié's quotation comes, there is an article on Bechet by Bob Wilber, now a firmly established musician in his own right but, in 1948, still strongly under the influence of Bechet, with whom he studied for several years. 'As a listener, Sidney has the intuitive ability to sense the value of any music he hears. I've never heard him say "That's an awful tune." He loves all music because he sees the way to play it . . . He plays the melody, and when he improvises, improvising on the melody. That, in brief, is his theory of jazz.'

Presented with the melody of 'Wild Cat Blues' by Clarence Williams, Bechet knew exactly how to play it. In the chapter on 'Dippermouth Blues' by King Oliver, I suggested that Louis Armstrong was the first musician to have an instinctive feeling for the rhythmic freedom of 12/8 time, though I added that 'Sidney Bechet seemed to have a pretty good grasp of it.' My caution in this instance derived from several other Bechet performances from the same period (hear a rather dreadful piece called 'Oh Daddy Blues' for a perfect example) in which he conforms with the ricky-ticky rhythmic conventions of the time in a way that Armstrong could not have done had he so wanted. This is slender evidence, I readily agree, upon which to withhold the conclusion that, in terms of complete rhythmic freedom and elasticity, Bechet and Armstrong were 'modernists' almost a decade ahead of their time.

Without doubt, Bechet's playing in 'Wild Cat Blues' shows that his familiar style of the Forties onwards was fully mature in 1923. In achieving this 'modern' sound, he was not entirely unaided. The even four-beats-to-a-bar upon which relaxed phrasing in 12/8 time depends is provided—happily without any audible assistance or hindrance—by the superb banjoist, Buddy Christian, a New Orleans man of Bechet's generation who does for Bechet what Johnny St Cyr did for Louis Armstrong, and with as much suppleness and accuracy. Nowhere is the maturity of Bechet's rhythmic approach more striking than in the series of breaks which the composition provides from the halfway key-change onwards. Once again, one is drawn into comparisons with Louis Armstrong, who was himself engaged at this time in making his first recordings with King Oliver's band. The way in which both men pounced with predatory zeal upon the opportunities for solo expression that such breaks offered (hear Louis in the Oliver recording called 'Tears') links them together again as the first 'modernists' to sense the full potential of solo improvisation.

One cannot leave Bechet at this point without touching upon the prickly subject of vibrato. When Bechet made his belated and much-acclaimed return to the centre of the jazz stage in the late Thirties, some otherwise well-disposed critics and fans complained of his broad vibrato, which was variously described as 'whinnying' and 'nannygoat'. Vibrato is the word for the artificial introduction of a throb or pulse in a note to give it added expressiveness. In 'classical music', violinists and cellists have always used quite broad vibrato, achieved by a controlled shaking of the left hand on the fingerboard when the strings are depressed. In orchestral playing, the wind instruments make much less use of applied vibrato, relying for the most part on the natural pulsation of the sound. At the unschooled or self-taught folk-music end of the musical spectrum, where hearts are worn more ostentatiously on sleeves, vibrato is used without restraint on all instruments, achieved by shaking the instrument against the mouth or, in reed instruments, rapidly moving the lips or jaw around the mouthpiece. It follows naturally from the above that, in New Orleans, the music which stemmed from the schooled background of the Creoles, as exemplified in the clarinet playing of Lorenzo Tio, Jr., George Bacquet, Jimmy Noone and Albert Nicholas, made modest and restrained use of vibrato. Sidney Bechet was a Creole, but he was also a self-taught rebel who naturally gravitated towards the more violently self-expressive music of black New Orleans that owed nothing to conservatory training. As a trumpet-player *manqué*, too, he was probably attracted to the rapidly-shaking, 'shimmering' sound which many of the New Orleans trumpet-players have adopted through the years.

Much of the hostility to Bechet's vibrato arises from the fact that his playing became well-known late in the day, by which time the advance of more formal teaching into jazz had modified the use of vibrato. (This has been a progressive tendency, reaching a point, in modern jazz, at which Miles Davis, decrying the use of any applied vibrato at all, recalled his first teacher telling him 'Play without any vibrato. You're gonna get old anyway and start shaking.') What's more, the sort of broad, rapid vibrato that had become an accepted part of the style of Louis Armstrong and Johnny Dodds and their respective followers had never been applied to the saxophone—or if it had, it had been discarded (in most instances, wisely) as a bad idea. In the article quoted earlier, Bob Wilber accurately describes Bechet's vibrato as 'steady and controlled and somewhat akin to a violin'. Significantly, few ever complained about the vibrato in Bechet's clarinet playing—and had he played trumpet or violin, the objections would probably have been equally muted. As it is, the Bechet sound, vibrato and all, must always be a matter of taste. My own view is that a musician's creative personality is indivisible. One has only to hear the weak and whining noises which less committed players got from the soprano in the Twenties—Buster Bailey, for instance, or Omer Simeon, both of them fine clarinettists—to recognise the intense passion which endowed Bechet's handling of the instrument with such command. The vibrato was not just a mannerism but a deeply-rooted expression of that passion.

In the light of what still appears to us, through the fog of primitive recording, to be splendid and formidable playing on a grand scale, it is astonishing that this chapter does not end with brief account of the influence which Bechet exerted on his contemporaries. Duke Ellington recalled, 'Sidney Bechet was one of the truly great originals. I shall never forget the first time I heard him play, at the Howard Theatre in Washington around 1921. I never heard anything like it. It was 'a completely new sound and conception to me.' The Duke translated his admiration into action when, for a brief time, he employed Bechet in his band in New York. Some time after the migratory Bechet had flown again, Ellington perpetuated some of his influence in the band by employing Johnny Hodges, a young Boston musician whom Bechet had taken under his wing and who, in both his alto and soprano playing, inherited some of the older player's lyricism and feeling for the blues. Apart from this, and the mild and unsuccessful flirtations with the soprano sax to which I have alluded, there is no aural evidence that Bechet made any lasting impact on the jazz of the Twenties. Much of the blame for this must go to his apparently unerring instinct for the wrong thing, the wrong place and the wrong time.

In the period between 1917 and 1921, when most of his New Orleans compatriots were establishing themselves in Chicago, Bechet was jaunting around Europe. He returned not to Chicago but to New York, where, as Louis Armstrong was to discover when he joined Fletcher Henderson in 1924, musicians had their own thing going and were resistant to ideas coming in from 'the West'. He never settled in a band long enough to allow his talent to infect other musicians, in the way that Louis passed on the ability to 'swing' to the stuck-up and cliquey Henderson men. By choosing to overcome the outcast in the saxophone family, he established himself as a 'loner'. It is no accident that jazz historians of today still cite Coleman Hawkins and Johnny Hodges as the first men to elevate the saxophone to a convincing jazz role, relegating Sidney Bechet and his soprano to the limbo of what the jazz popularity polls categorise as 'miscellaneous instruments'. Yet what 'Wild Cat Blues' reveals above all else is that Sidney Bechet was, by an impressive margin of several years, the first great jazz saxophonist.

Bessie Smith

THERE ARE MOMENTS when anyone setting out to discuss the blues must wish devoutly that the term had never been coined. To start with, there is the purely grammatical ambiguity which makes one vacillate feebly between the singular and the plural. In this context I had better make it clear that I work by no firm rule but use whichever form looks and sounds right at the time.

Then there is the problem of accurate definition. During the Jazz Age of the Twenties, the term 'blues' became fashionable and was used indiscriminately to denote a whole range of moods from hangover and ennui at one end of the scale to deep depression at the other. It is quite clear that what Noël Coward meant by his 'Twentieth Century Blues' was a million light-years removed from the subject matter of Bessie Smith's 'Empty Bed Blues'— but it is no easy matter to explain why.

As if this were not enough, confusion surrounds the actual musical definition of the blues. It is simple enough to establish that the basic format of the blues is a stanza or chorus of twelve bars in length with the three basic chords of tonic, subdominant and dominant—or, in the key of C, of C major, F major and G seventh. But one will very soon have the awkward task of explaining away a primitive blues by Big Bill Broonzy or Leadbelly that over-runs into anything from thirteen-and-a-half to fifteen bars or, worse still, of laughing off familiar 'standards' such as 'Limehouse Blues' or 'Jazz Me Blues' which are not in any sense of the term blues at all.

Let us content ourselves here with the tersest of definitions.

When an instrumentalist announces that he is going to improvise or 'jam' on the theme of a twelve-bar blues, he means that he is about to harness his improvisation to a harmonic sequence that lasts, each time round, for twelve bars and in which, in the key of C, the chords will be as follows:

bars	1	2	3	4	5	6	7	8	9	10	11	12
chords	C	C	C	C7	F	F	C	C	G7	G7	C	C

Of course, jazz has acquired harmonic sophistication over the years and these basic chords have been enriched with extensions and substitutions. But strum them out on the piano or guitar and you will recognise them as being the basis of well-known instrumental 'standards' such as 'In the Mood' and 'At the Woodchoppers' Ball' as well as literally countless jazz compositions and spur-of-the-moment inventions.

When a blues singer of great antiquity from a remote area of the Deep South advances on a microphone, guitar at the ready, to sing the blues, he will have something rather different in mind. Using the same basic harmonic structure, he will sing a line— say, 'I lay down las' night, turnin' from side to side'—which will occupy, and slightly overrun, bars 1 and 2. Over bars 3 and 4 he will fill in with an answering phrase on guitar, taking care of the progression to the new chord in bar 5. The same words will be repeated over bars 5 and 6, and bars 7 and 8 will again have some instrumental response. Then, over bars 9 and 10, he will sing a new line—'I was not sick, I was jus' dissatisfied'—that serves to resolve the thought or sentiment expressed in the first two repeated lines. And again, instrumental backing fills out bars 11 and 12 and leads to a new stanza. It is in this area of instrumental response between vocal lines that the very early blues often strayed from the rigid twelve-bar formula, as the singer virtually strummed away until he was ready to deliver the next line.

On the musical side, one further thing needs to be said. Far back in time, the blues evolved from the meeting of African and European musical cultures. On the European side there is the harmony which, as we have seen, can quite easily be set out in conventional musical symbols. When it comes to melody we find the two cultures in head-on collision. It is quite possible to set out the melody of a blues using the key signature, the diatonic scale and the notation of European music. Doing this, we would notice that, invariably, much use would be made of the flattened third, seventh and, sometimes, fifth degrees of the scale. These are the notes which are often referred to as 'blue notes' because their use gives the melody line of the blues its dark and melancholy quality. But if we compare the notes which we have written down with what a blues singer actually sings, we find that our blunt-fisted European notation is inaccurate. The 'blue notes' are rarely flattened by a true semitone, but are bent and twisted in a subtle way which defies notation.

As for the actual character of the blues, it is as complex and perverse as human nature itself. In its primitive early form, the blues was the medium through which the oppressed and subjugated black American on Southern plantation or levee ventilated his feelings about life. In view of the condition of that life, it is surprising to discover that the theme of the blues is not always one of hopelessness and despair. There is a fine blues by the pianist Richard M. Jones whose words, no doubt borrowed from some common store, speak for all the blues: 'Trouble in mind, I'm blue, but I won't be blue always—the sun's gonna shine in my back door some day.' Trouble there is in the blues, and plenty of it, ranging from the personal disasters of poverty, starvation, prison, booze, sickness and ill-fated love to the shared calamities of flood, drought or pestilence. But the blues were sung to alleviate pain, not to intensify it, and everywhere the unhappiness is tempered by hope, defiance or a wry philosophy. If good luck befell or a love affair succeeded, then the celebration of it in the blues song was, in its turn, modified by a deeply-instilled realism. In the stanzas of the blues, love may be passionate, tender, bawdy, violent or tragic, but never romantic.

From the blurred and indistinct picture that has so far emerged the reader will gather that the blues is as hard to ensnare and pin on to a specimen board as jazz itself. Like jazz, it has undergone growth and development and transplantation, surviving misconceptions, corruption and indignities along the way. Purists have pursued, as if it were the Holy Grail itself, the notion of ultimate 'authenticity', studiously separating the wheat of 'genuine blues singers' from the chaff of 'singers of the blues' who were not born to the style but acquired it. Nobody will ever know for sure when and where the first recognisable blues was sung. Since many of the earliest exponents were itinerant musicians who wandered far and wide across the Southern States, the trail rapidly became criss-crossed and confused.

Having once been something of a purist myself, I can recount a cautionary tale which illustrates the dangers of pontificating about authenticity. One night in the mid-Fifties, a gladiatorial contest took place in my club in Oxford Street between Big Bill Broonzy from Scott, Mississippi and Josh White from Greenville, South Carolina, both of whom were in London on separate engagements. Big Bill was at the time enjoying a professional Indian summer as 'the last of the Mississippi blues singers' (the first, as it turned out, of a long procession of surviving Mississippi bluesmen to visit Britain as the blues revival gathered momentum in the Fifties and Sixties). Josh White had moved to New York in his early twenties to embark on a successful cabaret career as a purveyor of folk-song that included black blues, work-songs, spirituals and penitentiary songs as well as folk-songs of England, Scotland and Ireland.

At the club on this occasion, Josh had to endure persistent ribbing from Bill Broonzy, who was in ribald mood and kept haranguing the audience with 'He cain't sing the blues! He's from the North—ain't never heard no one from the North sing the blues!' Singers from the Mississippi States always tended to regard the blues as their special preserve, much as the old New Orleans men talked of jazz. And doubtless Bill spotted the effect that a long sojourn in the alien field of sophisticated cabaret had had on Josh's style. But critics in the audience, myself included, nodded sagely at Bill's comments. This is what we had always said—Josh White was not an 'authentic' blues singer and here it was being confirmed, as it were from the horse's mouth! A few weeks later, from the same horse's mouth, came the admission that Big Bill Broonzy, whose career as a blues singer flourished in the Thirties in the urban environment of Chicago, had had to brush up and, in some instances, learn from scratch the country blues and folk-songs which his European promoter wanted him to sing.

I cannot answer for the other witnesses to that epic contest (it ended with both men singing a string of amicable and entertaining duets), but I thought then, and think now, that Josh White was not in the same class as Broonzy and that he didn't sing the blues very convincingly. But authenticity had nothing to do with it. Having acted in his youth as guide to several blind bluesmen of the calibre of Blind Lemon Jefferson and Blind Blake, he must have had a headful of the real stuff and could have learnt it as well as anyone had he the ear and voice to do it.

It is important to have got any preoccupation with authenticity out of the way, because by the time we join the story of the blues, it had undergone a metamorphosis. The British blues historian, Paul Oliver, has written a pictorial survey actually called *The Story of the Blues*, which I highly recommend and in which we can see, through the selected photographs, the change taking place. The early chapters, discussing the evolution of the blues, show pictures with a predominantly rural background. Guitar players and bandsmen clutching home-made instruments pose on ramshackle porches or in dusty-looking fields, wearing flimsy vests or awkwardly-fitting country suits. And then, after fifty-odd pages, the scene suddenly changes and we are confronted with an imposing regiment of women, theatrically-dressed against formal backdrops and looking more like prima donnas than purveyors of a simple folk-music. And that is exactly what they were, for by the start of the century the blues had become a formal song-form which was susceptible to theatrical presentation. In other words, it had made the quite considerable step from a folk-music to a popular music. And because its roots were so firmly embedded in the life of Negroes in the South, it became, in every area to which black entertainment spread, very popular indeed.

With some justice, the photograph which looms largest in the early part of this phase in Paul Oliver's story is that of a homely lady dripping with ornate jewellery and revealing in a broad grin a veritable Fort Knox of gold fillings. This is Gertrude 'Ma' Rainey, the first great exponent of what have come to be called the 'classic' blues. Ma Rainey (she never liked the title, preferring to be addressed as Madame Rainey) was born Gertrude Pridgett in 1886, and by the age of eighteen was married to one Will Rainey and was working with him in a travelling show under the name of Rainey and Rainey, 'The Assassinators of the Blues'. Contrary to widespread belief, 'Nigger Minstrel' shows were not the sole invention of paternalistic and condescending white entrepreneurs for the amusement of white audiences. In the last two decades of the last century, all-black minstrel shows were established in which, for some years to come, black entertainers would have the opportunity to work their apprenticeship. A good idea of the nature of these shows comes from Paul Oliver's description of one of the best known of them all, F. S. Wolcott's Rabbit Foot Minstrels. Writing of this team and its chief rival, Silas Green's from New Orleans, he says: 'It was the central location of both shows on the Mississippi that enabled them to draw so freely on blues singers, but they also featured a variety of acts. Wolcott's show had jungle scenes and olios, wrestlers, comics, jugglers and vaudeville teams as part of the show. The "Foots" travelled in two cars and had an 80′ × 110′ tent which was raised by the roustabouts and canvasmen while a brass band would parade in the town to advertise the coming of the show . . . the stage would be of boards on a folding frame and Coleman lanterns—gasoline mantle lamps—acted as footlights. There were no microphones; the weaker-voiced singers used a megaphone, but most of the featured women blues singers scorned such aids to volume. Few "classic" blues singers of note became famous without serving a tough apprenticeship in the tent shows, barnstorming from settlement to township to plantation, from Florida to Fort Worth, from North Carolina to New Orleans and from Missouri to Mexico.'

There is a famous story, almost certainly apocryphal, which serves to describe the special, theatrical quality which these women brought to the performance of the blues. It is alleged that Ma Rainey was onstage in a tent show, bringing all the majesty of her fine contralto voice to bear on her speciality, 'C. C. Rider', when the frail stage on its folding frame began to collapse. Without a tremor in the voice or a falter in the tempo she kept on singing with such authority that there was neither mirth nor alarm among the audience as she slowly sank from view in a welter of disintegrating timber. True or not, the heart of the story is to a large degree confirmed when we listen today to the many available recordings of Ma Rainey. Through the suspirating mists of ancient recording we hear the authentic sound of the 'classic' blues—a strong, clear, unequivocal melody line, rich in blue notes and delivered in tones which are not only poignant, melancholy and intensely moving but have, even at this distance, a regal command.

Authentic—that dangerous word reappears. I will justify it by claiming that, whether or not she was first in the field, Ma Rainey was the one who defined the 'classic' style by which we judge the work of her eminent rivals such as Ida Cox, Bertha 'Chippie' Hill, Clara Smith, Sippie Wallace and Bessie Smith herself. As for historical authenticity, a clear denial emerges from one sentence in Paul Oliver's book: 'She first heard the blues, she told John Work, when she heard a young girl singing a "strange and poignant" lament in a small Missouri town in 1902.' She was sixteen at the time and already embarked on a career as an entertainer. From that point onwards she used a blues of her own composition as an encore. But as time went on and the blues attained the status of popular music in Negro entertainment, she turned to them almost exclusively.

For some years the legend persisted that Ma Rainey and her husband heard Bessie Smith in her hometown of Chattanooga, persuaded—some versions say 'kidnapped'—her into joining their show, and that Ma Rainey then taught her how to sing the blues. Clearly the legend arose not only from the stylistic similarity between the two formidable contraltos but also from a need to find a link between the blues that Bessie sang and their rural and primitive origins. The truth, as it emerges in the fine biography of Bessie Smith by Chris Albertson (*Bessie*), seems to be that it was not the Raineys who 'discovered' Bessie, but a couple called Lonnie and Cora Fisher for whose show she auditioned in Chattanooga in 1912, when she would have been about fourteen years old. According to Paul Oliver, she always spoke of Cora Fisher as her inspiration. However, this is not to discount entirely the Rainey influence—Ma Rainey and Bessie did meet during Bessie's adolescence, worked together for a short while and established an allegedly strong mother-to-daughter relationship. Furthermore it seems probable that, through Ma Rainey's pre-eminence in the field of what one could call the 'theatrical' blues, the precepts which Cora Fisher handed down were essentially those of Rainey.

There is no need here to trace Bessie Smith's early career in minute detail. The Oliver and Albertson books, not to mention the eye-witness accounts that appear in Hentoff and Shapiro's *Hear Me Talkin' To Ya*, give a full account. One fact emerges—that Bessie Smith was a natural, unaffected artist with a 'presence', even in her teens, that overcame a rough manner, a non-existent dress sense and a tendency to overlay her statuesque beauty with ungainly fat. The most revealing picture comes from the New Orleans guitarist Danny Barker in *Hear Me Talkin' To Ya*: 'Bessie Smith was a fabulous deal to watch. She was a pretty large woman and she could sing the blues. She had a church deal mixed up with it. She dominated the stage. You didn't turn your head when she went on. You just watched Bessie . . . if you had any church background, like people who came from the South as I did, you would recognise a similarity between what she was doing and what those preachers and evangelists from there did, and how they moved people.' Years later, in the 1950s, a fine gospel singer came to fame who demonstrated this theory in reverse. Though Mahalia Jackson renounced the blues and jazz as 'sinful music', she did admit to having heard Bessie Smith as a child, and in her spellbinding style the influence was undeniable.

Sidney Bechet, whose recollection of a turbulent love affair with Bessie Smith was probably true in essence if not in detail, threw a light on the darker, offstage side of her nature which went deeper than the view of other contemporaries that she was 'rough'. 'She had this trouble in her, this thing that wouldn't let her rest sometimes, a meanness that came and took her over.' Speaking of her death in a car accident in 1937, he showed an insight into her real tragedy that is all the more forcible coming from a man who was no stranger to 'meanness' himself: 'Someways, you could almost have said beforehand that there was some kind of accident, some bad hurt coming to her. It was like she had that hurt inside her all the time, and she was just bound to find it' (*Treat It Gentle*).

It would take a psycho-analytical treatise for which I am in no way equipped to plumb the source of Bessie Smith's trouble. She was born into abject poverty—but so was Louis Armstrong who, through similar early vicissitudes, established a mood of sunny optimism which seldom deserted him through the rest of his life. In escaping the fate of a lifetime of ill-paid servility by the only route available—that of an entertainer in a black travelling show—she had a remarkable early success. In terms of comfort or glamour, the theatre circuits which she toured hardly deserved star rating, but before the demanding and highly critical audiences of her own people, she herself rapidly became a star. That she was called upon to do more than sing is evident from the recollection of James P. Johnson's wife, May Wright, who in *Hear Me Talkin' To Ya* described seeing Bessie's own show in Atlanta in 1921: 'You won't believe this, but Bessie was the smallest woman in that show. And you know how big *she* was. Well, that opening number was the funniest thing I ever saw. The curtain went up, and the floodlights came on, and there was the entire chorus dressed in close-fitting bloomers, bent over with their backs to the audience. The orchestra struck up "Liberty Bell", and there was that whole chorus shakin' every muscle in their bodies.' Singing, acting, dancing, hip-shaking were all part of the travelling entertainer's stock-in-trade, but it is improbable that Bessie, with her unbridled sexuality, her bawdy manner and her insatiable appetite for 'good times', harboured any resentment or frustrations over these intrusions into the sanctity of her 'art'. She seems to have been a heavy drinker almost from childhood and this no doubt contributed over the years to the mounting violence of her temperamental storms. But the stories of her portentous rages, tempestuous love-affairs, wild bouts of generosity, epic binges and not infrequent recourse to devastating fisticuffs—all of which stretch back as far as her public career itself—leave us with the impression of a totally untamed creature who remained, to the end of her days, immune from the restraints of manners or convention. Something of this uninhibited, almost menacing vitality emerges from the grainy images of a seventeen-minute film called *St Louis Blues* which Bessie made in 1929. The flimsy story line, for all it triteness, was at the same time centred firmly within Bessie's own personal experience. The woman she portrays, who is given the name Bessie, finds her boyfriend in what is known, in very un-Bessie-like language, as a compromising situation with a rival. She hurls the girl out of the room but is herself struck to the floor by the boyfriend who leaves her to drown her sorrows in, among other things, a dramatic version of 'St Louis Blues'. There is a brief but hollow reconciliation and the film ends with Bessie once again singing the blues. Everything that is good about the film emanates from Bessie Smith who overcomes the crackly sound track and a dreadfully unbecoming costume with voice and movements that are truly majestic.

To agree with Sidney Bechet that Bessie Smith's 'hurt' was probably deep within herself is not to discount the frustrations which confronted a black entertainer in America as the Twenties approached. An impresario called Irving C. Miller, who had touring shows in the South around 1912, remembers the young Bessie in the chorus of one of them: 'She was a natural singer, even then—but we stressed beauty in the chorus line and Bessie did not meet my standards as far as looks were concerned. I told the manager to get rid of her, which he did.' The slogan of Mr Miller's shows, 'Glorifying the Brownskin Girl', explains what otherwise appears to be philistinism of truly Goliath proportions. Bessie Smith was too black.

When, around 1920, the big recording companies began to grasp the commercial potential of black artists, especially those from the South, it looked for a while as though a similar rebuff was in store for Bessie. The very first blues record to appear in the lists was recorded in August 1920. The Okeh record company, having failed to contract Sophie Tucker, took a considerable chance on a little-known black vaudeville singer called Mamie Smith. Her first recordings, of undistinguished popular songs, did well enough to warrant a return visit to the studios. On this second session her manager, a persistent and energetic entrepreneur called Perry Bradford, persuaded the company to be even more reckless and allow her to sing a blues backed by a black band. 'Crazy Blues', sung in a manner indistinguishable from many white singers of the period, has little distinction other than that it was the first in the field. But half a blues was better than nothing for the huge audience which was ripe to receive it, and 'Crazy Blues' was a hit.

There can be little doubt that the success of 'Crazy Blues' took the record companies by surprise. Centred in New York as most of them were, such research as they might have done into the tastes of the black community would have been directed at the established Negro population which had settled in Harlem and which, as we have seen in the chapter on James P. Johnson, had high aspirations towards 'respectable' white culture. To them, the blues was the music of the rough, uneducated migrants from the rural South and, as such, definitely not nice to know. Once the record companies became aware that there was a much wider black audience to be tapped, they began to record more and more black artists for their newly established 'race' lists, aimed exclusively at the Negro market. In the fullness of time, many of these race records were to become the cherished possessions of avid jazz collectors from Stockholm to Sidney and Tokyo to Toronto. But in the early days it seems that the companies were paralysed with apprehension. In 1921 Bessie Smith auditioned for the Black Swan label which was newly founded by the erstwhile partner of composer W. C. Handy, Harry Pace. Despite their proud slogan, 'The Only Genuine Colored Record—Others Are Only Passing for Colored', Black Swan turned Bessie down, preferring to stay on safer ground with the more cultivated and lightweight style of Ethel Waters. News reports from the same year suggest that Bessie may have made some trial recordings for the Emerson Company, but if she did, they were never released. In January 1923, under the wing of the composer, pianist and entrepreneur Clarence Williams, she tried again for the Okeh label, but her style was once again adjudged too rough. 'Too black' might have been the exact comment of her judges in their private deliberation, for no other singer, least of all Mamie Smith, so characterised the essence of the blues with its subtle variations of pitch, sheer weight of melancholy and, above all, harsh and disturbing timbres.

It was Frank Walker, the man in charge of the Columbia

record company's 'race' lists, who eventually took the chance on recording Bessie Smith. The story that, having once heard her sing in the South, he sent Clarence Williams to find her and bring her to the studios loses some of its romantic gloss when it is noted that she was in New York two weeks earlier auditioning for Okeh. In fact, Clarence Williams had to go no further than South Philadelphia to summon Bessie to New York. It was on February 15, 1923 that Bessie Smith first went into the recording studios in earnest. 'She looked anything *but* a singer,' Walker recalled later, 'she looked about seventeen, tall and fat and scared to death—just awful.' A year or so later the sharp and superior musicians in Fletcher Henderson's Orchestra were to show the same blend of shock and amusement at the 'country boy' appearance of Louis Armstrong. New York considered itself to be the hub of the entertainment industry, and its denizens no doubt suffered some pain at the dawning awareness that these gauche bumpkins were giving them a lesson in musical sophistication. The bandleader Sam Wooding is quoted in the Albertson biography on the subject of Bessie's initial impact on them with her slow, drawn-out style. 'This is one reason she didn't go over too big with New York musicians . . . She would sing something like "Baby, I love you, love you mo' and mo' ''. I'd go to the bathroom, come back and catch the rest of the verse, "I hope you never leave me, 'cause I don't wanna see you go". She had dragged out each word so that I hadn't missed a thing.'

In the history of modern entertainment, there have been artists with a magnetic stage personality who have been unable to project it on to records. Bessie Smith was not one of them. It took two days to conquer nerves and unfamiliarity and produce a pair of marketable recordings, 'Downhearted Blues' and 'Gulf Coast Blues'. Once they were issued, Bessie experienced the same magical ascent to stardom that appears to have followed her teenage stage debut ten years or so earlier. She may have arrived in the studio looking like a frightened and clumsy teenager, but the singing that was transmitted to wax was, from the outset, mature, steeped in harsh experience and formidably commanding. Within six months, Bessie Smith's version of 'Downhearted Blues' sold 780,000 copies, obliterating all previous versions of the song. Discovering some 'irregularities' in her contract, Bessie and her husband Jack Gee severed relations with Clarence Williams in a brisk meeting which allegedly—and characteristically—left him in a dazed heap on his office floor. Frank Walker became her manager and, in the next five or six years, presided over a prolific recording career that ran to sales exceeding 8,000,000 and made her, within the limitations of black entertainment, a superstar.

It is this fact which confronts me at this point with a problem. Not all of Bessie Smith's recordings through the Twenties were 'classics'. Towards the end of the decade her turbulent lifestyle was reflected in a coarsening of the magnificent voice. The insatiable demands on her repertoire resulted in some numbers which conformed to a familiar pattern, others which did her little justice. But, like Louis Armstrong, Bessie Smith seemed artistically incapable of dispensing trash. From the most unworthy material, some trace of nobility can always be extracted. And, on top of the heap, there is the rich crust of widely acknowledged masterpieces. Having made the decision to deal with two recordings, the question remains 'Which two?' Can great performances such as 'Young Woman's Blues', 'Empty Bed Blues', the majestic 'Yellow Dog Blues' or the triumphant 'Cake Walkin' Babies' be left out? Each presents an important facet of her style. And when it comes to accompaniment, can I afford to neglect the great partnership with James P. Johnson, or the richly satisfying collaborations with her favourite cornet accompanist, Joe Smith? In the end, I have chosen two of her best-known recordings, confident that both are among her very best and mindful, too, that each puts her firmly in a jazz context.

The choice of 'St Louis Blues' makes it necessary to bring in one further character in the story of the blues. W. C. Handy will reappear later in this book, cast as a villain of the piece in one episode in the life of Jelly Roll Morton. He was a Memphis bandleader and cornetist, a trained musician who earned the Tin Pan Alley title of 'Father of the Blues' through a string of compositions which have since become standard material in the jazz and popular music repertoire. This soubriquet, often repeated and taken seriously in ill-informed jazz journalism, was the cause of much suspicion and obloquy directed at Handy as the 'authentic' blues came to light. Jelly Roll Morton could hardly find words to express his scorn at a radio announcer's suggestion that Handy originated jazz and blues, and there are johnny-come-lately blues pundits around today who recount with glee every instance of a W. C. Handy lyric which turns up in pristine form in some primitive blues from the common stock. It is perfectly true that Handy, born into a self-made middle-class Negro family in Florence, Tennessee in 1873, was not by any stretch of the imagination a bluesman. The few examples of his cornet-playing on record show him playing in a clipped, square ragtime manner innocent of any blues or jazz inflections. But it is also true that, when he came to write his autobiography, *Father of the Blues,* he made no pretence to be other than what he was, a schooled composer who heard and was intrigued by the rural blues on his travels, and who incorporated their form, and sometimes snatches of their words, in a series of blues compositions. When, in 1914, he achieved both fame and a modest fortune with his 'St Louis Blues', the time was ripe for just such a formal organisation of blues material. Ma Rainey was in full spate, Bessie Smith was just embarking on her career and the blues itself was making the transition from a folk to a popular music. Anyone who has actually read Handy's lyrics—the couplet ' I know the Yellow Dog District like a book, Indeed I know the route that Rider took' from 'Yellow Dog Blues' is a typical example—will find it hard to assert with a straight face that he stole his material wholesale from folk sources. And it would ill become a musician who has recorded, I hope with love and affection, such Handy classics as 'St Louis Blues', 'Memphis Blues', Beale Street Blues' and 'Yellow Dog Blues' to add fuel to the canard that W. C. Handy was simply a purloiner of other men's material. In the composed form in which we know them, with their carefully-structured and contrasting melodic themes, these pieces did not exist before Handy put them down on paper.

'St Louis Blues' is a fine example. It was to Handy's advantage that he was an active dance-band leader, to whom instantaneous audience response was important. Once, when he was playing for a vast audience at Dixie Park in Memphis, he noticed a curious phenomenon. 'It was the odd response of the dancers to Will H.

Tyers' "Maori". When we played this number and came to the Habanera rhythm, containing the beat of the tango, I observed that there was a sudden proud and graceful reaction to the rhythm. Was it an accident, or could the response be traced to a real but hidden cause?' Handy experimented with the undiluted tango rhythm of 'La Paloma', and 'sure enough, there it was, that same calm yet ecstatic movement'. What he had stumbled upon was the rhythm, originally called *tangana*, which originated in African music, was the basis of Jelly Roll Morton's 'Spanish tinge' that underlay New Orleans music, and often emerged in the work of primitive blues players, notably the pianist Jimmy Yancey. This tango rhythm became something of a hallmark in Handy's compositions. The original piano copy of 'St Louis Blues' starts with the G minor theme in tango rhythm as an introduction, a deliberate and clever move of the composer's when one thinks of the suspicion that the blues aroused at first in audiences attuned to the conventional dance forms. 'I tricked the dancers by arranging a tango introduction, breaking abruptly then into a lowdown blues.' The ruse succeeded and 'St Louis Blues' was an instant hit.

When Bessie Smith came to record it, 'St Louis Blues' had already been popularised by other singers on the theatre circuits, one of whom, Ethel Waters, had made it her own speciality. As usual, Bessie ran over this obstacle like a steamroller. Her version became definitive, putting back into the song the essence of the real blues which had originally inspired Handy to write it. With her in the studio that day in January, 1925 was Fred Longshaw, a competent and diligent musician with no jazz pretensions who elected to play harmonium on the occasion, and young Louis Armstrong who had arrived in New York some four months before to join Fletcher Henderson's Orchestra. By this time, Bessie had been a recording star for a full two years, and there is little reason, in view of her temperament, to disbelieve the legend that she was far from pleased by the booking of Armstrong in place of her preferred Joe Smith who was out of New York at the time. Musical considerations apart, the prospect of sharing the limelight with a young and no doubt bumptious musician who was currently being hailed as a phenomenon was hardly likely to appeal to her.

In the event, Louis approached most of the numbers which they recorded at the session with great seriousness and restraint (the only dubious exception being some jokey, out-of-place playing in a vaudeville song called 'You've Been A Good Ole Wagon', which Bessie converts into a solemn blues). These were, after all, two already great artists with an instinctive awareness of their own transcendant artistry. Whatever was said on the surface—and Louis himself claimed to prefer the records he made with a much lesser singer called Maggie Jones—it would have been surprising if they had failed to find a common artistic meeting ground.

That common ground is located in the very opening bars of 'St Louis Blues', which they transposed into the key of E flat. It is easy to be derisive about the contribution of Fred Longshaw and his asthmatic harmonium. If the quality of swing belongs to the angels, then the devil must have invented the harmonium expressly to destroy it. And yet, like a great many odd noises from the primaeval days of recording, its sound has become woven into the very atmosphere of the piece to the extent that, were technology to find a way of expunging it and substituting a crisply-recorded rhythm section, I should be loth to see it go. What carefully-contrived arrangement could be better than the husky and sombre B flat major chord which replaces Handy's tango introduction and, as it were, opens the curtain on Bessie's performance?

Fresh in my memory is a conversation about Louis Armstrong with the British trombonist George Chisholm, a Louisphile of long-standing. He made the point that Louis was one of the very few musicians who possessed such innate swing that he could establish a tempo with the shortest of phrases—sometimes even with one note. Bessie Smith shared this faculty. While Fred Longshaw is hard at work trying to establish co-ordination between foot-pedals and keyboard, she makes plain within the span of the words 'I hate to see . . .' exactly the tempo which she intends to maintain. It is significant, in the light of Sam Wooding's comments earlier about her slow, drawn-out style, that this blues tempo is much slower than anything to be heard in instrumental jazz at that period. It was not until well into the Thirties that musicians started tackling this sort of slow-drag blues. If we listen again to some of the famous instrumental blues that traditional jazz bands take at a crawling pace today—King Oliver's 'Riverside Blues', the Armstrong Hot Five's 'Savoy Blues', Jimmy Noone's 'Apex Blues' or Ellington's 'Creole Love Call'—we find that they trot along at what we now consider a medium tempo, presumably to give the dancers what they wanted. Bessie, used to singing to motionless or at any rate swaying audiences, could afford to set her own dramatic tempo—and she was lucky in an accompanist for whom music held very few surprises to which he could not instantly adapt.

No words about the rapport and musical understanding between Bessie Smith and Louis Armstrong can do justice to the opening chorus of 'St Louis Blues'. In a mood of experiment I once learnt off by heart the vocal and cornet lines so that I could play them on trumpet as one continuous melody. The result came as near to a perfect *instrumental* blues chorus as one could conceive. It is not just in inventive talent that the two principals were evenly matched. Passion is an elusive quality in music, often impersonated by a sort of spurious frenzy, a simulated hysteria that is all too familiar in contemporary pop music that boasts a black gospel-song influence. I have sometimes said that the great jazz giants whom I have heard in person—Louis Armstrong, Sidney Bechet, Coleman Hawkins, John Coltrane—have all made the same striking impression that, were the instrument to be suddenly wrenched from their lips, the music would continue to flow out of sheer creative momentum. Such is the great wave of passion on which 'St Louis Blues' is carried that I am similarly rather surprised that it doesn't continue to well out of the speakers when the amplifier is suddenly switched off or the needle lifted.

Each one of Louis Armstrong's responses is worthy of analysis. I will be content to pick out three. At the very beginning, in answer to Bessie's opening line 'I hate to see that evenin' sun go down', he reacts without hesitation to the dramatic mood which she has set by starting a descending phrase with seven E flat notes hammered out with great intensity. The whole phrase is imbued with a beauty and melancholy that disguise the fact that all Louis is doing in terms of structure is playing the straight five-note scale from E flat down to A flat that ushers in the subdominant chord of the second four bars. In this, he is bound by the meticulously correct but deadeningly unadventurous harmonies churned out by Fred Longshaw on the harmonium. Louis spent much of his musical career overcoming, and indeed glorifying, unimaginative backing, and this recording is a fine example. At the end of the first verse, Armstrong's feeling for harmony enables him to play a neat trick as he follows Longshaw's chord progression doggedly with a note pattern that changes only at the last moment, when it seems on the very verge of mockery. And then, in the very last verse of all, following a veritable clarion call to action by Bessie on the word 'Nowhere' that ends the minor tango section, Louis responds to the line 'I got the Saint Louis Blues just as blue as I can be' with a complex fill-in that almost comes a cropper. The snatch of melody that Louis plays, phrasing it recklessly across the beat, is one which crops up elsewhere in music related to New Orleans. It sounds as if its inspiration was the trio section of the famous march 'National Emblem' which, as we have already seen in the chapter on the ODJB, was always quoted by Louis Armstrong in his versions of 'Tiger Rag' and may possibly have had connections with that tune itself. In the tune 'Clarinet Lament' by Duke Ellington's Orchestra, featuring the New Orleans clarinettist Barney Bigard, the same phrase is elevated to the status of an introductory cadenza. Whatever its origins—and it is not inconceivable that Louis invented it himself—it fills the bill admirably in this instance, providing a fitting response to Bessie's stirring lament and showing, in passing, Louis Armstrong's uncanny, cat-like ability to recover from a bad mistake and continue on his way without the missing of a beat.

As for Bessie Smith herself, this is one of her masterpieces. Having said that, I shall not, to the reader's relief and certainly to mine, be following up with pages of detailed analysis. It was central to Bessie Smith's art that she simplified rather than elaborated her themes. In modern times the quality in black music popularly known as 'soul'—expressed in techniques directly borrowed from Negro church music—has been progressively exaggerated to the point where a simple blues becomes a positive firework display of shrieks and moans and wild vocal contortions. Neither the classic female singers nor the country bluesmen who preceded them went in for such antics. Bessie's way, taken up and carried forward right into the rock 'n' roll era by the great Kansas City blues singer Big Joe Turner, was to restrict the range of a song to no more than five or six notes and to construct her phrases so economically that a change in direction of just one note could have a startling dramatic or emotive effect. One example stands out in 'St Louis Blues'. The first two twelve-bar blues verses begin with identical phrases, sung to the words 'I hate to see that evenin' sun go down' and 'Feelin' tomorrow like I feel today' respectively. Bessie starts the second verse, as Handy intended, with a melody line that begins in exactly the same way as the first. But where the word 'see' in 'I hate to see . . .' descends to the E flat keynote as in Handy's original melody, the last two syllables of 'tomorrow' hover indeterminately in the 'blue note' area between the second and third notes in the scale, eventually making a little upward turn which creates an unimaginably desolate effect. Indeed, if I wanted examples to illustrate my earlier definition of 'blue notes' I need do no more than point to these two lines and to the words 'sun' in the first and 'feel' in the second.

There is another characteristic of Bessie Smith's style which goes a long way to explaining why many commentators, myself included, choose to regard her, not as the culmination of a tradition of blues singing, but as the beginning of a new tradition of jazz singing. Since a jazz critique developed a long time after the music itself had begun, we have had the luxury of making many of our definitions in retrospect. Thus the jazz singers to us are those who, like the musicians, have enhanced their chosen themes with a blend of insight, blues feeling and creative variation, whether improvised or not. A singer who sang 'St Louis Blues' note for note from the sheet music as Handy had written it down would not sound to us like a jazz singer, however sincere the interpretation. For one thing, much of Handy's phrasing is symmetrical, with matching phrases following hard on each other like flower patterns on a wallpaper. And this sort of tightly-knit symmetry is the very antithesis of the broadly-sweeping and imaginative composition which we recognise in the best of jazz. Bessie Smith shared with Louis Armstrong a sort of built-in musical radar which steered her unerringly away from approaching symmetry. Since the words of popular songs were often harnessed to fairly jerry-built construction, we find both Bessie and Louis often making a dog's breakfast of the the lyrics in the interests of improved musical architecture. A famous example of Bessie's cavalier treatment of the words occurs in the song 'Cake Walkin' Babies' where, in order to deliver a superbly rhythmic and swing-ing musical phrase, she sings 'The only way is to win is to cheat 'em'. Less extreme are the occasions in 'St Louis Blues' where, for purely structural ends, she inserts a breathing point right in the middle of a verbal phrase, knocking its grammar sideways. In the first verse, she sings 'It makes me think I'm / on my last go-round', emphasising the point by letting her voice fall off the syllable 'I'm' in a characteristic way. Likewise in the last verse, while Louis and Fred Longshaw faithfully reproduce Handy's repetitive melody to the words 'I've got the Saint Louis Blues just as blue as I can be', Bessie will have none of it. To turn the line into musical sense, she makes a dramatic pause on the second 'as', dropping off it in two steps in another of her striking manner-isms and cutting it off completely from the rest of the sentence. Paradoxically, this apparent sacrificing of the literary sense to musical construction actually deepens the emotional content of the song, a point to which I will return later.

The second Bessie Smith performance that I have chosen comes from a period, four years after the recording of 'St Louis Blues', when times had changed. Recording technique had made the giant stride into electrical reproduction, and singers no longer had to bellow into the cavernous mouth of a receiving horn as if aiming for the back row of the stalls. True, theatres continued to demand powerful voice projection—the era of whispering crooners was several years away. But the new recording methods could cope with subtler nuances now, and Bessie had plenty of these in her musical armoury. Unhappily, her career was moving rapidly towards a crisis. After almost a decade since Mamie Smith first opened up the blues market, the sales of blues records were beginning to decline. In an effort to boost sales, the managers of 'race' recordings began to stuff the lists with material in which 'blue' rather than blues was the operative word. Bessie Smith almost always managed to imbue the most relentless double entendres with a certain melancholy dignity, but nevertheless it is a sad experience to play through her output of this period and hear the great voice, fraying somewhat at the edges under the stress of furious living, applied to a succession of songs in which the same old harmonic progressions—and sometimes the same melody—are trotted out to prop up a string of double meanings.

And then suddenly, a gem appears. In view of the imminent collapse of Bessie Smith's career, it is tempting to read some sort of autobiographical significance into her recording of 'Nobody Knows You When You're Down and Out'. She had recently been involved in a disastrous Broadway debut, and her records were not selling as briskly as they once did. But she was still very far from down and out. What is more, her uncertain and dangerous temperament had long put such tenuous friendships as she acquired at risk without applying the test of poverty. Bessie Smith rarely treated a song with anything less than total commitment, as witness the impassioned, almost tragic, overtones which she lent to songs such as 'Alexander's Ragtime Band' and 'There'll Be a Hot Time in the Old Town Tonight'. Written by an entertainer called Jimmy Cox, 'Nobody Knows You When You're Down and Out' teeters on the razor's edge that separates the lyrical from the maudlin, but with a firm embrace Bessie guides it on to safe ground. She has the assistance of a five-piece band led by Clarence Williams but dominated by the fine cornet-playing of Ed Allen, who backs her in a manner reminiscent of Joe Smith.

With benefit of greatly improved recording, we can hear in this performance more characteristics that stamp Bessie Smith as a supreme jazz singer. The manipulation of tone—or more accurately, timbre—is one attribute which distinguishes the jazz musician from his 'straight' dance-band colleague. A melody line will be given all kinds of contrasting nuances through a great repertoire of thin notes and thick notes, sweet notes and sour notes, clear notes and hoarse or 'growled' notes. These are used purely as materials in the musical construction, without particular reference to the theme or mood of the song that is being played. The fact that Bessie is singing words does not deter her from deploying her tonal resources in a manner quite independent of the general portent of the lyric. We have an example of this at the very outset of 'Nobody Knows You . . .'. The opening two lines—'Once I lived the life of a millionaire/Spending my money, I didn't care'—seem on paper to demand a wistful interpretation, tinged with regret. And no doubt from a 'straight' cabaret singer they would have got it, complete with a dollop of self-pity. Bessie is clearly not too concerned with a literal reading of the words. She takes her inspiration from the melody to which they are attached, treating those opening lines as two matching phrases, built on major and minor chord sequences respectively, which follow each other like great breakers on a sea shore. One can imagine Louis Armstrong or Sidney Bechet—or, much later on, Ben Webster—giving the second line the same majestic swell.

A few lines later, something equally unexpected happens. The words 'I carried my friends out for a good time . . .' are shouted like a full-blooded blues, with a poignant flattening of pitch on the word 'friends'. And then, with the phrase 'buying bootleg liquor', Bessie suddenly lets her voice drop away so that the words are virtually spoken, with a profoundly melancholy inflection. The moment brings vividly to life guitarist Danny Barker's recollection that, in performance, 'she was unconscious of her surroundings. She never paid anybody any mind.' Heaven knows what emotion prompted Bessie to lapse into soliloquy on those words. We learn from Chris Albertson that Bessie always preferred home-made liquor, maintaining that anything sealed made her sick. So far as we know, there was nothing in her often riotous relationship with bootleg liquor to prompt such sudden sadness. Once again, it transpires that there is a compelling *musical* reason for the device. For after building steadily for three lines, the melody suddenly collapses feebly on those words 'Buyin' bootleg liquor, champagne and wine'. It is the kind of weak, one-note phrase for which jazz players have become adept at improvising an alternative. Bessie's does not merely bridge the gap, it endows the line with great emotional strength. The point is made again most forcibly when, after the beautifully apt cornet solo by Ed Allen, Bessie returns to the chorus but, this time, hums the first bars of each line, in the words of Chris Albertson, 'expressing the feeling behind the song more effectively than any words do.' This is the standard which Bessie Smith set for all jazz singers to follow, using improvisation in its fullest sense on the melody of a song to express a deeper meaning than that of the words on their own. It was an example which, a decade later, enabled Billie Holiday to make remarkable music out of popular ditties of the calibre of 'I Cried for You' and 'Back in Your Own Back Yard', not to mention 'Ooooooh, What a Little Moonlight Can Do'.

We cannot leave Bessie Smith without referring to the rhythmic aspect of her music. Elsewhere in this book, I make the point that, of all the musicians who recorded in the early Twenties, only three —Louis Armstrong, Sidney Bechet and Bessie Smith—seemed to possess the instinct to overcome and, indeed, change the rhythmic conventions of the day. Of these three, I would put Louis and Bessie together in the very top bracket. In some ways, Bessie had the more difficult task, since she had to handle words which were often harnessed to melodies conceived in the even quaver, eight-to-a-bar rhythm which ragtime bequeathed. I have already spoken of her habit of altering the words or the sentences to conform to her rhythmic notions. 'Nobody Knows You . . .' is full of such adjustments. For instance, Jimmy Cox's original words in the song's second line are 'Spending all my money, I didn't care' to match the syllables of 'Once I lived the life of a millionaire'. Recoiling from symmetry as ever, Bessie drops the word 'all', which enables her to sing the phrase across the beat, stringing the words 'Spending my money I' into one phrase. In several instances, her unerring rhythmic instinct, based like Louis Armstrong's on an underlying rhythm of twelve eighth notes (or four quaver triplets) to the bar, gets her out of difficulty with the lyrics. The very opening line, for instance, is almost impossible to sing in a 'straight' fashion without distorting the word 'millionaire'. If an even-quaver style is used, giving the notes of 'Once I lived the life . . .' equal value, then undue emphasis has to be put on the last syllable—'million-*aire*' to make it scan. If the quavers are dotted in more lilting style, then it is the first syllable—'*mill*-ionaire'—that has to be stressed. Free of both tight conventions, Bessie is able to drape the sentence loosely over the two bars so that 'millionaire' comes out exactly as it is spoken.

I hope I have made the case for regarding Bessie Smith, not simply as an exalted blues singer, but as one of the greatest of all jazz performers. Unfortunately for her, technology inflicted upon singing styles in the Thirties the kind of radical changes which instrumental jazz was not to suffer until the arrival many years later of electronics. Bing Crosby, like most of his jazz associates a great fan of Bessie's, was to develop an intimate use of the newly-perfected microphone from which 'crooning' emerged. Bessie Smith's career had already suffered two setbacks by the end of the Jazz Decade. The blues on which her early triumphs had been built had lost their popularity and, with the dramatic slump of 1929, the bottom fell clean out of the recording industry. In 1933, at the instigation of John Hammond (a young enterpreneur endowed happily with both money and taste, who, three days later, was to introduce a newcomer called Billie Holiday to the studios), she made a recording comeback after two years' absence. At her own request, no blues were involved, but the rowdy vaudeville songs which she sang on this occasion seem to be a throwback to the rorty atmosphere of the Twenties rather than a presage of the new mood of the Thirties. Neverthless, Bessie was in fine voice and apparently good spirits, and there has been much intriguing speculation as to how she would have fared had not her life come to its abrupt and violent end on a Mississippi road in 1937.

With the wisdom of hindsight we can understand why Hammond's courageous gamble with her in 1933 bore no immediate fruit. The singers who came to fame in the Thirties—among them Billie Holiday, Connee Boswell, Mildred Bailey, Ella Fitzgerald and, on the male side, a late-developing Louis Armstrong—all cultivated a light, confidential style well-suited to the improved sound techniques in both studios and theatres. Never in a million years could Bessie have trimmed her voice or her personality to the intimacy of the living-rooms into which rapidly developing coast-to-coast radio pumped popular music. But, in the very year of her death, the discovery of a legendary New Orleans musician called Bunk Johnson, who had played with Buddy Bolden at the beginning of the century and whom many believed to be long dead, instigated a revival of interest in early forms of both jazz and blues which was soon to grow into something of a craze. There is little doubt that Bessie Smith would have been sought after in the early stages of the New Orleans Revival. Whether her down-to-earth nature, deeply suspicious of anything smacking of the phoney, would have put up for long with the movement's inherent nostalgia and sentimentality, is another matter. Sidney Bechet's awful verdict makes such speculation appear trivial. 'It was like she had that hurt inside her all the time, and she was just bound to find it.'

Jelly Roll Morton

OF ALL THE SELECTIONS made in this book, that of a Jelly Roll Morton 'masterpiece' is likely to be the most arbitrary and controversial. To call him the Chopin of early jazz is no more absurd than these analogies usually are. Taken with a pinch of salt, it sums him up quite usefully. His reputation—a controversial one even to this day—rests on the cumulative effect of scores of piano compositions, many of which he himself adapted for small, New Orleans-style band, and some of which he lived to see converted into rabble-rousing swing band fodder in the Thirties.

Here's a paradox. The man who, in forty itinerant years, frequently neglected music to earn a living as gambler, pimp, vaudeville comedian or pool-room hustler, later poured angry scorn on the successful swing musicians whose arrangements of numbers such as 'King Porter Stomp' and 'Milenberg Joys' gave his music an extended lease of life. One assumes that the royalties which recordings by Fletcher Henderson, Bob Crosby and, more especially, Benny Goodman attracted made a vital contribution to his livelihood in the late Thirties when he himself was without a recording contract and, indeed, lapsing into complete obscurity. And yet here was this figure, according to contemporary reports, standing around on Harlem Street corners dressed in sharp, if rather out-dated style, and flashing the diamond inlaid in his front tooth as he held forth on the shortcomings of the younger musicians around him and proclaimed the elementary principles of jazz as he had 'invented' it in 1902. As he himself pronounced in an interview, 'Not until 1926 did they get a faint idea of real jazz, when I decided to live in New York . . . very often you could hear the New York (supposed to be) jazz bands have twelve, fifteen men; they would blaze away with all the volume they had. Sometimes customers would have to hold their ears to protect their eardrums from a forced collision with their brains.'

To savour the full audacity of this claim, I refer the reader back to the chapter on James P. Johnson, which describes the rivalry and competitiveness that existed within the 'Harlem school' of piano-players even before the outrageous loudmouth from the West stalked vociferously into their midst. Reactions were predictable. Years later Duke Ellington, usually generous or discreet about fellow-musicians, gave his unforgiving judgement: 'He played piano like one of those high school teachers in Washington; as a matter of fact, high school' teachers played better jazz.' The Duke's own idol, Willie 'The Lion' Smith, was more respectful. Indeed, he wrote in his autobiography, 'It used to make me mad to hear the New York cats who hadn't been out of Harlem making fun of Morton. Like myself, Jelly Roll had played in all kinds of places and that was the way you learned about life—playing in all the different back rooms.' But the pianist's fraternal sentiments had a sting in the tail . . . 'Jelly was a guy who always talked a lot. He used to be around the Rhythm Club every day and stand out on the corner and he used to bull and con all those fellows . . . I used to come around especially on Friday and Saturday looking for Jelly. I went round this one Friday and he was standing on the corner. "Look, Mister One-Hand," I said, "let's go inside and let me give you your lessons in cutting." So Jelly and I would go inside by the piano. I was the only one he would stand and listen to and then he didn't open his mouth. I must have played nearly everything you could name and when I got through, I said, "Well, Jelly, you'll keep quiet now." And true as I'm sitting here, Jelly would be quiet.'

But not for long. Jelly kept at it through thick and thin. And in the spring of 1938, exiled by circumstances to a tiny club in Washington, Jelly Roll Morton was finding times exceedingly thin when, suddenly, his persistent street-corner oratory achieved a kind of apotheosis. A chain of events that was to prove vastly important to the understanding of jazz history was set in motion when Morton chanced to hear a reference, on Robert Ripley's 'Believe It or Not' radio programme, to W. C. Handy as 'the originator of jazz and the blues'. It was the kind of sloppy, ill-informed comment that lay journalists have made ever since the word jazz was coined, for Handy, as bandleader and cornetist, was not a jazz performer at all, while his famous pieces such as 'St Louis Blues', 'Memphis Blues' and many others were formal compositions based on the blues rather than intrinsic blues material. But Ripley's gaffe hit Morton on a nerve excoriated by neglect, and he exploded. In a letter to 'Dear Mr Ripley' reproduced in the jazz magazine *Downbeat*, he unleashed the kind of extravagant polemic that his street-corner audiences had endured down the years. 'It is evidently known, beyond contradiction, that New Orleans is the cradle of jazz and I, myself, happened to be the creator in 1902.' And later . . . 'Mr Ripley, these untruthful statements Mr Handy has made, or caused you to make, will maybe cause him to be branded the most dastardly imposter in the history of music.'

It may well have been this eruption in the columns of *Downbeat* and the subsequent controversy that prompted Alan Lomax, the curator of the Library of Congress Archive of American Folksong, to invite Jelly Roll Morton to record his reminiscences for the archives. Be that as it may, the whole incident had certainly primed Jelly with such a mountainous sense of injustice and outrage that his story, rich in almost Biblical cadences, developed into a manifesto on behalf of New Orleans in general and Jelly Roll Morton in particular.

Fate could not have chosen a better time for him to make public all his bottled-up indignation. A movement to find out more about the origins of jazz had already begun to stir among jazz writers in the States. A year or so earlier Bunk Johnson, who once played in Buddy Bolden's prototype jazz band, had been discovered working in the Southern rice-fields and was all set to provide the New Orleans Revival, as it came to be called, with a legendary figurehead. In the ensuing years, Jelly Roll Morton's story, eventually transcribed and amplified by Alan Lomax in a definitive biography called *Mister Jelly Roll*, proved despite all the absurd bragging to be the most perceptive analysis of the nature and significance of New Orleans jazz ever expounded. The more one probes the thought behind the grandiloquent speech, the more one agrees with the clarinettist Omer Simeon that Jelly 'would back up anything he *said* by what he could *do*'.

And up pops another paradox. Jazz music's first intellectual, the man whose lifelong preaching for the cause of New Orleans roused generations of musicians to derisive fury, was a 'loner' if ever there was one. As one who achieved the status of a 'house pianist' in the red-light Storyville district in the early years of the century, his New Orleans was not the permanent carnival of street parades, bandwagons and rough cabarets that horn-men like Louis Armstrong and Sidney Bechet have described. As Morton was quick to point out, it was the piano-players—all-round entertainers with a repertoire of ragtime, classical and original music—who were the élite amongst New Orleans musicians. Their undisputed territory was in the lavish and expensive 'sporting houses' where, performing the function of one-man pit orchestras to the orgiastic goings-on, they had a certain standing and were no doubt regarded with some envy by the lowlier musicians who played in the 'joints' and on the streets. Jelly Roll asserted that he was about seventeen years old when he achieved the rank of a piano 'professor' in the District. As such, he remained somewhat aloof from the horn-blowers whose names crop up in fraternal terms whenever reminiscences of New Orleans have been evoked. In one of jazz critic Leonard Feather's 'Blindfold Tests' for *Metronome* Magazine in America, Louis Armstrong could only recall Morton as 'that boy who went to California in the early days'.

Indeed, by the time young Louis had begun to take an active part in New Orleans music, Jelly Roll Morton had long left the city, travelling, often in hobo style, through the South and mid-West in pursuit of easy money and a variety of ambitions that included recognition as 'the pool champion of all the world'. His activities as a pimp—a profession adopted without shame by many musicians as a 'filler' when the music business was slack—had him run out of more than one town, and his wanderings eventually led him as far afield as California where he settled for five years, making money in all sorts of ways, legitimate and otherwise, and spending it as fast.

The high peak of Jelly Roll Morton's career came in the 1920s when, like every other New Orleans musician with a nose for 'the action', he drifted into Chicago for a protracted stay. Even then, when the black South Side ghetto was crowded with bands and musicians with a New Orleans reputation, Jelly remained curiously aloof. He toured extensively, mainly as a bandleader. But unlike such compatriots as Joe Oliver, Louis Armstrong, Johnny Dodds and Jimmy Noone, he never became associated with any of the famous Chicago jazz haunts. It is more than likely that his proud insistence on his superior Creole caste deterred him from becoming too closely involved in the black ghetto with its dense population of migrant workers from the South. He clearly liked to think that he belonged elsewhere. One of his earliest recording sessions in Chicago finds him as a guest in the select company of the white New Orleans Rhythm Kings. And apart from his tours and his recordings, he earned his living working for the publishing firm of the white Melrose brothers.

Alan Lomax's research into the relationship between the tough, not unduly scrupulous members of the publishing family and the proudly independent itinerant pianist and composer whose work they published makes poignant reading even in the face of Jelly Roll's aggressive personality. Morton's business card at this time read 'Jelly Roll Morton, composer and arranger for Melrose Music Company', and he obviously regarded Lester and Walter Melrose as business partners *and* friends—probably the only friends he had. They, on the other hand, were cool in their recollections of him. 'Oh no,' said Walter, 'of course he didn't work for us. He used to come around sometimes to talk about numbers. That's all.' One doesn't need to be a profound student of the racial climate of Chicago in the early Twenties to appreciate the impact of Jelly's not altogether diplomatic arrival at the Melrose office that day in 1923, which Lester Melrose recalled twenty-five years later. 'A fellow walked into our store with a big red bandana around his neck and a ten-gallon cowboy hat on his head and hollered "Listen everybody, I'm Jelly Roll Morton from New Orleans, the originator of jazz!" He talked for an hour without stopping about how good he was and then he sat down at the piano and showed that he was every bit as good as he said he was, and better.'

The Memphis-born pianist Lil Hardin had been equally impressed when, on one of his earlier visits to Chicago, Jelly Roll Morton had dropped into a music store where she was hired to demonstrate the newly-published numbers and, as he had done to a hundred other piano-players across the States during his peregrinations, elbowed her off the piano stool to teach her a lesson in every sense. 'So one day Jelly Roll Morton came in. He sat down and he started playing. Oooh, gee, he had such long fingers and, oh, in no time at all he had the piano rockin' and he played so heavy and all goose-pimples were stickin' out all over me. I said, ooooh, gee, what piano-playin'! So I sat there and I listened and I stood up and I walked . . . I was so thrilled. So when he got up from the piano he did something like this as if to say "Let that be a lesson to you!"—and it was a lesson because, after that, I played just as hard as I could just like Jelly Roll did, and till today I'm still a heavy piano-player and I attribute it to my hearing Jelly Roll.'

Jelly Roll Morton's piano style remained remarkably constant and unaffected by fashion during his lifetime, so reference to any of the scores of piano solos which he recorded will give an idea of the playing that so impressed both Lil Hardin and Lester Melrose. It will also give us an insight into why players brought up in the 'Eastern', Harlem school of piano-playing—I have already quoted Duke Ellington and Willie 'The Lion' Smith—invariably put him down. James P. Johnson was politer than most. He heard Morton in 1911 when 'he came through New York playing that "Jelly Roll Blues" of his . . . Of course, Jelly Roll wasn't a piano-player like some of us down here. We bordered more on the classical theory of music.' No doubt Jelly's long, disdainful nostrils would have twitched at this comparison for, although he admitted that he was not a fast sight-reader, he prided himself on being able to rattle off by ear such classical standards as the 'Miserere' from *Il Trovatore*, the Anvil Chorus, the Overture from *Martha* and so on. But the fact remains that Jelly Roll Morton's style was quite different from that of James P.'s Harlem school. And yet both styles stemmed directly from ragtime, sharing some of its conventions—namely, the 'striding' left hand that sustained the beat, and the use, in composition, of two or three related themes. Wherein lies the difference?

The answer is, in New Orleans. Another of the paradoxes which seem to cluster like angry wasps around the person of Jelly Roll Morton is that the born 'loner', the aloof figure who virtually turned his back on New Orleans in 1907 and was never a close associate of any of the other New Orleans giants, nevertheless represents for us a one-man piano-playing encyclopedia of the New Orleans musical tradition. As he intoned into Alan Lomax's microphone in a characteristically resonant phrase, 'Jazz music came from New Orleans and New Orleans was inhabited with maybe every race on the face of the globe.' This in itself would not have produced the jazz of which Jelly Roll was so proud. Jelly's own family history encapsulates the process through which jazz emerged. His family were Creoles, once an elite amongst the officially-termed 'coloured' population. Alan Lomax sums up the Creoles' position in a paragraph: 'Under tolerant Spanish and French rule in Louisiana, mulatto children were sent to school, taught trades and given professional jobs. Freedmen of colour helped to win the Battle of New Orleans under Andy Jackson. Before 1861, these coloured Creoles accumulated fifteen million dollars-worth of property, much of it in slaves; they organised literary societies and musicales and published their own newspapers, while the craftsmen amongst them built lovely churches and homes in New Orleans and cast the lacy ironwork for its balconies and doorways.'

Ironically, it was the Civil War and emancipation which undermined this cultured community's position in the world. When all 'coloureds' were free, social distinctions became blurred. The Creoles were drawn inexorably downwards until, by the end of the nineteenth century, they had little left but their pride and the remnants of a culture. Near the very bottom of their descent, in the prosperous and volatile city of New Orleans, they met the black descendants of freed African slaves on the way up. These were musicians who had no practical experience of overtures or operatic arias from the European tradition. Their musical heritage was the self-taught, raw and intensely vigorous music of the rural South—notably the blues, that musical form (described in the chapter on Bessie Smith) of childishly simple structure which nonetheless was to prove capable of expanding to encompass an almost limitless expressive content.

In recent times, some commentators on the popular music scene have aspired to a sort of instant punditry by excitedly challenging the long-established proposition that jazz began in New Orleans. They have pointed to other regions in America where, co-existent with New Orleans jazz, syncopated improvised music with jazz characteristics was to be found. To be sure, jazz historians have acknowledged for a long time that New Orleans at the start of the century had no monopoly of bluesmen, Creole orchestras, street bands, brothel pianists, gospel choirs or any other of the basic ingredients that went into early jazz. Yet the fact remains that it was from New Orleans that the first masters came, scattering the seeds of a vital new music wherever they went. One need only point to the 'growling' trumpets and trombones in Duke Ellington's music that are descended from King Oliver, to the soaring clarinets of the Swing Era that were inspired by Jimmy Noone and Johnny Dodds, to a whole school of alto-saxophone players who can be tracked back through Johnny Hodges to Sidney Bechet —everywhere the New Orleans influence. And it was exerted not only through the great virtuosi. The 'collective improvisation' of so-called Dixieland or traditional jazz, whether it speaks with a Chicago, New York, West Coast, European, British or Australian accent, follows, however ineptly in Jelly Roll Morton's view, a model established in New Orleans.

In all of this activity, we find Morton, once again, a lone figure. He did not have the immediate influence on his contemporaries and successors that men like Armstrong and Noone exerted. Most piano styles in jazz derive from a combination of primitive blues piano and the sophisticated Harlem 'stride' school, with a substantial dollop of the ubiquitous Louis Armstrong influence thrown in. When Morton recorded his band masterpieces, most of them huddled together in two or three sessions by his Red Hot Peppers in 1926, the strictly disciplined New Orleans band style was already on its way out of fashion. Attention had begun to focus on Louis Armstrong whose 'Hot Five' recordings showed a break away from the bandmasterly approach of both

Oliver and Morton towards an altogether freer approach with emphasis on the soloist. So we can say that the recordings by Jelly Roll Morton demonstrated the very epitome of the New Orleans style at a time when that style had already begun to disintegrate. When, in the years after Jelly's Library of Congress exposition, a new generation of musicians set about reviving and reconstructing the New Orleans music, few of them pursued Jelly's line for very long, if at all. In the face of the loud and frantic Trad Jazz of today, not to mention the pop music that surrounds it, Jelly Roll Morton would undoubtedly have concluded that his strictures upon the New York (supposed to be) jazz bands of the Twenties had remained unheeded too long and that, among the customers, eardrums and brains were now inextricably entangled.

I have chosen the 'Original Jelly Roll Blues' for discussion not only because it is a favourite of mine, but because it is the complete demonstration, a text-book exercise if you like, of Morton's teaching. Fortunately, that teaching is available for all to read and hear. The recordings for the Library of Congress Archive of American Folksong have been issued on commercial disc in their entirety, and they also form the basis of Alan Lomax's Morton biography. Indeed, Morton's dictum that 'Jazz is to be played sweet, soft, plenty rhythm' has been quoted so often that it has become a rather quaint cliché, like the Victorian adage that 'Children should be seen and not heard'! But Morton said very much more than that, enough to surround the bed-head of any aspiring New Orleans-style bandleader with embroidered mottoes. Here are a few to start with: 'Always have a melody going some way against a background of perfect harmony.' 'Without breaks and without clean breaks and without beautiful ideas in breaks, you don't even need to think about doing anything else, you haven't got a jazz band and you can't play jazz.' 'If a glass of water is full, you can't fill it any more; but if you have half a glass, you have the opportunity to put more water in it. Jazz music is based on the same principles, because jazz is based on strictly music.' 'If you can't manage to put tinges of Spanish in your tunes, you will never be able to get the right seasoning, I call it, for jazz.' Most of these principles are self-explanatory, calling for such basic musical ingredients as melody, variety and dynamics. But the reference (another often-quoted one) to the Spanish tinge needs some explanation. What Morton spoke of as a tinge of Spanish was the range of rhythmic variations which Spanish music acquired from African sources and which form the basis for what we loosely describe as Latin-American music. The simplest of these variations—and the one most often found in jazz—is the *tangana* rhythm from which the Tango derived and to which, as we have seen, the composer W. C. Handy was drawn. Count a couple of bars of eight-to-a-bar and emphasise the first, fourth and seventh beats—*one*-two-three-*four*-five-six-*seven*-eight—*one*-two-three-*four*-five-six-*seven*-eight—and you have the basic rhythm. Superimposed on a straightforward four crotchets or quarter notes to the bar in a way that comes naturally to guitar or banjo players, it provides a certain respite from the regular beat and underlies in a subtle way many good New Orleans jazz performances. In his 'Jelly Roll Blues', Jelly Roll Morton decided to state it unequivocally by bringing in castanets at a strategic moment.

The first thing to be said about the performance itself is that it is based throughout on the twelve-bar blues. In accounts of Jelly's modus operandi in rehearsing a band for a performance such as this, there is at first sight a contradiction. According to his wife Mabel, whom he married in 1928, 'He used to tell his band "You'd please me if you'd just play those little black dots . . . you don't have to make a lot of noise and ad lib. All I want you to play is what's written." ' But according to the clarinettist Omer Simeon and guitarist Johnny St Cyr, both of whom were in on the classic Red Hot Peppers sessions, Morton allowed them a considerable freedom. Said Simeon, 'He was exact with us. Very jolly, very full of life all the time, but serious. We used to spend maybe three hours rehearsing four sides and in that time he'd give us the effects he wanted, like the background behind a solo . . . The solos, they were ad lib. We played according to how we felt.' Johnny St Cyr confirms this: 'Reason his records are so full of tricks and changes is the liberty he gave his men . . . he was always open for suggestions.' What we have to remember here is that on the greatest Red Hot Pepper sessions in 1926, Morton was surrounded mainly by New Orleans men who had been brought up on the same precepts. In Kid Ory he had not only the king of ensemble trombonists but a musician of vast experience. At the time that Mabel Morton recalled—that is, from 1928 onwards—he was increasingly having to drill musicians from a different background, which would explain his strictness.

The 'tricks and changes' to which St Cyr referred are what elevate 'Jelly Roll Blues' from a string of blues choruses to a composition of enormous grace and style. Morton's chime-like introduction establishes a fine, stately tempo and then immediately the fun begins. The guitar makes a statement which is answered by cornet and trombone in succession, and then we are off into a lilting New Orleans ensemble with its Crescent City sound established by John Lindsay's resonant string bass. (One important legacy of the operatic and orchestral tradition in New Orleans creole music is the high standard of double-bass playing. Some of the most primitive examples of New Orleans jazz recorded in the Twenties—by Sam Morgan's Band, for instance— are distinguished by accurate and peculiarly sonorous bass work.) The cornetist George Mitchell was not a New Orleans man— he came from Louisville, Kentucky, but had moved into Chicago early in his career and had clearly been influenced by King Oliver. Throughout this record he plays with a mute in Oliver style, using it to give additional bite to an incisive lead that must have delighted his leader. Many bandleaders would have been content to follow this effective first chorus with the mixture as before, but Morton has other ideas. A trill on the clarinet introduces a variation on the first four bars of the blues harmonies, and one which is to play an important part later in the composition. In this, the normal progression from B flat through B flat seventh to E flat takes another route, namely B flat, D seventh, G minor, B flat seventh, E flat. This progression, smacked out in the form of 'stop chords' by the band, leads into another ensemble, but this time punctuated by a clarinet break—another refinement which most bands would have overlooked. The third of these choruses in B flat has yet another change. The first four bars revert to the standard progression, but feature piano breaks in which a chromatic figure repeats itself in descending octaves before turning over on its back and surfacing into a third joyful blues ensemble.

'You have the finest ideas from the greatest operas, symphonies and overtures in jazz music,' preached Jelly Roll. 'There is nothing finer than jazz music because it comes from everything of the finest class music.' Certainly, the dignified and measured modulation which now follows is of impeccable pedigree, so redolent is it of those nineteenth-century European drawing-rooms in which quadrilles, mazurkas and stately waltzes were played. It leads into the key of E flat and to a series of choruses in which the variation used in the second chorus of the piece, suitably transposed into the new key, becomes a permanent feature of the rest of the composition. In the first of these choruses the castanets come into play behind George Mitchell's cornet lead, emphasising the Spanish tinge. Even this chorus, appearing at first hearing to be a cornet solo, is thoughtfully enhanced by some counter-melody from Omer Simeon's low-register clarinet.

The danger arises now that, if I continue to detail the variations which Morton explores—the piano figure behind the first clarinet solo, the unusually-placed stop chords behind the second and so on—the impression might be given that the piece stops and starts with a superfluity of tricks and devices. But Morton was too cunning a composer for that. Anyone who has ever played traditional jazz for dancers will have discovered that to contrast broken or legato passages with forthright New Orleans-style ensemble is a sure way to elevate the spirit and lighten the feet. (Boogie woogie piano-players who broke into the pounding rhythm with across-the-beat breaks were up to the same trick, if in a less subtle way than Morton.) Thus, Jelly Roll Morton gets his men to come back into the ensemble in the seventh bar of each chorus using identical phrasing each time so that, amidst the variation, familiarity keeps returning. Musical psychology plays a large part in the arranger's art, and Morton was a master of it. The same effect was used even more effectively in his 'Sidewalk Blues', made a few months earlier, when he brought in two extra saxophone players so as to contrast the legato 'Liebestraum' theme with the ensuing bars of jaunty New Orleans ensemble.

At the beginning of this chapter I referred, in what might have been a careless generalisation, to Morton's compositions being piano pieces, many of which he adapted for New Orleans-style ensemble. In fact, we have here a chicken-and-egg enigma. 'No jazz piano player can really play good jazz unless they try to give an imitation of a band, that is, by providing a basis of riffs.' As with most of Morton's rules, a queue of notable exceptions forms instantly in the mind. With Jelly Roll Morton's own music, it doesn't much matter how the ideas took shape, whether the gracefully melodic phrases were expressed through George Mitchell's cornet or by Jelly's hands on the keyboard. What does matter is that in Jelly Roll Morton, jazz found its first—and New Orleans jazz its only—thoroughgoing, fully-fledged composer.

Fletcher Henderson

IN THE PERIOD between 1910 and 1920, America went dance crazy. Up until then, popular song and music for dancing had been two separate commodities, the only link between them being that the majority of sentimental songs were written in waltz time. Otherwise, the music for the gallops, polkas and schottisches of dancing America were instrumental, custom-built pieces. It was the emergence of the Fox Trot—originally one of a whole series of dance steps in 4/4 or 2/4 time that included the Turkey Trot, the Bunny Hug, the Grizzly Bear and the Kangaroo Dip—that wrought the change. The main reason for the Fox Trot's survival through the ages is that it is a basic step (some killjoy once described it sourly as 'walking backwards through a crowded room encumbered by a member of the opposite sex') capable of sophisticated variation, which it received in the period immediately before World War I from a new breed of professional dancers headed by Vernon and Irene Castle. In response to the demand for popular music, the publishers begin to insist that new songs should have danceable rhythms or at least be capable of adaptation to the new dance steps.

The activities of the Castles was absolutely crucial to the development of modern dance music. For one thing, they lifted the social status of the dance-hall, which had hitherto been considered in respectable society to be a low-class sort of place in which it was not proper to be seen except, possibly, on the occasional reckless 'slumming' party. With the establishment of larger and larger ballrooms, it followed that the bands that provided the music began to grow. It has never been satisfactorily established who formed the first dance-band in the modern form. Vernon and Irene Castle took on as their musical director James Reece Europe, a black musician with formal training who, by 1910, had established himself in New York as an honoured representative of Harlem music at the respectable, white-orientated end of the spectrum. We can judge the measure of dignity which he attained and the style of presentation which he favoured, from a concert which he presented in 1914 at the Carnegie Hall which featured 125 musicians and singers. Apart from ten pianos, seven cornets and eight trombones, the bulk of the huge orchestra seems to have been made up of banjos, mandolins and such contemporary oddities as the bandolin and the banjophone. The saxophonist Garvin Bushell, who arrived in New York in 1919, recalls that elephantine orchestras were not confined to the concert platform. 'The Negro dance-bands I heard were often from thirty to fifty pieces . . . there were sometimes twenty men playing bandolins, a combination of the banjo and violin [mandolin, surely] that was plucked. They played pop and show tunes. The saxophone was not very prominent as a solo instrument, but the trumpet, clarinet and trombone were. The soloists, especially the trumpet players, improvised, and those trumpet players used a whole series of buckets and cuspidors for effects' (*Jazz Panorama*).

Garvin Bushell's reminiscence takes us forward from the era of Jim Europe (and other rivals of his, leaders like John C. Smith, Allie Ross and Ford Dabney) to a point at which the 'gutbucket' element began to infiltrate into the most respectable black orchestra. We have seen in the chapter on James P. Johnson how migrants from the South, moving into New York in increasing numbers during the second decade of the century, created a demand for the sort of vigorous, improvised music, well aquainted with the blues, that had been the basis of their country music back home. So many conflicting definitions of the term 'gutbucket' have been put forward that I will say no more than that it is handed down as an appropriate-sounding term for this rough music and the sort of dives in which it was to be found in its raw state. Buckets and cuspidors, part of the home-made tradition in poor country music that also involved washboard percussion

Eddie Edwards, Larry Shields, Tony Sbarbaro, J. Russell Robinson, Nick LaRocca

James P. Johnson.

KING OLIVER'S CREOLE
JAZZ BAND. *Left to right,
Baby Dodds, Honoré
Dutrey, King Oliver,
Louis Armstrong, Bill
Johnson, Johnny Dodds,
Lil Hardin.*

*The veteran Sidney
Bechet.*

Bessie Smith.

JELLY ROLL MORTON'S
RED HOT PEPPERS. *Left
to right, Andrew Hilaire,
Kid Ory, George Mitchell,
John Lindsay, Jelly Roll
Morton, Johnny St Cyr,
Omer Simeon.*

Fletcher Henderson.

LOUIS ARMSTRONG'S
HOT FIVE. *Left to right,
Louis Armstrong, Johnny
St Cyr, Johnny Dodds,
Kid Ory, Lil Hardin
Armstrong.*

*To Kid Muggsy
from
Louis Armstrong*

Coleman Hawkins.

*Bix Beiderbecke (l) and
Frankie Trumbauer.*

Bix Beiderbecke.

Duke Ellington.

Eddie Condon.

Benny Carter

Johnny Hodges

Dickie Wells

and cigarbox fiddles and guitars, no doubt found a ready acceptance among a dancing public that was hungry for novelty. And
'hot' improvisation was clearly given a hefty boost when the
Original Dixieland Band arrived in 1917 to spread jazz mania into
the upper strata of New York society.

Once the battalions of banjos and bandolins had become
redundant and were dismissed, there remained the prototype
dance-band, with two or three brass instruments and a clarinet
to give excitement and brilliance while a couple of saxophones
added to the required volume and provided tonal ballast. In the
rhythm section, the piano derived importance through its role
as accompanist for singers and dancers as well as its close historic
connection with the ragtime from which the dance music of the
early Twenties still drew rhythmic inspiration. From the plethora
of catgut or steel wire that had once surrounded this nucleus, a
solitary banjoist remained, and it was usually a tuba, otherwise
known as a brass bass, that supplied the foundation.

Of course, not all of these early dance-bands employed improvisation. It would have been during the formative years before
1920 that the great river of popular dance music began to divide
into two streams, the one carrying 'straight' or 'sweet' music that
stuck faithfully to written arrangements, the other heading off
towards more improvised 'hot' music that gave scope to jazz
soloists. How near did those first New York improvisers come to
jazz as it has since been defined? In Garvin Bushell's judgement
of the music he heard on his arrival in 1919, 'New York "jazz"
then was nearer the ragtime style and had less blues. There wasn't
an Eastern performer who could really play the blues. We later
absorbed how from the southern musicians we heard, but it
wasn't original with us. We didn't put that quarter-tone pitch in
the music the way the Southerners did. Up North we leaned to
ragtime conception—a lot of notes.'

By the start of the Twenties, there were good players active
in the Harlem area. The New Orleans notion of jazz had been
implanted by visitors such as the Original Creole Band led by
Freddie Keppard and the itinerant Sidney Bechet. The success
of Mamie Smith's prototype classic blues recording of 'Crazy
Blues', which hit the music shops early in 1921, led to an increase

in blues activity around New York. Mamie herself stepped up
her touring schedule, and it is hard to find one musician associated
with the Harlem scene at that time (and they include Bubber
Miley, Joe Smith, Garvin Bushell, Johnny Dunn and Coleman
Hawkins) whose potted biography does not include a stint with
Mamie Smith's Jazz Hounds. As we saw in the story of Bessie
Smith, other more accomplished and deep-dyed exponents of
the blues soon converged upon New York to give an object lesson
in how to imbue an improvisation with jazz feeling. Furthermore,
the touring itinerary took most of the musicians through Chicago
where, according to all their reminiscences, they took a crash
course in jazz playing at the feet of King Oliver and his Creole
Jazz Band. Garvin Bushell recalled having heard that band in 1921,
before Louis Armstrong joined Oliver. 'Bubber Miley and I went
to hear King Oliver at the Dreamland every night. It was the
first time I'd heard New Orleans jazz to any advantage and I
studied them every night for the entire week we were in town. I
was very much impressed with their blues and their sound. The
trumpets and clarinets in the East had a better "legitimate" quality,
but their [Oliver's] sound touched you more. It was less cultivated
but more expressive of how the people felt. Bubber and I sat there
with our mouths open.'

It was in the small, 'gutbucket' cabarets in Harlem that the
young musicians were able to exercise the skills in jazz-making
which they were rapidly acquiring. It appears that the first local
star that they produced, one as imposing in his 'attitude' as any of
the great piano-ticklers of James P. Johnson's circle, was the
Memphis-born trumpeter, Johnny Dunn. The saxophonist and
composer Don Redman, who will make a significant appearance
later in this chapter, remembered him in an interview reproduced
in *Jazz Panorama*: 'When I first came to New York, Johnny Dunn
was *the* trumpet player. He was a terrific salesman for himself and
he was the first one I knew to use any kind of mute. He'd set
himself up in a show with just himself and dancers. His valet
would come followed by all sorts of trunks, and I used to wonder
if they were all for one man. The valet would set them up against
the wall, and in them would be all kinds of pots and pans, flower-
pots, cans, anything to get a different sound out of his horn.

I think he was an influence on Duke [Ellington] because he really did get a lot of sounds out of his horn.' The examples we have of Dunn on record show a player full of drive but prone to over-use the effects and rather wooden and inflexible in his phrasing. It can be little surprise to us that, though he stayed around New York for most of the Twenties, he was soon outstripped as a manipulator of mutes by Ellington's star cornetist, Bubber Miley, and was left standing as an improviser and showman by Louis Armstrong and the formidable trumpet-men who followed in his wake.

This was the pattern of jazz development in New York in the early Twenties. With admirable objectivity, Garvin Bushell constantly returns in his reminiscences to the same theme. Johnny Dunn 'played the blues so it moved you, but not as soulfully as those blues players out of Louisiana.' Harlem was catching on, but there was much to learn. One musician who seems to have arrived in New York with a fully-fledged and quite independent style was the cornetist Joe Smith. He was born into a musical family in Cincinnatti, Ohio, and having been taught cornet by his father, left home in his teens to work in travelling shows. He arrived in New York in 1920, still only eighteen years of age. In some ways his development was very similar to that of Bix Beiderbecke in that he appears to have conjured out of his own head a calm, relaxed and rhythmically free style, coupled with a ravishingly beautiful tone on both open and plunger-muted cornet, that ran contrary to all those influences which other Harlem-based musicians were eagerly absorbing from the South—or the West, as the whole area from New Orleans up to Chicago was sometimes called by New Yorkers. 'To my mind,' recalled trumpeter Louis Metcalf, 'the controversy about the two different styles of playing, Eastern and Western, came to a head when Louis Armstrong joined Fletcher Henderson, taking Joe Smith's chair. It was a real jazz feud with all the musicians taking sides. Louis represented the Western style of jazz, while Joe Smith was the Eastern.' As we shall see when we come to' discuss Bix Beiderbecke, New York jazz throughout the Twenties was to polarise into what, in later parlance, came to be identified as 'hot' and 'cool' jazz styles. No doubt other musicians of that period played with a legitimate rather than a dirty tone, used vibrato sparingly and couched their solos in an unhurried, reflective manner. They would have been classed by Garvin Bushell as technically proficient but lacking in feeling. Joe Smith qualifies as the first of the 'cool' jazzmen in that, through what at that time were unorthodox means, he achieved the vocalised sound, the blues spirit and the swing which makes for convincing jazz performance—convincing enough for him to become, upon their first meeting, the favourite accompanist of that most exacting judge of 'blues feeling', Bessie Smith.

Indeed, it is as members of the backing bands for blues singers that Joe Smith and the other budding musicians in New York first got a fair hearing on record. I must stress here that the recognition of them as important jazz musicians is retrospective. In New York after the arrival and departure (on a European tour) of the Original Dixieland Jazz Band, the furious argument about jazz or jass centred upon the rackety, novelty-ridden music of the ODJB's imitators and the syncopated dance music of Jim Europe and his rivals. The jazz craze sparked off by the ODJB even brought a reaction among respectable Harlemites against Europe, whose orchestra was now billed as a jazz band and advertised as 'Fifty Joy Whooping Sultans of High Speed Syncopation'. In his book *Early Jazz*, Gunther Schuller sums up the situation as we now look back on it. 'In the midst of all this wrangling over true jazz and Negro music, a new generation of Negro musicians, unheralded and practically unnoticed, was quietly slipping into New York. They were men like the trumpet player Johnny Dunn, who came to New York with W. C. Handy's Orchestra from Memphis; trumpet player Joe Smith and clarinettist Garvin Bushell, both from Ohio; Fletcher Henderson and Wilbur Sweatman; while other men like Bubber Miley, June Clark and Perry Bradford had either grown up in New York or had already been there for some time before the jazz craze really burst on to the scene.'

Schuller goes on to make a significant point. These temporarily displaced jazz persons, who were kept in work by the craze for blues recordings, were for the most part literate musicians. Several of them—Coleman Hawkins, Bushell and Don Redman—had studied music at college and were well versed in reading and theory. Fletcher Henderson had a university degree in chemistry to add to musical qualifications acquired since the age of six. He moved to New York from Atlanta University intending to do post-graduate research, but became instead the song demonstrator for the publishing company that W. C. Handy and Harry Pace set up. When this company spawned Black Swan Records, specialising in black artists, Henderson became its musical director. It was in this role that he was established when the blues craze erupted.

The alert reader will have spotted by now that, in New York in the very early Twenties, a situation had developed which is fascinatingly similar to the explosive events that had brought jazz into being in New Orleans twenty-odd years earlier, and had created in New York itself the fruitful strain of Harlem stride piano. A schooled, sophisticated culture with no particular place to go was set on a collision course with a virile folk tradition on its way up in the world. As usual, the actual birth of big band jazz was a casual, accidental affair. Don Redman, who had come into New York with a short-lived band from Pittsburgh, told the story. 'I wasn't in town but a few days after that when I got a phone call to come and make a record date for Emerson. I went down to the studio and found Fletcher Henderson on the date. There was a band there, but it wasn't his band. He didn't have a band then, but was kind of house pianist for Emerson . . . On this date Florence Mills was singing.' The session led to others, in the course of which the ad hoc or, in contemporary terms, 'pick-up' band, was augmented. One session led to a successful audition for the Club Alabam'—'that was the Cotton Club of that era. When we went into the Club . . . we decided to make Fletcher the leader because he was a college graduate and presented a nice appearance.' There were also, of course, the not-inconsiderable connections that Henderson had built up in the recording and publishing world, which ensured that the band made prolific recordings from the very outset. An incident at the Club Alabam' throws light on the close, almost family bond that was characteristic of Hender-son and his men throughout the Twenties and beyond. Redman again: 'Edith Wilson was on the bill with us and she wanted Hawk [Coleman Hawkins] to come out on stage and play blues behind her. He didn't mind but he wanted to get paid for it. George White was the manager of the club and he told Fletcher to fire Hawk. Since we were doing terrific business and had gotten other offers from the Roseland and other places, we decided we'd give notice to a man if Hawk was fired. We moved over to Roseland and from then on we were the top band in New York. No one rivalled us then.'

Top band or not, the first big jazz band in the modern sense did not spring fully mature into the world. Just as in the collision between Creole and folk-music in New Orleans, and again in the meeting of schooled ragtime and country influences in the Harlem piano haunts, an uneasy hybrid existed for a while before proper fusion was effected. The Fletcher Henderson Orchestra's early recordings in 1923 suggest that the ambitions of the leader and his arranger, Don Redman, lay in the direction of creating a new-style of dance-band. Redman claimed that the Pittsburg band, Billy Paige's Broadway Syncopators, with which he came to New York, was the first band in that city to play arrangements. Certainly the recordings we have of Jim Europe's bands find all the melody instruments playing in unison, with thin harmony provided by piano and one or more banjo-type instruments. Redman's arrangements deployed the 'blowing' instruments in vertical harmony, in the manner which today is commonplace in bands both big and small. This differed from the method not only of Jim Europe but of Armand J. Piron's New Orleans Orchestra which came to New York in 1922 and 1923, on the second occasion preceding Henderson into the Roseland Ballroom. It was the custom of New Orleans bands of whatever size to play in the loose, polyphonic manner which is familiar to us through the jazz bands as 'New Orleans style'. Indeed, the only difference (if we forget about the leader's violin, which he often did himself!) between Piron's dance-band and the jazz bands from the same city is that Piron's men repeated their themes over and over in the same way, without the heated variations which the jazzmen would give them.

It is doubtful if Fletcher Henderson's band regarded itself as a *jazz* band in those early days. We have to remember that, among musicians with the. pride in their calling that strict technical training had engendered, the word 'jazz' was, in the early Twenties, given a bad name by the crude excesses of the ODJB's imitators. The efforts of the young white bandleader Paul Whiteman to make jazz respectable by dressing it up in symphonic guise (described briefly in the ODJB chapter) were almost certainly inspired more by the example of the huge Negro bands of Jim Europe's generation, with a possible nod in the direction of John Phillip Sousa, than by the brief sensation that the ODJB caused. Jim Europe's bands seem to have spawned two separate traditions, one of elephantine dance-bands with a concert potential (remember that Europe preceded Whiteman into the Carnegie Hall by a margin of ten years), the other of exciting black dance music with strong ragtime links, a 'hot' music in terms of vigour and syncopation if not of improvisation. Whiteman took up the challenge of the former, Henderson of the latter, only deigning to swap ideas much later in the decade. There is one piece of glaring circumstantial evidence to support this assumption. 'The soloists, especially the trumpet players, improvised,' recalled Garvin Bushell about the dance-bands that he heard in New York when he arrived there in 1919. In regularly hiring the elusive Joe Smith for his early recording sessions and in wooing, and eventually winning, Louis Armstrong away from Chicago to join him, Henderson clearly attached a special significance to the role of a good 'hot' trumpet-player who could beat all-comers in this department.

'I decided that the youthful trumpet-player would be great in our act.' This was Fletcher Henderson's somewhat phlegmatic recollection of hearing Louis Armstrong for the first time in 1922, when Louis was still in New Orleans and Henderson was on tour with Ethel Waters. His words, which must qualify as the greatest understatement in the history of jazz commentary, convey an impression which Henderson's subsequent handling of Louis in the orchestra bears out—that is, that Fletcher Henderson never at any time realised the full significance of Armstrong's impact on his band. Contemporary evidence abounds that he himself preferred the mellower style of Joe Smith, whom he no doubt found more 'musicianly'. And when, after fourteen months, Louis returned to Chicago, there is no hint in the history books of the kind of trauma on both sides that such a parting should have caused.

There are plenty of recordings available which show us how

Fletcher Henderson's band played before Louis Armstrong's
arrival. They do not inspire the jazz lover with enthusiasm. Of the
team which Henderson gathered around him, only one musician,
Coleman Hawkins, had any potential as an improvising jazz
musician—in the absence, that is, of Joe Smith, who does not
appear on every recording. And with Hawkins, the word 'potential'
needs stressing. Aged only nineteen when the Henderson band
began recording in earnest, Coleman Hawkins was nevertheless a
fully experienced musician, having previously toured for two years
with Mamie Smith's Band. To say that he stood head and
shoulders above contemporary exponents of the tenor saxophone
is to claim no more than that he was a giant among pygmies. The
clarinettist Buster Bailey, who joined Henderson shortly after
Louis, remembers Louis's comment on Hawkins—'Man, he
swings! He swings out of this world!' Hawkins himself recalled:
'I was aware of jazz right from the start as a kid. I used to sit up
and practise all day—all day long. Then when I was through with
my lessons I would play jazz all the rest of the day.' Since he
then goes on to recollect hearing Armstrong and Earl Hines in
Chicago when he was fourteen—that is, in 1918, some four or
five years before either musician arrived in the city—it seems that
his dates were a bit confused. Be that as it may, the truth is that
the recorded examples of his work before and during the period
when Armstrong was in the band reveal a musician who neither
swung nor played convincing jazz. The tone which was to become
legendary in later years was undoubtedly big, but cumbersome as
well. Melodically, his solos did little more than run up and down
the chords in the manner of an ensemble part, and rhythmically,
he played in the clipped, jerky manner—as different from the
relaxed phrasing of the New Orleans bands as a facial twitch is
from a broad smile—in which Redman and Henderson between
them wrote for the band.

Clearly, the lessons being slowly absorbed from the South by
New York musicians were not enough to effect a magic transforma-
tion upon the Henderson Band. Even when, at the time of Louis
Armstrong's arrival, it was further reinforced by a powerful
trombonist from the rather unpromising area of Nebraska, Charlie
Green, and by the Memphis-born clarinettist Buster Bailey, fresh

from King Oliver's band, it still suffered from one central problem. Don Redman did not know how to translate the essential elements of swing, blues feeling and 'hotness' into written arrangements, even if he fully comprehended them in the first place. If the Fletcher Henderson band had ended its career suddenly in August, 1924, the recordings handed down to us would have revealed no more than a competent dance-band bogged down in the mannerisms and rhythmic conventions of its time. To bring about any sort of explosive metamorphosis, it required an injection of the raw essence of jazz administered sharply in its ossified rump.

It received it in good measure on September 29, 1924, when Louis Armstrong arrived from Chicago. From the Louis Armstrong biography by Max Jones and John Chilton (*Louis*), we glean that the hip Harlem men in Henderson's band did not exactly greet Louis as a Messiah come to show them the error of their ways. First of all, Louis Armstrong's unfashionable appearance hardly impressed them. The drummer, Kaiser Marshall, recalled: 'I remember the day Louis showed up for rehearsal . . . the band was up on the stand waiting when he got there, and Louis walked across the floor. He had on big thick-soled shoes, the kind policemen wear, and he came walking across the floor, clump-clump, and grinned and said hello to all the boys.' Henderson, according to Max Jones, found Louis 'pretty much a down-home boy in the big city' who took a ribbing from the band and endured it good-naturedly. Don Redman summed it up elsewhere. 'He was big and fat and wore high-top shoes with hooks in them and long underwear down to his socks. When I got a load of that, I said to myself, who in the hell is this guy? It can't be Louis Armstrong. But when he got on the bandstand it was a different story . . . in fact, Louis, his style and his feeling, changed our whole idea about the band musically.'

Most of the Henderson men have since testified, with varying degrees of warmth, to the effect that Louis had on their music. The qualities which he showed, fresh from King Oliver's band, covered every aspect of the playing of jazz. His tone, even filtered through the straight fibre mute which frail recording machines then demanded, was full and commanding. Furthermore, he hit each note with an attack and a varied use of pulse or vibrato which gave it a life of its own, in striking contrast to the dead sounds that fell from the horns of his colleagues in the trumpet section. Every solo that Louis recorded with Henderson springs from its surroundings with such leaping energy that one might believe, had such a thing been possible in those days, that it had been 'edited' in from recordings of a later era. The flat-footed fox-trot rhythm that pervades the written ensembles is suddenly galvanised into something approaching swing, largely due to Armstrong's facility in placing accents all around the beat in an ever-changing rhythmic pattern.

I have to confess at this point that, with a few exceptions such as the masterly exposition of 'Everybody Loves My Baby' and the explosive 'TNT Blues', Louis Armstrong's solos within the context of the full Henderson orchestra are not among my favourites. It always sounds to me, especially in the earlier recordings, as if he had been typecast as a sort of cheer-leader for the band, to provide a virtuoso 'spot' and generally whoop up the proceedings. Had Fletcher Henderson or Don Redman possessed the musical acumen to tap the vein in Armstrong's playing that manifests itself in, say, 'St Louis Blues' with Bessie Smith or, indeed, in some of the relaxed records made with Clarence William's Blue Five or the Red Onion Jazz Babies, who knows how much sooner his influence would have shown itself in the recorded work of Henderson's own band?

As it is, there was a time lag. Through the thirteen months of Armstrong's presence, there was steady improvement. The most successful overall of the early recordings, 'Copenhagen', achieved a sort of unity by letting Louis rip in the ensembles, where he can be heard elbowing the whole thing along in a way that is reminiscent of the Oliver band's two-cornet power-section. And 'TNT Blues', made about a year later, has not altogether derisory written passages, despite a twittering clarinet trio (one of Henderson's trade marks initiated by Don Redman) and occasional pompous use of the tuba. For all these advances, it was not until Louis had left the band that his lessons seemed to bear full fruit.

'The Stampede', recorded four months or so after Armstrong's departure, shows a band totally revitalised. The tune was one which Fats Waller, whose legendary appetite for food was not matched by comparable monetary greed, allegedly sold to Fletcher Henderson in a job lot of nine compositions for the price of a dozen hamburgers. It has some of the characteristics of a piano 'shout' in the riffy first theme which matches simple figures from the trombone with answering phrases by trumpets and saxophones. And all the way through there is strong emphasis on rhythmic development rather than melody, which is left almost entirely for the soloists to provide. It takes no great effort to imagine the introductory passage, with its procession of little skipping phrases in the treble followed by a burst of improvisation over heavy oom-chah bass, played entirely on piano by Fats Waller himself. In the event, piano, saxes and brass handle the opening figures, and Rex Stewart, seemingly on the verge of explosion with eagerness, rips off the solo passage.

Rex Stewart, then only nineteen years of age, had been an ardent admirer of Louis Armstrong from the moment Louis set foot in New York. 'I went mad with the rest of the town. I tried to walk like him, talk like him, eat like him, sleep like him. I even bought a pair of big policeman shoes like he used to wear and stood outside his apartment waiting for him to come out so I could look at him.' When, after some persuasion, a shy and reluctant Rex Stewart was finally persuaded to follow Louis into Henderson's trumpet section, the idolatry still showed itself in every eager solo. It may have been this excessive reliance on the Armstrong model that prompted Henderson to send him away after a few months to do some more studying at Wilberforce College, where Fletcher's brother Horace led a student band. Stewart returned to Henderson after two years, contributed much fine work with the band and then found his own niche in jazz history as one of the most original voices in the Duke Ellington orchestra. Until he died in 1967, he remained faithful to that first love by continuing to play the short cornet when all other, including Louis himself, had long since changed to trumpet.

If Rex Stewart was still immature by Henderson's exacting standards—and there's no doubt that he lacked Louis Armstrong's poise and rhythmic sure-footedness in the heat of battle—he nevertheless suits the mood of this 'new' Fletcher Henderson band admirably. Everything about the opening passage has a forward thrust, a feeling of urgency, which had been entirely lacking in earlier Henderson performances except when Louis Armstrong took over the reins. Someone once described swing as the quality which not only makes people want to dance but would also cause them to fall over in a heap if the music stopped unexpectedly. By this definition, 'The Stampede' swings.

The opening 32-bar theme enables one to be more specific. There was one characteristic which so dominated Louis Armstrong's contributions to the Henderson records that it amounted to a cliché Indeed, it may have arisen from Armstrong's frustrated efforts to get the band's pedestrian phrasing off the ground, since he never overdid it in other surroundings. The best way to grasp it is to count four crotchets or quarter notes in a bar—one-two-three-four—then omit the first beat and move the other three back half a beat, so that, in fact, they fall on the three hyphens between one-two-three-four. In the chapter on Bix Beiderbecke, I refer to this three-note, before-the-beat phrase as being the springboard from which Louis launches into his solo in 'Potato Head Blues'. These anticipated beats have the effect of creating a forward momentum. Count several bars of them in a row and you will find yourself propelled forward as if you were leaping down a steep flight of steps, with the danger of falling flat on your face. Balanced against notes played strictly on the beat, they form the basis of the advanced syncopation which in the Thirties was to earn that decade the title of the Swing Era.

Louis Armstrong did not invent this syncopation, even though he was apparently born with a natural ability to handle it. One of the characteristics of Harlem stride piano, as demonstrated in James P. Johnson's 'Carolina Shout', was that the right-hand figures were phrased in advance of the metronomic oom-chah bass. Thus Fats Waller's tune, sensitively arranged by Don Redman and interpreted by the soloists in the swinging Armstrong manner, may justly be cited as a bridge linking the advanced rhythmic notions of Louis Armstrong and James P. Johnson on the one hand with the big band music of the Swing Era on the other. The first full chorus in 'The Stampede' has the delighted, faintly surprised air of a full orchestra, with its arranger on hand, suddenly discovering how to do it! While the banjo plays a steady four-in-the-bar, the phrases thrown to and fro between trombone and the rest of the front line anticipate the beat in a relaxed, 'hot' and faintly disreputable way which is not recognisable as being by the same po-faced Fletcher Henderson band of old.

Perhaps the most startling revelation of Louis Armstrong's liberating influence comes when Coleman Hawkins leaps out of the ensemble for his solo. Here for the first time is a glimpse of the tenor saxophone player from whom all rivals were to stand back in awe for the next decade. Not only is his solo couched in terms strikingly similar to Armstrong's up-tempo contributions, but the actual notes themselves have a vibrant life of their own. There are two notes at the beginning of the ninth bar which show how Hawkins had learnt from Louis the vitalising properties of a tiny pulse or vibrato in even the shortest note. It is an interesting historical point that the trumpeter Roy Eldridge, whose fast and furious playing in fluent 'saxophone' style revolutionised the jazz trumpet in the immediate post-Armstrong period of the late Thirties, has always claimed it was this thrusting Hawkins solo, which he learnt by heart, that sowed the seeds of his own style.

After Hawkins and a short modulation, another theme, starting in the minor, is introduced. It was a stroke of brilliance on Don Redman's part to bring in Joe Smith to elaborate upon it. After the scorching eagerness of Rex Stewart and Coleman Hawkins, Smith's uncannily placid chorus offers a cool oasis. I say 'uncannily' because there is mystery inherent in Joe Smith's playing. He uses no fewer notes, and only marginally less rhythmic impetus than his predecessors in the solo order, and yet the whole solo is pervaded by a feeling of calm. Towards the end of the passage, Fats (or Redman) provides him with a long phrase of rippling eighth notes which he plays in a singing, crystal clear way which is absolutely ravishing.

Trio passages for three clarinets were, throughout its life, a trade mark of the Fletcher Henderson Band. If not invented by Don Redman, they were certainly exploited by him from the outset, in a manner which, when harnessed to the jerky, rhythmically unsubtle style of his early writing, gave a silly, twittering effect which I have already remarked upon. In this department, as in all others, 'The Stampede' shows a dramatic improvement. After Joe Smith's solo, the clarinets come in wailing, anticipating by a year or so the eerie use to which Duke Ellington was to put them in some of his most sombre compositions. Previous appearances of what has come to be called the Henderson 'clarinet choir' were not marked by any great ambition or expertise, but here it plays a positive role, establishing a contrasting atmosphere to the jolly romp that surrounds it, and, in a break in mid-chorus that is reminiscent of one of Louis Armstrong's reckless leaps into space, a flash of technical brilliance, too.

It took musicians in general, and orchestrated bands in particular, many years to acquire the sort of rhythmic freedom which Louis Armstrong demonstrated. In the chapter on Luis Russell, I make what I hope is a convincing case on behalf of the Russell Band as a major forerunner in the advance into the Swing Era, with Pops Foster's New Orleans-style, four-in-the-bar bass playing pointing the way. Fletcher Henderson's Band, not only in 'The Stampede' but for some years to come, leaned heavily on the two-beat base given by the use of a powerful tuba-player alternating with the lighter beats of the banjo. For all the thrusting energy of Armstrong-inspired solos and arrangement, there is still something faintly inhibited about the ensemble that follows another fine Rex Stewart solo and rounds off the piece. It neither lopes to a blithe climax in New Orleans style nor builds up the massive tension and excitement of which Luis Russell's Band was capable.

But in introducing this qualification to the claim often made by jazz historians that Fletcher Henderson's band was the sole progenitor of the big bands which were to dominate the Swing Era, I have been guilty of criticism's most heinous crime—that is, of taking a performance to task for failing to achieve what it did not set out to do in the first place. We sometimes forget that many of the early bands—and some later ones, too—were engaged not for their contribution to high art, but to provide music for dancing. The Roseland Ballroom was a whites-only establishment whose customers would have required the band to accompany the Fox Trot and its sundry derivatives. Not for Henderson the luxury enjoyed by King Oliver with his black audience in Chicago's

South Side ghetto, or by James P. Johnson catering for the eccentric hoofers fresh from Carolina or the Georgia sea-islands. At the Roseland, Henderson played opposite the best white bands of the day, and in terms of the music which he offered the dancers, he had to conform to their standards. Seen in this light, 'The Stampede' stands out as a final triumph of art over expediency, of jazz over respectability. And in showing, under Redman's direction, how to handle to its richest effect instrumentation handed down by a random process of evolution from street bands and circus outfits, it set the pattern which all big bands, sweet or swing, would follow to the present day.

Louis Armstrong

THE 'HOT FIVES', a term invariably uttered in tones of deep reverence by students of jazz history, represent a towering peak in Louis Armstrong's career. Indeed, such is the collective impact of these recordings of the middle and late Twenties that they have sometimes distorted the picture of Armstrong the professional musician and performer.

'It's not like the old Hot Five days' was a sentiment quite commonly overheard, from the Forties onwards, as devotees of Louis on record came away from one of his 'live' performances in a state of mild shock at the manifestations of commercial 'showmanship' which they had just witnessed. In the forefront of their minds was a picture of a quite different Louis Armstrong of bygone days, a musician dedicated to pure art who created masterpieces of improvised jazz in defiance of commercial pressures.

In the interests of truth as well as critical fairness, it has to be stressed that, in this sense, 'the old Hot Five days' never happened. Louis Armstrong's Hot Five—sometimes augmented to the Hot Seven—was a band that existed, apart from one or two charity appearances, in the recording studio alone. And even there, its existence was sporadic. In three years from 1925 to 1928, the inspired music-making that profoundly affected the whole course of jazz occupied just twenty-two scattered days. For Louis, 'the Hot Five days' were no more than interruptions in a professional career that involved every facet of showmanship from featured solo spots to accompanying floor shows and, for a while, silent movies.

The Chicago to which Louis Armstrong returned in the winter of 1925 from his stay with Fletcher Henderson in New York had blossomed into a hotbed of jazz. In the so-called Black Belt that ran through the city's South Side, clubs, cafés, dance-halls and music stores had proliferated. History is confused as to whether it was Lil Hardin Armstrong or Joe Glaser, the manager of the Sunset Café who was to take control of Louis Armstrong's career ten years later, who first had him billed, on a banner across a club front, as The World's Greatest Trumpet-Player. It was to be some time before the world was to recognise Louis' talent. But in Chicago, he returned to find himself a star, so much in demand that he was able, at one period, to commute between three different jobs on the same night.

Many of the romantic notions about 'the old Hot Five days' stem from the belief that 'clubs' in the Chicago of the Twenties resembled the kind of informal, free-and-easy jazz clubs which in the post-war years have become familiar the world over. A reminiscence by the Chicagoan tenor-saxist Bud Freeman (*You Don't Look Like a Musician*) might help to dispel such misconceptions: 'In the middle Twenties Joe Glaser (who later became Louis Armstrong's manager) owned a night-club on the south side of Chicago. It was called the "Sunset Café." It featured the Carroll Dickerson Orchestra and a floor show. The show had the usual master of ceremonies who told a few jokes and ended his routine with a tap-dance. There was a chorus of girls who could *really* dance and sing and there were very funny comedians most of whom were to become famous in the Amos 'n' Andy television show ... A little man (by the name of Percy Venable) produced and directed the floor show. If he had lived longer (he died at an early age) he would have become one of the greats; his shows were way ahead of their time ... with all this talent, the most talented of them all was a not-too-well-known trumpet-player by the name of Louis Armstrong ... No one used the word 'Jazz' to define Louie's playing; everybody knew he was hearing a true master. After the floor show the band would play a short dance set. They would take a stock arrangement of some Broadway show tune that Louie loved to play (one in particular was Noël Coward's "Poor Little Rich Girl") and play the introduction, verse and chorus as it was written, down to the coda, and then Louie would play twenty or more improvised choruses, always to an exciting climax! I have *never* heard anything like it, nor do I expect I shall ever hear anything to equal it again.'

It was during the dance set that touches of informality, more compatible with the jazz image, would creep in. Then it was that the marauding trumpet-players, intent upon cutting Louis Armstrong down to size, would converge to sit in with the band. Earl Hines, who was musical director for Louis Armstrong's own band when it took over from Carroll Dickerson, tells a hilarious story concerning these episodes. Many of the sitters-in were 'hot' men, not too strong in the reading department. Sometimes a composer with a new tune to try out would come into the club and distribute the lead sheets around the band to be read at sight. On one occasion Fats Waller came in with one such arrangement, and sat in himself on piano. The bandstand was at the time overloaded with visiting musicians, who made heavy weather of the written parts. At one stage, says Earl, Fats lent over from his seat at the piano which was raised above the rest of the band, and shouted: 'What key are you guys *strugglin'* in?'

This sort of cabaret club was only one facet of Armstrong's activity. At the same time, he also played in the trumpet section of Erskine Tate's Orchestra which was resident at the Vendome Theatre. This was a movie theatre in which the band was expected not only to accompany the silent movies but also to provide an hour-long show several times a day in between showings. It was under Tate's leadership that Louis' talents as a showman were discovered and given some encouragement. From time to time he was allowed to come forward to solo in a 'classical' speciality—his favourite was a popular excerpt from 'Cavalleria Rusticana'—and also to air his talent for comedy, presenting a mock sermon under the name of the Reverend Dippermouth.

This is the musical context into which the Hot Five and Hot Seven recordings were periodically inserted. Had it not been for the strict segregation which then, and for many years, governed the appearance of black artists on records, it is in fact unlikely that the Hot Fives would ever have been made. They were commissioned, so to speak, for the Okeh recording company's 'race' catalogue, the sphere of recording activity aimed at the Negro market which the blues boom of the early Twenties had opened up. For those who constantly hold up the Hot Five recordings as the zenith of Louis Armstrong's recording career, it should be a sobering thought that, had a more liberal attitude prevailed in the recording studios, they would almost certainly not have happened at all, and it would have been 'Poor Little Rich Girl' and 'Cavalleria Rusticana' by which we would have come to judge Louis!

According to the musicians who took part, the Hot Five sessions themselves fell far short of solemnity. 'We'd work the tunes out in the studio, no trouble,' Louis recalled. 'Good atmosphere, so good that a trombonist, not Kid Ory, forgot himself and started blowing like hell into the wall instead of into the recording. A lot of those comments on the records were just as though we were talking to one another on a club date—real natural.' Kid Ory, too, remembered that 'the records I made with the Hot Five were the easiest I ever made. We spoiled very few records, only sometimes when one of us would forget the routine or the frame-up, and didn't come in when he was supposed to. Even then, we'd try and cover up.' From all accounts, it was not unusual for one of these precarious takes to end with these great men of jazz clinging to each other and bent double with painfully suppressed giggles like naughty schoolboys.

None of this, of course, detracts from the great historical and artistic importance of the Hot Five recordings. Indeed, the total absence of pressure, the blissful ignorance among the participants of the significance of what they were doing, almost certainly enhanced the music. Outside the studios, there were already a host of demanding fans who flocked to the Vendome Theatre or the Sunset Café to hear the man billed as 'The World's Greatest Trumpet-Player' hit the high notes. Lil Hardin Armstrong, Louis' wife at this time and a strong influence on his career, once told of his horror at discovering that people were coming to the theatre just to hear him play—or miss—high F. She gave him practical advice: 'C'mon and make some G's at home—if you can get a G at home, you won't worry about an F in the theatre!'

There is no evidence that anyone, not even the persuasive Lil, exerted any such pressure on Louis in the recording studios even though, with the Hot Five, he was feeling for the first time the responsibility of leadership. From first to last, a festive, off-duty atmosphere pervades the Hot Five sessions. Armstrong's development as a virtuoso performer is reflected in the music, but only in the most oblique way. In this respect, the carpers of later years were right. Nothing in Louis Armstrong's career, not even the work that he was doing at the time that the recordings were made, was quite like 'the Hot Five days'. For about the only time in his career, these recordings offer a picture of Louis Armstrong musically on vacation. The jazz history books, taking as they often do a simplistic view, have been pretty well unanimous in pointing to the Hot Fives as examples of Louis gradually bursting the established New Orleans ensemble style at the seams. But by the time the quintet first went into the recording studios in Chicago on November 12, 1925, the loose-knit New Orleans ensemble was already out of fashion. Even Louis' old mentor, King Oliver, had succumbed to the pressure for a saxophone section, and Louis himself had waved goodbye to the New Orleans ambience when he joined Fletcher Henderson's big dance orchestra in 1924. As Armstrong's diligent biographers, Max Jones and John Chilton, have pointed out, the frenzied, scorching trumpet heard on recordings with Erskine Tate's Vendome Orchestra in 1926 probably reflects Louis' 'public' style more accurately than anything from the Hot Five sessions of that time. By reverting to the relaxed collective improvisation of the New Orleans style for his recording sessions, and by retaining that basic style in the Hot Five's music for the full three years of its existence, Louis provided us with the opportunity of hearing his talent developing, as it were, in laboratory conditions.

'Potato Head Blues' was recorded almost exactly at the halfway point in the group's life. Stylistically, it represents a culmination. While the title (an uncomplimentary but jovial reference to some person unknown) reveals the light-heartedness of the occasion, the music shows a powerful cohesion throughout. Holes can be picked in the ensemble work. The trombonist who replaced Kid Ory (the same enthusiast who serenaded the brickwork in his abandonment?) does little but moo harmoniously, and Johnny

Dodds is not altogether at home with the harmonies that composer Louis—or more probably Lil—Armstrong specified. But somehow the blistering energy of Louis' trumpet carries everything along with it. Comparing the work of Johnny Dodds in the Hot Five and Seven setting of this period with contemporary recordings with his own little band (to be discussed later), some critics have noted a certain strain, as if Dodds were striving to match Louis Armstrong's virtuosity with an uncharacteristically florid style. As a soloist, Dodds was undoubtedly more at home with the simple blues and march harmonies of the New Orleans repertoire than with the rather more sophisticated chord progressions that crop up in 'Potato Head Blues'. But he bears down on his solo with a heroic determination and swing that commands respect.

Louis Armstrong has two solo spots, and in each he lays down unequivocally what will be demanded of the generations of jazz soloists who follow in his wake. After the first ensemble, he rips out an unaccompanied 'break' that leads into what, in popular music parlance, would be called the 'verse'—that is, a short secondary theme which returns, by way of an imperfect cadence, to the main theme. The verse in 'Potato Head Blues' starts with four authoritative notes, the first two firmly implanted on the beat. It would make simple, if not very exciting, sense if the rhythmic pattern of those first four notes were repeated symmetrically in bars 5 and 6 and again in bars 9 and 10. If the tune was ever committed to paper, that is almost certainly how it was laid out.

Jazz solo improvisation has been described as 'spontaneous composition', and Louis Armstrong's innate instinct for composition made him discard dull symmetry in favour of elegant, and exciting, variation. So, in the fifth and sixth bars, he alters the four-note phrase entirely, stretching the first note over three beats, squeezing notes two and three together to make room for it, and holding back the fourth so that it becomes, in effect, the first note of the ensuing phrase. Then again, in bars 9 and 10, notes from the underlying chord are borrowed to elaborate the original four notes with short arpeggios in yet another variation. 'Phrasing' is the term given to this sort of balanced construction, and Louis had a remarkable flair for it. It enabled him, on many occasions before and after 'Potato Head Blues', to bestow nobility upon undistinguished themes.

Exciting as it is, the verse in 'Potato Head Blues' is a mere prelude to the central Armstrong performance. At the end of the clarinet solo, Johnny St Cyr strums a short linking passage on banjo and then Louis literally launches himself into an improvisation against 'stop chords' by the band. Four years earlier, when Louis was with King Oliver's band, he recorded a tune of his own called 'Tears' in which, for one whole chorus, he improvised unaccompanied two-bar responses to the band's statement of the tune. At the time this was a pretty daring feat. It is hard to think of any musician (with Bechet and Beiderbecke as possible exceptions) who had the melodic and harmonic sense to maintain the music's impetus over the unbridged gaps. A certain similarity in the two tunes—the mingling of major and minor harmonies, for instance—leads Louis to repeat, in 'Potato Head Blues', the very phrase that, in bars 15 and 16, links the two halves of 'Tears'.

But if 'Tears' was daring, 'Potato Head Blues' is positively reckless. Here are no solid chunks of melody against which to pitch the responses, but single chords on the first beat of alternate bars which are there to help the listener rather than inspire or guide the soloist. Louis treats these staging posts with a certain amount of arrogant disdain, sometimes using them as launching pads from which to project a rhythmic phrase, at other times careering straight over them as it they were not there.

Anyone who listens again and again to this superbly constructed solo will discover his own magic moments in it. It might be the phrase that stalks majestically across the beat in bar 3, perhaps, or the augmented chord that is implied in bar 6 in place of the tune's more conventional dominant 7th, or again, the surprising but absolutely scintillating D flat against a D seventh chord which distinguishes bar 12. Apart from these technical niceties, there is the glory of that searing, burnished tone and the triumphant joie de vivre with which Louis emerges from the solo and rejoins his colleagues for the finishing straight. And above all, for anyone with a feeling for jazz history, there is the awareness that, after this, jazz would never be the same again. For better or worse—and surely only the most crabbed purist would say that it was for worse —the way was opened for a whole era of fruitful solo exploration.

Bix Beiderbecke

SOME TIME IN THE YEAR 1910, the *Davenport Daily Democrat*, a smalltown newspaper in Iowa, ran a feature article which began 'SEVEN-YEAR-OLD BOY MUSICAL WONDER, little Bickie Beiderbecke plays any selection he hears! Leon Bix Beiderbecke, aged seven years, is the most unusual and the most remarkably talented child in music that there is in this city. He has never taken a music lesson and does not know one key from another, but he can play in completeness any selection, the air or tune of which he knows.'

The happy concatenation of circumstances which converted a boy musical wonder into a jazz genius are laid out in the admirable biography of Bix by Richard Sudhalter and Philip Evans from which the above quotation is taken. For our purposes they can be summed up in a few pages. Davenport stands on the Mississippi river at a point where the excursion steamers from New Orleans, Cape Girardeau and St Louis moored and turned around. As a small boy, Bix was drawn to the music, from small bands and from the steam organs called calliopes, which poured from these pleasure boats and, on clear evenings, wafted up as far as the Beiderbecke home on Grand Avenue. At the same time, he was driving a piano teacher to distraction by using a prodigious musical ear and memory to circumvent the tedious business of sight-reading—and sticking to—the written notes.

A new, strange and exciting outlet for this inventive talent presented itself when Bix's elder brother Charles, home from the war, brought into the house a new wind-up gramophone and a batch of records which, among an assortment of operatic arias and overtures, included two freshly recorded numbers—'Tiger Rag' and 'Skeleton Jangle'—by the Original Dixieland Jazz Band.

To the precocious and at the same time anarchic Bix, the free and unfettered sounds of this early jazz were a revelation. It was not long before he borrowed a cornet and began tentatively to pick out the clear, incisive notes with which Nick La Rocca led the ODJB into action.

From this point onwards, the story falls into a familiar pattern. There is the formation of a schoolboy band, the sitting-in with local and visiting musicians, the taking-in of sundry influences. In 1919, Bix heard, and probably struck up a fleeting acquaintance with, nineteen-year-old Louis Armstrong, who pulled into Davenport aboard the SS Capitol as a member of Fate Marable's band. There is no aural evidence that Bix became a sudden convert to the Armstrong style. By all accounts Louis was already something of a virtuoso, and it is likely, that, as a learner still, Bix stayed with the more approachable music of the ODJB and Nick La Rocca whose example could be studied at leisure on gramophone records. A few years later, in Chicago, Bix was able to listen to Louis more consistently, but by this time he had already acquired a strong style of his own. Where from? Setting aside, as the main factor, his own innate originality, it is probable that the most impressive music that Bix could hear in the flesh during his formative years was provided by two young New Orleans musicians who worked in and around Davenport in 1921. One was Leon Roppolo, whose clarinet solos subsequently recorded with the New Orleans Rhythm Kings have a plaintive, legato quality which is shared by Bix's earliest work on record. The influence of Emmett Hardy—a few months younger than Bix but clearly a more experienced and accomplished player at that time—must be taken on trust, since he died of TB in 1925 without making his mark on record. When I first began to read the jazz magazines in the mid-Thirties, Hardy was painted as a romantic, almost Keatsian figure given to playing compulsively until his lips bled. Of such nonsense is jazz legend compounded. In this present context, we must be content with the comparatively boring conclusion that Emmet Hardy, a good player according to those who remember him, probably had some influence on Bix's style.

The first band of note with which Bix Beiderbecke played was a youthful group which took shape in the last weeks of 1923. It is alleged that they chose to call themselves The Wolverine Orchestra after Jelly Roll Morton's composition 'Wolverine Blues' which in the early days was a popular item in their repertoire. What is more certain, listening to the recordings which they made throughout 1924, is that The Wolverine Orchestra was a band of note solely because Bix was playing in it. Rhythmically, it played in the jerky, 'vo-de-o-do' style of the typical dance-bands of the time, but against this framework, Bix's clear and already distinctive cornet sound reveals some of the subtlety which, long before the wider record-buying public had ever taken note of his name, earned him the admiration of his fellow musicians.

It was an admiration which had, at first, to surmount Bix's **unpromising appearance. His eyes and 'silly little mouth' were** what first struck the pianist and songwriter Hoagy Carmichael. The young Eddie Condon also found Bix's eyes noteworthy, though it was the overall apparition that inspired some characteristically laconic Condon prose. He took in Beiderbecke as 'a kid in a cap with the peak broken. He had on a green overcoat from the walk-up-one-and-save-ten district; the collar was off his neck. He had a round face and eyes that had no desire to focus on what was in front of him.' Eddie Condon was not exactly enthralled at the prospect of working with Bix. 'I've made a mistake, I thought. I'm stuck with this clam digger for two months . . . how can a guy in a cap and a green overcoat play anything civilised?' The clarinettist Mezz Mezzrow's recollection of young Beiderbecke is perhaps the most surprising, contrasting with the pudgy, whey-faced, sleeked impression that the familiar photographs convey: 'Bix was a rawboned, husky, farmboy kind of kid, a little above average height and still growing. [Mezz's musical perception is clearly stronger than his human biology—Bix was over twenty-one when they met and presumably had reached full height.] His frog-eyes popped out of a ruddy face and he had light brown hair that always looked like it was trying to go some place else . . .'

Both Carmichael and Condon were reporting impressions received before they had heard Bix blow a note, and even Mezzrow had only heard the indistinct sounds emanating from records by the Wolverines. Musicians, and especially those of the tough jazz school, are not usually prone to attacks of the vapours, but nothing else will adequately describe the effect which the first notes from Bix Beiderbecke's cornet had on our three witnesses. 'Just four notes,' recalled Hoagy Carmichael, 'but he didn't blow them—he hit them like a mallet hits a chime. And his *tone*—the richness . . . He ruined me. I got up from the piano and staggered over and fell exhausted on the davenport.' Eddie Condon was on the train en route to an engagement when he first heard Bix actually play. 'With nothing to do but sit and stare at the scenery from there [Cleveland] to Buffalo, I began to wonder again about the cornet. I got out my banjo. Eberhardt [another colleague] dug up his saxophone and doodled along with me. Finally Beiderbecke took out a silver cornet. He put it to his lips and blew a phrase. The sound came out like a girl saying yes. Eberhardt smiled at me. "How about 'Panama'?" he said. I was still shivering and licking my insides, tasting the last of the phrase. "All right," Beiderbecke said, " 'Panama'." By itself, so it seemed, my banjo took up the rhythm. At last I was playing music; so far as I was concerned, it could go on for ever.'

Strangely enough it was Mezz Mezzrow, whose slangy literary style normally sagged beneath the weight of colourful hyperbole, who produced the clearest analysis of Bix's style. 'I have never heard a tone like he got before or since. He played mostly open horn, every note full, big, rich and round, standing out like a pearl, loud but never irritating or jangling, with a powerful drive that few white musicians had in those days. Bix was too young for the soulful tone, full of oppression and misery, that the great Negro trumpeters get—too young and, maybe, too disciplined. His attack was more on the militaristic side, powerful and energetic, every note packing a solid punch, with his head always in control over his heart. That attack was as sure-footed as a mountain goat; every note was sharp as a rifle's crack, incisive as a bite. Bix was a natural-born leader. He set the pace and the idiom, defined the style, wherever he played, and the other musicians just naturally fell into step.' This is fascinating stuff, seeming to contradict almost wilfully the picture which legend has built up—

the picture of an eccentric and weak-willed genius, the stereotype of the misunderstood artist driven by self-doubt and false friends into alcoholic self-destruction, with a musical persona that was correspondingly introspective and 'cool'. But if we forget altogether the Young Man With A Horn of Dorothy Baker's novel (allegedly inspired by Bix) and concentrate on the music, it is not hard to recognise the musician whom Mezz is describing, even if some of the magic is lost in the inhibiting atmosphere of the recording studio.

That the magic was potent is confirmed by the swift ascent which Bix, without any formal musical qualifications, made into the first league of the popular music business. With the Wolverines he went to New York towards the end of 1924. A reviewer for the showbiz magazine *Variety* found the band 'a torrid unit that need doff the mythical chapeau to no one'. More important for Bix, the celebrated and influential bandleader Paul Whiteman heard the band and filed away in his memory a highly favourable impression of the young cornet-player. But it was a bandleader from Detroit, Jean Goldkette, who was the first to tempt Bix away from the Wolverines. With Goldkette at the end of 1924, Bix's musical illiteracy brought problems, not least of which was the necessity, on recording sessions, for an extra trumpet-player to play the written parts while Bix stood by for the hot solos which the ever-conservative recording executives did not always want. Jean Goldkette had to let Bix go, but added 'I don't want to let him out of my sight. He's going to be very good indeed, mark my words.'

Sure enough, Bix Beiderbecke was back in the Jean Goldkette fold within eighteen months. But by this time he had renewed contact with a musician with whom, for the rest of his short life, he was to form a close musical partnership. In many ways, Frank Trumbauer was the perfect foil for Bix—an accomplished and forward-looking musician, but sober, disciplined and business-like where the other was erratic, unbridled and an increasingly heavy drinker. Their somewhat Laurel and Hardyesque career together (there would be many occasions when Trumbauer would have cause to say 'Another fine mess . . .') began in the autumn of 1925 when Bix joined Trumbauer's band for a season. From it,

they went together into the Goldkette Orchestra, Bix having by
this time marginally improved his reading but greatly enhanced
his reputation as a 'hot' man. Jean Goldkette, though a well-
schooled musician, was always a non-playing leader and, as he
turned his attention to the business side of things, Frank
Trumbauer took charge of the band in the field. It is relevant
to the huge influence which Bix had on his contemporaries, both
white and black, to record that the Goldkette band was good
enough to challenge—and rout—Fletcher Henderson's famous
orchestra in the Roseland Ballroom in New York, Henderson's
own home ground. Despite this, it was only a matter of eighteen
months or so after Bix rejoined before Goldkette disbanded.

From the band which had adopted—and earned—the title of
'The Paul Whiteman of the West', Bix Beiderbecke and Frank
Trumbauer moved on together into the Paul Whiteman Orchestra
proper. In terms of professional success, they could go no higher.
Although Whiteman's organisation was nothing if not commercial,
it was willing and able to draw on the finest talent in what was then
called the 'hot' field—assuming, of course, that the talent was
encased in a white skin. Integration on the bandstand was not to
come for another decade or so. Jazz legend for years indulged
itself in the simplistic theory—'cornfed' would have been Bix's
own word for it—that it was the restriction and sheer boredom of
big band work that drove Beiderbecke, the great artist, into
alcoholism and a premature and spectacular death. It was the
British jazz critic and musician Benny Green, in a perceptive
essay on Bix, who first propounded the belief, which Sudhalter
and Evans confirm in their detailed biography, that Bix's self-
destructive urge was fuelled by a deep sense of inadequacy. The
musicality which once drew little Bickie Beiderbecke to the
attention of the *Davenport Daily Democrat* had a strong conventional facet. He was reared in a middle-class home with the
strongest possible links with European culture. It would take a
full chapter, with a psychiatrist in attendance, to plumb the
complex causes of jazz music's yearning for respectability. The
symptoms are everywhere and extend from Paul Whiteman's
guying of 'crude jazz' in 1924 to the carefully-contrived concert-hall
image of the Modern Jazz Quartet in the Fifties. With Bix, we can

assume that upbringing, family environment, education and, perhaps, ancestry exerted a magnetic pull. It was reinforced by the genuine musical interest which he and many of his contemporaries had in the twentieth-century European composers. Bud Freeman has said to me, 'Apart from going to hear all the greats like Louis and King Oliver and Bessie, we didn't listen to *that* much jazz—it was more the classical composers for us.'

Some jazz historians with a 'New Orleans or bust' approach have called in Bix's involvement with European music as evidence to disqualify him as a 'jazz musician'. For anyone wishing to enter into a debate that leads straight into a quagmire of definitions and semantics, it can just as reasonably be used to prove the exact opposite—namely, that Bix, unlike some contemporaries whose use of the whole tone scale and advanced harmonies sounded like mere trickery, was able to absorb these diverse ingredients into an integrated style just *because* he was a great jazzman. Be that as it may, Bix Beiderbecke's fan-worship of Maurice Ravel and the like strengthens the proposition that he admired Paul Whiteman's Orchestra and that his frustration, which manifested itself in increasingly frequent and prolonged absences from the bandstand, arose from his belief that he could not live up to it. It has become fashionable to deride Whiteman's elephantine 'symphonic jazz' and to scoff at the title 'King of Jazz' which a Hollywood movie bestowed on him in 1930. The term 'jazz' had less sophisticated connotations in those days, and we should now be able to accept without rancour that, while offering no competition to true jazz artists of the calibre of Louis Armstrong, Duke Ellington, Jelly Roll Morton or Bix himself, Paul Whiteman did preside over an organisation which set itself a high standard of musicianship, from which jazz talent was not excluded. By the standards of a dance-band, a concert light orchestra or a show band (and his orchestra combined all three) he did not purvey tripe. The men who arranged for him—Bill Challis, Tommy Satterfield, Ferde Grofé—were friends of Bix and shared his musical aspirations. That he felt pride, rather than shame, in playing what they wrote is shown by the story, told by Sudhalter and Evans, that he sent home to his parents copies of every record he made with Whiteman, and was bitterly hurt when, on one of his leaves-of-absence from the band, he found all the packages unopened.

It was the story of Bix's last years, with their decline into alcoholism and broken health punctuated by sometimes violent breakdowns, that provided fuel for the legend, rather than anything which he consigned to gramophone records. Indeed, to some who, like myself, were first gripped by the more spectacular music of Louis Armstrong, the initial exposure to Bix's recordings was something of an anti-climax. I suppose we expected to hear music deeply imbued with tragic melancholy, lapsing into pathos as physical and mental deterioration progressed. What sprang from the grooves, however, was a joyous, clean-cut, extrovert sound, as clear as a bell and endowing every tune, however banal, with almost boyish enthusiasm.

After Louis, Bix's solo flights were, at first hearing, un-adventurous. It was only after patient and persistent listening that the truth became apparent. Starting from the same point in the development of jazz playing, Louis and Bix moved in dia-metrically opposite directions. Louis Armstrong's music ex-panded outwards, as if violently impelled by centrifugal force. It was not only the New Orleans conventions which he 'burst at the seams', to use the popular cliché. Melodically, harmonically, rhythmically and emotionally, he took off on an exploration into the unknown. Bix, seemingly more cautious by temperament, took the opposite course, staying within the musical conventions of his time but digging deeply into them and upturning little gems of subtlety and fresh discovery every inch along the way. One specific instance underlines the contrast. In a piece called 'Ory's Creole Trombone' by the Hot Five, Louis Armstrong, with a rush of imaginative zeal to the head, attempts a 'break' which, while recognisable as a musical thought, cannot technically be played on the trumpet at all. In a triumph of mind over matter, the idea comes through to us, but musically it is a very strange sound indeed. It is quite inconceivable that Bix would ever have allowed invention and execution to come unstuck in this way. When, in a series of famous encounters, he bandied spontaneous phrases with Frank Trumbauer, there are few, if any, moments when one literally gasps at the sheer recklessness of it all. What astounds here is the cool-headed, even laconic way in which phrases that seem set on some well-worn path suddenly dart off at a tangent or double back on themselves in a totally unexpected way.

The moment has come to broach the tricky subject of the terms 'hot' and 'cool' as they are used in jazz discussion. The trickiness arises from the fact that 'hot' has performed more than one role over the decades. At the time when Bix was establishing his reputation with the Goldkette and Trumbauer bands, he would have been known as a 'hot' man, a musician adept at improvising as distinct from a 'straight' man who was restricted to playing the notes put in front of him. Likewise, at the end of the Twenties when the word 'jazz' became temporarily unfashionable, the music which employed a large degree of improvisation was generally known as 'hot style'. Even when it became respectable in trendy circles to talk about 'jazz' again, the word 'hot' persisted. In France, where their devotion to the art was always rather more impassioned than among the phlegmatic Anglo-Saxons, 'le jazz hot' was what they enthused about. But nobody at that time talked about 'le jazz cool'. Hot jazz was simply a term to distinguish the real thing from all the novelty music and syncopated dance tunes which the uninformed media insisted on calling 'jazz'.

The distinction between 'hot' and 'cool' as an approach to jazz improvisation did not really start to be made until the arrival of the Modern Jazz Era immediately after World War II. This was a period when many long-established jazz notions were being overthrown. One belief, propagated more by jazz writers and fans than by musicians themselves, was that the type of musician who fired off passionate improvisations straight at an audience's gut sensibilities was part of a vanishing past. The new image of the jazzman depicted a musican withdrawn behind dark glasses who communicated, if at all, in monosyllables, regarded an audience as an intrusive but necessary evil and approached his music-making with a certain clinical detachment. Being wise after the event, the adherents of the 'Cool School' would point to two of the great heroes of the Swing Era, tenor-saxists Coleman Hawkins and Lester Young, as epitomising the old and the new.

Coleman Hawkins, who played with a huge tone encrusted with overtones and enriched by a breathy vibrato, was the 'hot' musician par excellence. By contrast Lester Young, with his light airy sound and soft, almost flabby, articulation, was taken to represent coolness.

Of course, the whole discussion, bound up as it was with fashionable attitudes, produced a lot of fatuous nonsense. Dizzy Gillespie, who inaugurated the craze for dark glasses, and Charlie Parker, from whom emanated the cliché of the modern musician turning his back on the audience, both rarely forged a solo at anything less than white heat. The modern musicians or beboppers were hardly more detached and cultish than the marihuana-smoking 'vipers' in Harlem in the Thirties, for example, who numbered Louis Armstrong among their founder-members and who assumed all the elements of a secret society from the language they spoke to the way they walked. And theory took a bad beating when Coleman Hawkins and Lester Young appeared onstage together in Norman Granz's gladiatorial show, 'Jazz At The Philharmonic' in 1946. For in that rabble-rousing arena, the apotheosis of Le Jazz Hot, it was the extrovert Hawkins who played blithely on his own sweet way without any special concessions to the audience, while the introverted, 'cool' Lester honked and riffed them into a frenzy.

To pour scorn on the trendy concept of 'cool jazz' is not to deny the existence of 'hot' and 'cool' elements in jazz. But they have nothing whatever to do with any one period or movement, whether fashionable or artistic. Nor indeed are they confined to music—when that passionate British political orator Aneurin Bevan called Labour Party leader Hugh Gaitskell a 'dessicated calculating machine', he was expressing in different words exactly what Eddie Condon, the ringleader of the tough but deeply sentimental Chicago jazz fraternity, thought of the modern alto-saxophonist Paul Desmond. Objective criticism cannot afford to take sides, especially when the core of the argument—'hot' versus 'cool', heart versus head, passion versus calm reflection—turns out to be no more than a whopping great human platitude.

But there is one way in which the word 'hot' and 'cool' can be endowed with some useful and constructive meaning. It lies in the contrast I have already made between the directions in which Louis Armstrong and Bix Beiderbecke travelled in their musical progress. There was Louis pushing into unknown areas which he *felt* rather than actually perceived, while Bix stayed within the conventional forms but explored them more deeply than anyone had yet done. It would not be far-fetched to link that break of Armstrong's in 'Ory's Creole Trombone', which in the heat of creation tried to transcend the trumpet's limitations and very nearly succeeded, with the eldritch shrieking of avant garde saxophonists no longer able to express themselves within the instrument's normal range. An arbitrary list of these flyers into space, the jazz astronauts, takes us from Louis on to Henry Allen and Rex Stewart, Roy Eldridge, Dizzy Gillespie (and here the baton passes to saxophone players), Charlie Parker, John Coltrane and the avant gardists. These, and other musicians through the whole range of instruments, pushed the boundaries of jazz further and further outwards, the cumulative effect of their key recordings giving the impression of men impelled by demons. If we label them the 'hot' men, this is not to elevate their role above all others —indeed, it could well be argued that the almost frenetic pushing outwards of jazz boundaries over the short space of five or six decades has not altogether been to the music's advantage. Fortunately for the richness of jazz, there is the creative direction, exemplified by Bix Beiderbecke, which has led musicians of equal genius to dwell upon, explore, refine and illuminate each new extension to the idiom. For all the influence which he had on the young modernists of the late Forties, Lester Young did not, in fact, make any major harmonic innovations. He worked as much within the musical conventions of the Thirties as did Bix within the established style of the Twenties. Miles Davis, in the early phase that culminated in his 'Sketches of Spain' collaboration with Gil Evans, likewise set to work on the new worlds which Charlie Parker and Dizzy Gillespie had 'opened up, burrowing into them when others were content to keep running round the surface. If we call them the 'cool' men, it implies no lack of warmth or intensity in their music, simply that they seem to us to have sought tranquillity rather than turbulence.

Of course, we are dealing here with crude over-simplifications.

Like male and female hormones, hot and cool elements exist, in varying proportions, within every musician. Lester Young, for instance, favoured the surging four-beat rhythm that distinguishes most 'hot' styles, and the taxi-horn honks and deliberate variations of pitch which he occasionally used, while in no way central to his style, nevertheless revealed occasionally the 'hot' man's urge to push outwards into unorthodoxy. Conversely, Louis Armstrong made in the mid-Thirties an artistic decision to abandon his explorer's role. His conscious explanation was characteristically mundane, since profound self-analysis was not in his line. He said: 'I stopped all that playin' for musicians, guys who'd come around the stand just to see what you could do. They never paid you a thing, but you could mess your lip up real good doin' all that!' But when we listen to his records of that period, many of them made with sloppy and poorly-arranged big band backing, what we actually hear is Louis taking a cooler, more reflective look at the idiom which he himself had been largely responsible for fashioning ten years earlier. Gone are the breathtaking imaginative flights and the fluffed notes and slightly tense articulation which went with them. Instead, we have relatively spare phrases, selected with majestic poise and a masterly sense of structure—and, incidentally, performed with an instrumental control that has rarely been equalled. I believe it was this cooler facet of Armstrong that has led Miles Davis to say in recent years: 'You know, you can't play anything on a horn that Louis hasn't played—I mean even modern.' Dig out the recording which Louis made of 'I Can't Give You Anything But Love' on June 24, 1938 and you will hear a solo which, within a firmly Louis-esque context, harks straight back to Bix Beiderbecke and 'Singin' the Blues'.

I have noted in the chapter on Fletcher Henderson that New York in the late Twenties was a city of musical extremes. Hot and cool existed side by side. To forestall any suggestion that there was a clear racial division between the two, it is worth making the point that, by offsetting the high and wild contributions of trumpeters Louis Armstrong and Tommy Ladnier with the more lyrical and placid solos of cornetist Joe Smith, Fletcher Henderson made in the trumpet department the same musically effective 'hot and cool' distinction that Count Basie was to make, a decade later, when he pitted such muscular tenor-saxists as Herschel Evans and Buddy Tate against Lester Young. Nevertheless, it is true that most of the white New Yorkers with whom Bix associated favoured the cool approach that had been established in popularity by such leaders as Red Nichols and Miff Mole.

Nowhere is this coolness more obvious than in the rhythm department. The opening bars of 'Singin' the Blues' provide a sharp contrast with the New Orleans style and its immediate derivatives that flourished in Chicago in the Twenties. Compared with records by Louis Armstrong's Hot Five and the McKenzie Condon Chicagoans—and they were different enough from each other, as we shall soon see—this music sounds almost lethargic. Contrary to superficial belief, the New Orleans jazz recorded in the early Twenties was not 'two beat' music. In the King Oliver and early Hot Five recordings, the rhythmic pulse was an even four beats to the bar. Even when Louis Armstrong employed a tuba-player to grunt away on the first and third beats, the underlying rhythm was still a pushing four-four. Here is an answer for those who, relying for a definition of 'hot' jazz on such blowing characteristics as the weight of tone or intensity of vibrato, have stumbled over piano or vibraphone players whose tone is built unalterably into the instrument. 'Hotness', according to the 'centrifugal' analogy that I have used, is very much a rhythmic thing. Listen again to 'Potato Head Blues' and, in the famous stop chorus without benefit of rhythm section, hear how Louis Armstrong seems increasingly to be straining at the leash towards the end of the chorus and beyond into the final ensemble. Such is the momentum that is built up that to lift the needle or turn down the volume sharply would invite an almost physical shock.

Cool deliberation does not thrive under such a momentum, which is why adherents to the reflective style of improvisation often lean instinctively towards the more measured pace that two-in-a-bar provides. In the fastest numbers that, say, Frankie Trumbauer's band essayed—and 'Clarinet Marmalade' from the Bix period is a good example—fidgety arrangement tends to disguise the fact that the playing is basically in the 2/4 style of a military march. In slower tempo, the choice of a side-to-side two-beat, in deliberate preference to the thrusting 12/8 rhythm that Louis Armstrong demonstrated, is even more marked. The introduction to 'Singin' the Blues' is the old-time dancing-master's '*one*-and-*two*' set to music!

About Frankie Trumbauer, who opens the proceedings with an elegant variation on the theme, strong subjective feelings have always been aroused. When the record came out, his solo attracted as much attention and praise from musicians and aficionados as that of Bix Beiderbecke. We know that the flat, polished tone that he got from the now obsolete C melody saxophone (pitched between the alto and the tenor) had a big influence on the light and airy sound that Lester Young was to bring to the tenor-saxophone a few years later. Today, the solo, while still admired for the gracefulness of its melodic line, is generally rated below that of Bix. Somehow, in Trumbauer's work, there is the feeling that an essential jazz element is missing. 'Some of you guys are all belly,' Lester Young is alleged to have told his great rival, Herschel Evans. By the same token, it could be said that Trumbauer was 'all head', with little sign of the raw spirit of jazz that Bix derived from his devotions at the feet of King Oliver, Louis and Bessie Smith. In music, the pulse or throb in a note that is called vibrato is not simply a device for prettifying a tone. As both Bix and Louis Armstrong showed in their own different ways, it performs an essential rhythmic function, even when, as with Bix, it is barely perceptible. Trumbauer's slack vibrato, no more than a faint quaver, does nothing to give his phrases buoyancy, and one or two otherwise interesting runs sound flat-footed as a result.

For contrast, we need only hear Bix Beiderbecke's opening note in the solo that follows. There is a learned thesis waiting to be written on the way jazz improvisers use opening notes to, as it were, 'tee up' a solo. Lester Young would often open with a single note followed by a gap of three or four beats, rather in the way that a speaker about to make an important point concentrates his listeners' attention with the word 'Now . . .' If we go back once again to 'Potato Head Blues' and the Armstrong stop-chorus, we hear that characteristic opening which Louis bequeathed to a host of imitators—three repeated notes played across the beat followed by a short one a third below. Apart from their actual rhythmic placings, there is a vibrancy in each note that somehow primes the ensuing solo with energy. To use another sporting metaphor, it's like the little hop and skip that a high-jumper gives before embarking on his run. Coincidentally, Bix Beiderbecke's two introductory notes are identically placed in the scale, but instead of Armstrong's three stabbing notes, Bix plays one, a gentle but taut note that puts him in perfect balance for the ensuing solo.

There is one thing further to be said about Bix and vibrato. Because he eschewed the broad, throbbing vibrato of New Orleans players in general and Louis in particular, many jazz commentators have used loose phrases like 'vibrato-less' or 'virtually no vibrato' in describing Bix's sound. Most people nowadays are sufficiently acquainted with the guitar to know how flat and lifeless is a plucked note that is absolutely devoid of vibrato. Yet I have been able to quote earlier a string of witnesses to the almost uncannily vibrant and ringing quality of Bix Beiderbecke's cornet tone. The singing effect that we can pick up on recordings such as 'Singin' the Blues' reminds me of nothing more than the poignant note that a master guitarist, be it Segovia or Django Reinhardt, will send winging on its way with an incisive attack and a subtle and well-timed vibrato. Ringing, singing or winging, Bix Beiderbecke's vibrato was not negligible, it was at the very heart of his magical sound.

In probing some of the secrets of Bix's 'Singin' the Blues' solo, I find it useful to remind myself that, when I first heard it, I was not greatly impressed. I have confessed earlier that the Bix legend had prepared me for something more emotionally charged. By comparison with the slurring and sliding and quivering music of Armstrong, Bix sounded at first like a man picking his way rather meticulously through a prepared script. The structure, with its shifting symmetry seemed, unlike Wordsworth's *Perfect Woman*, 'too good for human nature's daily food'. But familiarity, in this instance, bred a deepening respect. Hard as it is to believe, the testimony of Bix's friends and colleagues adds up to overwhelming evidence that 'Singin' the Blues', like every other Bix solo, was a spontaneous improvisation. He was simply not interested in repeating himself as long as the opportunity was there for further exploration. It may be that on that first occasion

I heard no further than the symmetry of the first four bars which, taken out of context, sound like a stanza of rather stilted verse. But of course, one must not stop there, for this formality is then beautifully counterbalanced by an asymmetric phrase of more complexity spread over the next four bars to make beautiful sense. And so it goes on—a perfect construction of balanced phrases, some of them a melancholy or seductive legato, some a triumphant, even dictatorial staccato. Within a single phrase there are notes that fall rigidly on the beat and notes that run ahead as if anticipating the next turn of melody.

I will content myself with one further point of detail. In rhythmic style, 'Singin' the Blues' belongs to the pre-Armstrong era. Had the same record been made by the same musicians ten years later, when Louis Armstrong's rhythmic freedom had been generally assimilated, the stilted two-beat would have been discarded as 'corny' and the piece would have loped along more loosely in a 12/8 time. Bix Beiderbecke personified the musical truth that rhythms do not in themselves go in and out of fashion or supersede each other in the advance of 'progress'. They simply exist, to be used or misused. As a 'cool' thinker according to my definition, it suited him quite well to stay within the two-beat conventions of the time and place. To see how restricting these could be if handled inexpertly, we need only move forward to the short solo by Jimmy Dorsey in the final chorus. He is so inhibited by the rigid framework that, before the eight bars are out, he practically expires from asphyxia. Bix on the other hand gloried in the opportunity for subtle variation which the framework provides. For one example, listen to the four bars that follow the fluent, tumbling break in mid-chorus. There is an explosive whip-up which is typical of many of Bix's excursions into the high register (it was another aspect of the inward direction of his exploration that he was usually quite happy to stay within the natural one-and-a-half octave range of the human voice). Descending from it with measured steps, he puts together another of his neat and logical couplets which most trumpet-players who know the chorus by heart (this writer included) interpret in an even-note style which underlines the meticulous construction of the musical sentence. But Bix's phrases were never so predictable, and close listening reveals that he does not play it like that. His first two bars use dotted notes in an almost jerky fashion—one-a-two-a-three—reminiscent of the 'vo-de-o-do' dance rhythms that the Wolverines used. In the second, answering phrase, the notes even out. Indeed, they so narrowly miss being straightforward even quavers or eighth notes that they would be almost impossible to describe accurately through musical notation. These extremely subtle rhythmic contrasts—between jerky and smooth, staccato and flowing, strictly on-the-beat and lazily across it—seemed to occur naturally and spontaneously in Bix Beiderbecke's improvisations, and it is through them that his solos have retained vitality over the years while those of his contemporaries have tended to sound increasingly mannered.

It would be blatantly unjust to leave the impression that 'Singin' the Blues' owes its peculiar magic solely to Bix's contribution. Fate played an important part in assigning to the session a recording engineer who was either a genius or an incompetent blessed with astonishingly good luck. Faced with a seven-piece band with a rhythm section weak in both numbers and efficiency, he cleared the airways effectively by consigning two of them to the limbo of inaudibility. In those days, drummers were encouraged to bring no more than one cymbal into the studio out of consideration for the recording equipment's sensitivity. So all we hear of Chauncey Moorhouse is an occasional splash of sound. As for Itzy Riskin, he can be detected vamping away manfully on the outer perimeter of the action, but it takes careful listening and I do not recommend it. For the virtual absence of these two warriors leaves the field clear for Eddie Lang, the only man in the rhythm section to match Bix and Trumbauer in stature. Born Salvatore Massaro, Lang inherited from his Italian background a schooled, 'classical' approach to the guitar. Compared with the fluent, wide-ranging work of successors such as Django Reinhardt or Charlie Christian whose melody lines, played on single strings, emulated those of trumpet and saxophone, Lang's rare solos in this vein sound rather laboured and pedestrian. His finest solos were just that—unaccompanied guitar solos in which he supplied both melody and chordal background in classical style, but with a rhythmic sense that belonged to a born jazzman. In the company of other musicians, he became a superb accompanist, and his reputation among jazz buffs to this day rests largely on great partnerships which he formed —with blues guitarist Lonnie Johnson (when Lang used the pseudonym Blind Willie Dunn) and, more especially, with his boyhood friend and fellow Italian, violinist Joe Venuti.

It is as accompanist, virtually single-handed, to the solos of Trumbauer and Bix that Eddie Lang shines on 'Singin' the Blues', contributing beyond measure to its quality and continuity. I will just pull out one plum—the silvery cascade of notes behind the twentieth bar of Trumbauer's solo which must have caused a few delighted smiles in the studio. Lang's virtues were negative, too. Having turned the Trumbauer and Bix solos into effective duets, he takes a back seat in the rather complex ensemble which follows Bix, leaving cornet and saxophone to decide, in a brief moment of confusion, who shall take the lead. The outcome is eminently satisfactory for the listener, for Trumbauer captures the melody line and leaves Bix to play a second part for eight bars which amounts to a continuation of the mood of his solo. After Jimmy Dorsey, there is no doubt who shall lead, for Bix assumes control in his most positive manner, giving the melody of Con Conrad and J. Russell Robinson its first unequivocal statement. Even here, the Bixian sense of rhythmic contrast prompts him to link the emphatic phrases of the tune with a beautifully-timed and nonchalant upward run that seems to pre-echo the break that Eddie Lang delivers a few bars later.

The reader may have begun to suspect, by this time, that there is no end to the refinements that I am capable of finding in 'Singin' the Blues'. Indeed, this is almost the definitive Desert Island Disc, three minutes of music with enough hidden treasures to keep a castaway digging away for years. Historically, it serves to pinpoint the effect which Bix—and his colleagues—had upon their con-temporaries, both black and white. Their 'cool' style impressed that hotbed of burgeoning talents, the Fletcher Henderson Orchestra, who actually recorded a 'cover' of 'Singin' the Blues' with cornetist Rex Stewart playing Bix's solo note for note. The black arranger and saxist Don Redman was strongly influenced by the white New York school and the band known as McKinney's

Cotton Pickers (booked, incidentally, by Jean Goldkette) bristled with Bixian and Trumbaueresque touches while Redman was its leader. Through Redman, this influence reached its most unlikely source, right in the heart of Louis Armstrong's band in 1928 when the Hot Five in its later form was augmented by Don Redman's alto saxophone. True, it was subverted almost instantaneously by the resolutely four-beat, thrusting style of Armstrong, Earl Hines and drummer Zutty Singleton. But there are moments in such Redman arrangements as 'Heah Me Talkin'' To Ya' and 'No One Else But You' when one can hear a New York two-beat feeling struggling to get out!

The influence of Bix himself was more widespread than most jazz historians acknowledge. I have been content to list such players as Jimmy McPartland and Bobby Hackett, who followed Bix's gentle and lyrical side. But fine as these players are in their own right, there was more to Bix than that, and others have found inspiration in the facet that Mezz Mezzrow stressed—the 'militaristic' attack, the 'solid punch', the notes 'sharp as a rifle's crack', which remind us more of such superficially unlikely Bix disciples as the rumbustious Wild Bill Davison, the terse Max Kaminsky, and the voluble Ruby Braff. It is not far-fetched to suggest that, through Rex Stewart, some Beiderbecke influence found its way into the formative styles of such black exponents as Clark Terry and Miles Davis. Certainly, a positive line of influence extended back to the New Yorkers when, in the first modern jazz era of the late Forties, 'cool' was promoted from a creative process to a way of life. Lester Young always insisted that he was attracted, as a learner, to the light, tranquil sound that Trumbauer achieved on C melody saxophone. When Lester's own influence affected the thinking of a whole generation of musicians in every branch of the saxophone family, it became easier still to hear Trumbauer —and perhaps, by association, Bix himself—in the sound of Paul Desmond, Lee Konitz and Stan Getz.

And so the ripples go on, transferring from 'cool' to 'hot' and back again. Ever since Bix Beiderbecke died, in 1931, at the age of 28, jazz enthusiasts have speculated as to the course he would have taken had he lived. Would his style have continued to develop until it reached the point from which the Cool School started in the late Forties? It's an attractive notion, but highly improbable. So much depends upon his own aspirations. Had they led him successfully in the direction which both Benny Green and Sudhalter and Evans have suggested, then the recording studios of Hollywood seem a more likely destination than the small and short-lived associations through which jazz innovators move most freely. But this is pedestrian, earthbound speculation, hardly worthy of a musical genius. For like many other geniuses in the creative universe, he flashed like a comet across the sky, leaving in his recordings some material evidence of the brilliance and magnificence of his passage.

Duke Ellington

THE YEAR 1923 IS to jazz history what 1066 is to the schoolboy's table of dates. In that year, King Oliver's Creole Jazz Band made the batch of recordings which are generally taken as the starting-point in the development of jazz on record. In them, the fully-fledged cornet of young Louis Armstrong was heard on record for the first time. Elsewhere, Bessie Smith, too, was making her first records, defying the technical shortcomings of the medium with the voice that literally elbowed its way out of the grooves to deliver the message of the blues.

In that same fateful year, Duke Ellington, after one false start, finally arrived, aged twenty-four, to find his fortune in New York. He was born on April 29, 1899, in Washington DC, and grew up in an environment which was, in the context of black America, middle class. His father, James E. Ellington, was a draughtsman in government employ, by Duke's account a fine fellow with a line in grandiloquent and outrageous flattery which he passed on to his son. (On tour with the Duke in Canada, he startled one of the local ladies by pronouncing: 'The millions of beautiful snowflakes are a celebration in honour of your beauty!') Duke Ellington's mother, to whom he was deeply devoted, appears in rare photographs to have been a lady of Edwardian style, beauty and elegance. Indeed, Edward Kennedy Ellington seems to have inherited a certain aristocratic stylishness long before a school friend of gregarious disposition dubbed him 'Duke' to enhance his own social status.

With the benefit of a solid education, Duke Ellington had earned a scholarship to art college before he left high school, but he never took it up. By this time, he was already earning 'a lot of money' by playing piano and by booking bands for dances. His art training was not entirely useless: 'When customers came for posters to advertise a dance, I would ask them what they were doing about their music. When they wanted to hire a band, I would ask them who's painting their signs.' In piano-playing, Duke had had early lessons from a formal music teacher called, incredibly, Mrs Clinkscales. When her pupils gave their recital in the local church, young Ellington was the only one who didn't know his part. 'So Mrs Clinkscales had to play the treble and I just played the umpy-dump bottom! The umpy-dump bottom was, of course, the foundation and understanding of that part of piano-playing I later learned to like.' The style of piano-playing which attracted the Duke flourished in places like Frank Holliday's poolroom, which appears to have satisfied Ellington's gracious standards by boasting lawyers, doctors and college graduates among its otherwise raffish clientele. The masters here were players like Doc Perry, Les Dishman, Clarence Bowser, Sticky Mack and Blind Johnny, some musically literate, some non-readers who nonetheless made their own original contribution.

Ragtime, with its florid, fulsome right hand and 'umpy-dump bottom', was without doubt the foundation of the solo piano style which these men practised. But it's probable that under the influence of the player-piano rolls which spread the new pianistic fashions emanating from New York as effectively as the gramophone was to do later, they were moving away from ragtime's almost militaristic 2/4 rhythm towards the more fluent, jazz-like style discussed in the chapter on James P. Johnson. Duke drank it all in. 'I was always a terrific listener. I'm taller on one side than the other from leaning over the piano, listening.'

And he went on listening when, already quite experienced as solo pianist, bandleader and entrepreneur, he and his close friends Sonny Greer and Otto 'Toby' Hardwick followed up a tip-off from Fats Waller and made the move to New York. Harlem was already a veritable university of advanced piano-playing and, as I have described apropos James P. Johnson, the lessons took the form of open contests. The 'professor' whom Duke admired most of all and who had the greatest influence on his own piano style, was the formidable Willie 'The Lion' Smith, scourge of any upstart with inflated ideas of his prowess. 'This was the big thing about The Lion: a gladiator at heart. Anybody who had a reputation as a piano-player had to prove it right there and then by sitting down to the piano and displaying his artistic wares. And when a cat thought that he was something special, he usually fell into that trap (or, you might say, into the jaws of The Lion) and he always came out with his reputation all skinned up, covered with the lacerations of humiliation, because before he got through too many stanzas The Lion was standing over him, cigar blazing.'

However, unlike Willie The Lion, James P. or Fats Waller, Duke Ellington did not graduate from this Harlem school to become a featured piano-player. Many early critics were led into underrating his abilities at the keyboard simply because he featured himself so sparingly. It is almost as if the 'terrific listener' was so preoccupied with listening to the musicians whom he gathered around him that he scorned his own contribution. Certainly, listening to, and utilising to the best advantage, the idiosyncrasies of his side-men proved to be one of Duke's great talents once the band which he formed in 1924 flowered into the Ellington Orchestra, ten or eleven strong, that took up residency first at the Kentucky Club and then in Harlem's most glittering entertainment showcase, the Cotton Club. Recordings by Ellington bands began late in 1924 and, significantly, acquired distinction only when soloists of real calibre joined the ranks. Even then, the characteristic which made Duke Ellington's music unique and the first example of 'jazz composition' within the big band meaning of the term was what, to anyone versed in straight composition, must appear to be an eccentric method of composing. Whatever inhibition it was that deterred him from becoming just another pianist-leader in the egotistical mould, also restrained him from imposing his will on the band in the manner of a composer-leader like, say, Jelly Roll Morton. The Ellington method entailed first of all gathering together musicians each of whom had a distinctive improvising style and tonal 'voice'. From that point on, it was a matter of using those voices to the full—and that meant taking suggestions from the musicians, altering preconceived ideas to suit them and coming as close as possible to 'improvising' through them.

Billy Strayhorn, the arranger who joined Duke in 1939 and thereafter became his compositional alter ego, described the process well: 'Ellington plays the piano, but his real instrument is his band. Each member of his band is to him a distinctive tone colour and set of emotions, which he mixes with others equally distinctive to produce a third thing, which I like to call the "Ellington Effect".

'Sometimes this fixing happens on paper and frequently right on the bandstand. I have often seen him exchange parts in the middle of a piece because the man and part weren't the same character.

'Ellington's concern is with the individual musician, and what happens when they put their musical characters together. Watching him on the bandstand, the listener might think that his movements are stock ones used by everyone in front of a band. However, the extremely observant may well detect the flick of the finger that may draw the sound he wants from a musician.

'By letting his men play naturally and relaxed, Ellington is able to probe the intimate recesses of their minds and find things that not even the musicians thought were there.'

I was once present in a hotel room when a group of rather earnest students were interviewing the Duke for a university magazine. One of them remarked on what he saw as the divergence of technical prowess within the ranks of the Ellington orchestra of the late Fifties. 'Let's be like the businessmen and talk percentages,' said the Duke, 'Nobody plays 100% of an instrument. Some guys like Clark [Terry] play 90% of their instrument. Someone like Ray Nance maybe plays 45% of the instrument—but he plays that 45% in a way that no one else on earth can play it!'

The first Ellingtonian of this calibre and stature was the cornetist Leroy 'Bubber' Miley. Born in South Carolina in 1903, Miley had been raised from the age of six in New York where, by the time he met Ellington in 1924, he had become a master of a style of playing that was prevalent—and extremely popular—in Harlem. 'Gutbucket' is what the musicians called it, and the word is certainly apt for the earthy, slightly ribald music that made much use of wah-wah mutes and 'growl' techniques. Jazz historians have discovered over the years the dangers that await anyone who attempts to deduce a chronological order of events by listening to gramophone records alone. It is all too easy to say that, because Joe Oliver recorded effective 'wah-wah' solos in 1923 and Bubber Miley is heard in similar vein in 1927, therefore Miley was influenced exclusively by Oliver. Another legendary master of the plunger mute was the Memphis cornetist Johnny Dunn, and both he and Bubber Miley were members of blues-singer Mamie Smith's band during the early Twenties. Miley also played and recorded in the band of cornetist Tom Morris, who did not enjoy Dunn's enormous popularity in New York, but who can be heard wielding a deft plunger on recordings made before any of the famous Oliver solos went into circulation.

This does not rule out Oliver as a direct influence upon Miley. Indeed, we have the evidence of Garvin Bushell (in *Jazz Panorama*), who travelled with Bubber Miley in Mamie Smith's Jazz Hounds, that Oliver did indeed make a great impression on the young cornetist. 'When we were in Chicago, Bubber and I would go to the Dreamland and hear King Oliver every night. Bubber got his growling from Oliver. Before hearing Oliver, he never growled. That's where Bubber changed his style and began using his hand over the tin mute that used to come with all cornets. It was hearing Oliver that did it.'

Let us, for the fun of it, assume that Oliver begat Bubber. This leads us to another intriguing facet of Duke Ellington the composer, and that is his eclecticism. I have already noted that, with considerable geographical licence, the music which came up to New York from New Orleans via Chicago was known as 'Western style'. The Eastern musicians—those operating on the Washington-Philadelphia-New York axis—were prone to look down on the Westerners. Louis Armstrong recalled encountering a cool breeze when he first moved up from Chicago to join Fletcher Henderson's band in New York. 'They simply ignored me to an extent, and so I don't say nothin' to them. But I'm saying to myself "This bunch of old stuck-up . . . !" ' Henderson saw Louis as 'pretty much a down-home boy in the big city'. And when Duke Ellington himself first encountered Willie The 'Lion' Smith, the latter invited him straight up to play. 'One of those Western piano plonkers just fell in—I want him to take the stool so I can crush him later.' Duke's account doesn't record who the piano plonker was—nor how he himself felt about being used as a decoy!

Contrary to the current trend, then, Duke Ellington showed no reserve towards Western style when he began to write his own music. He admired Sidney Bechet—'one of the truly great originals'—without stint, and even managed to pin down that notoriously unclubbable 'loner' in his band for a few months in 1926. (Indeed, the Bechet sound, to some degree domesticated, became an almost lifelong colour on the Ellington palette through the alto-playing of Johnny Hodges.) Further New Orleans colouring was deliberately added with the later inclusion of clarinettist Barney Bigard and bassist Wellman Braud. Duke seems to have been particularly receptive to ideas emanating from the King Oliver band of earlier years. The clarinettist who preceded Bigard was Rudy Jackson, who had played (though not recorded) in the famous band that included Louis Armstrong. In the long-defunct magazine *Jazz Music*, the writer and broadcaster Charles Chilton wrote of a conversation he had enjoyed with Jackson in Ceylon in 1945 in which the clarinettist recalled having enthused to Duke Ellington about Oliver's work, especially in the area of the blues. One piece which Rudy Jackson played over to the Duke was Oliver's 'Camp Meeting Blues' whose themes, filled out with fat harmonies and a liberal injection of the Ellington Effect, re-emerged there and then as 'Creole Love Call'. We may fairly assume that the Oliver-Armstrong 'break' from 'Snake Rag' which finds its way intact into Duke's 'The Creeper' owed its new lease of life also to Jackson's suggestion.

One further 'coincidence' brings us abruptly from the general to the particular. 'Black and Tan Fantasy' was written by Duke Ellington and Bubber Miley. It is generally accepted that the sombre opening theme was contributed by Miley, who is said to have based it on a church song that his sister used to sing. With a little acute listening we can go further than this, for the first eight bars of the theme are no more nor less than 'The Holy City' ('Jerusalem, Jerusalem') transposed into a minor key. This borrowing from 'The Holy City' has made quite frequent appearances in New Orleans jazz through the years and, more intriguingly still in the present context, it was used by King Oliver as a central theme for his piece 'Chimes Blues'! Fun though it is, this sort of amateur detection, which is open to anyone with a record-player and a pair of ears in good working order, is no mere self-indulgence. It gives an insight into the sort of mind—alert, inquisitive and unusually receptive—which recognised and drew in all the basic ingredients of jazz and then put them through the subtle culinary process that results in what Billy Strayhorn called the Ellington Effect.

In 'Black and Tan Fantasy' the Effect was pronounced and, as we shall see in a moment, controversial. Before going into the details of it, it is necessary to introduce one more distinctive and important Ellington 'voice'. Trombonist Joe 'Tricky Sam' Nanton was a prime subject for Duke's percentage calculations. He was born in New York in 1904, and wàs playing his own brand of 'gutbucket' in Harlem clubs when Duke hired him in 1926. He was brought in to replace Charlie Irvis, who had matched Bubber Miley in his experiments with the plunger mute. Between 1926 and 1948 when he died, Tricky Sam had virtually no musical existence outside the Ellington Band. As a straight trombonist, playing open horn, he was inclined to be staid and pedestrian and would scarcely have qualified for more than a passing mention in the history books. But when he put a cone-shaped metal mute in the bell of the instrument and manipulated a large rubber plunger in front of it, he became a poet. It was not a style that called more than ten per cent of the instrument into play—indeed, as Duke Ellington discovered when he wrote for him, there were no more than a handful of notes that could be pitched accurately under such a burden of mutes. But no one, before or since, ever produced such evocative sounds out of that ten per cent. I have already established that 'wah-wah' is the common onomatopoeic term for the kind of plunger work in which both Nanton and Miley specialised, but there are trombonists of my acquaintance who have almost worried themselves into a nursing-home trying to discover how Nanton's trombone seemed to say 'yah-yah'!

Duke Ellington subsequently referred to the opening minor-key theme of 'Black and Tan Fantasy' as the funeral-march section, and clearly Bubber Miley and Tricky Sam Nanton, plungers flapping lugubriously, are cast in the role of mourners. We do not

know who it was who put the 'jungle music tag' on Ellington's
music of this period—I would guess that it was someone on the
publicity rather than the musical side of the fence. It was a label
that came in handy when the Duke was called on to write music
for the lavish and exotic productions at the Cotton Club, but to
me it has always seemed a clumsy and obvious term to describe
the eerie, nocturnal and *open-air* effect which muted horns,
clanking banjo and a strangely reverberative studio acoustic
produced. If I say that it evokes for me an impression of the
American South rather than the African jungle, I have to confess
that I have seen neither. But nor, as far as I know, had Duke
Ellington!

In his book *Early Jazz*, Gunther Schuller pours some scorn
on the second strain of 'Black and Tan Fantasy' as compared
with those sections in which Bubber Miley clearly made a strong
contribution. Indeed, in comparing, to the Duke's disadvantage,
the difference in artistic levels at that time between Miley and
Ellington, he says: 'Whereas Miley's theme, his solos—and to a
lesser degree Nanton's—again reflect an unadorned pure classicism,
Ellington's two contributions derive from the world of slick,
trying-to-be-modern show music.' This is stern, schoolmasterly
stuff, but in the end the quality that has made 'Black and Tan
Fantasy' an acknowledged classic for fifty years has more to do
with the Ellington Effect than with 'unadorned pure classicism'.
And it would be unreasonable to expect that effect to exclude the
Ellington personality altogether. From the start Duke revealed
many musical facets, and they were often flatly contradictory. As
a composer, he often revelled in fast and furious stomping, and
in the early days he developed a brass section which was un-
beatable in that genre. The opposite side of his nature showed
itself fully from the mid-Thirties onwards in luxurious, almost
sybaritic, melodies such as 'Sophisticated Lady', 'Prelude to a
Kiss' and 'In a Sentimental Mood'. The second strain of 'Black
and Tan Fantasy', which Otto Hardwick plays here on alto
saxophone, is an early manifestation of this leaning. Until I read
Schuller's condemnation I had always accepted it as an attractive
snatch of melody and a typical Ellingtonian touch. Trying to be
modern? Well, there is a chunk of whole-tone scale at the beginning

of each eight-bar section, but it falls into place quite naturally and without pretension. Out of keeping with the rest of the record? At the risk of sounding truculent, one is tempted to ask 'Whose record is it anyway?' Duke chose to call the piece a fantasy, no doubt acknowledging a certain dreamlike cross-fading of images and impressions. Fifty years and innumerable performances later, that alto-sax interpolation is inextricably enmeshed in the fabric of the piece, and there is nothing much that any musicologist can do about it. Its very lushness seems to give added point to what follows.

At this stage in his career, Duke Ellington showed a cavalier attitude towards his contract with Victor Records and took his band from studio to studio under a variety of transparent pseudonyms—The Washingtonians, the Harlem Footwarmers, the Jungle Band and so on. As a result, 'Black and Tan Fantasy' was recorded no less than five times in eight months in 1927. Each version has its own character. Trumpeter Jabbo Smith replaced Miley in two 'takes' made on the same day, and on one recording the first solo after the alto-sax passage is played by Nanton on trombone. The version from an October session which I have chosen to discuss has, I believe, the best Bubber Miley solo. But each of these interpretations, and, indeed, all subsequent performances of the piece, retain, as though it were written into the score, the device with which Bubber Miley made his solo entry in the very first recording—a long sustained high note, tightly muted, that is held up like an arresting forefinger to drag the listener's attention back from sentimental fantasies to a fervent oration on the theme of the blues. Bubber Miley's solo in the version under review is absolutely superb. It is a passionate harangue in which everything that has ever been written about the influence of the vocal blues on instrumental jazz—the infinite variations in timbre, the bending of tones into 'blue notes', the use of throat sounds or 'growls'—is exemplified. Like King Oliver's solo in 'Dippermouth Blues', this is 'preaching trumpet' and the description cannot be bettered.

No piano style of the period could have sustained Miley's mood, and Duke's jaunty solo, couched in the two-fisted 'stride' style of the Harlem school from which he graduated, does little more than relieve the tension before Tricky Sam Nanton comes in with another oration. This solo is not by any means his most impressive, but in the last four bars he bursts into a macabre lamentation which shows the way in which his style was to develop. Bubber Miley's final solo, this time exhorting and scolding the congregation even more passionately, has again provided all subsequent interpreters with a model to which they have adhered more or less faithfully. It reaches a climax in the eighth bar with a surprising G seventh chord (Duke's inspiration rather than Miley's, perhaps) that gives a suitably dramatic lead into the quotation from Chopin's 'Funeral March' which forms an apt coda to a piece that breathes atmosphere.

The Chicagoans

THE NUCLEUS OF McKenzie and Condon's Chicagoans was a group of young musicians—Jimmy 'McPartland, Bud Freeman, Jim Lannigan and Frank Teschmacher—who had become hooked on jazz in the early Twenties while they were still at the Austin High School in Chicago. They learnt to play, like scores of embryo jazzmen since, by putting on records by their favourite bands (with them, the New Orleans Rhythm Kings topped the list) and stopping the turntable every few minutes while they learned the music off, bar by bar. According to Jimmy McPartland, 'In three or four weeks we could finally play one tune all the way through—"Farewell Blues". Boy, that was our tune!' Hearing these musicians reminisce, one is struck by their resemblance, in eagerness and enthusiasm, to the 'revivalist' bands which sprang up all over the world in the years immediately after World War II.

But the Austin High School Gang, as they came to be called, were no revivalists. For one thing, they were Chicagoans, at a time when Chicago was the hub of contemporary and forward-looking jazz. They had only to hop on a streetcar to hear, night in and night out, the very finest jazz that could be heard anywhere, from musicians such as King Oliver, Louis Armstrong, Johnny and Baby Dodds and Jimmy Noone. More important still, they were Americans, and it was no part of the mood of young Americans in the early Twenties simply to emulate the great jazz masters from a respectful distance. It would be unrealistic to evade the fact that they were white, too, and had access while they were still learning to avenues of employment from which their 'teachers' were barred. All of these factors served to give them and the associates whom they gathered round them the sort of brash confidence that was needed to establish them as stylists in their own right.

A wide range of critical views have been expressed about the Chicagoans and the so-called 'Chicago style' with which they have been accredited. A common verdict among those purists who accept the New Orleans style of collective improvisation as Holy Writ is that they tried to copy New Orleans jazz and simply got it wrong. All the evidence contradicts this rather lofty view. The listening habits of the Austin High School Gang seem to have been catholic if not downright indiscriminate. Jimmy McPartland has recalled: 'We sometimes went down to a Chinese restaurant, The Golden Pheasant, where there was a band by the name of Al Haid. They played pretty good, a semi-commercial brand of jazz, so we used to go down and eat chop suey and listen to the orchestra. It wasn't as good as the New Orleans Rhythm Kings— but we listened.' They listened also—and closely identified with— The Wolverine Orchestra which featured the brilliant young cornetist Bix Beiderbecke. Apart from his shining musical quality, Bix had other attractions for the young Chicagoans. I do not go along with the view that has sometimes been voiced that Bix Beiderbecke's reputation was inflated by his contemporaries in some sort of anti-black propaganda move. The frequent forays which the white musicians made into the black area on Chicago's South Side to hear their idols—and Bix himself often accompanied them—discounts any such racial bias. On the other hand, it was clearly encouraging for the young hopefuls in Chicago to have a hero who was not separated from them by age (he was only two or three years their senior) nor by any racial or social barriers. Bix was 'one of them' and his influence was enormous. To say that the style revealed by the young Chicagoans in their early records is simply a bad attempt at New Orleans style is to turn a deaf ear to the Bix influence in every bar.

Whether or not the early enthusiasms and explorations of the Austin High School Gang and their friends amounted to a definable 'style' is another matter. Certainly the musicians shared an attitude of mind about their music, a thrusting aggressiveness that seems to permeate the music of the McKenzie-Condon sessions and set them apart from the recordings of that period by New Orleans men. Jazz historians recognised this trait years ago and groped around for the cause. The city of Chicago itself—'tough, cynical, gangster-ridden'—took much of the blame or praise, according to the critical point of view. I should like to throw into the pool another theory which is, at least, more closely connected to the process of making music.

Let us first see how the McKenzie-Condon session actually came about. The principals who gave their names to the band were not from Austin High School. Indeed, they were not even Chicagoans by birth. Red McKenzie, from St Louis, Missouri, was an ex-jockey, a compulsive singer, an instrumentalist *manqué* who made good the deficiency by making quite convincing jazz noises through comb and paper, and an energetic entrepreneur with useful connections, in which role he appears on this record label. Eddie Condon, born in Indiana, had moved to within striking distance of Chicago with his family in 1914 and, almost as soon as he was old enough to hold a banjo in a band, threw himself into a one-man crusade on behalf of jazz in general and his Chicagoan friends and associates in particular. Condon knew the musicians, McKenzie knew Tommy Rockwell, the powerful head of Okeh Records. The result was a record session at the outset of which, according to Condon, Rockwell was 'polite but dubious'.

Eddie Condon shared the Austin High School Gang's fanatical devotion to jazz. Indeed, it is in his reminiscences of that period (*We Called It Music*) that we see the first glimpse of jazz and 'the public'—that is to say audiences, bookers, recording chiefs and anyone else who paid the piper—drifting apart. He recalls playing for a dance at the unpromising-sounding Gedney Farms Country Club in Westchester in 1928: 'There were three generations of Westchesterites present: the kids wanted "Tiger Rag", the middle-aged group wanted "Alice Blue Gown", the old folks asked for Strauss waltzes. The entertainment chairman came up and said, "I used to play drums at Yale. Trouble with your man is he doesn't syncopate enough." "He didn't go to Yale," I said.

'Nothing pleased anybody—the music was too fast, too loud,

too slow, and where was the melody? Finally we decided to turn our backs on the audience and enjoy ourselves. We took off on "Jazz Me Blues", "I Wish I Could Shimmy Like My Sister Kate", "I Ain't Gonna Give You None Of My Jelly Roll", "Royal Garden Blues", and "Clarinet Marmalade". Now and then I took a quick look at the dancers; they were shocked, disgusted, irritated, bored, and mad.'

Half-a-century later, musicians trying to earn a living in jazz will recognise almost identical symptoms of sales resistance, reading 'rock' for 'Tiger Rag' and 'Glenn Miller' for 'Alice Blue Gown'. They will find it surprising, if not comforting, to learn that it happened to Eddie Condon as early as 1928. True, the Original Dixieland Band had frightened New York to death when they first unleashed their 'jass' in 1917. And in the early Twenties, controversy over the new music raged in both musical journals and the lay press. But it's equally true to say that the originators of the music, the great black exponents such as Oliver, Armstrong, the Dodds brothers, Kid Ory and Jimmy Noone, felt no draught from the outside world. Their music had grown up freely in New Orleans without pressure from either commercial or artistic quarters. In Chicago, for a while at least, the same free and unselfconscious growth was able to continue. Themselves migrants from the South, the black musicians played to audiences who had come up the same way and shared the same culture. Furthermore, most of them had been active in music long before the term 'jazz' was coined, so they claimed no special identity for their wares. Faced with a situation comparable to Eddie Condon's Westchester débacle, they would have obliged with 'Alice Blue Gown' and even a Strauss waltz—and since they knew no other way to play than in their warm New Orleans style, it would have sounded wonderful!

Eddie Condon's problem was one which has beset jazzmen of every race and persuasion ever since jazz spread across the world —namely, how to 'sell' the music to people who were not culturally predisposed to accept it. It seems to me quite feasible that at any rate some of the nervous anxiety that is discernible in the Chicagoans' music, the fact that it lacked the freewheeling joy of the best New Orleans music and often sounded more feverish than 'hot', may have derived not so much from the character and environment of the musicians as from the defensive attitude of mind which they found themselves having to adopt. The recording session that produced 'Nobody's Sweetheart' bristled with it. Eddie Condon had booked the Austin High School team en bloc. The drummer Dave Tough, who had been playing regularly with them, had just taken off on a working trip to France, and Condon replaced him by general consent with an eager nineteen-year-old called Gene Krupa. The band was completed by pianist Joe Sullivan, a player who blended the styles of Earl Hines and Fats Waller with a rollicking Irish pugnacity that was all his own.

In his book, Condon recalled that, as the musicians set up for the session, an already nervous Tommy Rockwell observed Gene Krupa building up his drums: ' "What are you going to do with those?" Rockwell asked, "Play them," Krupa said simply. Rockwell shook his head. "You can't do that," he said. "You'll ruin our equipment. All we've ever used on records are snare drums and cymbals." Krupa, who had been practising every day at home, looked crushed. "How about letting us try them?" I asked. "The drums are the backbone of the band. They hold us up." I could see that Rockwell was leery of the whole business; drums or no drums, I figured, we are probably going to get tossed out. "Let the kids try it," McKenzie said. "If they go wrong I'll take the rap." "All right," Rockwell said, "but I'm afraid the bass drum and those tom-toms will knock the needle off the wax and out into the street." '

Well, the recording equipment survived and 'Nobody's Sweetheart' was passed on to posterity as an important piece of jazz history, a minor classic and, so it has always been said, the epitome of 'Chicago style'. Can the performance of a hastily assembled and notoriously unruly bunch of musicians, some of them musically immature, really be called a 'style'? Jimmy McPartland has shown himself doubtful. 'They say we got our particular style down well on that session. Of course, we didn't have a name for it or anything—it was simply the way we used to play.' And the way they played was extremely diverse. Jimmy McPartland himself had shaped his early playing in the Bix Beiderbecke mould, with such success that in 1924 he had gone to New York to take

Bix's place in the Wolverine Orchestra. As his lead playing and solo in 'Nobody's Sweetheart' reveal, he didn't possess Bix's striking clarity of thought, tone or execution. Indeed, in view of the widely-accepted image of Chicago jazz as hard-boiled and tough, McPartland's cornet playing is surprisingly soft-centred. Its main attraction, clearly absorbed from Bix, is its unpredictability. One is never quite sure in which direction the phrases, hemmed in by the tune's rather slow-moving harmonic structure, are going to make a dash for freedom.

Frank Teschmacher, who precedes McPartland in the solo order, was a musician of a different order. It is a source of great frustration to the jazz historian that a fatal car accident in 1929 deprived us of the chance to see how his talent would have developed. All that comes down to us now is the bespectacled, studious face in the photographs, some rather colourless recollections by his associates of a man deeply absorbed in music both jazz and 'classical', and some fervent, wildly expressive solos that ignited controversy almost as soon as they were committed to wax.

Analysis of his solo in 'Nobody's Sweetheart' isolates, without too much difficulty, three distinct elements in his style. We have a clue to one of them in the opening ensemble chorus of the piece. It was Teschmacher, we are given to understand, who designed the routines of these McKenzie-Condon recordings, setting out the order of events and writing out the occasional scored passages. The pattern that he used here, with a legato—and fairly 'straight' —statement of the theme in which the clarinet harmonises soulfully, followed at once by a contrasting 'hot' chorus with clarinet again playing a leading part, is, as we shall see, one which was used almost invariably by the New Orleans clarinettist Jimmy Noone in his small-group recordings of the period. It is known that Teschmacher was an ardent admirer of Noone's, and if that had been his only influence we might have expected him, in his solo chorus, to have set off, Noone-like, on a series of fluent but bustling runs over the whole range of the instrument, interspersed with stabbing high notes and wailing slurs. But with Tesch there was another clear influence, and one that worked in the opposite direction. I am referring, if you had not already guessed, to the ubiquitous Bix. Leaving aside the style in which it is delivered, the actual melody line of Teschmacher's half-chorus could be described as a Bix-style cornet passage transcribed to clarinet. Indeed, Tesch captures rather better than McPartland the commanding, parade-ground side of Beiderbecke's style. The Bix influence, calling for lines that were convoluted rather than wide-ranging, staccato rather than flowing, clashed with, and overcame, the Noone influence in Teschmacher's playing.

And yet it is clear, from every solo that he recorded, that Frank Teschmacher aspired to the passion, the intensity, the 'hotness' that he heard in the black musicians' work. This third element, emanating from the man himself, is the one which aroused all the controversy over his playing. Jazz commentators can be found, past and present, who dismiss Teschmacher's recordings on the grounds of their technical inadequancy. Compared with either Noone or Bix, whose actual instrumental sounds shared a certain schooled purity, Teschmacher played 'out of tune', used a 'squawky' tone and often let fly carelessly-articulated phrases. It is tempting to say, glibly, that he was not the first jazz musician deliberately to distort his instrument's natural sound and capability in the interests of self-expression. But on reflection he probably *was* the first. Throughout subsequent jazz history one can think of many musicians—from clarinettist Pee Wee Russell, trumpeter Henry Allen, cornetist Rex Stewart and trombonist Dicky Wells right through to 'moderns' like saxists Sonny Rollins and Roland Kirk—who have exploited 'wrong' playing to convey their individual message. Here was a musician who, according to fellow clarinettist Joe Marsala, had 'terrific technique,' who had studied violin at the Austin High School and who, like several of his associates, had a passion for music that extended to Ravel and Gustav Holst. It seems grotesquely unlikely that, after so much absorption in music, he would not have known how to tune a clarinet! No, what I hear in Frank Teschmacher is the assertion, albeit unformed and probably largely unconscious, of an alternative way of playing jazz, a freely-expressed, romantic, 'anything goes' approach which ignored the unwritten laws and precepts of New Orleans style.

In some ways, the same judgement applies to Lawrence 'Bud'

Freeman, although when 'Nobody's Sweetheart' was recorded, he was probably lagging behind his contemporaries in musical development. He was the only one of the Austin High School Gang who had undergone no musical training before taking up jazz. Eddie Condon described his first meeting with Bud, when he was sent to play a gig in a small-time cabaret in Chicago. 'When I got there the other musicians had arrived. One of them, Squeak Buhl, was setting up drums. A good-looking kid was trying to get notes from a tenor saxophone which was green with corrosion. It sounded the way it looked. A blond, solidly-built boy was watching him; he had a cornet. I introduced myself; the saxophone player shook hands with me. "My name is Bud Freeman," he said. "This is Jimmy McPartland." We sat down and began to play. Freeman seemed to know only one tune; everything sounded vaguely like "China Boy". McPartland had a strong rugged tone; he knew where he was going and enjoyed the journey. Buhl set a good beat and we all pushed it a little. Now and then Freeman hit a note that sounded like music.' Jimmy McPartland has also put down his recollections of Bud's earliest work with the Austin Gang. It was so bad that Teschmacher would say, 'Let's throw that bum out!' But McPartland stood up for him. 'There was one thing I could recognise in Bud then—he had a terrific beat. He still has. He began by just playing rhythm, getting on one note and holding it; I mean swinging on it, just that one note. He didn't change the harmony or anything, and we used to get so mad at him, you know. We'd yell at him "Change the note!" Still, as I remember, he had a great beat.'

By the time 'Nobody's Sweetheart' came to be recorded, Bud had found a few more notes and he swung them, in his short half-chorus, with a great beat. A short time before this session, Bud Freeman had heard the Fletcher Henderson Orchestra and had been floored by the playing of Coleman Hawkins, whom he had previously heard only on record. The inspiration of Hawkins was no doubt there in this performance, but Bud had little technique to express it except in the most skeletal way. And, as with Tesch, there was always the more insistent influence of Bix Beiderbecke, revealed chiefly in the rhythmic approach, that brought Bud's contribution in line with those of Teschmacher and McPartland. Excluding hindsight, there's nothing much in 'Nobody's Sweetheart' to suggest that, within three years, Bud Freeman would be fluent enough—and sufficiently his own man— to present fully-fledged to the world an alternative tenor-sax style to that of Coleman Hawkins.

In their solos, the work of these young Chicagoans seems to have been not so much a style, more schizophrenia set to music! Likewise, the ensembles show the tug of conflicting influences. Once again there is the model of Beiderbecke. In the second half of the final ensemble Teschmacher, have thrown off a Noone-type run, plays a legato phrase across the beat which is pure Bix. The rhythm combination of Sullivan, Condon and Krupa, however, lays down a pushing beat which is much closer to the steady four-four of the New Orleans bands than the rocking two-beat which usually accompanied Bix at this period. The juxtaposition of these two rhythmic notions—the one-two-three-four of the rhythm section and the variations on *one*-and-*two*-and from the front-line—gives the music an agitated feeling which is accentuated by the little tricks (the self-explanatory 'shuffle', 'flare' and 'explosion') which the lads thought up. I have left bassist Jim Lannigan out account since he produced an idiosyncratic style on the string bass which no subsequent jazz style preserved—a tuneless hunker-dunker which leads one to think that he must have overhauled his technique drastically before graduating to the Chicago Symphony Orchestra a few years later!

How do we assess the music of these Chicagoans? In his book *Really the Blues*, the clarinettist Mezz Mezzrow, a Chicagoan himself and one of the cronies of the musicians under discussion, analysed their early recordings—at which, incidentally, he was present and on some of which he played the tenor saxophone. Despite mutual compliments which passed between Mezzrow and Bud Freeman in later years, I sense that little love was lost between Mezz on the one side and Eddie Condon and the Austin High School graduates on the other. Mezzrow identified himself closely with the black race. When he went to jail in the Thirties on a narcotics charge, he actually declared himself a Negro and served his sentence in the black section. He was a brash, opinionated and, in some aspects of his posing, aburd man and it must have infuriated the keen and conscientious members of the McKenzie-Condon band to have him constantly around lecturing them on the error of their ways in departing from the principles of black New Orleans music. Mezzrow's stern judgement on his fellow Chicagoans was that, instead of sticking close to the New Orleans pattern and working to perfect it, they got too big for their boots. 'Trying to show how good they were, they got too fancy, sometimes, too ornate and over-elaborate, full of uncalled-for frills and ruffles.' It is sometimes difficult to ascertain whether Mezz's displeasure arose because they listened to him and got it wrong, or because, as seems probable as time went on, they ceased to listen to him at all.

Whitney Balliett, the distinguished jazz critic of the *New Yorker*, has taken up a position at the other extreme: '. . . a number of white musicians from the Chicago area suddenly coalesced and produced a new ensemble-solo music that is generally known as Chicago jazz . . . it seemed . . . very snappy, very modern . . . the white Chicagoans had the new-broom quality that bebop offered fifteen years later.'

Was Mezzrow right, or does Whitney hit the nail on the head? Or again, does the truth lie somewhere in between? The conclusion to which the thoughts in this chapter seem to have led is that the most significant thing about 'Chicago style' as exemplified in 'Nobody's Sweetheart' is that it was not a style at all.

Johnny Dodds and Jimmy Noone

I HAVE CHOSEN TO DISCUSS recordings by Johnny Dodds and Jimmy Noone in a single chapter for two reasons. One is that neither musician demands—or indeed offers—the sort of background information that I have given for, say, Jelly Roll Morton or Sidney Bechet. We know surprisingly little about them. They were not 'characters' with colourful careers nor, so far as we know, did they go in for much theorising about their music. They died within a few years of each other in the early Forties, before the great tidal wave of research and literature that accompanied the New Orleans Revival had got fully under way. And in the recollection of their surviving colleagues, it is their music rather than their personalities that looms largest.

The other reason for putting them together is that they are literally poles apart. I have gone into some detail in earlier chapters about what we might call the Explosion Theory of the creation of jazz which, in simplified terms, I have described as the result of a collision between Creole culture on the way down and 'slave' culture on the way up. In the schooled, classically-based music of the Creole families, the clarinet played an important role alongside the stringed instruments of the small, salon orhecstras. When, with the decline in social status that followed Emancipation, those orchestras became bands and the salon gave way to the dance-hall, the honky-tonk and the open street, the clarinet had the robustness and the versatility to survive. Furthermore, in the hands of the Creole musicians, it retained a high degree of its classical purity of tone and fluency of execution even when it found itself outnumbered by brass instruments of a rougher background.

One Creole musician proved the exception to the rule. He was Sidney Bechet, whose maverick personality drew him towards the more expressive, rough-and-ready music of the blues. In his reminiscences, he speculates modestly on the influence which he might have had on his contemporaries in New Orleans. 'There was Johnny Dodds about that time, he was with Kid Ory when I was with the Eagle Orchestra. Johnny, he's said I influenced him, that he got a lot of inspiration from me. Well, I'm proud to be told that. There was Jimmy Noone there too, I influenced him—that's what people who have written books have said he told them.'

If Bechet was one great influence upon young New Orleans clarinettists in the second decade of the century, there was another who is less well-known but equally important. Lorenzo Tio, Jnr., was a Creole whose father and uncle were both distinguished clarinettists. The few recordings which we have that show his work—he travelled and recorded in the early Twenties with Armand Piron's New Orleans Orchestra—impress more with the smoothness of his technique and the purity of his tone than with his creativity as a jazz player. His significance in our story is that he appears, from a glance through the biographies of early jazz, to have taught every single New Orleans musician who ever picked up a clarinet, from Bechet himself through Johnny Dodds and Jimmy Noone to the younger generation of Albert Nicholas and Barney Bigard. By his own admission Bechet proved a recalcitrant pupil: 'It's a funny thing about teaching, about all those lessons. They didn't really do for me. They weren't doing what had to be done. I guess you come right down to it, a musicianer has to learn for himself, just by playing and listening.' In his references to another of his teachers, the Creole George Bacquet, Sidney Bechet clearly defined the difference between the schooled Creole approach and the self-taught, intuitive method of music making that stemmed from the blues. 'What he played, it wasn't really jazz . . . he stuck real close to the line in a way. He played things more classic-like, straight out how it was written. And he played it very serious . . . there wasn't none of those growls and buzzes which is part of ragtime music, which is a way the musicianer has of replacing different feelings he finds inside the music and inside himself . . . all those interpreting moans and groans and happy sounds.'

It is not too fanciful to regard Sidney Bechet and Lorenzo Tio as the 'father and mother' of New Orleans jazz clarinet. The family that they raised was as diverse as any human family, inheriting in differing degrees the characteristics of each parent. Thus we can hear, in the blues-playing of Jimmy Noone, a fair measure of Bechet's 'interpreting moans and groans', although in the purity of his tone and the flamboyance of his technique he favoured the Creole style of Tio. Likewise in the work of Johnny Dodds, it is the close likeness to Bechet's throbbing, rough-edged blues sound that first strikes us as exclusive until we listen to some of his most fluent ensemble work, especially with King Oliver's Creole Jazz Band, and hear plenty of the decorative, liquid clarinet which was Tio's Creole heritage. So when I say that Dodds and Noone were poles apart, it means no more than that they represented the extreme differences in character that can exist within one family.

Choosing a Johnny Dodds 'masterpiece' presented the problem that has occurred elsewhere in this book. We know him more from an accumulation of varied recordings than from any one revealing work. It is with not so much regret as positive anguish that I have passed over two superb sides—'Gatemouth' and 'Perdido Street Blues'—recorded in 1926 under the name of the New Orleans Wanderers. My reason was that I wanted to find something as far removed as possible from the atmosphere of the Louis Armstrong Hot Five and Seven sessions which I have already touched upon in the context of 'Potato Head Blues', and the Wanderers did include four-fifths of the Hot Five. Some jazz critics of recent years have dismissed Dodds's work with the Hot Five, especially in the later years, on the grounds that he could not keep up with the great strides that Louis was making in the direction of more rhythmic and harmonic freedom. In agreeing with them to a large extent, I do not go on, as some have done, to deride Dodds's musicianship. In transforming his little five-piece recording band from a tight New Orleans-style ensemble into an arena for improvisational fireworks on the grand scale, it was Louis, not his colleagues, who was out of step. Johnny Dodds produced some fine solos, notably in 'Wild Man Blues', 'SOL Blues' and 'Potato Head'. But Armstrong's exploding talent put him under strain and introduced into the sessions a spirit of striving tension which was different from the blithe, relaxed feeling of a perfect New Orleans ensemble.

The recordings in which Johnny Dodds seems to me absolutely at home and in command are those which he made with his Washboard Band in July 1928. This was not an isolated session—in the years between 1927 and '29, he made forty-odd recordings with trios and small bands, including a seven-piece group with Louis Armstrong and Earl Hines in which Louis, perhaps because he was under contract elsewhere, played a subdued role which suited Dodds. But the Washboard Band date stands out for several reasons. Johnny Dodds, not a strong harmonist, as we noted in the analysis of 'Potato Head Blues', was in his element among the simple chord progressions of the blues. Even here, his approach was not one of great melodic or harmonic subtlety. His solos and ensemble playing, especially in the up-tempo numbers, were built upon simple arpeggios, innocent of the ninth and diminished chords which Louis Armstrong so eagerly exploited in the context of the Hot Five. And yet, upon this simple basis, Dodds seemed to be able to create endless variations, each of which had some distinguishing mark of its own. The Washboard Band session consisted of four blues numbers, two up-tempo and two slow, each pair showing such similarity that one might be excused for thinking on first hearing that it represented two 'takes' of the same piece. But there are key differences—the two up-tempo numbers are in B flat and F respectively, while both slow pieces are in C—and the set emerges as a four-part study of the blues in varying moods. And that is how I propose to examine it, treating the separate numbers as a whole rather than invidiously selecting one for special consideration.

The band which Johnny Dodds leads on these records was one which, with occasional personnel changes, enjoyed a six-year residence at a club called Kelly's Stables from 1924 onwards.

With the exception of its piano-players—Lil Hardin Armstrong and Charlie Alexander are the two who appear with Dodds on records—the band featured New Orleans men, and its music was strongly representative of the home style. The two brass players, cornetist Natty Dominique and trombonist Honoré Dutrey, come down on records as extraordinarily fitful players, veering between on and off days in an inexplicable way. July 6, 1928 was happily a good day for both of them and, with only occasional lapses by Dutrey, they fulfilled perfectly the uncomplicated roles which the carefree blues session demanded of them. For many years, discographers scratched their heads over the identity of the piano-player, who on this date was manifestly not Lil Armstrong. With or without a cautious question mark, the name of Charlie Alexander is now generally accepted, although his contribution is unlikely to elicit more than mild curiosity from most listeners.

One of the great joys of this session is the well-recorded and splendid bass-playing by Bill Johnson, who has already made an appearance in this book as the banjoist on King Oliver's 'Dippermouth Blues'. I shall have more to say about the contribution of New Orleans to the art of jazz bass-playing when I come to the work of Pops Foster in Luis Russell's Band. All I need do here is draw the listener's attention to the great variety of sounds and rhythms which Johnson employs, sometimes booming away two-in-the-bar with a resonance that suggests that he is using the bow in places, and at other times slapping out a resilient four-beat rhythm with frequent variations. As for Baby Dodds, we are confronted here, as elsewhere, with a problem. Johnny's rumbustious younger brother, often spoken of with some awe by the normally unshockable Louis Armstrong as a formidable hell-raiser in his youth, survived his staid, teetotal brother by a margin of nineteen years (he died in 1959) and so made a significant contribution to the post-war New Orleans Revival. I was one of those fortunate enough to hear him in person playing with Mezz Mezzrow's Band at the first International Jazz Festival at Nice in 1948. His performance there, distinguished by a driving rhythm, feather-light press rolls on the snare-drum and a whole firework display of exploding noises from every corner of the kit, confirmed for me his reputation as one of the great masters of New Orleans drumming to whom a generation of younger men, including Gene Krupa and George Wettling, bowed in homage. It has to be said that I never heard a record which did even a hint of justice to him, and often have difficulty in convincing friends that he was not the rather clumsy thunderer that often comes across on disc. In this session, pounding a washboard with thimble-capped fingers, he has little chance to do more than show a spritely line in time-keeping.

'Bull Fiddle Blues' gets off to a shaky start with a trombone break by Dutrey who fluffs a note at a rhythmically inopportune moment. But this is not frail, finely-poised music likely to be thrown by a minor accident, and with joyful disregard, the ensemble takes up the chorus. From the first, Johnny Dodds shows who is in charge by establishing the beat with a few notes hit firmly on the nose. And then he is off, weaving and bobbing in a sustained manner reminiscent of his early work with King Oliver. At once, we notice one of the chief characteristics of Dodds's playing, which is an insistence on driving home the beat at every stage in his flowing variations. 'My brother was serious, but he had play days too,' Baby Dodds recalled—and for all the poignancy of Johnny's blues-playing at all times, there is in these up-tempo numbers a great sense of exhilaration, too, a joyous romping which lifts the spirit. Much of it derives from the way in which, in the opening bars of each chorus especially, Dodds usurps the trumpet's dominating role and lays down the beat with a string of dictatorial crotchets.

At times in these performances, this reminder of the beat was not only stimulating but strictly necessary. When, in accordance with recording demands, the bass and washboard abandon Charlie Alexander at the start of his brief piano solo, his urgent desire to reach the end of it intact plays havoc with the number's steady rhythm. Likewise, poor Dutrey, handicapped by lung damage incurred on war service, is often found battling with technical and time-keeping problems in his up-tempo breaks. But it is no mere sentimentality to say that these flaws really do not matter. Indeed, I positively welcome them, if only for the ecstasy of hearing the ensemble with Johnny Dodds at its head pick the performance up by the seat of its pants and boot it on its way!

In 'Blue Washboard Stomp', it is Alexander's carbon-copy solo (he seems, from the evidence here, to have been equipped with no more than two ideas for all-purpose use in fast and slow tempos respectively) which gives the impression that this is just another version of the first piece. Apart from the change of key from B flat to F, there are other differences. Natty Dominique, who showed considerable reticence in 'Bull Fiddle Blues' outside of a pleasant solo, asserts himself more strongly. Much of the critical scorn which his playing has attracted over the years derives from the fast and rather uneven vibrato which has been put down to feebleness in the holding of a tone. From the increasing number of recordings of native New Orleans music which have become available since the Revival, we recognise that 'nanny-goat' vibrato as a conscious characteristic of one school of New Orleans playing. It was fundamental to the style of one of the legendary New Orleans men, 'Papa' Mutt Carey, who recorded some fine sides with Kid Ory in the Forties. That it was no mere instability of lip or lung is shown in the ensemble choruses of 'Blue Washboard Stomp', when Dominique uses it deliberately as a rhythmic device, rather like a roll on a drum, to link staccato phrases. In other ways he contributes to the highspots of this blues piece, coming up with some across-the-beat phrasing, in the chorus after the bass breaks, which reminds us of the way old Bunk Johnson played during his brief Indian summer in the Forties. And again, in the very last chorus of all, he holds a sustained note in the upper register which offsets Dodds's restless clarinet figures perfectly, while Bill Johnson's bass pounds out an unexpected drum rhythm.

When it comes to Johnny Dodds's turn in the break choruses which are a feature of 'Blue Washboard Stomp', we have a demonstration of his resourcefulness in varying the simplest of blues choruses. He has already played a solo of similar construction in the first number. On this occasion he gives each break a different character with a legato phrase here, an expressive upward glissando there. Compared with some of his contemporaries—Bechet, for example, or Jimmy Noone—Johnny Dodds did not boast a fast or flashy technique. For one thing, the heavy tone which he cultivated, with its broad vibrato and incisive edge, did not lend itself to rapid runs over the full length of the instrument. Indeed, there are occasions in his recorded work when it seems as if he is loading the long-suffering clarinet with more emotional weight than it can stand. But the ability suddenly to charge the most skittish of breaks with a sudden surge of passion amply compensates for any lack of pyrotechnics.

When we move into the two slower blues pieces in B flat, we find Johnny Dodds in his most intense mood. On clarinet, Sidney Bechet and the British player, the late Sandy Brown, are the only rivals to Dodds in the ability to feed a high-voltage current of sustained passion into a solo built upon long, throbbing notes. At the outset of 'Weary City', an old friend from a previous chapter reappears—namely, an introductory quotation from the 'Holy City'. It serves to establish a mood which I can only describe as one of melancholy dignity in which it is Johnny Dodds and not the reticent Dominique who gives the ensemble its character. It is interesting to note, with Dodds, that the emphasis on the four beats to a bar which gives his up-tempo work such lift is not abandoned in these slower tempos. Nobody except Bessie Smith ever made it quite so clear in the first bar of a blues exactly what tempo was required. The on-the-beat style would be rhythmically stiff and unyielding were it not for the elasticity which is given to each beat by the whole band from Baby Dodds and Bill Johnson upwards. This ability to expand what, on paper, would be written as four crotchets or quarter-notes to the bar into loping, unhurried steps that are rhythmically linked to each other is what, in the Twenties, distinguished the New Orleans style from all others. It saved much music which, as in this Johnny Dodds band, was based on the eight-to-a-bar rhythmic approach, from sounding jerky and square, and it gave to Louis Armstrong the impulse to abandon that rhythm for his own more loping 12/8 style. I can best describe it in non-musical terms by saying that, in their early recordings, the New Orleans bands bounced on a trampoline when others marked time on a barrack-square.

It was the treatment of these two blues pieces, 'Weary City' and 'Bucktown Stomp', that confirmed me in my decision to treat the four numbers as one whole, developing work. (Incidentally, it seems probable to me that the titles became muddled up somewhere along the way, a not unusual occurrence in early recording. 'Bucktown Stomp' is the most inappropriate name for the bluesiest of the four pieces and I suspect that it was at some time confused with 'Bull Fiddle Blues'). When Charlie Alexander has delivered his one slow blues idea and Dutrey and Dominique (the former much happier in this slower tempo) have contributed good solos, it is Johnny Dodds who, consciously or intuitively, develops the theme from one piece to another. 'Weary City' finds him in his most sober mood, lending such a serious air to the proceedings that, when Baby Dodds takes his turn on the tuneless washboard in a series of breaks with piano, trombone and bass, we are disinclined to giggle. The low-register clarinet solo, centred upon the fifth degree of the scale around which it swoops and stalks with a searing melancholy, is a beauty, with an assertive, almost theatrical entrance that contrasts with the shy and unspectacular image of the man himself that has come down to us.

Listening to the two C major blues pieces one after the other, one might think, if one did not know it to be far-fetched, that Johnny Dodds was deliberately holding back in 'Weary City' in order to pull all the stops out for the final 'Bucktown Stomp'. This piece starts with a C major chord which sounds as if it is to be a reprise of the previous number. But no, the chord is a launching pad for a break by Dodds which soars into the high register in a positive shriek of anguish and announces that this is to be Johnny Dodds in the emotive mood which nudges the very limits of the boundary that separates the sublime from the ridiculous. Many clarinet-players in the New Orleans Revival of the Forties and Fifties adopted the Dodds manner in tackling the blues, and all too many of them, aiming for high tragedy, succeeded only in achieving a sort of ludicrous pomposity or, in theatrical terms, pure 'ham'. The danger lies in the elaborate runs in which Dodds seems to take his inspiration not from standard clarinet practice but from the more angular contortions of the blues guitarists. The electric guitar inhabited the realms of science fiction when Dodds recorded his finest solos in the Twenties, so there is something prophetic in the similarity between the introductory break in 'Bucktown Stomp' and the wild, heavily vocalised wailing of a modern blues guitarist like B. B. King.

From the opening break onwards, Dodds is in charge of 'Bucktown Stomp'. He takes the lead in the first chorus as if he had temporarily forgotten that the other front-line men were present, and Natty Dominique has to insinuate himself into the proceedings as best he can. Much is always made of Sidney Bechet's tendency on soprano saxophone to elbow the trumpet out of the dominant role in the front-line. Here and elsewhere, Johnny Dodds was quite capable of doing the same thing, and without the assistance of a soprano saxophone! Through these first two majestic choruses of 'Bucktown' he has the best of both worlds, stating his theme with typical trumpet phrases heavily on the beat *and* filling in with impassioned guitar-style runs. When it comes to his solo, he sings the blues in the same unrestrained way, sustaining until the anguished break at the very end of the piece a mood which is totally consistent and convincing. Indeed, if I may borrow a cliché from contemporary critical jargon, it is the commitment which Johnny shows to all of the numbers in this set of four—and, I should add, to any number that he ever played—which in the end puts the scoffers and the flip imitators to shame.

Johnny Dodds was a blues player at heart. He always worked with small bands heavily slanted towards the blues. During the Thirties, when his New Orleans contemporaries were either retired or reaping the rewards of the new-style swing music, Dodds remained in Chicago, leading his bands in little clubs remote from the attentions of recording companies. In 1938 he was brought to New York for a recording session organised by Lil Armstrong in which his 'Chicago Boys' were mostly hip young New York musicians to whom he gave a salutary lesson in how to play the blues.

It is a strange thing that Jimmy Noone hardly fared any better. With a few adjustments—one or two isolated recording sessions in the Thirties, for instance—the story told in the preceding paragraph applies equally to Noone. Indeed, in one respect he was less fortunate than Dodds whose reputation was well established by prolific recordings in the Twenties in such prestigious surroundings as the bands of King Oliver, Louis Armstrong and Jelly Roll Morton. Jimmy Noone's presence on some Oliver recordings was only fully established quite recently after years of deliberation and head-scratching by discographers. A few records which he made with Louis Armstrong in 1928 cast them as accompanists for Lily Delk Christian whose non-jazz—and come to that, non-musical—singing until recently kept record-collectors at bay. Much the same deterrent effect was exerted by Doc Cook's Dreamland Orchestra, a cumbersome dance-band with which Jimmy Noone worked on and off through the Twenties.

The reason I find it strange that Noone met with as little commercial success as Johnny Dodds is that his clarinet style and his repertoire were both more accessible than those of Dodds. The records which he made with his Apex Club Orchestra in 1928/9 consisted largely of popular songs aimed at a much wider audience than the 'race' market towards which Dodds's blues recordings were directed. And Noone was always careful to stress the melody, often playing it himself in a limpid, seductive way far removed from the jangling angularities of Dodds. It was Noone rather than Dodds who had the greatest impact on the succeeding generation of clarinet men. If we take account of Albert Nicholas's playing with Louis Russell and Louis Armstrong, of Barney Bigard with Ellington and of both Jimmy Dorsey and Benny Goodman with their own celebrated orchestras, it is hard to think of any area of the Swing Era of the Thirties which was untouched by Noone's influence.

If we are bewildered by Noone's failure in the commercial field, it is perhaps less hard to see why jazz enthusiasts over the years have tended to pay him more lip service than genuine heed. Jimmy Noone was a Creole, heavily influenced in his upbringing by the Creole tradition of light music and the role of the clarinet within it. The manifestly self-taught blues styles of Bechet and Dodds were an exception among the first recorded generation of New Orleans clarinettists. The rest of them were taught to treat the clarinet as the versatile instrument that it is, and acquainted themselves with the rapid fingering, fast tongueing, pure-toned aspects of conventional clarinet style. Jimmy Noone epitomised this approach. Quite a large corner of his repertoire over the years was set aside to demonstrate his acquired technique, with the result that the explorer into the territory of Noone recordings has to step fastidiously around some rather quaint and old-fashioned clarinet doodling in 'speciality' vein and the occasional quagmire of syrupy sentimentality.

The recording I have chosen as a Jimmy Noone masterpiece is not widely acknowledged as such. I suppose most jazz collectors would pick 'Apex Blues', a fine blues performance whose succession of riffs have become standard in the traditional jazz repertoire. I have tried instead to find something which typifies the method of ensemble playing which Noone handed down to the likes of Nicholas and Bigard and at the same time shows us something of the instrumental brilliance which, through its impact on Benny Goodman and Jimmy Dorsey, paved the way for the clarinet's dominating role in the Swing Era that was to come.

The clarinettist Mezz Mezzrow, in his book *Really the Blues*, defined these qualities of Noone's with his usual blend of perception and purple prose. 'What Jimmy didn't do with that clarinet of his, weaving in and through and all around those cats like an expert hackie in heavy traffic, just ain't been invented yet . . . He played strictly New Orleans style, with a soulful tone instead of the shrill twittering effects you hear today, and he played all over that instrument from top to bottom, hitting every register but the cash one. The little flourishes he came up with "in the windows", fill-ins at the ends of phrases where the other players took a breath, were really amazing. He was always inventing new things, but they were in the New Orleans idiom every time.'

The only point at which I take issue with Mezzrow is in his belief that there was some abstraction called 'New Orleans style' or the 'New Orleans idiom' to which all players had a duty to pay homage. It was the musicians who forged the New Orleans style, and much of what we retrospectively acknowledge today as the very epitome of New Orleans clarinet-playing emanates from recordings made by Jimmy Noone towards the end of the heyday of New Orleans music.

It is one of these recordings, a version of a popular song by Jimmy McHugh called 'Every Evening', which I have selected as my Noone masterpiece. In the light of Mezzrow's comments, it is ironical that the little band from the Apex Club with which

Noone recorded some of his best pieces did not conform to the classic New Orleans line-up of cornet or trumpet, clarinet and trombone. Noone's only partner in the front-line was Joe 'Doc' Poston, a saxophone player from Alexandria, Louisiana who had been a colleague of Noone's in Doc Cook's Dreamland Orchestra. A negligible jazz soloist, Poston nonetheless did all that was expected of him in this little band, which was to provide a straight-forward melody line around which Noone could demonstrate his mastery of the art of contrapuntal clarinet. The only other star name in the band was that of the Pittsburgh pianist Earl Hines, who had arrived in Chicago in the mid-Twenties and was, at the time of this recording, on the point of making his mark as one of the greatest and most influential jazz pianists.

'Every Evening' starts deceptively with what sounds like a dance-band arrangement of a typically platitudinous popular song of the period. But in the event the relatively straight statement of the verse serves to heighten the sense of exhilaration when, with the arrival of the main chorus, Jimmy Noone peels off into his more familiar ensemble role, diving and swooping around Poston's stolid alto lead like a swallow harrassing a crow. What raises his work above mere fussy decoration is the rhythmic lift which he gives to the proceedings with ever-changing patterns in which the sudden incursions into the high register are used much in the way that a drummer will use explosive beats to create shifting accents. And of course, the whole performance is enhanced by the most ravishing clarinet tone in all of jazz.

Outside of Jelly Roll Morton's band work and that of the best Harlem stride pianists, jazz piano solos had up until this point been rather diffident, hangdog affairs, clogged with heavy chording and obfuscated by inadequate recording. With every leaping, cocksure solo that Earl Hines contributed in the late Twenties, he seemed to give notice, like a militant shop steward of the Amalgamated Union of Ticklers and Allied Keyboard Operatives, that never again would the pianist be regarded as the work-horse of the jazz band. For many years, jazz historians, wise after the event, attributed what they called Earl Hines's 'trumpet-style' piano-playing to the influence of Louis Armstrong. 'Trumpet-style' is really quite a good description of the way in which Hines produced a strong, unequivocal melody line with the right hand playing strident octaves rather than chords and arabesques. And it is certainly true that, having devised this way of playing, his melodic variations did owe something to Armstrong. But his own explanation for the origin of the style is less romantic: 'I got sick of playing a lot of pretty things and not being heard ... we had no microphones then, and I figured that if I doubled the right-hand melody line with octaves, then I would be heard as well as the trumpets and clarinets.' Whatever its origin, the device was immediately effective. I shall have more to say about Hines in later consideration of his recording with Louis Armstrong, but the listener to 'Every Evening' will not fail to notice the interesting harmonies with which he transforms the ordinary tune, the rhythmic 'trumpeting' in the right hand, and the way in which the left hand, totally emancipated from its previous oom-chah role, now takes a more important harmonic and rhythmic part than had ever been conceived before.

After the piano solo, there is a typical Noone passage in which, for half a chorus, he has the rest of the band playing the sort of choppy phrases usually supplied to tap-dancers while he performs some tricky runs on the clarinet that are not far removed from tap-dancing in their staccato agility. This nimble work, pointed up with some fast tongueing that makes each note in the tracery distinct, continues to the end of the chorus when the ensemble has returned to normal. And then comes one of Noone's most effective devices, a short glissando up to a piercing high note which leads into the final chorus, followed by stabbing notes in trumpet rather than clarinet style, giving the chorus a thrilling climax which owes nothing to Doc Poston and his stolid reiteration of the tune. Halfway through this chorus, the drummer rolls a fierce crescendo that drops immediately to eight bars of whispering ensemble before flaring into furious life again for the ride-out. This was another Noone device, borrowed and reproduced in a rather less subtle way by the young enthusiasts from the Austin High School who haunted the Apex Club and took in Jimmy Noone's lessons.

Indeed, the jazz of the white Chicagoans, and of the musicians from far and wide who spent time in Chicago, reflected the dual influences of Johnny Dodds and Jimmy Noone in varying strengths for some years to come. The odd thing, in the light of the very simple and straightforward model for New Orleans-style clarinet-playing which Noone presented, is that when young musicians in their twenties all over the world began to recreate New Orleans jazz in the Revival of the late Forties, it was Johnny Dodds's more idiosyncratic and difficult style which they emulated. Bob Helm in San Francisco, Sandy Brown, Wally Fawkes and Cy Laurie in Britain, Claude Luter in France, Pixie Roberts in Australia, all could be heard in their early days emoting tremulously in the Dodds manner. And when more primitive New Orleans jazz superseded old Oliver and Armstrong records as the inspiration, it was the cue for the sound of New Orleans veteran George Lewis to take over. Perhaps this chapter, together with the greater availability in recent times of the complete Noone recordings, will reassert what the young musicians who commuted from Kelly's Stables to the Apex Club and back again will have understood—that Johnny Dodds and Jimmy Noone represented in extreme forms two indivisible facets of New Orleans jazz.

Louis Armstrong and Earl Hines

IT IS DIFFICULT, in the dry process of retrospection and reassessment, to imagine the excitement that must have been in the air in the Chicago of 1927/28. Jazz was everywhere, in literally scores of dives, dance-halls and movie theatres. Crime was everywhere, too, and its impact on the music scene is succinctly encapsulated in two oft-quoted sentences by Chicago drummer George Wettling: 'At the Triangle Club, the boss was shot in the stomach one night, but we kept working. After that he walked sort of bent over.' But the jazz histories which harp on the details of gangsterdom underestimate the musician's capacity for detaching himself from his surroundings. Speakeasies and shady clubs provided the environment in which jazz could flourish, but they had as little effect on the music itself as did the pimps and prostitutes in the red-light district of New Orleans.

In the jazz context, the genuine excitement in Chicago at that time is measured in terms of creativity. Most of the great men from New Orleans were still active in the city. Their young disciples, rallying around the team from Austin High, were in the heady throes of making their first recordings. Furthermore, the finest representatives of the jazz that had been blossoming in New York through the decade—the stars of the Henderson and Whiteman orchestras, the classic blues singers and their accompanying bands—constantly passed through the city on tour or moved in for extended seasons. And over everything, inescapably, the giant shadow of Louis Armstrong, reaching the very height of his creative powers. Bud Freeman tells a story that exemplifies Louis ' standing in the city, the power of his presence. 'In the days in Chicago, before Louis became world famous, he spent a great deal of time walking the streets of his neighbourhood on the south side . . . One afternoon, as he strolled along 35th Street, he noticed a small crowd gathered around two street musicians. He stopped and listened and much to his delight, the trumpet-player was playing Louis' improvised chorus of "Struttin' with some Barbecue". At the finish of the number, Louis walked over to the street musicians and said: "Man . . . you're playing that *too slow*!" "How would you know?" they challenged. "I'm Louis Armstrong . . . that's my chorus you're playing!" The next day the street musicians had a sign next to their tin cup. The sign read . . . "PUPILS OF LOUIS ARMSTRONG".'

Louis was not alone on the Olympian heights. The reminiscences of jazzmen who were on the scene are peppered with the names of trumpet-men who were 'as good as Louis at that time'—June Clark and Louis Metcalf, two young lions from New York, and the formidable Jabbo Smith who had the technical ability to match and even surpass Louis in speed and range, if not in the taste and nobility of his invention. None of these claimants to the crown left any evidence on record that they had the measure of Armstrong. Much more important in terms of results was the discovery by Louis of a friend and colleague who was, by 1928, his equal in every respect.

Earl Hines had worked with Louis Armstrong as pianist and musical director at the Sunset Café for some months before he replaced the second Mrs Armstrong in the Hot Five recording band. I find quite credible the story that it was Hines who persuaded the loyal and easy-going Louis to replace the New Orleans men in the Hot Five with musicians who were more attuned to the modern ideas which Louis himself had been largely responsible for propagating. The fact that two of the new men—Jimmy Strong the clarinettist and Fred Robinson on trombone—were lightweights without the authority of Johnny Dodds or Kid Ory is sometimes used by purists to suggest that Hines was a bad influence on Louis in seducing him away from the straight and narrow path of New Orleans jazz. I hope to have shown in the references to Louis in these chapters that in the course of nature

Louis Armstrong had a different rhythmic concept from almost all of his contemporaries. It was not just that he fully realised the 12/8 implications in the relaxed and loping New Orleans beat. Within that rhythm he had a freedom that enabled him to move around, across and over the beat with an instinctive poise that was remarkable. In Earl Hines, he found a colleague who had the same capability. And all considerations of modernity or trendiness apart, it was inevitable that Louis would move away from the carefree atmosphere of the first Hot Five into a musical environment that stretched him more fully.

With the New Orleans drummer Zutty Singleton, two years older than Louis but another forward-looking musician, Louis and Hines made up three swashbuckling musketeers on the Chicago jazz scene. At one point they went into business together, booking premises and attempting to start a club of their own. In view of the close links between Chicago nightlife and the highly organised underworld, it is hardly surprising that their venture was a total failure. But the experience did not appear to do more than temporarily split up the formidable trio. Hines recalled: 'Louis was wild and I was wild, and we were inseparable. He was the most happy-go-lucky guy I ever met. Then Louis and I and Zutty formed our own group, and I don't know what happened but we like to starve to death, making a dollar or a dollar and a half apiece a night, so we drifted apart ...' But the association continued in the recording studios, where Louis, Hines and Singleton continued to make records under the name of Louis Armstrong's Hot Five which were to inspire a new generation of young jazz musicians who would emerge as trend-setters in the mid-Thirties.

The partnership of Louis Armstrong and Earl Hines is epitomised in their duet recording of 'Weather Bird'. It was not, as is often suggested, the first trumpet and piano duet in a long line of such collaborations that stretch up to the present day. King Oliver and Jelly Roll Morton had made two fine duets back in 1924. But certainly Louis and Earl, in that studio in December 1928, established records for rapport and brilliant daring which have not been broken to this day. We can argue with equal confidence that 'Weather Bird', in presenting two musicians of genius unencumbered by lesser mortals, is the most perfect recording to be made during the entire decade of the Twenties.

Having said this, I am assailed by a reluctance to embark upon an analysis of the piece. The tune itself is one that Louis and King Oliver wrote for Oliver's band back in 1923. As recorded by that band (under the title 'Weather Bird Rag') it is a spritely tune in three-part march format, amply suited in its simple chord structure to the joyful, stomping treatment, full of breaks and driving ensemble, that it receives. The way that Louis and Earl convert it into a bravura performance of enormous complexity has such a feeling of spontaneity and freshness that detailed discussion of it brings to mind Duke Ellington's cautionary dictum about critics: 'They take a flower and say "Isn't that beautiful" . . . then, to show how beautiful it is they pull off the petals, strip the leaves, split the stem and in the end—no flower!'

In *Early Jazz*, Gunther Schuller dissects 'Weather Bird' with a musician's care, including a chart of the latter part of the record when the two musicians abandon the set format of the tune in order to challenge each other more keenly with phrases hurled across an irregular number of bars. I mention this not only to direct the reader to a fine piece of critical analysis but also to warn him, when it comes to listening to the record, that if, as I did for some years, he tries to link the Armstrong/Hines exchanges to the original shape of the tune, he is inviting a brainstorm.

The introduction epitomises swing. The notes are not only timed with split-second accuracy, but each one has a spring and resilience of its own. In the very first chorus we see how Louis and Earl propose to go about things. Louis takes care of the melody, more like a snake than a bird in its curling and twisting lines. Hines clearly has no intention of merely providing 'oom-chah' accompaniment. He realises quite well that, between them, he and his partner have enough innate rhythmic sense to carry the beat without assistance, and he is content therefore to suggest it from time to time, but otherwise to leave it to be implied while he places stabbing chords all around it in the most exhilarating way. Meanwhile, as I noted in the chapter on Jimmy Noone which introduced Hines, he had devised his 'trumpet-style' octave playing in the right hand that enabled him to play forceful melodic lines to match those of any blowing instrument. Using this technique and applying it to the lower half of the keyboard, he is able here to furnish a counter-melody to Armstrong's lead. Whether he was influenced by Armstrong's phraseology or simply thought along the same lines, the result is the nearest one could get, on the days before electrical 'dubbing', to *two* Louis Armstrongs in duet.

The reader will be well practised by now at picking out little gems of construction and invention from an Armstrong performance of this period. 'Weather Bird' is not an easy tune to play, especially on trumpet. Its melody line weaves and dodges in a way that defies supple phrasing, and yet Louis gets around it with the poised agility of a lightweight boxer limbering up. Listen to the fifth and sixth bars of the opening theme, where he gives the awkward phrase a special sinuousness by allowing the three notes at the very end of bar four to vanish practically out of earshot. This device pre-dated by some seventeen years a favourite dodge of the modern 'bebop' musicians led by Charlie Parker and Dizzy Gillespie. Then the practice of barely articulating certain notes in a long and rapid phrase in order to give it rhythmic variation became known as 'ghosting' the notes. Louis does it throughout 'Weather Bird' as though born to the idea.

To get a notion of how Armstrong's instinctive rhythmic ideas are assisted and, no doubt, triggered off by Earl Hines, stop a while at the fourth bar of the secondary theme. Here again there is a bit of melody which, in the original King Oliver version, is a raggy, symmetrical phrase punctuated by short breaks. We know from previous examples that Louis Armstrong, like all the great solo-builders who followed him, had a built-in radar which foresaw and automatically steered away from dully symmetrical phrases. In this instance, he alters the second matching phrase by extending it across that fourth bar with a legato triplet of quarter-notes. Simultaneously, Earl Hines suspends the steady left-hand rhythm and substitutes instead one of his octave 'trumpet' phrases, very Louis-ish in its conception right down to the suggestion of a whip-up at the beginning. The result is a stroke of musical wit of which any composer, having laboured over it for days and nights, would feel justifiably proud. That it emerged in the course of a few minutes' spontaneous improvisation is nothing less than a miracle.

But such miracles abound in 'Weather Bird'. Take, for example, the rhythmic gymnastics with which Earl Hines challenges himself when it comes to his turn to play a solo variation on the secondary theme. Anyone who is not quite sure up to now what 'trumpet-style' means apropos Earl's piano-playing will find here a perfect example. He leaps straightaway into a bit of melodic improvisation hammered out in octaves that could have come straight from the trumpet of Louis Armstrong, complete with a vigorous tremolo in the fourth bar that simulates the trumpeter's rapid vibrato or 'shake'. After the halfway mark, however, he abandons this in favour of a percussive, hand-to-hand karate assault on the basic rhythm, throwing the accents to and fro in a cavalier fashion which must have frightened the daylights out of every other pianist within earshot. In a television interview when he was around seventy years of age, Hines spoke of his habit of constantly exploring new harmonic devices to reach a certain point in a familiar tune. He said, in effect, 'I'll never take the same route twice—and when you see me smile, that means I'm lost!' Similarly, he has never outgrown an apparent compulsion to try and trip himself up rhythmically, chopping the beat up in such a way that, many times, the listener is encouraged to believe that he is lost, only to find when the regular rhythm is resumed that he has not missed a fraction of the beat.

This rhythmic challenge, thrown at Louis Armstrong and eagerly taken up, is what eventually elevates 'Weather Bird' to the level of a supreme masterpiece. We get a hint of what is to come when, after Louis Armstrong has played a reprise of the first theme, there is a short interlude or 'bridge' into the third strain. Gunther Schuller sets out this passage in conventional notation. The complex result looks more like a chemical formula than a piece of music. I can testify to the fact that, fifty-odd years later, the bridge remains impossibly difficult to play solo with any degree of conviction. For two musicians to create it spontaneously and successfully at one attempt (there was no second 'take' of 'Weather Bird') leads us once again into the realm of miracle.

From here on, the piece builds with mounting complexity. For the listener who finds the trumpet/piano exchanges hard to follow, it is helpful to know that, once Earl Hines has taken a full 16-bar piano solo on the third theme, the duettists pay little heed to the actual shape of that theme. On paper, they are simply splitting the sixteen bars into two sections in which a two-bar break is followed by six bars of duet. Reading 'ensemble' for 'duet', this is the format that is followed on the original King Oliver recording. But in that performance, notwithstanding its exhilarating drive, there is nothing to confuse or tax the mind— every cadence is in its predictable place, clearly signalled. What Louis and Earl do is to ignore the natural rise and fall of what is, after all, a pretty basic theme and to play instead a catch-me-if-you-can game with fragments of free melody no more than one or two bars in length. The result is that when they return to base each time with a four-bar phrase identical to the ending of the very first theme, that phrase often appears to crop up in the wrong place. In its way, this final section of 'Weather Bird', leading inexorably to the complex coda out of which Louis climbs triumphantly to a high C finish, comes nearer to the ultra-modern conception of 'free improvisation' than anything that was to be recorded in the Thirties or Forties. Only by purging his mind of preconceptions and abandoning it to the music can the listener do full justice to its glories.

Luis Russell

EMILE COUÉ, the French psychotherapist whose advocacy of Auto-Suggestion had as much impact on America immediately after World War I as the music of the Original Dixieland Jazz Band, coined the therapeutic slogan 'Every day, and in every way, I am getting better and better'. As a cure for individual depression and self-doubt, it may well be effective. But when it comes to mankind's outlook in general, no such slogan is necessary. It is an understandable human tendency for each new generation to speak of any kind of development—in education, technology, scientific discovery, the arts—in terms of improvement. Without any semantic justification, the word 'progress', meaning simply 'to move forward', is taken to imply a move *upwards* in the direction of something better or more valuable.

If we are discussing civilisation, in the sense of learning how to live together sensibly and comfortably, the concept of gradual improvement is not altogether absurd. It is possible to picture an ultimate goal, a vague Utopia in which today's wrongs are eventually righted. Bringing it down to its most mundane and materialistic level, we can at least argue that, in having our houses heated by radiators or concealed wiring, we have 'progressed' from mediaeval times when they piled logs in the middle of the living-room floor.

When we apply this interpretation of 'progress' to the arts—and jazz writers have been arch-offenders in this over the years—we are on much more hazardous ground. Progress towards what? 'The Search for Truth' is the nearest that philosophers have come to formulating an artistic goal to which all the creating and exploring and theorising aspires. And it doesn't get us very far. Deprived of even the foggiest notion of what Perfection is, we nonetheless cling to a touching belief that we are moving towards it. One jazz 'history' written in America in the Fifties (its very partisanship in that highly partisan era has happily led to its own relegation to past history, so I have no need to identify it) epitomised this belief. Taking the 'modern jazz' of that time as a criterion in which he could apparently see no blemish, the author treated the work of all the early jazzmen—with the obligatory exception of Louis Armstrong—with massive condescension, splashing words like 'crude' and 'primitive' about and conceding to them little merit other than that they 'paved the way' for the glorious things to come. One might say, in mitigation, that he was over-reacting against the vociferous New Orleans Revival movement which at that time was putting forward the equally insubstantial view that Utopia, in the form of the 'pure' New Orleans style, had already been and gone. The advocates of 'modernism' and 'traditionalism' were—and in some areas still are—both making the same mistake in criticising musicians for the tools that they used, rather than in the light of the use they made of them.

This brief homily has been necessary because, in the course of this survey of some of the jazz masterpieces, a theme has emerged. In talking about it, I am bound, short of tedious circumlocution, to use the words 'progress' and 'advance', and I want to make it clear that these imply no judgement, for or against, on things that simply happened. I made the point, in the chapter on Bix Beiderbecke, that rhythms—and the same goes for the various conjunctions of notes which we call harmonies—do not themselves go in and out of fashion or supersede each other. They just exist, to be used or misused. Let's take the two most striking examples of musicians who were 'ahead of their time'. Louis Armstrong, from the first recording that he made, showed an instinctive feeling for rhythms more complex than those employed by most of his contemporaries. Bix Beiderbecke, a devotee of Debussy and Maurice Ravel, revealed in his solos (on piano especially) a familiarity with the harmonic devices of modern

European music which jazz musicians in general did not acquire for almost a decade. The prophetic aspect of their genius was amazing, to be sure. But it was not this that made their music great. For a long time after each musician was first heard on record, superb jazz was played which owed nothing to their example. Had Bix never lived, it was inevitable that musicians would eventually have made use of the harmonic ideas that already existed in the works of the modern European composers. Louis Armstrong's impact on the rhythmic notions of the time was rather more fundamental, for reasons which I shall come to in a moment. But even so, it was during his lifetime that musicians such as Horace Silver and Herbie Hancock chose to revert, in much of their work, to the once 'corny' eight-to-a-bar rhythm from which Louis departed. And contemporary jazz–rock music has gone on to make a new fashion out of the old-fashioned beat. If we measure musical stature simply in terms of quasi-scientific discovery, then both Louis and Bix were made totally redundant when avant-garde musicians in the Sixties discarded the whole notion of basic harmony and regular metre as having been exhausted. From which cautionary tale we learn that we would be wise to avoid the assertion, so often made, that artists like Louis and Bix were great because they influenced generations, and to stick to the safer premise that they influenced generations because they were great!

The theme that runs through every chapter so far has been the gradual change in the rhythmic approach to jazz improvisation and writing during the Twenties. It may be thought that I have given too much attention to this, and not enough to the melodic-cum-harmonic advances which were made. But if we leave out of account the experiments which Bix Beiderbecke and some of his white associates and disciples made in adapting the sophisticated harmonies of modern European music to jazz—experiments which were not taken up and extended on any large scale until the end of the Thirties—we find that the chordal foundation on which jazz musicians improvised were limited to virtually the same simple harmonic progressions, borrowed from European church and military music, which underpinned New Orleans music. Indeed, it was well into the decade before some very elementary extensions of the basic diatonic system were fully assimilated. I noted, in the chapter on Louis Armstrong's 'Potato Head Blues', that Johnny Dodds was not altogether at home with the harmonies. Specifically, there is a point in the twenty-eighth bar of his solo when, against the D seventh chord of the tune, he plays his break resolutely on the tonic chord of F. Recorded in 1927, this aberration harks back to some of the King Oliver band recordings four years earlier when, in blues that are pitched in B flat, the rhythm section (guided no doubt by the classically-trained Lil Armstrong) started in the eighth bar the now familiar alternative sequence of G seventh, C seventh, F seventh, B flat, while the front-line men pursued the simpler course of B flat, F seventh, B flat. Years later, when the New Orleans Revival brought into the limelight musicians who had never left the city, a similar indifference to harmonies other than the basic blues chords, especially in the sequence which I have just outlined, was noticeable in recordings by, for instance, George Lewis's Band.

But the relatively slow harmonic growth of jazz in the Twenties is not my only reason for putting emphasis on the rhythmic changes. Harmony, in the specific sense of a system of chord 'progressions' on which melody is based, is not an essential ingredient of music. Nowadays, most of us are familiar with the sound of Indian *raga*, which makes no use of that kind of harmony. African drum ensembles, dispensing with both harmony and melody and concentrating instead on rhythm and pitch, achieve a rhythmic complexity far beyond anything that Beethoven could possibly have conceived.

Spokesmen for Western civilisation reach for the word 'primitive' whenever they encounter a music with strong rhythmic foundations. It is a word which cropped up frequently when critics and record reviewers, brought up in a predominantly European culture, first turned their attention to jazz recordings. Their preoccupation with harmonic elegance and the genteel manners of the concert-hall led all but the most perceptive to patronise, if not openly condemn, musicians like Johnny Dodds or Jelly Roll Morton while turning with unfeigned relief to the polite and house-trained music of Red Nichols. The London

Melody Maker, in its infant days in the late Twenties, affirmed, in chorus with many other critical organs, that the records by Red Nichols represented 'the ultimate in "hot" style'. Their record reviewer was not entirely deaf to the charms of Johnny Dodds, conceding, in the introductory remarks about one of his recordings, that 'the nigger has a heart as big as his great woolly head'. To be fair to that paper, it was one of the very first to run any kind of regular review of jazz recordings, and within a very few years the fine critic and musician Spike Hughes, writing under the name of 'Mike', was urging its readers to turn away from Nichols and lend an ear to the music of such men as Armstrong, Ellington and the great soloists in Fletcher Henderson's Orchestra.

But the fact remains that, at the outset, critical appraisal of jazz demanded that the basic European rules of harmony should be observed. As late as the Forties and Fifties, the New Orleans Revival focused attention on some unknown elders who had remained, semi-active in music, in the city of New Orleans throughout the lifetime of jazz. Their music was frequently derided, even by those who were amiably disposed towards the traditional forms of jazz, as being 'out of tune' and riddled with 'wrong chords'. I put those terms in quotes not because the allegations are untrue by European standards, but because they are irrelevant by the standards of the musicians concerned. It transpired that the music of, for example, Jelly Roll Morton's Red Hot Peppers at their best did not represent the earliest form of jazz, as many people had believed—especially those who had already labelled it 'primitive'. On the contrary, it appeared to be a comparatively polished culmination of the New Orleans tradition. If we listen to recordings made around the same time by Sam Morgan's Band, still operating in New Orleans, we hear something much more like the music that George Lewis was to introduce about twenty years later. This is music in which the building up of rhythmic impetus and complexity clearly had higher priority than the harmonic conventions.

A perfect example of what I mean was recorded by George Lewis and his band in 1944. The number they chose to play was a ragtime composition by James Scott called 'Climax Rag'—a tune, incidentally, which Morton also tackled in quite a different way in a 1939 session shortly before his death. Like all ragtime pieces, the composition has more than one theme and goes through quite a range of conventional harmonic patterns. The Lewis Band launches into the piece like a cavalry charge getting under way, scattering 'wrong chords' in all directions. Half-way through the record, when the simpler final theme has been safely reached, they have attained a smooth gallop, careering along with a joyful abandon. I once played this record on an old-fashioned portable record-player with the sound turned down to a whisper and my hand resting on the closed lid of the machine. In this situation, what came through to me strongest was the rhythm of the music, transmitted through the lid to my hand. It was an extraordinary experience to feel the complex vibrations at my finger-tips and to realise that, with the melodic and harmonic content almost completely faded out, what was left was something much nearer to an African drum ensemble than a conventional jazz band, an exciting and compelling tapestry of rhythms.

George Lewis and his men led us to see that there was a phase, in the very early days of jazz, when conventional harmony played a minor role. One thing that listeners brought up on the Dixieland music of the Twenties and Thirties noticed when the so-called primitive end of the New Orleans jazz spectrum came to light was that the trumpet, clarinet and trombone players did not always deploy themselves into separate three-part harmonies, but played the melody virtually in unison with a certain amount of that sour but evocative dissonance which one finds in the instrumental folk-music in many areas of the world. And, of course, the very same pattern existed in the development of the blues, which did not reach the formalised harmonic framework of the 'twelve-bar blues' until a fairly sophisticated stage in its evolution.

Once conventional European rules of harmony had been assimilated into jazz, it was inevitable that jazz musicians would begin to explore, as a basis for improvisation, the ramifications which already existed in so-called 'classical music'. In the mid-Thirties, the trumpeter Roy Eldridge deliberately sharpened his facility and speed so that he could 'run changes' like a saxophone player—in other words, base his improvisation on the notes of a rapidly-changing progression of chords. Bebop, the earliest manifestation of modern jazz in the Forties, demanded even greater agility from the soloist, to the extent that, inexorably, the reserves of feasible 'new' harmonies were exhausted. What the advance guard of jazz improvisers have been doing from the late Fifties onwards is to search for a new basis of improvisation once 'running changes' no longer presented a challenge. This is not the place or time to go into them all, but it is sufficient to say that, in advanced forms of jazz in the Seventies, harmony in the sense of chord progressions has become redundant. Indeed, in some extreme instances, linear melody too has been spurned, with identifiable notes being replaced by sounds and harmony giving way to 'texture'.

It is possible, then, to imagine a history of jazz in the foreseeable future which will treat harmonic development as an episode through which the music passed. The concept of rhythm is not so easily shrugged off. Any two notes—or even sounds—that follow each other in time suggest a rhythm. The very movements that are used to produce the sounds—the raising and lowering of a stick or mallet, the action of the fingers on keys or valves, the actual breathing between phrases—contain their own rhythm (anyone who saw Louis Armstrong in action will remember how, holding the fingers of his right hand stiff, he whacked them down on the trumpet valves as if he were tapping a drum). While some avant garde musicians long ago discarded what is generally accepted as melody and harmony in their work, it would be a brave and foolhardy musical revolutionary who harboured ambitions to divest his music of rhythm. The outward symptom of rhythm is that forward-moving impetus which jazz people call 'swing'. It is significant that the devotees of ultra-modern performers who have discarded all the normal rhythmic conventions such as regular tempo, bar-lines and time-signatures still assert that their music 'swings', thereby implying that somewhere at the heart of seeming chaos a rhythmic pulse is beating.

So it can be argued—and I have been arguing it for the past few pages—that the really fundamental changes in jazz over the years, changes that have distinguished one style or epoch from another, have been rhythmic. On this premise we can specify more accurately still the theme which links these jazz masterpiece^S of the Twenties. It is one of musicians slowly coming to term^S with the new rhythmic concept revealed in the work of Bessie Smith, Sidney Bechet and, above all, Louis Armstrong. In almost every recording (Jelly Roll Morton's being a notable exception) there are signs of rhythmic schizophrenia, whether it be Louis conflicting with his colleagues in King Oliver's Band and the Hot Five or Bix overcoming the two-beat straitjacket of Trumbauer's Orchestra. And yet, within a very few years everyone, from the West to the East, was swinging away in the loose-limbed 12/8 manner over a steady, thrusting four-in-a-bar beat. There must, one feels, be a missing link somewhere between the records I have discussed so far and the jazz that was to earn for the Thirties the title of the Swing Era.

Indeed, there was such a link, and it is to be found in the Luis Russell Band in general and in the playing of George 'Pops' Foster in particular. Luis Russell, born in Panama, moved to New Orleans in his teens. In Chicago in the Twenties, he spent several years in the rather cumbersome band which Joe Oliver led after the break-up of the Creole Jazz Band, showing himself on records to be an indifferent pianist whose solos had a disconcerting habit of parting company with the rest of the rhythm section and running uncontrollably downhill. His talents clearly lay in organisation. When Oliver's Band played in New York in 1927, Joe Oliver was offered, and refused, a residency at the new Cotton Club, and the job went, with historic results, to the young Duke Ellington. It was no doubt managerial gaffes such as this that disaffected several of Oliver's ambitious sidemen, including Luis Russell. He left Oliver and, within months had become leader of his own band in New York, gathering together a highly talented team of musicians, several of whom had been with King Oliver. With Ellington and Fletcher Henderson already established in the city, the arrival of trumpeter Henry Red Allen, clarinettist Albert Nicholas, trombonist J. C. Higginbotham and drummer Paul Barbarin to join Russell, not forgetting the brilliant Boston-born altoist Charlie Holmes who was already on hand, led to a formidable concentration of jazz talent in Harlem from 1927 onwards, and one which swiftly transferred the focal point of jazz from

Chicago to New York.

George 'Pops' Foster, who joined Russell in 1929 and whose contribution to the band's style will be discussed in detail later, gave an idea in his autobiography of how the Russell band operated at that time. 'We worked seven days a week and we loved it. We'd rather be working than be at home. It was like it was back in New Orleans. Back then I used to sit around wishing I could go to work. It was a pleasure to work in those days. Russell's band was romping so good in twenty-nine we had everything sewed up around New York. We were playing the same style we played in early New Orleans.'

Anyone scouring the personnel of the band on record sleeve or in a discography might well raise an eyebrow at the last sentence. For by the standards of the day, Luis Russell's Orchestra, with two or three brass, three saxophones and a four-piece rhythm section, was nearer to a full-sized dance band than a small New Orleans-style ensemble. And at first hearing, the recordings themselves confirm this impression. The band not only romped, it roared. Using arrangements for the introductions, statement of the themes, modulations and solo backings, the five or six front-line instruments often played as a single section, moving en bloc in a striking departure from the polyphonic New Orleans pattern. Sometimes, coming nearer to the modified New Orleans style which King Oliver had used once saxophones had invaded his band, two of the saxophones were given a busy, bustling part to read while trumpet, clarinet and trombone improvised loosely around them. And sometimes again it was each man for himself in a mêlée of collective improvisation.

What gave the Russell Band its great feeling of informality and joie de vivre was the manner in which the arrangements were played—and this in turn arose from the musical personalities and backgrounds of the musicians themselves. The trumpeter Henry Allen was clearly and audibly a disciple of Louis Armstrong, achieving much of Armstrong's luxuriant, fur-lined tone. The facet of Louis which Allen took to naturally was the intense, dramatic and sometimes wild playing, full of slurred notes and impassioned 'shakes', with which Louis brought high drama to blues and stomps alike. Where Allen differed from Louis—and

by the time he joined Russell he was very much his own man—
was in the direction in which this high emotional intensity pushed
him. Where Louis would harness it to his strong feeling for
structure to produce majestically-conceived and very explicit
melodies, Allen was given to more oblique utterances, building
up a mood, an impression, with tense bursts of sound rather than
creating a new melody as Louis did. Henry Allen's own masterpiece, 'Feelin' Drowsy', recorded in the same period, is a fine
example of this 'impressionist' approach, one which anticipates,
by thirty years or so, the avant garde musicians who 'painted
pictures' in sound. Allen's emotional temperament happily spilled
over into his ensemble-playing, with the result that he paid more
attention to the spirit than the letter of Luis Russell's arrangements. The relaxed, joyous feeling that illuminates almost every
Luis Russell recording in 1929/30 springs to a high degree from
the loose interpretation which Allen put on the arrangements in
front of him.

The trombonist J. C. Higginbotham was a perfect foil for
Allen, and indeed they struck up a musical partnership which
lasted on and off into the Fifties. If the credit for first giving the
jazz trombone a fluent solo voice belongs to Miff Mole, it has
always seemed to me unjust that Higginbotham's name is rarely
put at the very top of the list of those who geared that mobility
to the fast and furious pace of jazz in the late Twenties. The use
of saxophone sections, albeit small to begin with, to supply a full
set of harmonies to the ensemble relieved the trombone of a great
part of its harmonic role. You will not hear J. C. Higginbotham
pumping out the root harmonies in the manner of the New
Orleans 'tailgate' men. Much of the time he can be heard providing
an independent part at the lower end of the ensemble, its impassioned tones reminiscent of the free harmonising of the bass
singer in a black gospel choir. His solo work was quite unrivalled
in the Twenties for its mobility and ferocious attack. He overcame
the heavy-handedness inherent in the instrument's awkward
mechanism by a lip-control that could produce fast trills and
'slurs', the latter being the technical term for a rapid alternating
between notes a major or minor third apart. It is a rare Higginbotham solo that does not utilise either or both of these effects.

Albert Nicholas, a contemporary of Louis Armstrong's and a boyhood friend of Sidney Bechet, was a Creole (in New Orleans the name was given the French pronunciation, 'Nicola') who inclined naturally to the fluent, technically-agile style epitomised by Jimmy Noone. With a tone which was drier and less seductive than Noone's, Nicholas nonetheless followed Noone's way of weaving and dodging through the ensemble, using the whole range of the instrument and occasionally starting a downward run with a piercing and electrifying high note.

The career of Charlie Holmes epitomises the chance factor in the entertainment business. He was born in Boston where his boyhood friends were Harry Carney and Johnny Hodges. Holmes moved into New York with Harry Carney in 1927, and when Carney almost immediately went into the Ellington Band, Charlie Holmes might well have joined the Duke too, on Carney's recommendation. But when a vacancy did arise in the Ellington Band, it was Johnny Hodges who caught the leader's eye, or ear. Judging from recordings at that time, there was very little to choose between the two alto men, who played in much the same style. Jazz history records fully how Hodges, working in a band which was built around the individual 'voices' of its soloists, flourished with Ellington and became, in effect, the first great master of the alto saxophone in jazz. With Luis Russell, Charlie Holmes contributed some fine solos, comparable to those that Hodges recorded with Ellington. But by the standard of Duke Ellington's own oft-quoted definition of success—'doing the right thing at the right time, in the right place, before the right people'—Charlie Holmes was in the wrong place in Luis Russell's band. The roaring, stomping band of the period under discussion declined, in the 1930s, into a quite ordinary big band whose work was undistinguished by talented arrangements or original compositions. When the band was virtually taken over by Louis Armstrong in the mid-Thirties, the scope for its other soloists, on record at least, dwindled further. Charlie Holmes remained until 1940 and thereafter sank into obscurity and partial retirement from music. Listening to his solos throughout his time with Russell, and especially in the 1929/30 period, it is hard to understand how a career could so sadly misfire.

The other important and influential member of the Luis Russell Band was its bassist, George 'Pops' Foster. Born on a Louisiana plantation in or around 1892, Foster moved into New Orleans at the age of ten, so it is fair to speak of him as one of the distinguished breed of New Orleans bass-players whose talents we have already encountered in the work of Bill Johnson with Johnny Dodds and John Lindsay with Jelly Roll Morton. In *Early Jazz*, Gunther Schuller analyses in some detail the peculiar qualities shown by these string-men from the Crescent City. Some early jazz 'histories', ill-informed and badly researched, gave the false impression that the original bass instrument in jazz was the brass tuba, which at some time in the Twenties was superseded by the double bass. To this oversimplification was added the frivolous and unlikely legend that an unnamed bass-player in a Dixieland Band once broke his bow in the excitement of the moment and there and then invented the plucked-string, or pizzicato style. The facts, borne out by reference to photographs of early New Orleans bands, are that most of those bands from the very first days of jazz used string basses in a sedentary or indoor situation. Marching bands would use the tuba for the obvious reason that it is easier to carry and has a greater volume. To get regular work, most bass-players would naturally 'double' on both instruments. With the arrival of recording in the Twenties, similar adjustments had to be made. In the primitive days when bands simply huddled round a huge cone-shaped horn, it was no doubt difficult for a string bass to get a note in edgeways. We have seen how two important bands, the King Oliver Creole Band and Louis Armstrong's Hot Five, dispensed with a bass instrument altogether, delegating its role to the pianist, banjoist or, in some Oliver performances, a bass saxophone. Another obvious solution was the tuba, whose incisiveness and audibility compensated, for a while, for the lack of mobility and versatility which eventually rendered it obsolete.

In extolling the superior capacity to 'swing' of the string bass, Gunther Schuller drew overdue attention to the great variety of rhythmic subtlety which bassist John Lindsay contributed to Jelly Roll Morton's recordings. 'We can hear how perfectly he alternated the basic two-beat rhythm (2/2) with the hard-driving

4/4s on one hand and whole-note single beat passages on the other. These changes of pace do not occur at phrase junctures, but are apt to break in at any point in the sixteen and twenty-bar phrases, balancing with and reacting to the soloists and ensembles.' The style was not John Lindsay's alone. We have come across it to great advantage on the Johnny Dodds recordings with Bill Johnson. Students of Duke Ellington's recordings with the great New Orleans bassist Wellman Braud will call to mind many instances of an ensemble or solo passage being given a sudden rhythmic boost when the bassist switches from two to four beats in the bar in response to innate musical instinct. And in Pops Foster's own autobiography as told to Tom Stoddard, Foster recalls that 'in New Orleans we'd have two pick notes in one bar, then you'd go to six bars of bowing, and maybe have one note to pick.'

Pops Foster was no musical theoretician. When I first met him and heard him in the flesh at the 1948 International Jazz Festival at Nice, we had in our British contingent a bass-player of 'modern' inclinations who, though little impressed by Pops Foster's 'old-fashioned' style, felt that he should approach the famous man for some advice. The response he got left him more bewildered than ever. 'When you get tired, stop playing and smile at the girls.' The American bassist Bill Crow, quoted in the Foster autobiography, was once equally dismayed to hear Pops expounding his harmonic theory in a New York club between sets: 'Hell, I just play any old go-to-hell note, as long as it swings!'

When these sage utterances were recorded, Pops Foster was approaching his sixtieth year, and he may have felt that he had handed out enough free advice for one lifetime. Whether or not he ever formulated his musical ideas more concisely, he was certainly a musician who knew what was required in any musical circumstance—and how to deliver it. What was required in the New York-centred jazz of the late Twenties was a coherent rhythm section style to complement the new rhythmic ideas that had stemmed from Louis Armstrong and were rapidly being assimilated into all of jazz—something, in fact, to resolve the rhythmic schizophrenia which was apparent in most of the recordings hitherto discussed. The tuba, short-winded and slow to move, had helped to perpetuate a stolid two-in-a-bar backing when the general movement was in the direction of a steady, surging four-in-a-bar. Soloists, becoming in Armstrong's wake ever more fleet and ambitious, demanded rhythmic support which sustained their fluent and thrusting improvisations. The answer was already to hand, within the armoury of the New Orleans bassists. Their big, resonant notes, endowed with what wine-bibbers call 'length', had, since they first appeared on record in the mid-Twenties, conformed to the relaxed twelve-eight feeling that Louis Armstrong introduced. The rhythmic variety—two beats here, four there, and occasionally just one—that Gunther Schuller noted, contained an element which Pops developed into a speciality. He played a four-beat style and 'when I went to New York playing that way, everybody wanted to do it. Right after that, about 1929 or 1930, they started writing arrangements that way, with a four-to-the-bar bass part.'

Here we are, then, on the threshold of the Thirties, a decade that was shortly to blossom into the Swing Era. Benny Goodman and his Orchestra, streamlining many of the arrangements already recorded by Fletcher Henderson, were soon to spearhead the attack by big band jazz upon a mass audience, a development which led jazz historians, ready for easy answers, to trace the seeds of Swing Music in all its ramifications to the Henderson Band exclusively. But if it is continuity we are after, it would be sounder to start with the rhythmically mature rhythm of the Luis Russell Band, whose pumping, four-in-a-bar beat dominated by the bass is surely a natural forerunner of the Count Basie rhythm section with Walter Page, the Duke Ellington rhythm section with Jimmy Blanton, the Woody Herman Herds with Chubby Jackson and his successors, and indeed those often frenetic but wildly swinging jam-sessions that have been staged under the banner of 'Jazz At The Philharmonic'.

I have chosen 'Panama' from the repertoire of Luis Russell recordings because, from its opening bars, it typifies this rhythmic maturity. It needs to be said at the start that 'Panama', originally a stately dance tune by Will Tyers, consists of four distinct themes, the first of which is dispensed with in this arrangement. It is characteristic of the Russell band's headlong, let's-get-going approach that after a jaunty introduction it goes straight into the final rip-roaring theme with Pops Foster driving it along four-to-a-bar as if time was already running out. Here is the band phrasing en bloc with that passionate abandon which, if it lacked the meticulous precision of the leading white bands of the period, certainly saved the arrangement from the clipped jerkiness which puts a date on so many of the big band performances in the early Thirties. This is particularly applicable as the band moves in similar style into the second theme, which has in this arrangement some choppy and angular phrases which need—and receive—relaxed interpretation to round off the sharper corners. There is a long and, in musicians' terminology, 'round the houses' modulation from E flat to A flat in which, through some wide gaps, we get an uninterrupted sound of Pops Foster's magnificently resilient and sonorous bass tone. In his autobiography, he explained: 'When we used to pick the bass we'd hold on to the bow at the same time, now they have little things called bowcaddies you put the bow in while you pick. I still usually hold on to the bow while I pick unless I'm going to slap the strings too.' We can see why in 'Panama', for within seconds of pumping out those muscular pizzicato 'breaks', Pops is underlining the legato character of the third theme with some rich two-in-a-bar bowing under Henry Allen's solo.

It is difficult to describe in words the furnace-hot thirty-two bars which Allen contributes here. If we take the word 'hot' literally, then all the manifestations of heat are there—a searing tone, steaming energy, phrases that leap like flames and then die off in a wisp of smoke. Throughout the forthcoming Thirties—and indeed on into the era of modern jazz—trumpeter-players in bands far bigger than Luis Russell's were to be called on to rise up (often under the gaze of Hollywood cameras) and generate spontaneous excitement with wild and high-flying solos. Few ever did so as naturally and constructively as Henry 'Red' Allen. His great strength is that he made no forced effort to 'swing'. Indeed, he sometimes seems deceptively to be striving in the very opposite direction, stringing a phrase lazily across the beat in a manner very typical of several New Orleans trumpet-men—Louis Armstrong to some degree, Lee Collins very markedly. This very controlled pacing of a solo, in however scorching a tempo, rendered Red Allen's work invariably passionate and exciting but never hysterical.

In 'Panama', the superb J. C. Higginbotham follows hot (in every sense) on Henry Allen's heels. When one thinks of the limited role which the trombone had played in jazz for most of the Twenties—the inflexibility of its tone, the awkwardness of its action and its inability to do more than grunt and stutter at fast tempos, then one can only marvel at the strides which a single generation of trombonists starting with Jimmy Harrison and Jack Teagarden and spreading to Higginbotham, Benny Morton and Claude Jones, made in the space of a few years. Here, Higginbotham's solo abounds with his familiar trade marks—the agile phrasing, ferocious 'shakes' and whooping incursions into the high register. Later, between two ensemble choruses, he comes up with another, a burst of machine-gun quavers that tumble chromatically in a sort of rhumba rhythm with accents on the first, fourth and seventh quaver.

If the trombone can be said at this stage to have been fully emancipated from its brass band role, then the tenor saxophone, only recently given an authoritative voice by Coleman Hawkins, had yet to come of age in similar fashion. Greely Walton was by no means an inferior player by the standards of the day, but the hollow, rather puddingy tone and flat, unexpressive phrasing fixes his solo in an era when the instrument was still on the threshold of its full flowering. After him, the ensemble takes over again, flaring up after the trombone break into what is usually the climactic, or in jazz terminology, 'ride-out' chorus of the tune. Such was the informality of recording in those days that we cannot be absolutely sure that the band did not intend to end there, but received a signal that there was more time in hand. Certainly there is a brief moment of indecision at the end of the chorus, in which the redoubtable Pops Foster holds things up virtually single-handed. And from this point until the end of the record, there is no more formal arrangement—things simply career onwards in what was later to become the characteristic jam-session style.

Whatever the truth of the matter, we end up with more treats in store. First, Albert Nicholas leaps in with a bustling clarinet solo couched very much in the manner of his idol Jimmy Noone but with more spiky asperity in the tone. Then Charlie Holmes takes over to show that any reservations which we may have about the tenor saxophone in this period does not apply to the alto. There are still vestiges of the 'running' clarinet style in his playing, but the phrasing has great swing and buoyancy and the tone and vibrato have shed all trace of the cloying sentimentality which the instrument had always assumed in its dance-band environment. In this period and for many years to come, solos by Charlie Holmes invariably provided unmitigated pleasure.

One aspect of this alto solo is worth discussion, and that is the spontaneous backing which the rest of the front-line, dominated by Henry Allen, play behind Holmes. Riffs, that is to say short phrases or figures repeated over and over with minimal alteration to accommodate changing harmonies, have been a feature of jazz for years. And not only of jazz. Anyone who ever heard Negro church music—often called 'gospel' music—will be familiar with the interplay between preacher and congregation or lead singer and choir. We have already come across it apropos the ring-shouts. It is the familiar 'call and response' characteristic of much black American music, being reflected in the rhythmic worksongs of the railroad and chain gangs and the relationship between early blues singers and their accompaniment. The formula is always the same, striking a contrast between the free voice of the leader and the repetitive backing from chorus or band. In the contrapuntal music of New Orleans the 'call and response' pattern was not marked, although there are traces of it in the King Oliver Band's work when Oliver, as in 'Dippermouth Blues', got to work on one of his declamatory 'wah-wah' muted cornet sermons over the ensemble. When bands began to get bigger, the enlarged front-lines were unsuitable for the New Orleans style of collective improvisation, for the simple reason that, under the pressure of an instrumental traffic-jam, the contrapuntal lines became an unholy mess. Written arrangements were an obvious solution, and where they were not available, simple formulae were devised which could easily be committed to memory and were known as 'head arrangements'. Somewhere along the line, the 'call and response' pattern, already familiar in the black churches, was brought into service as a simple way of deploying the instrumental resources. Recorded jazz abounds in examples of this formula, in which the soloist or vocalist assumes the role of the leading voice while the rest of the ensemble plays a repeated phrase or riff in response. In some of the early Count Basie Band recordings in the late Thirties, it was sometimes one section of the orchestra—the trombones, say, or the saxophones—which chanted a 'call' while the rest responded.

On the basis of very limited research I would hesitate to assert that the use of the 'call and response' formula in band jazz began with the Luis Russell Band. But I can think of no previous recorded performances in which it had been so marked. Church influence seems to have been strong in the Russell band. Several of their recorded titles reflect it—'On Revival Day', for instance, and 'Feelin' the Spirit'—and in a piece called 'Saratoga Shout', there is the first reference on record to the now ubiquitous hymn, 'When the Saints Go Marching In' (which, surprisingly, did not appear on jazz records under its own title until the same Luis Russell band, under Louis Armstrong, recorded it in 1936). When, in 'Panama', the band is finally left to its own devices, one of those devices is an exact reproduction of the modus operandi of a black church choir. While Charlie Holmes says his piece, Henry Allen leads a 'choir' behind him, chanting a three-note phrase which only changes minimally to follow the harmonies of the tune.

The essence of an effective response or riff is its monotony—which is perhaps why British and Continental jazz musicians have never been at home in this type of playing. Long before the repetition has achieved the hypnotic effect which is its main purpose, they become embarrassed and changed to something else. Luis Russell's men suffer from no such inhibition. When Charlie Holmes has finished his solo, he takes over the same riff with the remaining saxophone and the trombone while, in a curious but exciting blend of traditions, Henry Allen rides out in true New Orleans street parade style with Albert Nicholas's clarinet running rings around him and piercing the ensemble with dazzling high notes. They end with one of the extended endings so much beloved by the King Oliver Band, with Paul Barbarin's joyous tom-tom beats reminding us that his drumming, chiefly on the snares in true New Orleans style, has up to this point been the soul of rectitude and discretion. 'We'd rather be working than at home,' said Pops Foster. And listening to 'Panama', who could doubt it?

Enter
the Giants

Louis Armstrong

LOUIS ARMSTRONG DIED in July 1971, within two days of his seventy-first birthday. Three years earlier, he had visited Britain to play a two-week season at the Variety Club in Batley, Yorkshire, blowing well enough on the good nights to reward the hundreds of devotees who made the pilgrimage to hear him. From this point his playing career stretched back, virtually uninterrupted, beyond the earliest days of recorded jazz. There were no periods of idleness or obscurity, no times when changing musical fashion threw him temporarily off course, no occasions, despite shoddy and slapdash accompaniment and sorties deep into the hazardous territories of commerical show biz, when his trumpet playing fell far below the high standard of honesty and integrity which he set himself in the Twenties.

It is a record unrivalled in all of jazz. And it seems to have been achieved by dint of a deep-seated instinct for survival. This drove him along a path of apparent ruthlessness which contrasts strangely with the surface image of a cheerful, warm-hearted and, in his early days, insouciant man. King Oliver, Fletcher Henderson and Lil Hardin Armstrong, Louis's second wife, all had a decisive influence on his rise to pre-eminence in the Twenties—and all were abandoned, conclusively but with a surprising absence of rancour, when they had ceased to be of use to him. Lil Armstrong seems to have viewed the ultimate break-up of their marriage, which took place around 1930, with a resigned sense of the inevitable. 'You don't need me now you're earning a thousand dollars a week. We'll call it a day,' was how, in her recollection, she

concluded the matter. Jazz critics over the years have been slower
to resign themselves to what they have regarded as a divorce, of a
more generally distressing kind, between Louis Armstrong and
the jazz ideals to which he appeared to have been wedded in the
days of the famous Hot Five recordings. I say 'appeared to be'
because we always have to remember that it took little more than
three weeks, spread over three or more years, to commit to
posterity the much-admired recordings by Louis Armstrong and
his Hot Five. The band had no existence outside the studio, and
for the rest of the time, Louis was enjoying himself hugely in his
publicized role of 'The World's Greatest Trumpet Player', performing with bands of all sizes in cabaret, between shows in a
movie house and for dancing. His own conception of his role in
life was based as much on these performances as on what he
regarded as high-jinks with his old New Orleans chums in the
Hot Five.

Nevertheless, it is true that, during the Twenties, Louis brought
about a single-handed musical *coup* that revolutionized jazz and
influenced thenceforward every branch of the music from solo
improvisation to big band arranging. It is also true that the
retrospective wailing and gnashing of teeth over Louis's post-1930
career that peppers the jazz histories is so much baying at the
moon. In asking that Louis should have continued to blaze the
trail while the rest of the jazz world stood still, the writers have
called for a superman, not a human being with finite resources of
creative energy. When they suggest that he somehow abandoned
high artistic principles for the fleshpots of commercial entertainment, they wilfully turn a blind eye to the professional life that he
was actually leading in the Twenties. And, in imagining that his
adoption of a solo career was a surrender to some egotistical urge,
they have failed to accept that, as British writer Victor Schonfield
has pointed out in a strongly argued review of Louis's music
between 1925 and '30, Louis's style ever since his recording of
'Cornet Chop Suey' in 1926 had 'reduced everyone else to the
level of accompaniment and riveted all the attention on his
trumpet.'

The Hot Five and Hot Seven era ended with the last small-
group recordings in 1929, by which time Louis, with Earl Hines

at his shoulder, had risen clear of the collectively improvised New Orleans-style ensemble. Acknowledged masterpieces such as 'Tight Like This', 'Muggles' and 'West End Blues' were essentially solo-and-accompaniment performances in which Louis and Earl Hines starred while the other horn men played a valuable but less dramatic supporting role. While in Chicago, Louis had made several recordings in the bigger-band setting in which he did his regular cabaret and theatre work, but the few titles made with the Carroll Dickerson and Erskine Tate orchestras give no more than a glimpse at the manner in which he was earning his everyday living. There are plenty of eye-witness accounts, however, to indicate quite clearly that his emergence as a showman-trumpeter in front of a band was a more gradual process than the discographies, with their sudden jump from quintet to big band, suggest.

In March 1929, Louis made a brief sortie to New York, playing a couple of dates with Luis Russell's Band and doing a recording session which included the extraordinary jam-session performance of 'Knockin' a Jug' (discussed in the chapter on Jack Teagarden) and two sides made with a contingent from the Russell band. 'Mahogany Hall Stomp' may be said to be an extension of the sort of informal small-group recordings that Louis had been making in Chicago. With New Orleans men Pops Foster, Paul Barbarin and guitarist Lonnie Johnson in the rhythm section, the music has a more relaxed, down-home flavour than some of the frenzied, up-tempo work of the latter-day Hot Fives, but the fact that Albert Nicholas's clarinet is conspicuously absent in the ensembles means that the Armstrong trumpet, prominent on the top of a trombone and saxophone ensemble, is once again virtually producing a solo with backing.

It is the other title recorded on the same day which gives an insight into the near future. The tune is the Jimmy McHugh–Dorothy Fields song 'I Can't Give you Anything but Love', which had been written the year before for the all-black review, *Blackbirds of 1928*. Louis had recorded popular songs before—indeed, much of the material recorded by the Hot Five had come straight from the floorshow at the Sunset Café, where Louis worked at nights. And the recordings that he made with Bessie Smith, Clarence Williams and others were nothing if not commercially

orientated towards a mass audience. But the style of show-business
that Louis had experienced in his developing days was a chummy,
happy-go-lucky, parochial affair compared with New York in the
late Twenties. Hollywood and talking-pictures had yet to assert
themselves as a musical influence, and it was on Broadway and in
the lavish Harlem tourist traps that stars were made. Furthermore,
the rapid growth of radio and the juke-box industry had begun to
expand the empire of Tin Pan Alley worldwide. To Louis, even
on that short first visit, the atmosphere must have been awe
inspiring—and challenging.

His response was foreshadowed in the recording of 'I Can't Give
you Anything but Love'. Here for the first time is Louis Armstrong shouldering the responsibility for the whole performance.
I have to dissent from the view of several writers who have
suggested that the extraordinary vocal chorus represented Louis
Armstrong's way of showing his contempt for the 'Tin Pan Alley
slop' that he was called upon to deliver, rather in the way that
Fats Waller would later guy the lyrics of sentimental songs. In
Louis, such a demonstration, however subtly concealed, would
have been entirely out of character. This was a man who, according
to his wife Lil, would prowl around their house in Chicago
worrying about his ability to deliver the high notes that his
audience expected; who had, on two occasions in the previous
year, accompanied the commercial singer, Lily Delk Christian
with manifest warmth and wholeheartedness, in songs whose
syrupy lyrics make the Fields-McHugh favourite sound positively
frigid; and who had just embarked on a love affair with the sweet
music of Guy Lombardo's Royal Canadians which was to baffle
earnest jazz students for years to come. Is it conceivable that, on
a visit to New York that was presumably aimed at getting a toe-
hold in that city, such an experienced professional would subvert
the whole exercise in defence of some high artistic principles? It
seems more probable that the eccentricity of this vocal refrain,
with its melodramatic wailing and grunting, arose from Louis
Armstrong's uncertainty about how to treat these new 'pretty'
songs.

Louis was a singer before he ever touched a trumpet. Before he
reached his teens, he was roaming the streets of New Orleans with

a youthful quartet. In his autobiography, *Treat It Gentle*, Sidney Bechet recalled: 'It was Bunk Johnson who was the first to make me acquainted with Louis Armstrong. Bunk told me about this quartet that Louis was singing in. "Sidney," he said, "I want you to go hear a little quartet, how they sing and harmonize". He knew I was crazy about singing harmony ... They were real good—they had a way. There was a little fellow singing there, Little Mack was his name, he was the lead. And Louis, he sang tenor then.' Whenever Louis himself recalled those days in an interview, he would sing a snatch of lyric with great feeling and tenderness.

When Lil Armstrong recorded her reminiscences for Riverside Records, she recalled another aspect of Louis's musicality. It was at a time when she was beginning to push Louis to leave King Oliver and go out on his own. 'I could hear Louis coming home whistling for, oh, much more than a block away. He had the most beautiful shrill whistle, and all those riffs that he later made in his music, he used to whistle them—such beautiful riffs and runs and trills and things, you know—and I said to myself, "Maybe one day that guy'll play like that." Just crazy thoughts, you know, but it turned out all right!' The nearest Louis came to whistling on record was on three occasions, with King Oliver and with his own Hot Five, when he recorded solos on the slide, or Swannee, whistle. Despite the obvious inadequacy of the instrument with its sliding pitch that makes it virtually impossible to play the notes perfectly in tune, Louis as always threw himself heart and soul into the solos in 'Sobbin' Blues', 'Buddy's Habit' and 'Who's It?' So unashamedly sentimental are the results that, for many years, discographers were reluctant to believe that it was Louis at all, ascribing the solos to drummer Baby Dodds.

The picture that emerges is of a man with a strong, well integrated and rapidly expanding musical conception that expressed itself through whatever medium he chose. His love of singing did not find regular expression in his professional life until he returned to Chicago after the Fletcher Henderson engagement. Neither Oliver nor Henderson encouraged it, although fellow-Hendersonians have testified that Louis constantly badgered Henderson to allow his voice an airing and was rewarded with the chance to bellow a few ribald, vaudeville-style lines at the end of 'Everybody Loves My Baby'.

Because the singing appeared late in the day, it has been customary for writers to say of Louis that he sang exactly as he played the trumpet. Chronologically, it is almost certainly more accurate to say that, when he took up the cornet, he played exactly as he had sung with his roving quartet. But such chicken-and-egg discussion is irrelevant. Either way, the music was always the same. One of his earliest vocals with the Hot Five, in the 'Heebie Jeebies' of 1926 vintage, makes the point perfectly. This is as good a moment as any to bury, beyond reach of disinterment, the legend enthusiastically propagated by Louis himself that, half-way through the vocal chorus, he dropped the songsheet and, in carrying on wordlessly, invented 'scat-singing'. For one thing, he had already sung a complete lyric, such as it was, word perfectly when amnesia struck so conveniently at the very outset of the second chorus. For another, it is not conceivable that the primitive recording equipment would have continued to pick up Louis's voice if, as is alleged, he was floundering about the studio floor trying to grab the errant piece of paper. It was a good story, and it may have been that Louis, or someone at the recording studios, felt that it was necessary to put it about to explain a style of wordless singing which, though not invented by Louis, was new to the record-buying public. In a similar instance in a 1930 recording of 'I'm a Ding Dong Daddy', Louis repeated the trick, interjecting the line 'an' I done forgot the words' into a section of scat-singing that was clearly planned and premeditated.

The important thing about this interjection, the scat syllables that surround it and, indeed, the words of any song which Louis sang, is that they were all subordinated to the musical sense of what was, in effect, an instrumental solo without the instrument. The lyrics of 'Heebie Jeebies' are far short of intellectual in the first place. Louis divests them of any verbal sense they might have, flattening out their silly syncopation and replacing it with the relaxed, rhythmically charged phrasing that distinguishes his opening statement on cornet. The result, paradoxically, is to make the song seem much less nonsensical that it does in its natural state. In writing about Bessie Smith in *The Best of Jazz* Volume

One, I pointed to the phenomenon of jazz vocalizing through which, by making the words subservient to an overall rhythmic and melodic conception, consummate jazz singers like Bessie, Louis and Billie Holiday have fed back into a song a higher emotional content than its words are able to sustain. In Louis's vocal, the words 'Come on And do that dance' sound more like an urgent and irresistible entreaty than a jaunty invitation.

Where Louis Armstrong's singing diverged from his cornet playing in the early days was in quality and warmth of tone. We need not attach too much importance to this, recording equipment at the time demanding a degree of voice projection which Louis, a totally untrained singer, could only achieve by shouting. As it improved, so did he and, as the Hot Five years passed, his voice, while losing none of its expressive outer crust, acquired a more tender and attractive central tone. By the time he came to record 'I Can't Give you Anything but Love', trumpet and voice were as compatible as their physical characteristics would allow.

It follows that, for an explanation of Louis's somewhat eccentric vocal rendering of the Fields-McHugh song, it would be safer to refer to his trumpet playing of the period than to read into it implications of musical or literary criticism which were quite uncharacteristic of him. The striking thing about Louis Armstrong's playing in the latter days of the small-group recordings was its huge emotional range. If we pick out some famous titles at random—'Basin Street Blues', 'Save it Pretty Mama', 'Muggles', 'Tight Like This', 'St James Infirmary'—we find no two performances exactly alike. One is dramatic, the next tender, the third imbued with the simple strength of the blues and so on. There could be no greater contrast than between the stately, controlled melancholy of 'St James Infirmary' and the style of 'Tight Like This', without doubt the most intense and emotionally highly-charged passage of jazz improvisation that had up till then been captured on record. In each instance in which Louis sings, the vocal either matches or complements the trumpet playing.

The singing on 'I Can't Give you Anything but Love' takes its mood from the trumpet playing, with various grunts and gasps put in to simulate the violent and distorted notes which burst from the horn. If the one mocks the Tin Pan Alley product, then so must the other, and that is inconceivable. What perhaps makes the version seem satirical to us (but not to the contemporary record-buying public, with whom it was a hit) is the unduly heavy emotional weight which Louis piled upon a rather frail little love song. So far from trying to be funny or derisive, he seems to me to have carried forward the tragic mood of 'Tight Like This' on to a vehicle which would barely take it.

If I am right in this belief, then Louis very quickly acquired a sense of balance. After a brief return to Chicago, he travelled to New York with Carroll Dickerson's Orchestra for a more protracted stay. A study of his subsequent career that relied solely on recording details might lead one to think that, when the Carroll Dickerson Orchestra broke up, Louis embarked upon a new role as a bandleader. The truth is that at no time during the subsequent forty-odd years did he show any inclination to shoulder the responsibility of leadership, and the various organizations that recorded under the name 'Louis Armstrong and his Orchestra' during the Thirties, turn out on close inspection to have been either assembled or actually led by others. In all but nominal respects, the career that he embarked upon from the middle of 1929 onwards was one of virtuoso solo artist.

In this capacity, Louis became more and more closely involved with popular entertainment. While the Carroll Dickerson Orchestra was fulfilling a cabaret residency at Connie's Inn, Louis 'doubled' as featured soloist in a review called *Hot Chocolates* staged by the Inn's Connie Immerman at the Hudson Theatre. The music for this review was written by Fats Waller and his lyricist, Andy Razaf. It is ironical, in the light of all the retrospective criticism levelled at Louis for his alleged defection to commercialism at this stage, that his belated arrival on that scene at the age of twenty-nine should have been in collaboration with another respected jazzman who had been immersed in Harlem showbiz for the past four or five years. There have been plenty of jazz historians ready to lament Louis Armstrong's choice to begin recording the popular songs of the day. Few, if any, have come forward to berate Fats Waller for writing them! But that is another story, and it will be taken up in the chapter on Fats himself.

A more justifiable source of regret is the undoubted deterioration, once Louis had moved to New York, in the quality of his accompaniment on record. Here again, history has tended to put this down to some sort of artistic dereliction of duty on the part of Louis Armstrong himself. The judgement ignores the fact that every black artist and band had, since recording became a major industry in the middle Twenties, been tugged this way and that by the ebb and flow of commercial tides. In an interview recorded for Riverside records in 1956, Coleman Hawkins looked back on the Fletcher Henderson Orchestra of that period and said, 'That was during the time when Fletcher was . . . exchanging arrangements with other bands and getting to sound too much like other bands . . . all the big time bands.'

The big time bands were those of Jean Goldkette and Paul Whiteman, and a cursory browse through the Fletcher Henderson output in the late Twenties and early Thirties will reveal plenty of examples of their direct influence. But Henderson was not the only one. In *The Best of Jazz* Volume One, in writing about the influence of white musicians such as Bix Beiderbecke and Frankie Trumbauer on their black contemporaries, I noted that it had infiltrated, through the arranger and alto saxophonist Don Redman, into the Louis Armstrong small-group recordings in which he took part. Two records—'Symphonic Raps' and 'Savoyager's Stomp'—made in 1928 by Carroll Dickerson's Orchestra with Louis and Earl Hines to the fore, again show that the orchestrator, possibly Redman, had an ear cocked in the direction of the successful white orchestras, especially in the rocking two-beat of the middle-tempo 'Savoyager's Stomp'. The clarinettist and tenor saxophonist Jimmy Strong, much maligned for having failed to maintain the earthy, New Orleans tradition of Johnny Dodds in Louis's Hot Five recordings, shows himself here and in other solos to have anticipated Lester Young by several years in his admiration of Frankie Trumbauer.

This was the band which, without Earl Hines who stayed on in Chicago, travelled to New York with Louis Armstrong in mid-1929. There, according to Mezz Mezzrow in his book *Really the Blues*, they found the Harlem juke boxes pouring out the saccharine music of Guy Lombardo's Royal Canadians. Louis had fallen in love with this band when it played a season in Chicago the previous year. But even without this startling fact, it would have been surprising if a band which had already toyed with the cute, ear-catching rhythmic 'effects' of the successful white arrangers had turned a totally deaf ear to the success, *among black audiences*, of Lombardo.

The trouble is that, while the influence of Whiteman and Goldkette had been, at best, stimulating and, at worst, harmless, that of Lombardo was wholly deleterious. The hallmark of the Royal Canadians was a repetitive formula in which brass and reed sections took turns to churn out the melody. The band proudly featured a saxophone section, dominated by the oily vibrato of Guy's brother Carmen, whose phrases rose and fell dramatically, like the bosom of a silent movie heroine in distress. Someone, no doubt with Louis Armstrong's acquiescence, decided that this sort of backing was ideal for projecting Louis as a successful recording star. It didn't happen all at once, and in most of the bands assembled around him, there were some saving graces. In the Dickerson Orchestra, for instance, both Jimmy Strong and trombonist, Fred Robinson, prove themselves, when comparisons with Johnny Dodds and Kid Ory are put aside, to be capable and attractive soloists. On drums, more felt than heard in the imprecise recordings of the time, there was the great New Orleans drummer, Zutty Singleton, laying down a propulsive rhythm that would have given the Royal Canadians hysterics.

And there was Louis. As a trumpet player he was now at the height of his powers. Jazz was rich in trumpet men by the end of the Twenties. Bix Beiderbecke, Tommy Ladnier, Jabbo Smith, Henry Allen, Cootie Williams, Bobby Stark and Rex Stewart were all making important, individual and indispensable contributions at the time. But as a jazz virtuoso, Louis, with his combination of burnished copper tone, majestic range, unerring rhythmic sense and massive warmth of feeling, stood head and shoulders above them all. Gone were the occasional over-ambitious flights of fancy, the notes that tripped themselves up in the rush of ideas, and the slight tenseness that can be felt in some of the wilder exchanges with Earl Hines. There is a feeling of intense exhilaration in the playing, stemming from complete instrumental command.

The programme of recording popular songs, on which Louis embarked with the version of 'I Can't Give you Anything but Love', cast a revealing spotlight on an aspect of his playing which had always been present, though never before illuminated with such clarity. This was his instinct for re-phrasing a slender and repetitive melody so as to strengthen its line, broaden its emotional range and endow it with rhythmic characteristics of which it was entirely innocent when it rolled off the Tin Pan Alley assembly line. The first sessions that Louis undertook on his return to New York in the summer of 1929 included four numbers from the Fats Waller show *Hot Chocolates*. Two of them, 'Sweet Savannah Sue' and 'That Rhythm Man', were up-tempo romps of no great distinction. But Louis also recorded his feature in the show, 'Ain't Misbehavin' ', and a song which was sung on stage by Edith Wilson, 'Black and Blue'. Much retrospective abuse has been hurled at 'Black and Blue' for its lyric by Andy Razaf. Certainly, the line 'I'm white inside' is unlikely to commend itself to modern thinking. But in fairness it should be said that the song showed a certain unique courage in suggesting, through the Tin Pan Alley medium, that being black in the America of 1929 was not all a matter of strumming banjos down on the levee or beating ecstatic feet on the Mississippi mud. Louis Armstrong's statement of the melody on trumpet divests its minor-key melancholy of any hint of self-pity, redistributes the repetitive four-note phrases of the tune so that they lose their predictable symmetry and, in the second eight bars, replaces the actual notes of the tune with arpeggios that somehow contrive to suggest both the melody and the harmony. One has only to hear the saxes, in the final eight bars of this opening chorus, playing the tune 'as written' to see what a transformation Louis wrought. The same sort of enhancing treatment is given to 'Ain't Misbehavin' '. Fats Waller was a jazz musician as well as composer, and he knew as well as anyone how to interpret and expand upon the notes and chord symbols outlined in a song copy. For this reason, his tunes, however hurriedly they may have been dashed off, always had a solid structure on which the interpreter could build.

But as Louis's career as an itinerant soloist and prolific recording artist progressed, he was called on to tackle songs which often fell far below Waller's unassuming standards. The effect he had on them can only be described as magical. No great effort in the direction of window-dressing arrangement or routining is apparent in the recordings, which mostly follow the same casual and unambitious pattern. In this respect, early jazz writers who referred to Louis Armstrong's solo performances as 'concerto style' implied a relationship between Louis's trumpet and the accompanying orchestra which did not exist. On a preponderant number of records, all the orchestra is asked to do is supply either sustained chords or else blurting explosions of sound on the first and third beats of the bar which, in orchestral terms, do no more than apply the principle of full employment to the 'stop chords' which a rhythm section can provide on its own. And yet those writers were not entirely wrong. For all the sloppiness of the arrangements and the inadequacy of most of the bands, Louis did somehow bestow a certain grandeur on the proceedings, piercing the turgid tapestry of sound with dazzling threads of gold that pull it all together into the semblance of opulent splendour. A musician with a greater sense of his own artistic importance might sound to us as if he were fighting against, or at least attempting to ignore, the uninspiring accompaniment. Louis sounds inspired because that is exactly what he was. Hard as it is for us to accept, he was in his element luxuriating and stretching himself on that bed of foam-filled Lombardo-esque saxophones.

The period is full of striking performances. In his recorded 'Musical Autobiography' made in 1956, Louis recalled having heard a trumpeter called B. A. Rolfe, 'a man that inspired me to play high notes. I never heard a man stand up and play what he played on a trumpet in my life. He stood up and played a tune called "Shadow Land" an octave higher! It inspired me so, I went down to the studio the following week and made "When You're Smilin' ". ' The first half of 'When You're Smilin'' is undiluted Lombardo, right down to a middle-eight on quavering violin. Louis may well have imagined that his vocal and high-note trumpet solo were continuing in the same vein. Certainly, neither offers the slightest evidence of tongue-in-cheek. If it was his wish to flatter Messrs B. A. Rolfe and Guy Lombardo by imitation, then it was happily thwarted by his inability to produce the cheaply ingratiating commercial style. Freddy Fisher's fatuous tune, which has since found its true niche in popular music history as the 'get off' number for generations of stand-up comics, acquires on Louis Armstrong's entrance a massive dignity far above its station. It is one of countless examples of Louis salvaging a crumpled scrap of musical ephemera from history's waste-paper basket and re-instating it as something of value.

I have chosen as a masterpiece from this period a song written by Carmen Lombardo which the lovers of 'sweet' music will always associate with the Royal Canadians. Their first record of 'Sweethearts on Parade', made in 1928 (the year of publication), is surprisingly 'hot' in flavour, but subsequently the tune was given the standard Lombardo treatment in which the cloying melody was passed from section to section while those instruments not otherwise employed filled in with coy bugle-call effects. When Louis recorded the tune in December 1930, he was in California playing an engagement at the Sebastian New Cotton Club in Culver City. The backing orchestra had included, on earlier recordings, the fine trombonist, Lawrence Brown, who shared solo spots with Louis. By December he had gone, and the band, now led by a young saxophonist called Les Hite, boasted only one name familiar to jazz lovers, that of the teenage drummer, Lionel Hampton. Despite this, Louis sounded happy enough with the band for one of his biographers, John Chilton, to be able to cite the twelve consecutive recordings which Louis made in California as the best possible example of Louis's amazing consistency at this time. He himself would in later years react to anyone who raised an eyebrow at his enthusiasm for Guy Lombardo by pointing the doubter firmly in the direction of 'Sweethearts on Parade'.

To be sure, there is plenty of evidence of Lombardo-ish intent from the outset, what with the heaving bosom of the saxophone section and tinkerbell interjections from the upper end of the piano keyboard. But solid four beats in the bar from the banjo—and how often does one thank Providence for a banjo?—and some crisp accents from Lionel Hampton provide welcome rhythmic muscle that leaves Louis Armstrong's muted trumpet free to outline the melody in quite a free fashion. The arrangement is curiously ambiguous in that four bars of trumpet over a sustained tonic F chord lead straight into the theme without a break and, since that starts on an F chord too, confuse the listener as to when the tune actually begins. If the arranger assumed that Louis would help by stating the tune note for note, he was led sadly astray. What Louis does is to toy with the bugle-call motif of the Lombardo version over the introductory chords, but in a ruminatory rather than militaristic way, carrying the idea through into the first two bars of the tune. All in all, six bars go by without Louis playing one note that falls outside the major chord harmonics of a bugle. If one didn't know him to be a totally intuitive improviser, one might say that he was deliberately translating the martial overtones of the song's title into music in a subtle and witty fashion.

Instant composition of this kind abounds in the opening chorus. The bugle-call idea is not entirely abandoned until the seventh bar of the tune, when Louis, who has already established a feeling of total relaxation by spacing measured, on-the-beat phrases around long gaps of bare accompaniment, abandons the beat altogether and drapes thirteen notes lazily across two bars as if stretching himself in preparation for more strenuous exertions ahead. For the next eight bars he addresses himself more purposefully to the actual notes of the tune, though once again he wanders off, in the second half of the section, into areas unimagined by Carmen Lombardo, this time introducing blues inflexions with a characteristic minor third in bar six and, in bar seven, the anticipation by a bar and a half of the F seventh chord leading into the middle-eight.

Early in the middle-eight there is a typical Louis touch which shows how independent his musical conception was of the things going on around him. He hurries the first phrase ('I'd love to join their fun' in the lyric) and delays the second ('but they bar me'), giving himself time to insert a note in between, the sole purpose of which is to suggest a harmony that he hears in his mind. The note, an A flat, belongs to an F diminished chord which he clearly, and rightly, thinks should link the B flat of the first two bars with the F of the third, but which has occurred neither to the composers nor to Les Hite's arranger. Louis was not a trained harmonist like some of the improvisers who were to follow him, but his references to harmony, usually in the form of single guiding notes or rapid descending arpeggios, often suggested fresh harmonic routes that gave added subtlety to a tune.

About the vocal chorus, I would like to make one central point. Here is a perfect example of the unity of conception between Louis Armstrong's playing and singing. All along the way, extra syllables and phrases are added to the lyric, starting with the word 'Oh' that precedes the opening 'Two by two' and going on to the carelessly articulated 'baby' after the words 'they go marchin' through'. If one interprets these odd sounds verbally, they will probably seem irrelevant, sloppy, humorous or even grotesque. But they are not there to convey a literal meaning, but to complete and fill out musical phrases for which the lyric is inadequate. One extreme example occurs at the end of the second eight-bar section, on the reprise of the words 'Sweethearts on Parade'. In literary terms, Louis makes a dog's breakfast of the actual words, which emerge as 'Oooh, sweethearten . . . earts on parade'. But the musical phrase to which these dismembered syllables are put, delivered in that gruff, pained voice, convey a feeling of loneliness far beyond the sentimental intentions of the lyricist. Once again, we come back to the paradox underlying great jazz singing—that by torturing, smothering and mutilating the actual words in the service of purely musical ideas, the singer will put back into the song a greatly enhanced emotional meaning.

With the words out of the way, there is a rather flabby and fumbling call to arms on the alto saxophone, and then Louis sallies forth, with Lionel Hampton faithfully and attentively at his elbow, on a triumphal march that completely transforms the wistful mood of the song. After two identical declamatory phrases, Louis hammers out a rhythmic pattern on one note to which Hampton adds some quick-witted complementary accents in an exhilarating exchange which reminds one of the way Lionel Hampton has often attacked single notes with the mallets since he graduated to vibraphone. It soon transpires that with this heightening of the rhythmic tension, Louis is winding himself up for a leap into the stratosphere. One of the charges laid against Louis in this period is that he too often fell back on reworking material

that had burst into life during the spontaneous improvisation of
the Hot Five sessions. Leaving aside the possibility that they may
have burst into life on the bandstand of the Sunset Café during a
dance routine, the important question is whether the phrase sounds
fresh and fits logically into its new context. Louis had used the
two bars borrowed from Alphonse Picou's clarinet variation in
'High Society' on previous occasions, notably in the 1928 recording
of 'Squeeze Me'. To my ears the 'Sweethearts on Parade' break is
more fluent and successful, the familiar passage, condensed into
one bar, being effortlessly carried on to form a perfectly balanced
break.

What happens immediately after this break throws further light
on the advanced rhythmic—and technical—ideas which can still
be found lurking in seemingly casual Louis Armstrong performances. Most of the unorthodox effects—the long upward
glissando, the rapid 'shake', the dying fall at the end of a note—
which Louis introduced or perfected, were made by hand, e.g. by
shaking the instrument, manipulating the valves and so on. But
at the mouthpiece end, too, where the combination of lip, tongue
and mouthpiece actually produces and pitches the note, he was
busy breaking rules. No lover of his work on popular ballads in
the Thirties will need to be reminded of the strange, flagging
articulation which gave such expressiveness to the legato phrases.
Where the normally tongued note is attacked with a crisp 'too
too' sound, Louis contrived to soften the attack into something
like 'phloo phloo'. What he did was to use the tongue, not to
articulate the notes separately, but to give them a gentle push
slightly ahead of the beat. This technique of using the tongue for
rhythmic emphasis rather than straightforward attack was to
prove indispensable to Dizzy Gillespie years later when he came
to introduce more complex rhythmic patterns into the trumpet
solo.

But we do not need to wait for Dizzy for an example. In the
passage in 'Sweethearts on Parade' immediately following the
'High Society' break, Louis plays a phrase that sounds simple
enough—indeed, for its first bar, it appears to sit rather squarely
on the beat. But if we listen closely to the apparent crotchets or
quarter notes on the first and third beats, and again on the first

beat of the second bar, we find that they are articulated *twice*, albeit barely perceptibly. To establish the exact value and context of the notes, we have to remind ourselves that Louis Armstrong's phrases were built, not on the one-and-two-and-three-and-four rhythm of early jazz, but a one-and-a-two-and-a-three-and-a-four rhythm in which the four crotchets to the bar of conventional four-four time were broken up into four sets of quaver triplets— 'da da da, da da da, da da da, da da da'. If we take the 'double' notes to which I have drawn attention as representing the first two notes of a triplet, with the silent third note represented by a hyphen, we find that what Louis actually plays in this phrase would not be out of place in the complex, cross-rhythmic context of an African drum ensemble—'da da -, da - da, da da -, da - da, da da -' etc. Being Louis, with the solo responsibility of taking care of all the rhythmic variation himself, he finishes the four-bar phrase with broad notes that are seemingly stretched at random across the beat, but which in fact imply a three-four rhythm straddled over bars two and three. To the layman whose mind is reeling under this barrage of technicalities I would say—relax, in the assurance that the feeling of elation, buoyancy and swing which you receive from this and similar Louis passages have their origins in a brilliant rhythmic conception which is all the more remarkable in that it was never exploited or shown off for its own sake.

Having expended such enthusiasm on two or three bars which are by no means the most spectacular in the solo, I can only leave the listener to explore for himself the secrets of the remaining highspots—the searing break that ends the second eight-bar section, the opening of the middle-eight in which the upward trend of the song's melody is consummated with a high note that takes off and explodes like a rocket, scattering notes in all directions; the break coming out of the middle-eight which once again puts a familiar Armstrong phrase to new and spectacular use, and the return to the bugle-call motif at the end, which is saved from banality when Louis stifles almost to extinction the final note of the second phrase in order to give passionate weight to the final martial notes. Behind many of Louis Armstrong's finest performances, a great drummer will be found beavering away, often in acoustically unflattering circumstances. It is not overgenerous to add the teenage Lionel Hampton to a list that includes Baby Dodds, Zutty Singleton, Chick Webb and Sid Catlett. Here and on the other recordings made in Los Angeles during this period, Louis seems to respond to Hampton's crisply timed accents like a sprinter leaping from the starting-gun.

To me, and I hope to the reader, it seems grotesque that a performance such as 'Sweethearts on Parade' should ever be relegated, with expressions of faint praise tinged with reproach, to the mere middle reaches of Louis Armstrong's achievement. Had his entire output in the Twenties been, through some catastrophe, totally lost to posterity, the recordings which he made in the early Thirties would surely have established him immediately as a giant. Indeed, for many fans and musicians, it was just these recordings, and the public performances from which they were distilled, that initiated what can only be described as idolatry.

Nor did the magic end there. When I 'discovered' Louis as a schoolboy, the records which I and my friends bought belonged to a much-maligned series issued, in the middle and late Thirties, on the British Decca label. How we enthused over such gems as 'Struttin' with some Barbecue', 'I Double Dare You', 'Jubilee' and 'Swing that Music', bewildered by constant assertion by the pundits of the musical press that these represented a betrayal of Louis's previous standards! Louis Armstrong, the great survivor, had by this time put his career under the total protection of Mr Joe Glaser, a strong man before whose flinty gaze such pressing problems as intrusive gangsters, importunate managers, turbulent womenfolk and marauding rivals all faded away. It may have been the persistent challenge from fellow-trumpeters trying on every occasion to pit their talents against those of the champion that, together with the unwelcome attentions of the underworld which saw in him a hot and negotiable property, sent him fleeing to Europe in 1932 and again, for a longer spell, in 1933. There, for the best part of two years, he spent his resources, both onstage and off, with furious abandon, fronting a band in a variety act that outraged the regular theatre-goers and startled even the avowed jazz lovers with its display of unbridled power and ferocious energy. It was the last the world was to see of Louis the carefree and profligate spender of his talents. When he returned to America in January 1935, beset by unresolved lawsuits and a troublesome lip, it is as if Fate, in the incarnate form of Joe Glaser, put a restraining hand on his shoulder. From now on the trumpet playing, still majestic in its tone, range and technical command, would be less volatile, more considered. As his career broadened into films, comedy and increasingly commercial recording, the material and the quality of the backing would more and more often give the purist cause to wince. But the cooler approach, in which Louis seemed to be re-examining and refining his earlier discoveries, produced, in circumstances as widely different as a collaboration with the Mills Brothers and a reunion with his old colleague, Sidney Bechet, much commanding and moving stuff. Had I the luxury of a volume the width of a London omnibus, I could pick more than one masterpiece from this period for illuminating analysis. But new names and fresh innovators claim attention, and I must move on.

Fats Waller

IN THE STORY of twentieth-century popular music, Louis Armstrong and Thomas 'Fats' Waller share a unique position. Acknowledged and revered by fellow-musicians and *cognoscenti* as masters in the esoteric field of jazz, they found their way separately and by rather different routes into the affections of a wide public that knew nothing about jazz and regarded them as lovable and talented entertainers.

Of the two, Fats was the more unlikely contender for the role. True, he had an infectious and accessible piano style, an outgoing personality and a line in irreverent clowning which in his childhood 'slayed' his school friends and often turned aside adult wrath. But he showed none of Louis Armstrong's powerful urge for survival in the entertainment world. Appetites as gargantuan as his massive frame were indulged without thought of the consequences, which not infrequently involved engagements either missed altogether or in which the star attraction was found, at curtain-up, taking a recuperative nap under the piano. His assets as a radio performer, quickly recognized by a Cincinnati radio producer in 1932 and later followed up in New York, were offset by his penchant for provocative and risqué ad-libbing, one outrageous bout of which prompted a radio announcer to close a show with the words 'And now it's time to say goodbye to Fats Waller and his music . . . and if it wasn't time, it would be a good idea'. Indeed, the very factors which earned the recordings by Fats Waller and His Rhythm a cult following all over the world in the late Thirties—the mocking of sentimental lyrics, the stentorian off-the-cuff commentary, the atmosphere of inspired chaos—flew in the face of show-business protocol, by which artists were expected to sell the song first, themselves afterwards.

With the bracketing together of Louis and Fats in this context more interesting comparisons emerge. In the hagiography of jazz, Louis Armstrong is usually depicted as a Hamlet who resolutely pursued the path of clown. Fats Waller, on the other hand, is drawn in the more conventional image of the light entertainer inside whom a serious and frustrated artist was screaming to be let out. No doubt there has been some wishful thinking in this respect by jazz commentators raised in the European tradition of 'high culture' and disappointed with heroes who do not always behave as 'great artists' should. But allowing for this, there remains weighty evidence from those close to Fats to support the picture of a thoughtful and sensitive musician trapped within a restricting musical environment. His son Maurice Waller, in a book about his father (*Fats Waller* by Maurice Waller and Anthony Calabrese) recalls an interview Fats gave after his return from Europe in 1938.

'When a reporter asked him about the difference between American boogie and the music preferred in Europe, the hamming ceased. "For years I've been trying to sell the idea of softer stuff over here. I used to tell 'em down at Victor I ought to tone it down, but they'd just say, 'No, go ahead and give 'em that hot primitive stuff.' Dad wasn't just attacking boogie woogie this time. Fats Waller was going through something of a transition. He was becoming more introspective, considering his achievements and potential as a composer. He constantly talked about his admiration for George Gershwin's "Rhapsody in Blue" and "Concerto in F". He was introducing more and more classical themes into his music.'

Eugene Sedric, the tenor-player with Fats on most of the rumbustious recordings in the Thirties, gives a colleague's opinion. 'He wanted to do great things on the organ and piano, which he could do. There were many times when . . . he felt like himself and wanted to play great. But when he played as musically as he could, many people in the audience would think he was laying down and they'd yell, "Come on, Fats!" He'd take a swig of gin or something and say resignedly, "Aw right, here it is." Fats really was a great artist . . .'

It sounds a familiar story, not unlike the one which, for many years, was repeated about Bix Beiderbecke. Detailed biographies of Beiderbecke eventually established that what drove him to drink was not the frustration of a dedicated jazz musician forced to earn his bread in the commercial Whiteman orchestra, but the confusion of a musician with doubts as to the validity of his jazz work and an innate inability to fulfil higher ambitions. Similar thoughts arise about Fats Waller, demanding consideration if his standing as a jazz musician is to be accurately assessed. It will help if we briefly summarize his development from musically precocious child to world-renowned entertainer, a story well documented and authenticated in at least three full biographies.

One point of some significance which emerges from all these biographies is the prodigious ease with which Fats seems to have assimilated keyboard technique. At the age of six he was a regular visitor to an upstairs neighbour's apartment which, unlike the Wallers' own overpopulated place (Fats was one of the five survivors from a family of eleven) boasted an upright piano. His childish skill at picking out tunes induced his parents to acquire an instrument of their own, on which they fondly believed that either Tom or his sister, Naomi, would lay the foundations for a career as concert pianist. Edward and Adeline Waller were quite typical of the strict, strait-laced, church-loving families who were in the van of the black migration into Harlem. Edward Waller had built up a haulage business which kept the large family adequately fed and clothed, but it was the church which was central to their lives. As soon as he was able to wheeze out simple chords on the harmonium, little Thomas Waller was recruited into the street-corner meetings at which Edward preached and Adeline sang the hymns. It is not hard to imagine the family scenes and upheavals when Thomas's predilection for 'the devil's music'— that is to say, all music associated with secular entertainment— led him into the decidedly unholy realms of nightlife which were blossoming rapidly not more than a block or two from the Wallers' sedate area.

The first haunt to which Fats—he earned the nickname as a

schoolboy—was attracted was a movie house called the Lincoln Theatre. It was not the films that attracted him, but the accompanying piano music played by a Miss Mazie Mullins, who must rank with Duke Ellington's early teacher, Mrs Clinkscales, as one of the unsung—and unconscious—heroines of the jazz story. Day after day Tom Waller bought a ticket and took a seat as near as possible to the pit, where he could watch and listen. Then he would go home and try to reproduce what he had heard on the piano. Since it is alleged that he weighed over fourteen stone (two hundred pounds) by this time, it is hardly surprising that Miss Mullins began to notice the huge boy in short trousers watching every move of her fingers. She invited him into the pit to sit alongside her, and within days, so the story goes, she was allowing him to take over for short spells while she took a breather. The Lincoln Theatre boasted an expensive pipe organ too and, even more incredibly, Fats was soon taking his turn on this more complex instrument, to such good effect that he was given the job permanently.

The Lincoln Theatre was no backstreet flea-pit. As well as movies, it presented live shows at weekends, and the finest black musicians and vaudeville artists would appear there, drawing an audience that would often contain white composers such as George Gershwin and Irving Berlin as well as theatrical bookers and agents. In the light of this, Fats Waller's success story might seem hard to swallow. But the reader should be warned that short pants have played a prominent and often misleading role in jazz legend. Careful scrutiny of the relevant dates suggest that, if the eye-witness accounts are true, male juveniles in America were condemned to a longer spell in truncated leg-wear than their counterparts in modern times. For, short pants or not, Fats was fifteen years old when he gained professional access to the Lincoln Theatre organ. Even in the full biographies, the nine years or so between the Waller family's acquisition of a piano and Fats's professional début are condensed and vague. We know that after early abortive piano lessons, he studied piano and violin at school, and that the religious activity of his parents in the local community provided him with access to both piano and organ in the church. He learned to read music and this, combined with an

acute ear which enabled him to reproduce in rough and ready
fashion whatever music he heard, would have furnished him with
some kind of a repertoire. Although it would not have been jazz
in any currently accepted sense, his music was seemingly sufficiently tainted with inflaming syncopation for it to cause the
schism within the Waller family.

So it was no fumbling beginner who insinuated himself into the
professional ambience of the Lincoln Theatre. But there was one
area in which his basic musical education was incomplete. Fats
Waller's impressionable adolescence coincided with the rapid
growth of Harlem from a quiet and rather stuffy suburb into a
teeming urban community. The centre of black entertainment
shifted from the rough San Juan Hill area known as The Jungles,
where pianists such as James P. Johnson and Willie 'The Lion'
Smith had achieved renown, to almost within earshot of the
Waller home. From basements and store-fronts, piano music
wafted into the street continuously, and Fats took it in greedily.
He was too young to go into the clubs and cabarets, so actual
tuition in this field of piano playing was harder to acquire.

One of the lesser lights among the Harlem pianists was Russell
Brooks, whose younger brother, Wilson, had been one of Fats's
school cronies. In 1920, when Fats was sixteen, his mother died
suddenly, her heart failing under the cumulative strain of child-
bearing, obesity and diabetes. Despite the frequent hostilities
with his father regarding his devotion to the 'music from the
devil's workshop', Fats had enjoyed a warm and secure family
life. With Adeline's death, it came to an end. Not long afterwards,
still in a state of shock, Fats left home and it was to the Brooks
household that he gravitated. They took him in and it was agreed
with Edward Waller that it would be best for him to stay with
them.

A new phase in his career began. For one thing, the Brooks
family owned a player-piano, the forerunner of the phonograph
and record-player as a mechanical disseminator of music, and just
as important to the young musical explorer. When a paper roll
was inserted in the instrument and the automatic mechanism
brought into play, rectangular holes cut in the paper in appropriate places to correspond to musical notes would activate the

piano in such a way that the keys would be automatically depressed as if manipulated by ghostly hands. To Fats, the great boon of this apparatus was not only that it brought him close to the music of idols such as James P. Johnson, but that, by slowing down the machine at certain points and fitting his fingers into the depressed keys, he could learn the fingering of complex chords which his ear could not identify. (It would have been a few years earlier that Duke Ellington, back home in Washington, D.C., learned James P. Johnson's 'Carolina Shout' by exactly the same method).

The Brooks family's player-piano advanced Fats Waller's career in a far more important, if indirect, way. Russell Brooks, who lived away from home, came by to see his mother one day and came upon Fats teaching himself 'Carolina Shout' from the piano roll. He was so impressed by the boy's keenness that, the next time he saw James P. Johnson, he persuaded him to give Fats a hearing. James P. did not normally undertake piano tuition, but when Fats played for him, the combination of precocious talent and the big, suppliant brown eyes conquered him as swiftly as it had Mazie Mullins at the Lincoln Theatre.

The relationship between James P. Johnson and Fats Waller reminds one strongly of that between King Oliver and Louis Armstrong in New Orleans, as recalled by Louis. The Johnsons took Fats under their wing, Lillian Johnson making an important contribution to his career by sending him out to buy his first pair of long pants. James P. Johnson initiated Fats into the art and technique of compulsive swinging which lies at the heart of Harlem stride piano. The pupil made such rapid progress that Johnson soon began to take him around the nightspots as his protégé, encouraging him to get up and play.

Time came when Fats had to be introduced to James P. Johnson's friend and principal rival, Willie the Lion Smith. The meeting was at a club called Leroy's, the most prestigious venue for the Harlem pianists. Willie the Lion recalled in his autobiography *Music On My Mind*, 'Leroy Wilkins was . . . a stickler for high-toned manners and good conduct. He was the first cabaret man to insist on the proper clothes for the floor managers, the waiters, and the musicians. On weekends *everybody* had to wear tuxedos, including the customers.' Into these showbiz surround-

ings walked Fats in the wake of James P. As was customary, his
long trousers were unpressed and spotted with grease and, according to Willie the Lion's memory, he was sucking a toffee apple.
When the Lion caught sight of them, it was Johnson who got the
mauling. 'Who the hell's the punk kid with you?' roared the Lion.
'Fats Waller—' 'Fats Waller? He looks more like Filthy Waller!'
It is a measure of the respect which Fats earned that night through
his piano playing that the nickname stuck. The Lion bestowed
permanent nicknames only upon his closest friends—some time
earlier, James P. Johnson had been dubbed 'The Brute', allegedly
because of the big, hairy overcoat that he used to wear. It was
only a matter of months before the Lion, the Brute and Filthy
were roaming the Harlem piano haunts together, a triumvirate of
invincible keyboard masters.

We can get an idea of Fats Waller's style at this period through
his first solo recordings, made for the Okeh company in 1922.
'Muscle Shoals Blues' is not a very reliable guide since it was a
publisher's tune that Fats was hired to play, with an eye to the
newly discovered market for the blues in the black community.
The stiffness of the performance suggests that Fats was paying
diligent attention to the sheet-music. The biographies by Fats's
manager of later years, Ed Kirkeby, and by his son, Maurice
Waller, both tell, in first-hand, fly-on-the-wall style how Fats,
called on to provide something for the B side of the record, immediately improvised a piece which he called, on the spur of the
moment, 'Birmingham Blues'. It is an improbable story. The very
completeness of the tune, furnished with a verse and recollected
in every detail for three choruses, suggests that it was a piece that
Fats had already composed with some thoroughness and that
perhaps only the title was an off-the-cuff invention.

Comparison of 'Birmingham Blues' with James P. Johnson's
'Carolina Shout', recorded the previous year, shows the two
pianists very strongly in a master-and-pupil relationship. Johnson
was totally in command of all his effects and variations, which
included a bass line which was rich in invention and right-hand
figurations which flowed smoothly and with assurance. Fats
Waller was already taking advantage of the ten-note reach afforded
by his huge hands, but the excessive use of broken tenths in the

left hand, with much too heavy an emphasis on the upper 'thumb' note, produces a cumbersome rhythm. In the second and third choruses there are examples of the frisking about at the treble end of the piano which was to become one of the most exhilarating ingredients of his later style. But here again, the fingering is not properly mastered and there is some uncertainty as to how to match the treble figures with the movement of the bass. Despite these youthful deficiencies, it is clear to the listener that, in Willie the Lion's words, 'The kid's got it.'

The story behind Fats's first recording opportunity is characteristic of him and throws some light on his attitude to music. He had been befriended by Clarence Williams, the pianist from New Orleans who had established himself in New York as composer, publisher, leader of studio bands and all-round entrepreneur. Anxious to help the promising young musician, Williams persuaded the Okeh recording company to use him as accompanist to the blues singer, Sara Martin. When he called Fats to tell him of the date, the reply he got was something less than grateful. 'I don't need the money, and I don't want to accompany anybody.' Williams gave him a lecture on his responsibilities as a professional musician and Fats finally agreed. However, it was to no avail—the session came and went without Fats putting in an appearance, and Clarence Williams deputized for him, launching himself on a lucrative studio career in the process.

In effect, though Fats Waller and James P. Johnson remained firm friends and associates, it was Clarence Williams who acted as the chief catalyst in the next phase of Fats's career. He was impressed by the ease with which Waller seemed able to trot out catchy melodies, and urged him to bring some in for publication. In the first batch was the 'Wildcat Blues', Sidney Bechet's performance of which, with a band led by Clarence Williams, was the subject of a chapter in *The Best of Jazz* Volume One. This was followed by 'Squeeze Me', a tune which Fats is alleged to have developed from a rude ditty called 'Boy in the Boat' that was much in demand at rent-parties when the merry-making had ripened. It has always seemed a somewhat irrelevant piece of historical information, since no one has been able to glean any clear indication of how the original tune went, other than that it was in limerick form—which 'Squeeze Me' is not, except possibly in the first two lines of the verse. It is marginally more interesting to note that the harmonic basis of Fats's piece—a rotating sequence of three chords relieved by modulation at the half-way and concluding marks—occurs in the second strain of a James P. Johnson composition called 'Fascination'.

However it came into being, 'Squeeze Me' was a hit for the Clarence Williams publishing firm and established Fats in the song-writing business. In those days, this was a casual, none-too-scrupulous activity that suited Fats well. He had married his first wife, Edith, on the rebound from the shock of his mother's death, and his first son, Thomas Jnr., had followed soon afterwards. There were mouths to feed, rent instalments to pay and, when a manifestly incompatible partnership inevitably dissolved, alimony payments to be found. Publishers would pay from twenty-five to fifty dollars for a song, often buying tunes which had already been sold to a rival down the street. Copyright went to the first firm to print the song, so it was a fair gamble. As for the composer, all that was left for him, after pocketing the cash, was the satisfaction of seeing his name on the song-copy or, not infrequently, the frustration of seeing someone else's name on it!

In their book, Maurice Waller and Anthony Calabrese list thirty-eight known Waller compositions, published and unpublished, in the year 1924 alone. Many of these were written in partnership with Andy Razaf, a young poet and lyricist with whom Fats struck up a partnership after a casual meeting, and who was later to acquire fame largely on the basis of his work with Fats. I say 'later' because the fact is that, despite quite prolific song-writing activity, with or without Razaf, few if any of the pieces written in the five years between 1924 and 1929 mean anything today in popular music terms, and only a handful survive in the affections of jazz enthusiasts. Collectors' pieces such as 'I'm Goin' Huntin'' and 'Georgia Bo Bo' recorded by Louis Armstrong and 'The Stampede', 'Whiteman Stomp' and goodness knows what others played by Fletcher Henderson's Orchestra (Fats is said to have sold one job lot of nine tunes, including 'The Stampede', to Henderson for the price of twelve hamburgers) attest not only to the facility with which Fats turned out original melodies but also to Clarence Williams's readiness to put them about and get them recorded.

It was not until the late Twenties that Fats Waller the composer was swept into the big time on the crest of a wave. In the years since Fats had made his precocious début at the Lincoln Theatre, Harlem had blossomed as an entertainment centre. Jazz history, justifiably absorbed in extracting and isolating the jazz essence from the rest of the great musical cocktail in which it spent its early years, gives us a lop-sided view, suggesting that, while first New Orleans and then Chicago nurtured the very finest musicians, New York was a late developer in assimilating the new music. But if we take black music and dance as an entity of which jazz was a part, then there is no denying that Harlem from the early Twenties onwards was burgeoning with talent.

Behind the handful of names that Tin Pan Alley, Broadway and Hollywood have helped to immortalize—Florence Mills, Bill 'Bojangles' Robinson, Bert Williams, Ethel Waters—there existed a regular army of hoofers, singers, comedians and musicians, all contributing to a rich entertainment scene which was one of the attractions which brought hordes of white New Yorkers with money to spend into night-time Harlem. Another reason, related to the first, was the growing fascination with Negro culture among New York intellectuals, with the 'liberal' journalist and author, Carl Van Vechten, as the movement's chief propagandist. Paternalistic and selective as it was (Harlemites with neither talent nor beauty derived little warmth from it), it did contribute a lot to creating the Harlem which, to a wide-eyed Duke Ellington on his arrival in 1923, looked 'like the Arabian Nights'.

The third attraction was very much more down to earth. Joel Vance sums it up succinctly in his biography, *Fats Waller—His Life and Times*. 'With the hedonistic defiance of Prohibition among whites, there came a taste for the exotic, the taboo, and the generally frowned upon.' He might have added 'the dangerous', too, for the elegant and lucrative tourist traps, ready outlets for the illicit liquor trade, soon came under the control of 'downtown' gangsters. The former proprietors who yielded gracefully to the take-over were often left in charge as front-men and managers. One who did not was Barron D. Wilkins, brother of the owner of

Leroy's and himself a frequent employer of the Harlem stride men in his ritzier establishment, Barron's. In 1926, he was knifed to death by a professional hit-man called Yellow Charleston.

Jazz, as represented by the Harlem pianists, was at the very centre of all this activity. As Willie the Lion Smith wrote about the clubs in which he and James P. and Fats played, 'The pianist had duties and responsibilities. He played solo piano, accompanied the singers, directed whatever band was on hand, and watched the kitty to be sure no one cheated on tips ... The piano was *it*! The man in charge ... he had to be an all-round showman and it helped if he could both dance and sing. It was like being the host at a party, you were expected to greet everyone who entered to establish favourable feelings.' As the shows became larger and more lavish, the pianist was also expected to write the songs. *Shuffle Along*, the first all-Negro show to make a surprise impact on Broadway in 1920, had songs written by Eubie Blake. Three years later, James P. Johnson gave the decade its theme tune— 'Charleston'—among the songs he wrote for the review *Runnin' Wild*. A rival show *Go-Go* in the same year had music by Luckey Roberts.

In the mid-Twenties Fats Waller, busy in an unspectacular and diffuse way with resident theatre work, vaudeville touring, a sojourn in Chicago and sporadic radio shows, made tentative inroads into this field with two shows written for the Lafayette Theatre. Neither *Tan Town Topics* nor *Junior Blackbirds* rates more than a footnote in the showbiz history of the times, though the first provided Fats and his collaborator, Spencer Williams, with a nationwide hit in the now forgotten 'Senorita Mine'. Equally obscured beneath the dusts of time is a song called 'Willow Tree' with which Fats and Andy Razaf scored a success in *Keep Shufflin'*, a Broadway review to which James P. Johnson also contributed, and in which they made a personal appearance, playing the entr'acte music on two pianos.

But Fats's real chance came through two old associates, Connie and George Immerman, for whose delicatessen store he had worked some years before as an errand boy. The Immermans had entered the show-business world when they opened a club called Connie's Inn in premises next to the Lafayette Theatre. In 1928, they decided to cash in on the vogue for all-Negro reviews with a show called *Load of Coal*, for which Fats and Andy Razaf wrote some songs. 'Zonky' and 'My Fate is in your Hands' were successful featured songs, but a third 'Honeysuckle Rose', was relegated to the backing for a soft-shoe dance by the chorus, and had to wait some fifteen years before it became one of Fats's most popular compositions and a favourite work-out for jamming musicians the world over.

Load of Coal was followed at Connie's Inn by *Hot Chocolates*, for which Waller and Razaf wrote even more numbers—twenty in all. The chronology of *Hot Chocolates* is somewhat confused in the Waller biographies which give the impression that Louis Armstrong's band (the Carroll Dickerson team from Chicago), newly arrived in New York, were booked from the outset. The facts seem to be that the review opened as a Connie's Inn floorshow in the early summer of 1929, without Louis Armstrong or his band. On 20 June, with a strengthened cast and some new tunes added, it opened at the Hudson Theatre on Broadway. A review in the *New York Telegram* began: 'With most of its gold teeth and no little of its tediousness removed, Connie's new tanskin revel is a far better show than it was a couple of weeks ago in the Bronx Windsor Theatre. Nowadays, at the Hudson, *Hot Chocolates* is faster, funnier and a good deal franker.' This indicates that the arrival on Broadway was by a rather more devious route than the potted histories suggest. Another source of confusion is the fact that the show never actually left Connie's Inn for Broadway. As soon as the curtain came down at the Hudson, the cast would hotfoot it back to Harlem to perform a curtailed version at the club. It was here that Louis Armstrong's band, booked for a four-month season from 24 June, would have first made a supporting appearance in the show. Within days, Louis himself was picked out of this floorshow version and added to the theatre cast. A review of the show prior to his joining noted: 'There is a song called "Ain't Misbehavin'"' on which much reliance is placed. Almost everybody in the show sings it at one time or another, and as there are a good many in the show, the song gets sung pretty often.' With Louis Armstrong's arrival, yet another performance of it was added—this time the definitive one.

If the above appears to indulge in some nit-picking about the exact sequence of events surrounding *Hot Chocolates*, there is a purpose to it. In the prevailing fashion for 'tanskin revels', *Hot Chocolates* would probably have enjoyed ephemeral success without Louis Armstrong. But, as I have noted in the chapter on Louis, he was at this time poised for take-off into a new phase in his career. Ever since the Dreamland Ballroom in Chicago had billed him as 'The World's Greatest Trumpet Player', Louis had enjoyed a reputation as a virtuoso performer which spread, through his series of spectacular recordings on the Okeh 'race' label, to black audiences across America and to musicians and record collectors across the globe wherever jazz itself had taken root. With the maturing of his talent for singing into a style which could encompass popular songs, and the application of his phenomenal trumpet technique and range to a new repertoire of gallery-fetching effects, he was ready to reach a wider audience that was less concerned with the musical refinements than with the overall entertainment value. It has become a platitude to say that a great many of Tin Pan Alley's more run-of-the-mill products from 1929 onwards had a long life and a distinction above their true station in life bestowed upon them by Armstrong performances.

In July 1929, Louis recorded four of the tunes from *Hot Chocolates*—'Ain't Misbehavin'', 'Black and Blue' (sung in the show by Edith Wilson), 'Sweet Savannah Sue' and 'That Rhythm Man'. The two latter, plus some other rhythm numbers from the show, were recorded around the same time by Duke Ellington. (Apart from 'Ain't Misbehavin'', which became a standard fixture in his repertoire, and a piano solo version of 'Sweet Savannah Sue', Fats did nothing in his own recording sessions to plug the tunes from the show, a fact which is less surprising when we learn that, with characteristic irresponsibility, he had sold them all in one job lot to the publisher and band-agent Irving Mills for the derisory sum of five hundred dollars.) But it was the Armstrong recordings which were significant. As popular songs divorced from the context of the *Hot Chocolates* revue, 'Sweet Savannah Sue' and 'That Rhythm Man' had no great distinction, the former in particular harking back stylistically to the 'Peg o' my Heart' type ballads of at least fifteen years earlier. Nevertheless, the power and personality of Armstrong's versions are such that, almost certainly, some band somewhere in the world is still trotting them out nightly in response to popular request. But it was 'Ain't Misbehavin'' and 'Black and Blue', the two songs added to *Hot Chocolates* to strengthen its Broadway production, which were projected by Louis Armstrong into their rightful place among the evergreen standards of popular music, hoisting their composer up with them.

So, by 1929, Fats Waller's career had blossomed along what, for Harlem 'stride' men, had become conventional lines. He had recorded piano solos of his own compositions (and, in the early days, some piano rolls, too). He had done his stint as accompanist for blues singers and had popped up on sundry band recordings. He had become a local celebrity on the rent-party circuit, had toured in vaudeville and had made a successful breakthrough into the wider area of show-business represented by Broadway reviews. He had also broken new ground of his own with his recorded work on pipe organ, presumably reflecting the kind of music which he played during his long residencies at the Lincoln and Lafayette Theatres. The jazz fraternity has not, on the whole, shown much enthusiasm for these, and it is doubtful if posterity will revise the verdict that, attractive and impressive as they are beside other Wurlitzer performances of the period, they fall down as jazz simply because of the instrument's tonal and mechanical shortcomings.

Mike Lipskin, an authority on Harlem 'stride' piano and a one-time pupil and protégé of Willie the Lion Smith, has written about Fats: 'His being a star was a kind of accident. Nobody had any idea that he was going to be that big, least of all him. He never looked for it; it just happened to him. If it hadn't happened to him, he could still have earned a very good living as a sideman on record dates, even without the songs he wrote. He could read, he was a good arranger, he could make guys want to play on a session —make them happy while they were doing it—and they had to record a lot of junk material . . . Nobody could have heard of the famous Fats Waller, and he would still have been one of the busiest musicians in the country . . .'

Let us stay in the realms of supposition and imagine that Fats's career ended abruptly in 1929. What would our judgement be today on his contribution to jazz? That he had already made his mark on jazz history is clear. Tunes like 'Squeeze Me', 'Honeysuckle Rose', 'Ain't Misbehavin' ' and 'Black and Blue' were destined, through the recordings by Louis Armstrong alone, to survive as 'standards'. Solo piano recordings such as 'Valentine Stomp', 'Numb Fumblin' ', 'Handful of Keys', 'Smashing Thirds' and 'African Ripples' would have been enough to single him out as a stride pianist of enormous power and potential. He was already a more modern player than both Willie the Lion Smith and James P. Johnson, whose work always bore rhythmic traces of their ragtime origins. With Fats, the forward momentum of stride was streamlined and interior sprung, assisted by a keyboard technique that outstripped that of his mentors. For instance, he exploited his enormous hands to devise a bass pattern involving left-hand intervals of tenths moving smoothly upwards and downwards in parallel, a rich harmonic ploy which was later developed by Art Tatum. The piano compositions (the personal rags which were an obligatory part of the stride man's armoury) had a new look about them, too. By 1929, when Fats recorded his most important batch of solos, ragtime was a thing of the past, and the pattern of sixteen-bar march-like themes on which most of James P. Johnson's compositions were based, had begun to sound oldfashioned. The new popular music was based predominantly on themes of thirty-two-bars' length, arranged either as variants of the time-honoured ABAC format, as in Jimmy McHugh's 'I Can't Give you Anything but Love' (1928) or in the AABA form popularized by George Gershwin and exemplified in his 'Oh, Lady Be Good' (1924). These are the twin formulae which came most naturally to Fats and formed the basis of his most successful pre-1930 solos.

Let us take an example. 'Handful of Keys' was first recorded in 1929 and, strictly speaking, falls outside the brief of this volume. But in this instance, time is irrelevant. Had Fats conceived the piece in 1939, it would have sounded no different, so characteristic is it of his style at any period. A mood of boisterousness is established at the outset with the frisky, kitten-on-the-keys-type introduction, and then we are off at full steam ahead. The opening theme conforms to a familiar Waller pattern, a two-bar figure repeated, with minor harmonic variation, to cover an eight-bar section. The format of this opening theme is AABA, so that after the eight-bar section is repeated, it gives way to a 'middle-eight' before returning. What gives the piece such a rollicking start is the rhythmic interplay between right and left hand. Even when overt clowning was kept in check, humour was never far below the surface in a Fats Waller performance. Here it is exemplified in the way the upward octave run in the right hand skips away from the heavy first bass beat of the bar as if challenging it to desert its solid regular metre and take off in pursuit. The left hand resolutely spurns all such temptation, its firmness accentuated by the 'broken tenth' which Fats uses in place of a single bass note on the first and third beats of the bar. In simple terms, this means that the little finger strikes a keynote in the bass, the thumb the third note of the octave above. This tenth is 'broken' by the thumb note being struck fractionally after the lower note, and with rather more force, so that what gives the listener his sense of the direction in which the bass harmonies are moving is not the root notes of the chords but notes in effect a third above—the E in the case of a C chord. It is an effective device, heavily exploited in ensuing years by Earl Hines, and varied with great subtlety by Art Tatum and Teddy Wilson.

The middle-eight B section of this first theme is based, as countless middle-eights have been since, on the corresponding section of George Gershwin's song, 'I Got Rhythm', and this emphasizes the popular song origins of Fats's thematic material. Unlike the bars that surround it, this middle-eight has no mandatory 'tune'. In subsequent performances of the piece, Fats played it differently. (Indeed, there is one 1939 Musak recording, a rare example of Fats sounding patently too drunk to play, in which he substitutes the middle-eight chords from his own 'Honeysuckle Rose' in fuddled error). The vagueness of this middle section enables him to introduce into his party piece some straightforward jazz improvisation, an element which, so far as one can tell from recordings, was new to such stride performances. In the first chorus, he pounds out a simple melodic line of the kind which Andy Razaf would have had no difficulty in equipping with words, had he been called on to do so. Fats comes out of this section with a favourite device, a series of phrases covering two beats with a little triplet 'turn' on the first beat. In the second chorus, in which Fats follows his customary pattern of repeating the first main theme in the piano's upper register, this curlicue triplet motif rebounds from Fats's subconscious to become a skittish variation covering the whole middle-eight bars.

After the two opening choruses there is a four-bar interlude leading into a new theme in a new key. This is a straightforward thirty-two-bar harmonic theme, a first cousin once-removed of the harmonic basis of the trio in 'Tiger Rag' or, going back still further into popular music, of Hughie Cannon's hit of 1902, 'Won't You Come Home, Bill Bailey'. Once again, there is no dominant melody to this section. As in much of James P. Johnson's work, we have a basic harmonic framework on which complex rhythmic patterns are superimposed. This brief secondary theme is stride piano *par excellence*. In its first eight bars there is ex-hilarating interplay between pumping, on-the-beat notes in the bass and ahead-of-the-best phrases in the right hand. For the next eight bars the harmonic sequence is followed with the out-line of a melody expressed in percussive chords again struck ahead of the beat and culminating in a typical Wallerism, a descending scale in the bass in which the right hand is brought in to double the notes, so that the pianist is literally drumming on the keys. The second half of the chorus shows how Fats's method differed from that of James P. Johnson, whose carefully worked out scheme of things would have demanded a reprise of the rhythmic pattern of the first eight bars. But Fats in full flight seldom concerned himself with such niceties of construction. Stomping chords devolve into another device which Fats inherited from Johnson and developed along his own lines. Basically, it is a pattern in which changing thirds played by the inner fingers of the right hand are rocked between appropriate notes played by little finger and thumb. No need to search around for an onomatopaeic aid to describe the effect. Fats provides one himself in the ribald verbal coda to his recording of 'Dinah' which starts 'Oh, ji-bee-ji-bye-ji-bee-ji-bee-ji-bo'. If one takes the long syllables to be thirds with appropriate harmonic variation and the 'ji' syllables to be notes above and below them played alternatively with little finger and thumb, we get a rough idea of a device with which Fats would often link his phrases or, on occasion, build a whole chorus.

The rest of the thirty-two-bar section in 'Handful of Keys' is made up of the sort of declamatory phrases which a trumpet player or a blues singer would use in similar harmonic circumstances. This is Fats expressing himself in orchestral rather than pianistic terms, and shows how simple he must have found it to churn out easily adaptable themes for Fletcher Henderson's use. In general, this thirty-two-bar section provides a strong contrast to the busy scampering of the opening theme. Having served this purpose, it is not developed. A brisk modulation takes us back to the opening theme, the rising scales of which Fats spreads in the first eight bars over three octaves. The fact that he doesn't repeat this happy notion in the second eight bars, as James P. Johnson would undoubtedly have done, stresses again the different approach of the two men. Fats is impatient with structural symmetry, eager all the time to push the performance on to a higher momentum. After a powerfully rhythmic middle-eight, he doesn't return to the theme but replaces its decorative line with a variation which is purely rhythmic. We can see why. Stride pianists liked to refer to their most spectacular keyboard inventions as 'fingerbusters', and Fats was on the run-up to his. He doesn't re-state the theme but literally submerges it in variation in which the left hand suddenly abandons its 'oom-chah' role to join in the fun.

The final 'fingerbuster' represents the kind of technical gymnastic display which the Harlem ticklers used to hold in reserve for the moment when an importunate rival needed to be put to rout. Following the harmonies meticulously, he spatters the keyboard with staccato phrases like a machine-gunner raking the field with fire. Fats used basically the same device in a contemporary solo which he called 'Smashing Thirds', and the words describe it perfectly. A less thoughtful player than Fats—or indeed Fats himself in his more abandoned moments—might have barged on through the middle-eight with sustained impetuosity. But with a brilliant stroke, he interrupts the forward movement with two breaks involving reflective broken chords that contrive to increase, rather than relieve, the tension. There is only one way to end the piece, and that is in the grand, ride-out style of Louis Armstrong, right hand punching out trumpet phrases across the beat. The coda, a descending bass figure combining the 'drumming' technique described earlier with James P. Johnson's 'interrupted bass', is an instrumental foreshadowing of those manic verbal overflows with which Fats's later commercial recordings would often career to a halt.

Earlier, I summed up Fats Waller, the pianist, at this stage in his development as a stride man of enormous power and potential. Before we go on to see the extent to which that potential was resolved, it is necessary to examine more closely my assertion that Fats Waller was a more 'modern' player than either James P. Johnson or Willie the Lion Smith. First, we must clear our minds of any suggestion that to be 'more modern' implies superiority. On more than one occasion in *The Best of Jazz* Volume One, I made the point, apropos of jazz rhythm, that new discoveries do not (or should not) devalue or render permanently obsolete all that went before. The piano pieces which James P. Johnson and, to a lesser extent, Willie the Lion recorded stand today as gems of keyboard composition. Indeed, Johnson is still shamefully underrated in this respect. But times were changing. Radio began to rival the piano as the chief agency of home entertainment. Through the Thirties, those families who still gathered round the piano of an evening would prop up on the music rack, not keyboard pieces specially written for the piano, but the published sheet music of the popular songs which were plugged on the radio and on gramophone records. By 1929, when Fats recorded the great majority of his solo pieces, the rich vein of keyboard composition that had started with the first published ragtime piece thirty-two years earlier had been worked out. The thrilling improvisational flights of Louis Armstrong and those exponents of every instrument who came under his influence engendered in musicians and audiences alike an impatience with the orderly and restrained dispensation of theme and variation which characterized the music of the ragtime players and their immediate descendants—and, to some extent, the band music of Jelly Roll Morton and King Oliver. It is no coincidence that the young pianists such as Fats Waller and Duke Ellington chose to cut their musical teeth on James P. Johnson's 'Carolina Shout', the most forward looking of his compositions with its thrusting rhythmic momentum and capacity for improvised extension.

This circumstance must surely be taken into account and added to all the varied explanations which have been put forward to explain Fats Waller's personal and artistic shortcomings. The dichotomy between his training in the sternly disciplined school of Harlem stride and the new romanticism that was sweeping through jazz must have mirrored the tension in his childhood, between his strictly religious family background and the creative opportunities offered by Harlem's uninhibited and 'sinful' night-life. Had his career ended in 1929, none of the theorizing nor the myth-making that now accumulates around his memory would have come about. Knowledge of his drinking habits and convivial nature, already fully developed, would have been confined to his close accociates, and nothing in his recorded output up to that time would have prompted anyone to investigate or analyse them. We would know him today as the composer of two of Louis Armstrong's greatest hits who popped up with some exhilarating solos of records by Fletcher Henderson and the little-known Tom Morris Hot Babies, and whose solo piano recordings constituted a fine and final flourish to the parlour piano era.

But it didn't end there. Surviving—nay, rampaging—into the Thirties, with the vogue for all-black Harlem revues on the wane, Fats needed to discover a new role for himself, a task to which he applied himself with characteristic insouciance, carousing his way from one impromptu recording session to another and, at one stage, prising himself away from his beloved Harlem long enough to make what, for jazzmen of that period, seems to have been an obligatory pilgrimage to Paris. Then fate took a hand. His success as a broadcaster, a role in which he played, sang and gave rein to ribald and often risqué off-the-cuff humour, suggested to his manager that the time was ripe for him to be equipped with a band for stage, ballroom and recording work. When it finally took shape, the band known as Fats Waller and his Rhythm proved ideally suited to Fats's impromptu style of presentation. In reed-men Gene Sedric or Rudy Powell, guitarist Al Casey, and trumpeter Herman Autrey, he had three regular soloists of distinctive style, the latter capable of explosive, if often erratic, ride-out trumpet in the Armstrong manner in response to Fats's verbal encouragement. Fortunately for our peace of mind, none of these sidemen were outstanding enough to arouse in us resentment at the constant stentorian interruptions from the piano stool that often obliterated their work.

Verbal participation played quite a prominent part in the presentation of stride piano. Both Willie the Lion and Eubie Blake have been known to punctuate both recorded and stage performances with running commentary, and in the atmosphere of a rent-party cutting contest, badinage between rivals and cross-talk from player to audience and back no doubt added to the excitement. One theory is that when he started broadcasting, Fats compensated for the absence of a visible audience by indulging in backchat with the station's master of ceremonies as he played. Whatever its origins, Fats Waller's capacity for maintaining a stream of chatter throughout the proceedings became an instant feature of his band recordings. The interruptions, which range from exhortations to the musicians to lengthy dialogue with some imaginary female presence, are not just laboured attempts to whip up 'atmosphere'. Some of them seem to be taking place within a private hallucinatory world in which voices are answered, insults are returned, manic laughter is induced and strange surrealist notions are pursued. Sometimes this stream of consciousness is inspired by the title or the content of the song, sometimes by the playing, or even the name of a musician taking part. When he recorded with a British group in 1938, a tenor solo by one Ian Shepherd initiated a line of thought. 'Yeah! What? Shepherd of the flock? Blow, my lamb, blow! He's up in the mountain!'

It was the success of the recordings by Fats and his Rhythm, sparked off in 1935 by a best-selling version of a previously unsuccessful new ditty called 'I'm Gonna Sit Right Down and Write Myself a Letter', which led to the orgy of critical heart-searching that has centred upon Fats Waller's role in jazz history. Could a man whose major contribution to the art form between 1934 and his death in 1943 consisted of churning out unrehearsed versions of generally trashy popular songs, mocking the lyrics and burying the tune in ribald commentary, really be counted among the giants?

Before we venture any sort of answer, we must counter some of the myths that have been erected to explain away the phenomenon. Most dubious of these is the theory that commercial pressure forced Fats to play the clown against his own inclinations. Other musicians, notably Louis Armstrong, Billie Holiday and Teddy Wilson, operated under the same kind of recording contract, playing inferior songs forced upon them by the studio managers and aimed at the same market. There is no evidence that they were expected to lay on the comedy—and plenty of evidence that Fats's managers were, indeed, begged from time to time to restrain their artiste's audible conviviality. Nor does the theory that the newly acquired mass audience created a demand for frivolity cut much ice. Fats's most successful hits were such songs as 'I'm Gonna Sit Right Down and Write Myself a Letter', 'When Somebody Thinks You're Wonderful', 'My Very Good Friend the Milkman' and 'Until the Real Thing Comes Along' in which the music has a danceable lilt and there is a minimum of horse-play. Further to this, there is nothing of the ingratiating, Uncle Tom crowd-pleasing in Fats Waller's humour. In his few film appearances he made a firm stand against having to utter the stock, 'Yassuh, boss' lines of the stage Negro, and the familiar Wallerisms—'One never knows, do one', 'I wonder what the poor people are doin' tonight' and the valedictory 'Well, a-a-a-ll right, then' came from his own personal vernacular and often had a derisive cutting edge.

A variation on the above theme suggests that the fearful grievous bodily harm that Fats inflicted on the lyrics of much of his material expressed his anger and disgust at the trash that he was called on to perform. Certainly, he had lethal ways of dealing with sentimentality—in 'It's a Sin to Tell a Lie' the line 'If you break my heart I'll die' becomes 'If you break my heart I'll break your leg and then I'll die'—and other sugary or melo-dramatic sentiments are delivered in a childish falsetto or a quivering operatic bass. Any notion that this often extremely funny lampooning of the songs was a one-man demo against the fatuities of Tin Pan Alley will not long survive the fact that, while some truly dreadful lyrics escape unscathed, Fats's own songs, with the relatively sharp and clever lyrics by Andy Razaf, came in for the treatment. In an early version of his 'Crazy 'bout my Baby', the repetition of the word 'baby' strikes him as funny—or, perhaps, embarrassing—so he milks it for laughs by singing 'Crazy 'bout my ... *bebby, bebby's* crazy 'bout me'. In another version, the title line acquires, at the end, a spurious dignity by being translated into 'I'm exasperated about the offspring, the offspring's exasperated about me'!

Dick Wellstood, one of the post-war generation of stride men and an objective admirer of Fats, wrote in the magazine *Jazz Review* in 1960, 'It's so hard to tell what Fats could do because he was always trying to entertain, and so made his playing entertaining at the damndest times ... the trouble with a lot of the guys of that age is that they really in a sense are ashamed of jazz.' If we take 'to entertain' in this context as meaning 'to make people laugh', then the judgement is in keeping with the early picture we have of young Fats rolling his eyes and wiggling his eyebrows for the amusement of his schoolfriends. This, and the available aural evidence, contradicts another of the Waller myths—that he was a deeply serious musician who was frustrated and angered by the refusal of the public to appreciate or even listen to the more sober and considered aspects of his work. It may be true—we have no reason to doubt the stories—that closeted with friends behind closed doors he would enthral his listeners with deeply reflective improvisations and performances of his favourite classics. It is not a side of him which makes much impression on record, though he had the opportunity to reveal it. A large number of the tunes which he recorded were ballads—i.e., relatively slow popular songs of the kind which inspired thoughtful and often noble interpretations in his contemporaries. That he could play in this vein is hinted at in several of his solo pieces, which show him indulging in the sort of harmonic exploration and melodic paraphrasing which can turn a modest Tin Pan Alley theme into fine jazz. But for his ballads he chose instead a more obvious, fulsome style, rich in decorative embellishment, full of heavy, organ-like chords and ready to pounce on any turn of phrase that invited some eyebrow-wiggling fun. There are a few recorded examples of him playing themes from the classics, in the established stride tradition, but they hardly nourish the image of the misunderstood artist. When he played the Quartet from *Lucia di Lammermoor*, for instance, he reduced the melody to triviality by rendering it in a series of right-hand trills for which the eyebrows must have been providing some hyperactive visual accompaniment.

The search for another Fats Waller, a Thomas Waller, perhaps, who will offer himself as a more seemly candidate for the jazz hall of fame, has led some commentators to lean heavily on the piano solos, of which 'Handful of Keys' was just one. Is it as a composer of piano rags in the stride idiom that we should salute him? Yes—and no. Yes, because recordings such as 'Valentine Stomp', 'Smashing Thirds' and 'African Ripples' provide exhilarating collections of the formidable weapons in Fats's stride armoury. No, because if we listen to them carefully, we soon detect that they are not carefully considered compositions at all, but demonstrations of Fats's ability to sit down and rattle off a convincing and catchy melody at will, sometimes using second-hand spare parts when originality failed. The facts speak for themselves. The opening theme of 'Valentine Stomp' is based on what I have described as the 'curlicue' triplet device used in the second middle-eight of 'Handful of Keys'. The second theme in 'Valentine Stomp' bears a strong family likeness to the second theme of 'Handful of Keys' sharing, in fact, its final sixteen bars. The third section of 'Valentine Stomp', a minor-key variant of the opening theme, turned up again in 1939 as the 'Piccadilly' section of the London Suite, which Fats is said to have 'composed' at miraculous speed at the keyboard. The first strain of 'Gladyse' in 1929 performed the same duty in 'African Ripples' in 1934. And the phrases on which most of these pieces are based occur, everywhere, in the solos in Fats's band recordings.

Fats Waller employed a similar technique of instant production in the writing of his show tunes. It in no way lessens the great virtues of such songs as 'I've Got a Feeling I'm Falling', 'I'm Crazy 'bout my Baby', 'Keepin' out of Mischief Now', 'Ain't Misbehavin' ' and 'Black and Blue' to say that many of the tunes which he polished off in the legendary ten or twenty minutes sounded like potboilers. Maurice Waller's biography lists three hundred and twenty-five Waller compositions, published and un-published, of which a mere handful live on in the public con-sciousness—hardly enough to set him among the Jerome Kerns and George Gershwins. The flaw in Fats's composing method shows up strongly in 'Honeysuckle Rose', a tune based on phrases that flow effortlessly from a stride pianist's hands. The melody is awkward to play on a blowing instrument, almost impossible to sing unless reduced to a manageable tempo, and sounds best when played on the piano by Count Basie, Earl Hines or Fats himself.

The object of the foregoing paragraphs is not to debunk Fats Waller as a man of many talents. It is simply to point out that those talents were not concentrated in any major body of work but were distributed, with profligacy and abandon, in handfuls of small fragments. To dismiss the Fats and His Rhythm output and search for 'the real Fats Waller' elsewhere is to court disappoint-ment or self-deception—and to miss a lot of fine jazz. His achieve-ments as they stand are not inconsiderable. He wrote a handful of memorable songs and played a barrelful of excellent piano solos, on his own or with the band. His harmonic and rhythmic innova-tions, rarely assembled in one piece but scattered all over his recorded work, influenced Art Tatum to the extent that he told an interview, 'Fats, that's where I come from—and it's quite a place to come from.' Most of his contemporaries and many musicians of a subsequent generation have paid tribute to him, either in words or in musical dedications. In an era when most informal jazz led an underground, after-hours existence, he stormed the best-selling charts with a band that swung and stomped like a sort of institutionalized jam session. It was not in his line to ennoble the popular songs of Tin Pan Alley by musical trans-formation, as Louis Armstrong and Billie Holiday did. Instead, he brought them down, with a relentless barrage of good-natured chaffing, from the sentimental, sickly sweet, escapist clouds to the world of merry-making, woman-chasing, wife-deceiving, in-nocence-pleading, trouble-fleeing and payment-dodging that he inhabited himself. As an entertainer in the broad sense—and almost all jazz musicians prior to 1945 performed that role in one way or another—he was extremely funny in a way that made no concessions to popularity and yet reached a vast audience outside those who would profess to be jazz enthusiasts. Several of these activities appear on paper to be conflicting and yet he reconciled them.

To choose one record from the three hundred or so that Fats made with his Rhythm between 1934 and 1942 is like trying to pick the juiciest from a barrel of apples. There are few out-and-out duds—the band had a formula for coping with the most intractable material, and throughout the years of almost permanent carousing, Fats's piano playing was remarkably consistent in its swing and buoyancy. Some of the slower songs nudge the borderline between jazz and superior dance music, especially when Fats plays rippling decorative figures around Gene Sedric's crooning sub-tone clarinet in a manner that clearly influenced the strict tempo music of Victor Sylvester. But lower the stylus at random on to any of the Waller Rhythm collections and the odds are good that you will hear a hot, driving jazz performance graced by some superlative stride piano and infused with an unforced party spirit.

The very first recording which the group made was wholly characteristic. Called 'I Wish I were Twins', it lacked the benefit of Sedric's distinctive and versatile playing (he didn't settle permanently with the band until late in 1935) but had an adequate substitute in Ben Whittet's dry-toned clarinet. Herman Autrey is in fine stabbing form, and the two front-line men share the opening chorus. The song, with such lyrical highspots as 'you great big babykins', gets gentle treatment from Fats, who was perhaps not yet into his full destructive stride. It enables us to hear that, with a voice with less tonal warmth and consistency than Louis Armstrong's, Fats nevertheless knew how to phrase a song in the jazz manner, and even the spoken or bellowed inter-jections have a certain rhythmic relevance. After the vocal there is the leader's piano solo in which, as is often the case, he converts the popular song into an exercise in stride piano, following the harmonies of the tune but substituting a whole procession of figures, arabesques and percussive chords for the melody. Then the horn men return for a chorus of jamming in which Herman Autrey generates a fervid head of steam with a succession of Louis-esque sustained notes, some with a downward glissando at the end, some shaken ferociously and some literally blurted out as if they could be contained no longer.

The above synopsis, varied sometimes to the extent that Fats's solo often opened the proceedings, could apply to almost every one of the Rhythm's up-tempo recordings. The one I have chosen as among the very best is a version of Euday Bowman's 'Twelfth Street Rag' recorded in 1935. On this occasion Rudy Powell played clarinet, but his style was so similar to Sedric's that the substitution makes no difference to the band's approach. The choice of material seems an odd one. 'Twelfth Street Rag' was first published in 1914, and subsequently hung about for four decades until Pee Wee Hunt gave it the *coup de grâce* in the Fifties. For a tune which is virtually unplayable in its pristine form except as a joke, it has had some distinguished interpretations. Louis Armstrong's Hot Five raised it far above its station in life with a stately, impassioned performance in the mid-Twenties, and it has been played by such distinguished leaders as Duke Ellington, Count Basie, Lionel Hampton and Sidney Bechet.

Fats gets around the problem of making musical sense out of the silly tune by ignoring it. After a crashing introduction that sounds as if the Harmful Little Armful had momentarily hopped kitten-like on to the keys, he takes off with steady momentum into a stride chorus based solely on the tune's harmonies. While the left hand follows the correct changes, the right hand plays a repetitive pattern of alternating adjacent thirds—those favoured 'smashing thirds' again—which seem to mock the sterile nature of the original tune without actually duplicating it. In the second half of the chorus, the figure is varied rhythmically with more percussive effect. If one probes beneath the surface impression that Fats Waller's solos were spontaneous firework displays of assorted stride effects, a sound sense of construction reveals itself, often expressed in the sandwiching of solid, strongly rhythmic passages in between the bravura playing. In this instance, lightness returns at the end of the chorus in the form of the triplet curlicues that made their early appearance in 'Valentine Stomp'.

At some stage in the life of 'Twelfth Street Rag', someone by the name of Sumner provided a lyric. Typical of the 'hot' numbers of the first jazz age, the words divide their allotted space between instructions on how to dance to the number ('first you slide . . . then you glide') and exclamations as to what irresistible fun it all is ('I can't get enough of this . . . play it over 'gain'). Apart from a cry of 'Here she comes—look out for that funny feelin' now!' half-way through, Fats uses the words as written but distributes them in a rhythmic pattern against shifting guitar figures to produce what, for all the sense which the words impart, could be described as an effective scat chorus.

What happens between the end of the vocal and the record's explosive conclusion can best be described in terms of two con-current strands of activity. In one, Rudy Powell and Herman Autrey deliver characteristic solos. In this period, Powell played clarinet with a persistently rasping tone, not very attractive in itself, but geared, like his restless, angular phrasing, to generating heat. Herman Autry was capable of fine playing in a style pitched somewhere between Louis Armstrong and Henry 'Red' Allen, and this is one of his best solos. The entrance, a note sustained over two bars in which Fats establishes a heightened, two-handed beat, gives masterly notice that a frontal assault on the senses is about to begin. An obvious rapport existed between Fats and his trumpeter arising, no doubt, from the latter's lack of inhibition in responding to his leader's musical and verbal call to frenetic action. Sometimes the result is erratic to the point of incoherence, but in 'Twelfth Street Rag' Autrey successfully builds up the tension with terse phrases pitched on and across the beat, remini-scent of Henry Allen's 'impressionistic' manner.

The second strand of activity involves Fats himself. I have noted earlier the surrealistic, hallucinatory quality of much of his verbal interruption. Close study of the band recordings, including some alternative takes, reveals Fats actually devoted some thought to the shape and style of the seemingly *ad lib* comments. Often related to the sentiments of the song, they create a scenario that hangs together—of Fats in altercation with a landlady or pursuing an unsuccessful courtship or, as in this instance, in the throes of a hectic party. Most of the noises behind Rudy Powell's solo suggest someone engaged in an ecstatic dance, at one point regaling his partner with 'Look what you can get for nothing, baby!' The trumpet solo seems to arouse an appetite. 'Waiter get some hot

dogs ready. Get some chitlins, too. Or hot potato salad,' are the
cries which intersperse the action here. It is worth noting that
while some of the utterances are quite independent of the music—
uncannily so when one considers that the perpetrator is simultaneously pounding out on-the-beat piano—others play a rhythmic
part in the proceedings. Obvious examples are the exclamations
of 'My, my!' and 'Ah, mercy!' which act as riffs behind the
soloist. But it is interesting, too, that, for example, the words
'Waiter, get some hot dogs ready' match, in the rhythm of their
syllables, the one-note trumpet figures that Herman Autrey is
playing.

The notion of Fats Waller's voice as a third member of the
front line, and not simply extraneous buffoonery in the background, strengthens when, in response to Fats's persistent injunc-
tion to 'Turn it loose!', the band roars into the final chorus. Now
the two strands of activity come together. Herman Autrey assumes
his favourite role, that of blasting out crackling single notes at
judicious intervals while the clarinet frisks around his ankles. On
this occasion, Fats answers his declamatory notes with shouts of
'Yeah!' which must have dislodged plaster from the studio ceiling.
And all the time the piano is pumping away in support, celebrating
the turn of the chorus with a glissando that rips from one end of
the keyboard to the other. I know few other performances which
demonstrate so unashamedly the sheer joy of taking part in
spontaneous jazz creation when total rapport and momentum have
been reached. That Fats presided over scores of such performances
in sessions designed for the commercial market is all the more
wondrous.

The end of 'Twelfth Street Rag' brings joy to its culmination.
Fats overruns the ensemble with portentous descending octaves
culminating in crashing Chopinesque chords, Herman Autrey
blows a derisive 'that's all' phrase on trumpet and then Fats
unleashes a final ear-splitting shout of 'YEAH!!!'

I can think of no better way of summing up Fats Waller's
contribution to life. Since his early death from aggravated pneu-
monia, in 1943, the huge gap which he left has been filled by
frequent reissues of all his recordings. It takes nothing away
from James P. Johnson and the other great stride men to say that,

in the public mind, the rich, roundly satisfying piano style that emanated from Harlem in the Twenties is known as 'Fats Waller piano'. Other musicians played jazz, offering a body of work for the sober and austere judgement of posterity. Fats Waller *lived* jazz, radiating music which one must either take or leave, because it was indivisible from his personality. At the end of it all, there is only one thing to be said.

YEAH!!!!

Coleman Hawkins

NOTHING SUMS UP the development of jazz in the 1930s better than the career of Coleman Hawkins. He appeared in the first volume of this series as a founder-member of what I described as 'the first jazz big band in the modern sense'. Fletcher Henderson's Orchestra in the early Twenties was strong on musicianship—most of its members, including the teenage Hawkins, had studied music formally—but manifestly weak on jazz. The influences that converted it from a stiff and jerky dance band into a convincing jazz unit were undoubtedly more varied than the history books of old tended to suggest. There is a good excuse for giving all the credit to Louis Armstrong. Most of Henderson's musicians acknowledged at one time or another the vitalizing influence which Louis had on the band when he joined it for a year or so in 1924. It was Armstrong's advanced rhythmic ideas, his ability to 'swing', which brushed off on Henderson's men. But the thrusting, forward-moving rhythm that was the foundation of Armstrong's style could be found, before his arrival, in the music of the Harlem stride pianists, and I do not believe that it was a coincidence that Henderson's first convincing recording in jazz terms —'The Stampede'—was written for the band by Fats Waller.

'The Stampede' marked the emergence of Coleman Hawkins on record as a jazz soloist of giant stature. His achievement was not simply to acquire a mature and integrated style of his own. He had also to provide a convincing jazz voice for the tenor saxophone. The clarity, vibrancy and eagerness of response which made instruments like the trumpet, clarinet and trombone so ideal for azz expression are not qualities indigenous to the saxophone. I shall say more about this when we come to discuss the impact that Lester Young made upon jazz in the mid-Thirties; it is enough to say here that Hawkins overcame the problem in such an emphatic way that he dominated the field for a decade and was still challenging all-comers for several years beyond that.

In a sphere of human endeavour that resounds with stentorian claims to priority and originality, it is refreshing to find that Coleman Hawkins invariably brushed aside suggestions that he 'invented' the tenor saxophone as a jazz instrument. Interviewed by jazz encyclopedist, Leonard Feather, for the 1957 publication The Jazz Makers, he said, 'Why, I heard saxophones on record when I was just a little kid. There was one trio with a tenor sax that was about the earliest music that I can remember. There was a whole lot of ofays [white musicians] playing tenor, even when I was just beginning; and before I'd really started making records and everything, there was Happy Caldwell in Chicago and Stomp Evans out of Kansas City, and Prince Robinson . . . no, I certainly wasn't the first.' The nearest he came to acknowledging the legend was to say, 'Well, yes, I suppose you could say I was responsible for the making of the tenor.'

From a man whose life revealed an atavistic urge to achieve and retain tribal leadership and domination, this modesty and generosity towards rivals may seem unconvincing. But to Hawkins—and indeed to the general discussion of his place in jazz—the basic question was irrelevant. The making of music is not a definitive achievement, like climbing Everest or running the four-minute mile. If, within the next year or two, someone succeeds for the first time in producing a series of convincing jazz solos on the bassoon, the event will be of negligible significance unless that musician goes on to reveal himself to be a jazz improviser of consistently high talent. If and when that happens, the fact that he brought a recalcitrant instrument into the jazz fold will be added to his laurels. Stomp Evans—or 'Stump', as he was alternatively, and probably more aptly, nicknamed—died young in 1930, but nothing that he left on record in the Twenties suggests a promising jazz musician. Both Prince Robinson and Happy Caldwell were active throughout the Thirties and beyond, but contributed no more than a handful of pleasant, unambitious solos. It matters little if they were the first. Coleman Hawkins was the best by a street—and he knew it.

The development of the jazz style of Coleman Hawkins can be charted by a succession of key recordings. One of them, 'The Stampede', was discussed in *The Best of Jazz* Volume One. Here the saxophone was wielded in the manner of a trumpet, stabbing out phrases based on crotchets or half-notes played ahead of or all around the beat and beginning to 'swing' lustily in the Armstrong manner. This was clearly a starting-point. Encrusted like a well used candle with keys, pads and connecting rods, the saxophone was designed for more nimble work than the echoing of a trumpet's voice. By the time we reach the next landmark, Hawkins had expanded his conception to make fuller use of the instrument.

'Hello Lola' and 'One Hour' look, in the discographies, unlikely material for classic recordings. The session was organized by entrepreneur, singer and comb-and-paper specialist, Red Mc-Kenzie, the man who had a few months earlier negotiated the recording début of Eddie Condon and his Chicagoan associates under the heading of the McKenzie-Condon Chicagoans. Mc-Kenzie had for some years led a novelty, kazoo-based group called the Mound City Blue Blowers. When his talent as a hustler gained him access to the recording studios, he seized the opportunity of augmenting the Blue Blowers with contemporary jazz stars, while at the same time keeping a firm grasp on his comb and paper. The results were not as bizarre as one might imagine, for McKenzie had a good understanding of jazz phrasing (his voice was considerably tastier strained through paper than *au naturel*) and, by limiting the routines to a string of solos sandwiched between cursory introductions and codas, he avoided drawing attention to the incompatibility of the instruments.

The first M.C.B.B. session with Hawkins in November 1929 quickly established itself as a milestone in the tenor saxophonist's career. It was the first time that he had been heard on record in informal, small-group, jam session surroundings. And the choice of material—an up-tempo piece borrowing the surging, hold-on-to-your-hat rhythms of the then sensational Luis Russell Band, and a popular James P. Johnson ditty taken at dreamy tempo—

brought his playing into sharp focus. In the fast piece, his solo shows why he was the scourge of every other tenor-saxophone player within reach. Letting off a series of rhythmic toots to warn of its approach, it is suddenly upon us in top gear, like an express train coming round the side of a mountain. The suggestion of steam locomotion is heightened by Hawk's use at that time of a heavily-tongued attack by which the notes were ejected forcefully from the instrument like explosive puffs of steam. For all their overwhelming vigour and bursting confidence, the 'Hello Lola' choruses still reveal innumerable signs of immaturity. The style of improvisation, with its rooty-tooty articulation and skipping arpeggios, bears more than a fleeting resemblance to the flamboyant 'speciality' pieces through which non-jazz exponents of the saxophone achieved fashionable distinction in the Twenties. As if to counteract this, Hawkins invests each chuntering fusillade of eighth-notes with a sense of passion and urgency against which the instrument often seems to rebel. High notes intended to crackle fiercely in trumpet style succeed only in whinnying desperately. The uncontrolled application of vibrato to short notes gives some of the fast phrases a wobbly feeling that weakens their rhythmic effect. And every now and then, a passionate outcry seems to get stuck in the instrument's gullet with choked results. It is an amazing, awe-inspiring solo in conception, but one is left with the feeling that player and instrument were not, at that stage, fully agreed on how it should come out!

Turn to the slow number, a charming eighteen-bar love song by James P. Johnson called, in full, 'If I Could be with You one Hour Tonight' and behold a different musician altogether. There are few, if any, suggestions in the previously recorded solos of Coleman Hawkins with Fletcher Henderson of the slow tempo tenor-saxophone style which Hawkins presented, fully fledged, in 'One Hour'. Gone are the indiscipline, the haphazard phrasing, the staccato attack and the feeling of rather breathless over-excitement of the up-tempo work. Instead, the huge tone is richly controlled, the vibrato is steady and expressive, the phrases ride serenely over, under and across the beat. Where before we had a careering express train, here is a stately ship at sea, all sails to the wind.

A 'rhapsode' is defined in the dictionary as an ancient Greek minstrel or reciter of epic poems. A 'rhapsody' originally meant the poem or part of a poem thus declaimed. And presumably through the emotionally exaggerated style of that declamation, the word acquired the secondary meaning of an 'enthusiastic, extravagant, high-flown utterance or composition' and an 'emotional, irregular piece of music'. In the light of these definitions, I suppose it was inevitable, and indeed reasonable, that writers in the early days of jazz criticism would apply the word 'rhapsodic' to the manner in which Coleman Hawkins played slow and middle-tempo tunes. Enthusiasm it certainly had, and extravagance, too, which often carried emotion dangerously close to the brink of sentimentality. In 'One Hour' the phrases, airborne on great gusts of tone, soar and billow in fine declamatory style, paying as little attention to the beat to which they are anchored as a high-flying kite does to the insignificant figure holding the string far below.

Since this chapter is moving towards the apotheosis of the rhapsodic Hawkins style, we should pause here to speculate on its origins. We know enough about jazz evolution to suspect that it didn't spring unprompted from the imagination of Coleman Hawkins. Since we have already established that there were no jazz tenor saxophonists of significance before Hawkins, we must look elsewhere. The 'ofay' saxophonists whom Hawk had heard in his early days need not detain us. There is no evidence in primeval dance-band recordings that the tenor saxophone was ever used in such a lush, extravagant way. If it had been, its influence on his style would surely not have been so long delayed. Was there any other jazz instrumentalist of the period whose music had a 'rhapsodic' feeling?

There were, in fact, two. Asked once about the musicians who impressed him on the Chicago scene in the Twenties, Coleman Hawkins cited Louis Armstrong, Earl Hines and Jimmy Noone. The clarinet playing of Jimmy Noone had three distinct facets. In fast numbers he played rapid runs and figurations with a machine-gun articulation, tongueing each quaver or eighth-note sharply. Without labouring the point, I submit the notion that if the Hawkins solo on 'Hello Lola' were transcribed meticulously for the clarinet, it would remind the listener strongly of Jimmy Noone. In his slower-tempo blues playing, Noone often used slurs and flourishes that, in vocal terms, came nearer to the singer of sentimental songs than to the shouter of down-to-earth blues. And when he actually tackled a sentimental song, all restraint went out of the window and a treacly sentimentality ruled the day. It was this area of Noone's playing, full of oily smears and fulsome *portamento*, to which the Hawkins rhapsodic style came perilously close in its more extravagant moments.

My second candidate may well seem a perverse choice. When Louis Armstrong left Coleman Hawkins and the other Henderson men late in 1925 to return to Chicago, his influence on their music did not cease. The steady stream of recordings which he made with the Hot Five and its various permutations over the next three or four years set a standard of virtuosity which challenged musicians everywhere. These records showed a rapid expansion of his own style, usually summed up in the history books by the cliché that he 'burst the New Orleans format at the seams'. That style did not develop in a vacuum. Chicago in the second half of the Twenties was a burgeoning entertainment centre, rivalling—and in terms of jazz talent, surpassing—New York itself. For three years, Louis undertook a range of work which in addition to playing for dancing, called for solo performance and accompaniment in theatrical surroundings. Aimed as they were at the so-called 'race' market, the Hot Five recordings were largely confined to the sort of stompy, blues and vaudeville-influenced material which that market demanded. In *The Best of Jazz* Volume One, I quoted Bud Freeman's first-hand account of a typical night at the Sunset Café, where Louis played for dancing, accompanied vocal and dancing acts and undertook several solo spots himself which would draw on the popular show tunes of the day. From his earliest playing days in the honky-tonks of New Orleans, when the prostitutes used to scream for the blues, and right on through the King Oliver and Fletcher Henderson experiences, the music Louis played was influenced by popular taste. Throughout his life, every utterance of his on the subject of his profession revealed that the notion of himself as a jazz 'artist' committed to ignoring or converting the public was totally incomprehensible to him. It follows that changes in musical fashion were readily reflected in his own playing style.

By 1927, the frenzy of Scott Fitzgerald's 'Jazz Age' was beginning to wane, despite the desperate efforts of successive generations of 'bright young things' to sustain it. The dance craze of the immediate post-war period had developed from a fever into a steady social habit. Popular music had lost much of the obsession with frenetic physical activity of which the composer, Constant Lambert, complained somewhat belatedly in his book *Music Ho!* in 1934: 'The most irritating quality about the Vo-dodeo-vo, poo-poop-a-doop school of jazz song is its hysterical emphasis on the fact that the singer is a jazz baby going crazy about jazz rhythms. If jazz were really so gay one feels that there would not be so much need to mention the fact in every bar of the piece. Folk songs do not inform us that it's great to be singing in six-eight time, or that you won't get your dairy-maid until you have mastered the Dorian mode . . . What should we think of a concert aria which kept harping on the fact that the singer's mouth was open and that her vocal chords were in prime condition?'

It takes nothing away from this splendid stuff that the pieces Lambert had in mind—'I'm going to Charleston back to Charleston', 'Crazy Feet, I've got those Crazy Feet', 'Rhythm is the Thing' etc.—were not intrinsically jazz pieces. We know what he meant, and it did jazz no harm when the epidemic of St Vitus Dance which his examples suggest began to subside.

Most cursory summaries of the history of popular music attribute the decline of 'hot' music to the trauma of the Wall Street crash in 1929 and the subsequent depression. But closer investigation reveals that the shift to songs sweet and sentimental had begun some time before that. If we want to pinpoint one particular cause, it would be simpler to pick on the fact that, with the foundation in America of the Columbia Broadcasting System in 1927 in competition with the existing National Broadcasting Company, radio established itself as the prime entertainment medium. To a degree which made the previous recording boom seem like a minority cult, music became as readily available in the home as water or electricity. One need not strain the imagination to grasp the effect which this had upon the material broadcast. Bawdy vaudeville songs, rich in *double entendre*, were hardly the stuff for domestic family listening, and at the same time it was no longer always necessary for writers of popular songs to harness them to the needs of a dancing public insatiable for excitement.

Louis Armstrong, a devotee of pretty music in all its forms, responded to these gradual and subtle changes with the acuteness of a sophisticated barometer. The first sign of an extension of his style in the direction of what, to avoid pejorative overtones, we may call the romantic side of popular music, occurs without warning in a 1927 recording of 'Savoy Blues'. I say 'without warning' because, at the outset, the piece sounds as if it is to be just another in the series of powerful, declamatory blues in which the Hot Five excelled. But instead of ripping into impassioned blues phrases in his customary manner, Armstrong's trumpet croons a couple of gentle, reflective choruses, phrased soothingly across the beat and completely devoid of the flattened third and seventh 'blue notes' that one would expect. It's an extraordinary departure. Six months later, in the next Hot Five session with a different personnel, the new mood reappears in an equally unexpected place.

While joining in the universal acknowledgement of 'West End Blues' as a supreme Louis Armstrong classic, some latter-day analysts have criticized the contribution of Earl Hines for introducing a foreign element of romanticism into what they consider to be a classic exposition of the blues. Whatever one thinks of this view, the charge is unjust to Hines. For in the preceding chorus, swapping vocal phrases with Jimmy Strong's clarinet, Louis himself lapses into the withdrawn, soliloquizing mood anticipated in 'Savoy Blues' and, as in that performance, totally at odds with contemporary blues practice. I used the word 'croons' advisedly in relation to the 'Savoy Blues' solo because this style, brought into heightened focus in the vocal section of 'West End Blues', has a close family likeness to the kind of lazy, off-the-beat phrasing that characterized Bing Crosby's popular singing style several years later. In the context of Armstrong's own development, 'West End Blues' is curiously isolated. The voice that he uses is a dramatic change from the extrovert bawling and scatting that had gone before. And, although there are suggestions of it in subsequent vocals such as 'Squeeze Me' and 'Save it Pretty Mama', it doesn't really re-emerge until the period, well on into the Thirties, when Louis seemed to realize his potential as a popular singer. It is customary to see the influence of Bing Crosby in the smoothed-out style of those later years. In the light of the above, should it not be the other way round?

If we seem to have strayed from the subject of Coleman Hawkins, let me return to it abruptly with another question. What else are the 'Savoy Blues' solo and the vocal in 'West End Blues' but 'rhapsodizing' in the Hawkins sense? One must always move with extreme caution when stalking artistic influences. Louis Armstrong was not the only jazz musician to be aware of, and affected by, trends in popular music. The earnest jazz buff shocked by the revelation of Louis's allegiance to Guy Lombardo must brace himself to receive the news that, a few years later, jazz saxophonists of the calibre of Johnny Hodges and Chu Berry were extolling the virtues of Freddy Martin, in whose smooth and sentimental tenor-saxophone playing no vestige of jazz could ever be traced. There is no contradiction here. Musicians are usually more concerned with craftsmanship than with artistic judgements, and the clear boundaries which now exist in our minds between the jazz and the popular entertainment music of past eras have been traced in retrospect. At the time, they were blurred to the point of invisibility.

It is possible that, without any prompting from Louis Armstrong, Coleman Hawkins arrived, by way of the same or similar influences, at an almost identical 'rhapsodic' approach. Possible, but not probable. He and his New York associates would have kept up with the trail-blazing recordings by Louis, especially after he was joined by the equally awe-inspiring Earl Hines. Red McKenzie, for example, reveals in 'One Hour' that he is well acquainted with the vocal obbligato in 'West End Blues', since he performs a grotesque comb-and-paper parody of it. His solo, followed by that of Hawkins, could fairly be described as a demonstration of the wrong and right way to do it!

The rather lop-sided nature of Coleman Hawkins's development persisted into the Thirties. The rhapsodic slow-tempo style altered little, so well rounded and mature was it in its first manifestation in 'One Hour'. If we jump forward four years—a big jump in the headlong career of jazz history—to the much admired recording with Fletcher Henderson of 'It's the Talk of the Town' in November 1933, we find that the tone has shed some of its booming volume, the vibrato is more intense, and the rhapsodizing —full of phrases that swell and burst, scattering a shower of decorative notes—is even more extravagant and operatic. But the style itself has needed no refurbishing or modernizing.

Fast tempos, on the other hand, continued to present a problem. It was not a matter of technique. On the contrary, a flag-waving Henderson version of 'Chinatown, My Chinatown', recorded in 1930, finds him flashing around at breakneck tempo with the agility of a clarinettist. The trouble is that the solo *belongs* to the clarinet, built as it is on a procession of the sort of finger-fluttering runs that Jimmy Noone bequeathed to disciples as diverse as Albert Nicholas, Jimmy Dorsey and Benny Goodman. We could sense, even if the slow-tempo performances had not already revealed it, that Coleman Hawkins had altogether grander ideas for the tenor saxophone than simply producing clarinet-type runs in a lower register. They began to emerge, spasmodically and explosively, in the Henderson recordings of the early Thirties. In 'My Gal Sal' there are two sensational saxophone breaks that rival Louis Armstrong in reckless daring. In the same year, 1931, an updated arrangement of King Oliver's 'Sugarfoot Stomp' (*né* 'Dippermouth Blues') produced from Hawkins an electrifying solo. Disdaining to dabble cautiously with the familiar phrases of the original, as his colleagues have done in succession, he launches his solo with a thundering pedal note that continues to boom like an irregularly chiming bell throughout the twelve-bar chorus while linking higher-register phrases leap excitedly around it. The way in which Hawkins places those notes on or around different beats in the bar echoes the rather careful and contrived orchestral stop-chords that punctuate previous solos. It is as if Hawkins were saying, 'Right, if we're going to play rhythmic games, let's *do* it!' Continuing into a second chorus, he follows this daunting precedent in the best way that he knows, by moving full steam ahead into the old express train delivery in which some of the chuffing eighth-notes are attacked so violently that they seem on the point of letting out a shriek of protest. It's a solo which, for all its imperfect form, jumps out of its surroundings as vividly as did Louis Armstrong's solos with Henderson six years earlier.

In 'Sugarfoot Stomp', the polarization of the Hawkins tenor style at that time is emphasized. At one extreme is a rhythmically free, around-the-beat extension of his rhapsodic style into faster tempos. At the other, there's the 'Hello Lola' express train, slightly more streamlined, making up in sheer irresistible energy and excitement what it lacked in rhythmic flexibility. The formula through which Hawkins generated this instant head of steam remained the basis of his up-tempo style until the end of his life, through a whole series of stylistic modifications. It consisted of building a solo out of phrases, or blocks, of two or four bars in length, with each beat of the bar given two notes. This may seem to be saying that he simply rattled off a machine-gun burst of quavers, or eighth-notes, but it didn't quite work like that. The second of each pair of notes falling on the beat was weaker than the first, sometimes imperceptibly, and sometimes so markedly that it almost disappeared from earshot altogether. One way of simulating this rhythmic pattern is to sing two and four-bar phrases to the syllables 'DOOdle, DOOdle DOOdle'—though it has to be said here that the way Hawkins attacked those syllables was the very antithesis of doodling! A better and more significant way is to beat out the eighth-notes hand to hand on a table top, starting with the right hand (or left if you are left-handed). In the nature of things, you will find that the left-hand beats tend to be weaker, and it is quite easy to soften them even more. It may be argued—and probably will be before we're through—that the whole rhythmic development of jazz from its beginnings right up to the a-rhythmic departures of modern times has reflected the efforts of improvising musicians to overcome the 'right-handed' tendency to stress the first and third notes in any combination of four.

If Hawk's own musical development was impeded by these early rhythmic limitations, his standing as the Tenor Saxophone Champion of the World was certainly not. To hear how he could overwhelm the most promising of challengers, we have only to listen to the all-star band which the British musician, composer and critic, Spike Hughes, assembled for some New York recordings in 1933. In that band was Chu Berry, six years Hawk's junior and regarded by many musicians and critics as his first serious rival. In a piece called 'Firefly' the two saxophonists solo side by side. Chu Berry, with his softer attack, is rhythmically less hidebound than Hawkins at the medium-fast tempo, but his efforts to match the older man's wilder flights of fancy lead to a disorganized rush of ideas and some technical faltering. In the first half of his chorus, Hawkins gives a lesson in how to rhapsodize with poise, and then he's off down the track in familiar blunt-nosed fashion, swinging purposefully enough to shove Berry brusquely into a siding.

Despite Hawk's obvious supremacy at this stage, the contest is close enough to indicate the sort of pressure under which he was working in the early Thirties. Chu Berry was not the only rival. Over the years, more than one musician has told of an epic battle between Coleman Hawkins and some of the Kansas City tenor men during this period. The pianist, Mary Lou Williams, recalls it as an outright defeat for Hawkins. 'The date must have been early 1934, because Prohibition had been lifted and whisky was freely on sale . . . The word went around that Hawkins was in the Cherry Blossom, and within about half an hour there was Lester Young, Ben Webster, Herschel Evans, Herman Walder and one or two unknown tenors piling in the club to blow. Bean didn't know the Kaycee tenor men were so terrific and he couldn't get himself together though he played all morning.' The story ends with the beleaguered Hawkins overshooting the departure-time for the next Fletcher Henderson engagement in St Louis and burning out his new Cadillac in the effort to make it.

The drummer, Jo Jones, saw the same episode less in the light of an internecine struggle. 'That was the first night Hawkins was really challenged. But when I say "challenged" I mean it was a respectful challenge . . . most of the time at sessions guys would just be trying to show Hawkins how they had improved since he had last heard them.' Several contemporary musicians have suggested that such animosity as existed between the rival tenorists

Lester Young and Herschel Evans in Count Basie's Orchestra, arose from the fact that, in challenging Hawkins with a quite different style of tenor-saxophone playing, Lester was showing disrespect for the master.

I was given, in recent years, an insight into this curious ambivalent relationship between Hawkins and his erstwhile rivals. He was appearing towards the end of his life at Ronnie Scott's Club in London and I went to hear him. Inside I found Ben Webster, who had, of course, made many appearances at the club as a jazz star in his own right. Ben had sat himself in a prominent position by the entrance and was waiting for Coleman Hawkins to arrive. He kept saying to me, 'Bean's really gonna play tonight . . . when he sees me here, he's really gonna play.' Ben knew, as did most other followers of jazz, that 'Bean's' playing had become sporadic, sometimes rousing itself into action with some of the old fire, but often ambling through the motions with little show of interest or energy. In due course, Hawkins arrived and greeted Ben warmly. Alas for Ben's expectations, it was not to be one of the good nights. Whether through flagging energies or the strange, secretive cussedness with which colleagues, journalists and others had become acquainted over the years, Coleman Hawkins lit no fires during that last set. Ben, himself an elderly and far from fit man, showed little compassion for a fellow-performer on his last legs. Indeed, his reaction was one of mounting indignation. Eventually, he heaved himself up from his seat next to me, grabbed an empty chair and ostentatiously marched with it towards the stand, sitting himself down right in front of Hawkins. When I left some minutes later, he was still there, glaring fixedly at the unresponding figure on stage as if to will him into greater activity. It was as though his mind had gone back to those Kansas City days when he and the other young contenders had turned out to show Hawkins what they could do, and he expected Hawk to repay the compliment.

The story does give some hint at the enormous pressure which was upon Coleman Hawkins in the early Thirties. Like 'the fastest gun in the West' he had established a nationwide reputation and, whether he liked it or not, he was called on by friend and foe alike to justify it on all occasions. In the interview with Leonard

Feather quoted earlier, he seemed to suggest that this constant challenge contributed to his abrupt decision, in 1934, to leave Henderson and travel to England. Articles in the London *Melody Maker* by, among others, Spike Hughes under the pseudonym 'Mike', were read by musicians in the States and indicated clearly that he was a celebrity over there. 'I didn't know until then that they knew me over there. I was too busy around here just striving to stay in front of some of the boys that were coming up—Herschel and Chu and everybody—trying to cut me all the time.'

The idea of spending some time as a celebrity in a foreign land, free of serious challengers, no doubt had a strong appeal. There may have been other reasons, too. The Max Jones-John Chilton biography of Louis Armstrong makes it clear that Louis's departure for Britain two years earlier was prompted by quite different pressures. Prohibition had forged a strong link between entertainment and the underworld. As hot properties, star jazzmen resembled the top football players of today—but their transfer fees tended to come, by express delivery, in the form of small pieces of lead. Whatever the reason, Hawk's decision was precipitate. He was talking vaguely about a European trip to a fellow-musician, who suggested that he should get in touch with Jack Hylton, then leader of the leading dance-cum-show-band in Britain. He got straight into his car, drove to the nearest Western Union office and dispatched a telegram addressed to 'Jack Hylton, London, England' which read: 'I am interested in coming to London. Sgd Coleman Hawkins'. In true fairy-tale fashion an invitation arrived the following day and, within a week, Hawkins was off on a trip that was to keep him away from the American arena for four years.

Financially, the gamble was a safe one. In terms of jazz journalism, Europe was far ahead of the United States in the mid-Thirties. The man-in-the-street in Wilhelmshaven or Watford was far more likely to be aware of the style and stature of Coleman Hawkins than his counterpart in Wisconsin. In England, and subsequently in France and Holland, leading bands and musicians fell over themselves in the scramble to appear and record with the Great Man. Artistically, Hawkins was on less sure ground. There is an intriguing parallel between his sudden departure from the centre of the action and Sidney Bechet's similar defection from the New York scene almost a decade earlier. To be sure, the vastly improved media of communication saw to it that Hawkins did not disappear from view as completely as did Bechet in the late Twenties. Furthermore, Hawkins was not isolated—a steady stream of his compatriots made their way to Europe during the same period, some on short visits, others to stay. Nevertheless, there were dangers inherent in the sudden switch from a highly competitive and demanding environment to one in which un-questioning adulation took the place of rivalry. It took a musician of high personal standards and an iron discipline to resist the temptation to tread water lazily—and indefinitely—in European hero-worship.

Happily, Coleman Hawkins was just such a musician. The many recordings which he made during his European sojourn reveal that the already rounded and mature rhapsodic style continued to blossom. 'Lost in a Fog', 'Lullaby', 'Stardust', 'Meditation' and numerous other ballads were extensions of the 'One Hour' con-ception, enriched by ever more searching harmonies. Even more impressive was the development of his up-tempo style. A record made in Paris in March 1935 with Michel Warlop's Orchestra finds him playing to the formula which he had tended to adopt since the 'Sugarfoot Stomp' days. The tune is 'Avalon' taken at a brisk tempo. In his first chorus, Hawkins plays as if the piece were a slow number stretched over half the number of bars. This allows him to rhapsodize independently of the beat, with broad, sweeping phrases. Once into the second chorus it is brakes off and full steam ahead, as we have come to expect. But there is a difference. The notes are no longer attacked with such violence that they quiver under the impact.

There are two ways of articulating a note on a single-reed instrument. One is to apply the tongue to the underside of the reed sharply as if pronouncing the letter 't'. Utter a string of rapid eighth-notes in this way and you get the staccato 'tooty, tooty, tooty' effect of the Hawkins 'Hello Lola' period. At the other extreme, there is the technique of 'slurring' notes which, to the confusion of the layman, has nothing to do with slithery up-and-down movements from one note to another. Notes that are slurred simply move from one to the other without separate 'tongueing' or articulation. It is even possible, on both reed and brass instruments, to 'slur' the first note of a phrase, by keeping the tongue *hors de combat* and passing a strong enough column of air over the lips or the reed to start a vibration. The technique was elevated to an endearing mannerism by the late Ben Webster, whose opening note in a solo was often wafted in, with a gentle 'phooooh' sound, on the crest of a stiff breeze.

Coleman Hawkins had a natural predilection for 'tongueing', born perhaps of the necessity in his far-off apprenticeship days to keep up with all the tricks of the trade. In those days, 'slap tongueing'—that is, producing a freakish, hollow tone by slapping the reed against the mouthpiece rather than vibrating it—was a fashionable gimmick and, according to Rex Stewart, who saw him with Mamie Smith's band in 1919, the fifteen-year-old Hawkins was a master of it. Few of the tenor saxists who followed in the wake of Hawkins in the early Thirties gave the reed such a drubbing as he did, and comparison with Chu Berry's work on the Spike Hughes sessions shows the master still using rapid tongueing at fast tempos while the disciple eschewed the habit.

Some time around 1934–5, Coleman Hawkins seems to have ironed this heavy attack out of his playing. That he did so more from an urge to try something new than under compulsion to keep up to date with new methods is indicated by the fact that, in the Fifties, he reverted to the heavy attack, telling one interviewer, 'I got fed up with all that slurring . . .' The effect on his up-tempo playing of the smoother progress from note to note was pronounced. The basic formula of four pairs of notes to the bar in quaver, dotted-quaver conjunctions remained, but it received more varied treatment. If we revert to the hand-to-hand rhythms on the table top, we can simulate the new Hawkins approach by striking each strong, right-hand beat at a different strength, ranging from gentle to explosive. Played in this manner, Hawk's solos became impassioned and rhythmic orations in which the voice rose and fell dramatically, and constantly shifting emphasis gave added meaning to notes and phrases. Freed from the rather rigid patterns which the 'tooty-tooty' articulation suggested, the improvisations pursued a much freer course. More often now, a phrase would come to its natural conclusion somewhere in between the obvious two-or four-bar resting-points, and with a hurried snatch of breath that was often picked up by the microphone, Hawkins would be off in pursuit of a new idea. And instead of being kept apart in different areas of the solo, emotive legato phrases and rapid-fire passages were freely intermingled.

The masterpiece in this particular genre was recorded in Paris in 1937. Having made a number of records with the rather ponderous backing of big continental dance bands, Coleman Hawkins was in congenial surroundings on that day. His erstwhile Fletcher Henderson colleague, Benny Carter, having crossed the Atlantic in 1935, was available on alto saxophone and trumpet. Two top French musicians, André Ekyan and Alix Combelle, joined them on alto and tenor respectively, the latter doubling for one number on clarinet. Stephane Grappelly (as he was then spelt) was as ham fisted at the piano as he was fleet fingered on violin but, fortunately, he did no more than provide a discreet oom-chah in the background. His two colleagues from the Quintet du Hot Club de France, Django Reinhardt on guitar and Eugene d'Hellemes on bass, provided all that was needed in terms of chugging rhythm, and the drummer was another expatriate American, Tommy Benford, who had played with the bands of Elmer Snowden and Jelly Roll Morton in the Twenties.

For the version of 'Crazy Rhythm', Benny Carter, a fine arranger with a particular talent for extracting deep-piled sounds out of a four-piece saxophone section, scored the opening chorus. Then the four saxophones went through their paces in turn, with Hawkins taking two choruses as befitted the nominal leader of the group. On the record, the informality of a jam session is simulated when someone, probably Benny Carter, urges Coleman Hawkins on into a second chorus with the words 'Go on, Bean, go on!' As a youthful jazz fan I was mightily impressed by this evidence of spontaneity in the studio, though subsequent listening made it plain that at no stage did Hawkins harbour the faintest intention of stopping.

By European standards at that time, both the French musicians were good players with a fair idea of jazz improvisation derived, manifestly, from listening to a lot of Coleman Hawkins on record and in the flesh. Their solos on 'Crazy Rhythm' reveal the credit and the debit side of the worldwide Hawkins influence. They play in a confident, forthright, 'hot' manner which compares favourably in terms of swing with some of the tentative sounds emanating from European bands. But the effort of maintaining the impetus, of keeping the ball up in the air, leads to some rather tense and jagged phrasing. In the third and fourth bar of his alto chorus, André Ekyan runs awkwardly up and down a gratuitous diminished chord in a way that contrasts most strongly with the effortless, smooth way in which Hawkins altered and negotiated the harmonies. Combelle, an unashamed Hawkins devotee, starts off purposefully but, again, can only sustain the Hawkins-like flow for short bursts at a time. Benny Carter's solo is discussed further elsewhere: after the over-eagerness of the Frenchmen, it is an object lesson in poise and elegant construction, riding on the beat rather than trying to push it along.

At the end of Carter's solo, there are a few off-stage notes from Coleman Hawkins indicating that, as in 'Hello Lola', he is straining at the leash. His opening phrases constitute one of the most thrilling 'Look out, here's me!' entrances in all of jazz. The riff with which he opens his solo had, by the end of the decade, become a Swing Era cliché. By an uncanny coincidence, its crucial opening bar appeared almost simultaneously (just over two months later, which is 'almost simultaneously' in recording terms) as one of the climactic riffs in Count Basie's 'One O'Clock Jump'. Riffing—the playing of short, rhythmic phrases repeated over and over to build up tension—has audible connections with the preacher-and-congregation 'call and response' pattern of American Negro church music, and first made a prominent appearance in jazz in Luis Russell's supercharged band in the late Twenties. Fletcher Henderson's band made use of the device in such early-Thirties arrangements as 'Hot and Anxious' (where the familiar 'In the Mood' riff made an early appearance), 'Comin' and Goin' ' and 'Yeah Man'. In Count Basie's early band, hot from Kansas City, the riff was a fundamental *modus operandi*, with many of the first Basie compositions consisting simply of three sets of riffs, by trumpets, trombones and saxophones respectively, superimposed on each other. Small groups took up the idea which, used to excess, eventually helped to give the Swing Era a bad name. Coleman Hawkins was one of the very first musicians to make use of the riff in solo performance. Indeed, in the early Forties, he recorded a couple of solos in the context of poll-winners' all-star conventions, in which, for some perverse and possibly malevolent reason, he did little more than repeat one single phrase with minor variations. The amateur sleuths who abound among jazz enthusiasts would find limitless food for conjecture and research in the apparent fact that Hawkins anticipated a stylistic trend when he was thousands of miles from the centre of fashion in the relatively 'olde-worlde' surroundings of European jazz. That the riff which so effectively launches his solo in 'Crazy Rhythm' was no inspirational flash in the pan is shown by the appearance of the very same riff, used slightly differently but with the same rhythmic purpose, on two separate occasions in his solo in 'Honeysuckle Rose' recorded at the same session.

The effect of Hawk's entrance in 'Crazy Rhythm' is to increase at once the whole momentum of the performance. It is as if those opening phrases, uttered with such force that the last note is literally hurled away, are a warning to the listener to hold on to his hat and prepare for a rough but exhilarating ride. A player with less idea where he was going—Alix Combelle, dare one say it without offence—might come to the end of the riffs after four bars or so and go off on a different tack, leaving them in the air. Hawkins, on the other hand, hangs on to them tenaciously, like a dog attacking and worrying a bundle of rags. He chews over the two-bar phrase three times, seizes the last two notes and flings them around on to different beats in the bar, makes as if to go careering off in the ninth bar and then returns to give them a final shake in bar ten, completing a perfect rhythmic pattern. It is a fine example of how a great jazzman can 'compose' at breakneck speed.

Nor does it end there. I have put the word 'compose' in cautionary inverted commas because it can mislead. This sort of improvised solo, which in the unrestricted location of a club would probably last ten times longer, can best be likened to the flow of words of an orator speaking without notes. A great speaker, carried along by the passion of the moment, will develop his theme in an inspirational way, choosing his words and balancing his sentences intuitively, sometimes excitedly pursuing a new idea, sometimes subconsciously echoing an earlier phrase, always building his argument with a combination of taut logic and emotional power. Looked at in this light, the two Hawkins choruses in 'Crazy Rhythm' amount to a masterly oration, a miracle of sustained, concentrated invention. You can search them in vain for the faltering phrase, the uncertain pause, the insertion of those nondescript, space-filling notes that are the musical equivalent of the 'ums' and 'ers' of human discourse. Gone, too, are the melodramatic, almost gushing outbursts which often brought earlier Hawkins solos to the very brink of absurdity. Passion is now expressed in the sustained ebb and flow of the melody line, the controlled fervour of tone and vibrato and the irresistible rhythmic impulse generated by constantly shifting accents.

Reverting to our earlier analogy, there is a point midway through the second chorus when it seems as if the express train must surely crash headlong into the buffers erected by Benny Carter's snatch of arranged coda and disappear in a stream of wreckage down the hole in the middle of the record. But Hawk's mature sense of construction applies the brakes, and the solo comes to rest in the most satisfying way with a couple of fleeting references to the opening riff.

'Crazy Rhythm' comes as near as the old three-minute 78 could to the competitive tournament atmosphere of the jam session through which jazz giants tested the mettle of their rivals in the Thirties. It shows beyond doubt that the absence of Coleman Hawkins from the New York arena had in no way impaired his ring fitness. Indeed, it gave warning, to all who cared to hear, of the fighting form of the man who, after luxuriating in the adulatory atmosphere of Europe for a further two years, returned to America in the autumn of 1939.

The story of that return, recounted with relish by more than one eyewitness, has something of the epic quality of the poems that kept the Ancient Greek 'rhapsodes' in business. The bassist Milt Hinton recalls with a certain degree of poetic licence, 'The night Hawk came back from Europe, all the fellows came to play for him. He was sitting at a front table. They wanted him to see how they had improved.' Note once again the suggestion of filial respect, sustained no doubt during Hawk's absence by the fact, recalled by Hinton, that, 'We'd listen to a lot of Hawk's records. He was making some in Europe that we'd get.' In his book *Jazz Masters of the Thirties*, Rex Stewart draws a far more dramatic picture: 'But then the word spread like wildfire: Bean was back! Hawk started falling into the joint every night, immaculate, sophisticated and saxophoneless. The tension continued to build— is this the night he will play? Coleman just sat there sipping, with a smirk on his face, as they all paraded their talents before him.'

Rex's account of the eventual dénouement is quoted in my chapter on Lester Young. His picture of the freshly repatriated Coleman Hawkins biding his time was confirmed by Hawkins himself in a long interview in 1956 which was issued by Riverside records in a double album called *Coleman Hawkins: A Documentary*. Unfortunately, printed quotations cannot reproduce the rich chuckles, pregnant pauses and other manifestations of barely-suppressed glee with which Hawk's reminiscences are punctuated. The events described took place at an after-hours spot called Puss Johnson's at 130th and St Nicholas, where musicians would go to play when their regular work was over. On his return from Europe, Hawkins gravitated to it without prompting. 'Wherever there's good musicians, you'll always find me!' There is something strongly reminiscent of the Hollywood western in the picture of Hawkins riding back into town and heading straight for the saloon where he knew his rivals were gathered. Hawkins relished the drama of this scenario when he looked back on it seventeen years later. 'You know, when I came back, they were layin' for me. I could tell they figured I'd been in Europe so long, now this was the real chance to catch me. Because I tell you, they been wantin' to catch me ever since I been a kid. I don't know why, they never did leave me alone. They got to cut *me*, if possible, and all that, you know? Well, boy, they was waitin'!'

As Rex Stewart recalled, Hawkins took his time to sum up his opponents. The smirk on his face no doubt derived from the growing belief that all they had with which to combat his gleaming and scrupulously-maintained six-shooter was a musical armoury that was rusty and out-dated. 'So I used to go around and I'd say to myself, they ain't gonna cut me playin' *that*—not what I just got through listenin' to. I mean, there must be somethin' they're holding back . . . if that's the best they're gonna play, not like that, they won't.'

At this point it is necessary to break off and say something about the nature of the jazz musician. He is an amalgam, in varying proportions, of artist, craftsman and scientist. Unlike, say, the painter or the composer of 'serious' music, the jazzmen of the generation under discussion tended to push the first-named *persona* into the background, holding the view that if technique and musical research were taken care of, the 'art' would look after itself. We have to remember that, in the musical climate of the times, what they were primarily called upon to communicate, in common with bands that had no pretensions to jazz creativity, was entertainment and a solid rhythm for dancing. It was the jazz musician's preoccupation with the technical side of his work which very often threw him out of step with a lay audience that tended to judge the music in terms of such abstractions as 'sincerity', 'excitement', 'soul' and so on. It explains such apparent aberrations as the appearance of Guy Lombardo, Freddy Martin, Rudy Vallee, Tommy Dorsey and even Mantovani in the list of great jazz musicians' favourites.

But absorption in the nuts and bolts of composition and execution could also interfere with a musician's judgement of his fellows. The role of musician as scientific researcher is one which is rarely taken into account by the outsider. A man like Coleman Hawkins would spend a large part of his waking hours analysing the structure of the music that he played and experimenting with theories that emerged from it. The fact that he would refer to the process unromantically as 'practising' or 'woodshedding' should not detract from its seriousness. It is not fanciful to think of the sort of after-hours jam session that took place at Puss Johnson's as a *conversazione* in which musicians aired their findings and presented progress reports on their researches. The danger in this otherwise valuable and stimulating activity lies in the scientist's quite natural belief that he and his particular line of research are at the very hub of the universe, and that those pursuing other exploratory routes or, indeed, still examining previous concepts are *hors de combat*.

In the light of this, we can understand Hawk's harsh judgement on the New York scene to which he returned in 1939: 'There wasn't any soloists around who interested me—they didn't seem to be playing anything. They didn't make the changes good—the changes were kinda sad.' Changes—that is to say, the harmonic progressions used in improvisation—were Hawk's speciality. A piece called 'Queer Notions' which he wrote for Fletcher Henderson's band in 1933 showed that he had a knowledge of the harmonic and scalar developments of modern European music which few jazz musicians outside of Bix Beiderbecke and some of his associates had boasted before. His method of improvising was to explore the harmonic possibilities underlying a tune with a sort of running commentary which moved smoothly and logically from one chord to another—'running changes' is how some musicians described it. While a rhythm guitarist's or a pianist's left hand will state a series of chords vertically, in a simultaneous cluster of notes, a melody instrument will outline them horizontally, contriving a series of notes, a melodic line, which will make use of significant notes in each successive chord. In a striking instance of art concealing art, the good improviser will construct a melody that is so strong, coherent and attractive that the listener is not made aware of the ingenuity underlying it. As a craftsman, what Hawkins complained of was the *lack* of ingenuity in this field. 'I was surprised, you know, 'cos I been over there for so long and I thought by the time I came back, the musicians here would be much more advanced. But they was just like when I left . . .' That his strictures took in the work of Lester Young, then at his peak, demonstrates how absorption in one aspect or theory of music can deafen a musician to experiments going on in other fields.

All this drama and speculation took place in those highly esoteric conclaves of musicians and hangers-on to which the general public is seldom privy. When that public was given the opportunity to make its views felt, they were startling. On his return from Europe, Coleman Hawkins got a nine-piece band together to work in a New York club called Kelly's Stables. In November, 1939, he undertook a recording session for Bluebird, a subsidiary of RCA-Victor that had its studios at Camden New

Jersey. In preliminary discussions on the session, the company's A & R man suggested that Hawkins should record 'Body and Soul', the seductive ballad number which Hawk used as a 'get off' encore at Kelly's. The idea took Hawkins by surprise—the other numbers for the session were two up-tempo swing arrangements designed to conform to current big-band trends, and a commercially orientated version of 'She's Funny That Way' with vocal by Thelma Carpenter. As for 'Body and Soul', 'that's nothin'—who wants to hear that?' was Hawk's reaction. Leonard Joy, the man from Victor, told him that some of the 'boys from Camden' had heard him do the piece at Kelly's and were raving about it, 'so I think you should do it for them'.

The story thenceforward has all the familiar, fairy-tale elements that have surrounded so many hit recordings. Still protesting that he had no arrangement for it, Hawkins was persuaded to record a cut-down, three-minute version of the treatment which he gave to 'Body and Soul' at Kelly's Stables, where he would play several choruses accompanied by rhythm section only, and then a final chorus with some makeshift chords from the band. Recording time allowed for just two choruses, and in the interests of condensation, Hawkins limited his statement of the tune to eight richly ornamented bars before setting out on an improvised exploration of the piece's harmonic structure. Article Number One in the producer's creed, ever since that obtrusive middle-man appeared on the recording scene, has always been that the public will not accept any piece of music unless its basic message, the tune, is stated and reiterated continuously in recognizable form. In the light of this, 'Body and Soul' as played by Coleman Hawkins should have been a recipe for oblivion. A few weeks after he recorded it—'I didn't even bother to listen to it, just packed up my horn and walked out'—he was sitting in a bar called Fat Man's when he heard the record being played in the influential Martin Block radio show. It was the first intimation he had that 'Body and Soul' was a hit.

Looking back on the event in his Riverside interview, Coleman Hawkins was still almost speechless with surprise. The reason goes beyond the creative artist's natural scepticism about popular taste. From the moment that he first walked into Puss Johnson's club to hear what the New York musicians had been up to in his absence, Hawkins realized that, in his grasp of harmony, he was ahead of them. 'Body and Soul' epitomized this gap in musical development.

'A lot of them used to say I was playin' wrong notes . . . when the record first came out, everybody, including Chu Berry and everybody, said I was playin' wrong notes in it.' That sentence could quite easily lead us into a lengthy treatise on harmonic developments in jazz. In these essays I have tried to avoid the sort of complex musical discussion which might make the lay enthusiast put the book down with an uncomprehending shake of the head. So let me just focus on one particular point, one which Coleman Hawkins himself cited as an example. The simplest and most familiar final cadence in music involves the mi-ray-doh, 'Three Blind Mice' sequence of notes, accompanied, in the key of C, by the chord sequence C, G seventh, C. The G seventh chord involves dissonance in the juxtaposition of the notes G and F at its upper end. As anyone knows who has ever hammered out the treble part of the elementary piano duet 'Chopsticks', the two notes on their own are a discomfort to the ear until the dissonance is resolved by the F note moving down to E. Incorporated with the rest of the notes in the G seventh chord, the two notes do not strike us as being discordant. Indeed, the inclusion of the F is necessary to give the chord the richness we expect. The history of the various fundamental changes in harmonic fashion over the centuries shows that the human ear will become accustomed, given sufficient exposure to it, to almost any combination of notes. Progress towards the acceptance of new sounds in this context has been impeded, not only by the ear's slowness, but also by the fact that that slowness has, so to speak, been institutionalized in a series of rules which it has been the advanced musical thinker's role to defy.

Jazz harmony, derived in the very earliest days from the harmonies of European hymns and marches, made very faltering steps in the Twenties towards catching up with modern European 'classical' music. The predominant reason for this is that the musicians themselves were, with a few exceptions, not particularly concerned with broadening the harmonic basis of their music. The collectively improvised ensemble, with its several contrapuntal lines moving independently, provided all the richness of texture that was required. And the great soloists, from Louis Armstrong down, were largely intuitive musicians who achieved their effect by expanding and enriching the melody of a tune while paying no more attention to its harmonies than was necessary for musical accuracy.

Pianists were the exception, of course, playing an instrument that demanded not just a melody line but instant 'orchestration' from the soloist. It is significant that in discussing the influences on his music, Coleman Hawkins was scornful of the notion that it was only other 'horn' men that he studied. 'I don't listen to any particular instrument to get an idea from. I mean, I'd just as soon listen to piano players. I can get just as much from a piano player, especially if it's the right one. I hear a lot of things that they play that I like, and I try to make that on my horn.' Rex Stewart attributes the development of Hawk's style in the late Twenties to the influence of Art Tatum who, among other things, was an advanced and accomplished harmonist.

On his return from Europe what disappointed the musician in Coleman Hawkins (while at the same time reassuring the gladiator) was that, though musicians had acquired the speed of execution with which to follow his method of harmonic exploration, the actual harmonies which they employed in their improvisations were still fairly simple extensions of the familiar diatonic harmonies. Like many jazzmen before and since, he was vague in his actual definition of the 'new' harmonies of which he made use. 'At that time, you make some kind of a D change goin' into D flat—that was wrong. At that time you had to make an A flat seventh goin' into D flat, *strictly* A flat seventh—they don't know that's a relative chord to D anyway, but I mean, they just didn't know these things and they couldn't see it that way. If they heard that D, it had to be ooh, that's terrible! It's nothing but a flattened fifth form and things like that . . . but they couldn't hear it. That's *extremely* common now, but it certainly wasn't common before I made "Body and Soul", I can tell you that now!'

'Body and Soul' is in the key of D flat. What Coleman Hawkins did, in carefully selected places, was to arrive home at that D flat key note, not by way of the 'Three Blind Mice' route of F, E flat D flat, but in shorter, semitone or 'chromatic' steps: E flat, D, D flat. There is a choice of harmonies with which that D note may be accompanied: by making a full-blooded chromatic progression from D seventh to D flat; or by using the normal A flat seventh dominant chord but flattening its fifth note from E flat to D. The 'flattened fifth' became something of a bogey in the Modern Jazz era of 1945 onwards. Aspiring 'modernists' seized on it as a passport to the realms of bebop, while adherents to the more conventional jazz forms interpreted it as the symbol of everything that was freakish and 'far out' in the new music. Its appearance as part of Hawk's harmonic armoury in 'Body and Soul' in 1939 may have been the reason for Thelonious Monk's apparent bewilderment in later years at the record's success. Monk, who as a young musician was employed by Hawkins in the mid-Forties, said to Hawk more than once, 'You never did tell me how did these people, these old folks and everybody *go* for your record of "Body and Soul".'

Hawkins himself was equally bewildered, though his wonderment was based on the belief that the general record-buying public wanted to hear the melody all the time. 'Where is the melody? There ain't no real melody in the whole piece!' He meant by this of course that, apart from the cursory reference to it in the first eight bars, he never actually states Johnny Green's original tune at all. The truth is that he took considerable liberties with its harmonies, too. Despite his assertion that the chord progressions that he used were indigenous to the tune—'The changes that I made in "Body and Soul"? That's the only changes to make in "Body and Soul"—what I mean is, that *is* "Body and Soul" '—the original piece has no such refinements as chromatic progressions or flattened fifths. Written in 1930, the tune was daring for its time, with the unusual excursion into three different keys in the space of its thirty-two bars. But reference to the original songsheet or to early recordings (viz. Louis Armstrong's successful version recorded in the year of the song's publication) shows no sign of the sophisticated harmonies that Hawk used. To take two clear instances, the conventional chord for the end of the second bar, right after the words 'sad and lonely', and for the second half of the seventh bar, behind the words 'yours, body and soul', is an A flat seventh. Indeed, a singer who tried to sing Johnny Green's melody as written over the Coleman Hawkins chords would find several notes clashing dreadfully with the accompaniment.

This doesn't mean that Coleman Hawkins was wrong in saying that his chords *were* 'Body and Soul'. When a popular song is adopted by jazz musicians, it is as if it were leased to them indefinitely for the purpose of improvisation. They are under no obligation to stick to the composer's original conception—they would be pretty poor improvisers if they did. It is a truth which I hope songwriters themselves would admit that a performance by a great jazzman—Louis Armstrong, Art Tatum, Coleman Hawkins —has often shown an insight into the character of a melody that the composer, with his limited aspirations towards producing a singable popular song in the shortest possible time, has missed. You may take it from me that many well-known songs, including 'On the Sunny Side of the Street', 'I Can't Get Started' and 'Moonlight in Vermont', would sound wrong today if played from the original songsheet. Coleman Hawkins may fairly be said to have completed 'Body and Soul' as a finely crafted piece of music and, had not the song already a superfluity of composers in Messrs Green, Heyman, Eyton and Sour (the last three required to produce the very ordinary lyric), I would suggest that his name should be added.

In bringing modern and sophisticated refinements to a popular song, Coleman Hawkins was clearly unprepared to find his own contribution popular in the same sense, especially when other musicians were finding it full of 'wrong notes'. But in dismissing the whole 'Body and Soul' episode as a freakish aberration on the part of the public, Hawk did them and himself an injustice. (By coincidence, Jerome Kern made a very similar misjudgement in the same year, including 'All the Things You Are' in a show with the strong reservation that, with its 'advanced' harmonies, the song was 'too hard' for the public.) Music of quality and distinction may be rare in the Hit Parade, but it is not completely unknown. What record salesmen know as 'the public' is not one huge, amorphous mass with a single response. While a lot of people were no doubt going about their business in 1939 whistling and humming such nonsense as 'The Hut Sut Song', 'Three Little Fishes' and 'Scatterbrain', there were enough who preferred the more sophisticated 'Deep Purple', 'I Get Along Without You Very Well' and the reincarnation of Victor Herbert's 'Indian Summer' to establish them as 'standards' that would survive until the present. As Coleman Hawkins so often said, the people who bought 'Body and Soul' in such quantities knew nothing about music. The man in the street would not know a flattened fifth if it jumped out from behind a lamp-post and flattened *him*. What he responds to are such abstractions as a romantic feeling, a good beat, a pretty tune. 'Body and Soul' fulfilled the first of these requirements in such generous abundance that it didn't matter if the other two were not over-stressed.

And here's a paradox that is not unusual in jazz. Unlike Louis Armstrong with his insistence on pleasing the people, Coleman Hawkins was no philanthropist. In his attitude to audiences he came closer to the dismissive, take-it-or-leave-it line of the post-1945 modernists than to the jazzmen-entertainers who were his contemporaries. In person relationships, he appears to have taken a malicious, Mephistophelean glee in the discomfiture of others. The Riverside interview from which I have quoted opens with him blandly informing his questioner that he was born at sea. The inflections of the disembodied voice alone suggest to us that it is a blatant invention which eventually degenerates into a sort of deadpan crosstalk act.

'How did that happen? Were your folks travelling to Europe?'
'They were comin' back.'

On the one occasion when I had the perilous task of interviewing him backstage before a concert, he responded to my enquiry as to whether he remembered various friends from the London visits in the Thirties with a flat 'No', nad then stared at me unwaveringly as if to savour my confusion. Buck Clayton once told me of an epic row between trumpeters Roy Eldridge and Henry Allen which was entirely engineered by Hawkins, who conveyed to each of them in turn fictitious slanders allegedly uttered by one against the other. And there is something not altogether kindly about the story, which Hawkins himself was fond of telling, of how, in the Fletcher Henderson days, he worked the trombonist Charlie Green, up into a fever of jealousy by loudly holding forth in his hearing about the fickleness of musicians' wives.

Despite all this, the initial impact of 'Body and Soul' is of a great heartwarming blast of human warmth and loving kindness. This is heightened rather than otherwise by a much greater discipline in the rhapsodizing than of yore. Gone are the earlier extravagances, the tendency towards histrionics, the quavering descents from the upper register that came so dangerously close to sentimentality. The tone is now full, firm and virile in every register, and the two choruses unfold with an inexorable logic and feeling for dramatic construction that is more powerfully moving than the more impassioned exhortations of the earlier style. Poor old, much maligned Joe Public showed himself in some respects to be more advanced than those musicians who chided Hawkins for playing wrong notes. To him, the arrival at the D flat keynote by way of 'some kind of a D change', which happens in the second bar of the first chorus, was no jarring musical solecism or aggressively 'modern' innovation, but a device that prompted a warm and caressing turn of phrase. Furthermore, in accepting Hawk's variations and departures from the basic melody without complaining 'Where's the tune?', he showed himself capable of 'hearing' the unstated melody which, after eight years and innumerable interpretations, must have been quite familiar to him.

There are three more signposts that I would like to erect before leaving the reader to explore for himself all the ramifications of this rich performance. One of the most effective devices which Coleman Hawkins had perfected by this time is the one known as 'doubling up'. This simply means treating one bar as if it were two, playing four sixteenth-notes or semiquavers to each beat instead of two eighth-notes. This improvisational ploy has two advantages. It enables a soloist who is, like Hawkins, eager to pursue all the harmonic twists and turns inherent in a tune to give attention to transient chords that more widely-spaced notes would overlook. And, by suggesting a tempo twice as fast as the original, 'doubling up' endows a slow ballad with some of the drive and swing usually associated with more lively pieces. For examples of this, listen to the serpentine movement through changing chords with which Hawkins modulates into the key of D between bars fifteen and eighteen of the first chorus, and to the way in which he is able to respond to the heightened tension introduced by ensemble chords in the second chorus by bringing into play some of the elbowing aggression of his up-tempo style.

The two remaining pointers can be summed up briefly. I have given some attention to the fresh devices which Hawkins brought into play with 'Body and Soul'. The performance would not have attained the status of a masterpiece had not these innovations been used with the utmost discretion and taste. Many a jazz solo has been ruined or impaired through a musician's eagerness to show off some newly discovered trick. The chromatic movement of which I have written at length is not used by Hawkins to the exclusion of more conventional harmonic progression. For instance, his treatment each time of the D major passage in the first half of the middle-eight makes use of the relatively naïve, diatonic harmonies of the original songsheet. The effect, no doubt intuitive rather than studied, is of opening a window and letting sunshine in on a cloudy and brooding atmosphere.

Similar restraint is used in the deployment of emotional resources. We have Hawk's testimony that the recording of 'Body and Soul' was a condensed version of the nine or ten choruses which he often lavished on the number at Kelly's Stables. The mouth waters at the thought of them, but it is hardly conceivable that they attained greater emotional impact than that which Hawk achieved, with a great actor's control and timing, in three short minutes. In common with another miracle, Louis Armstrong's 'West End Blues', this performance leaves one with the impression that one has been carried high aloft and lowered to earth again on a vast wave of passion. And yet the moment of climax is masterfully delayed until eight bars from the end of the piece and then restricted to four bars in which Coleman Hawkins makes a series of chromatic leaps into the upper register, choosing deliberately unseductive intervals and implying chords far more complex and dissonant than any that have been suggested before. It's a startling and dramatic moment, a sudden explosion of fury that dissipates as quickly as it came as the piece subsides towards a coda which brilliantly, and this time with ineffable gentleness, reiterates the chromatic idea. It stimulates one's optimism about human nature wonderfully to reflect that one of the most successful jazz recordings was, in its own way, also one of the best.

Jack Teagarden

IN ITS TERMINOLOGY, the story of Jack Teagarden's arrival in New York tends to sound like the scenario for a corny western. Accounts by musicians who were on the spot are curiously vague as to the exact date and circumstances, but the consensus is that Jack arrived in town in the autumn of 1927. Jimmy McPartland recalled that he, Bud Freeman and Pee Wee Russell were sitting in a speakeasy on 51st Street when Pee Wee, who had been enthusing about the trombonist as 'the greatest thing I ever heard in my life', went off to round him up so that they could judge for themselves. Bud Freeman's recollection is that Pee Wee Russell called him in the middle of the night to say that Jack Teagarden, the best trombonist in the world, just 'blew in' from Oklahoma City and was in action at a speakeasy on 53rd Street. According to Eddie Condon, it was Bud Freeman who called *him* in the middle of the night, long-distance, and got Teagarden to play some blues over the telephone. Condon, who was in New York, said, 'Put a brand on his stomach and bring him in.'

The probability is that Pee Wee Russell made the introductions, since Jack Teagarden was no stranger to him. Both men had played, in the mid-Twenties, for the Texan pianist and bandleader, Peck Kelley. (Conforming to the theme, the band's name, Peck's Bad Boys, sounds like one of those gangs of marauding horsemen around which cowboy epics are built!) It is not hard to understand Russell's enthusiasm for his old colleague, nor the feeling of excitement that Jack Teagarden's playing spread among the New York musicians. Eddie Condon and his associates had themselves only lately arrived in New York from Chicago, where the trombone was respected for its supportive role as exemplified by the great Kid Ory, but not admired, as were the trumpet, clarinet or piano, as a vehicle for solo virtuosity. The evidence of gramophone records, with their spurious selectivity that favours those who were in the right place at the right time, is notoriously unreliable, and one must exercise extreme caution in using terms like 'the first' or 'the best' in respect of the jazz pioneers. For example, records reissued in comparatively recent years have shown that, in Texas during the late Twenties, the locally re-nowned Alphonse Trent Orchestra boasted, in 'Snub' Mosley, a trombonist who, in terms of sheer speed of execution, was a front-runner, if not way ahead of the field. In the book, *Jazz Masters of the Thirties*, Rex Stewart lists several influential players in New York at the same time, some of whom—Jake Green, Jake Frazier, Teroy Williams, Billy Kato, Herb Gregory—we must take on trust. But those with whose work we are familiar on record, such as Charlie Green, Charlie Irvis and Joe 'Tricky Sam' Nanton, show themselves strongest in the broad, sweeping measures of the blues. At brisker tempos, they were no match for the other horns.

The player most consistently credited with the feat of liberating the trombone from its restricted supporting role was a studious-looking New Yorker called Milfred 'Miff' Mole. The Original Memphis Five, with whom Mole made his recording début in the early Twenties, was the most successful of the bands which rode into fashion on the crest of the wave of jazz mania created by the Original Dixieland Band. With superb instrumental control that involved a wide range of dynamics, he devised a style which grafted the melodic agility and unpredictability of Bix Beiderbecke on to the staccato rhythmic manner of the ODJB's Eddie Edwards. His solos throughout the Twenties—and there are hundreds of them on record—are undoubtedly the most interesting trombone improvisations of the period. Full of daring intervals and un-expected turns of phrase, they offer melodic ingenuity and grace from an instrument more accustomed to supplying emotive bursts of raw passion. Indeed, it is on the emotional level that Miff Mole's work falls short of the best of jazz. Unlike Bix Beiderbecke, with whom he shared a strong sense of musical discipline and construction, Mole seems to have been impervious to the raw spirit of black American music. Consequently one waits in vain for his solos to flair into fervent life in the way that Bix's so often do.

By the late Twenties, Miff Mole, in loose partnership with the cornetist Red Nichols, had virtually cornered the market in what were then termed 'hot style' recordings in New York. Together and separately, with groups that recorded under a wide variety of names, they set a fashion for elegant, sophisticated jazz, giving plenty of room for 'hot' solos while keeping firm control of the temperature. Rhythmically, their music leaned heavily on the first and third beat of the bar, with the phrasing couched in the even quaver, one-and-two-and-three-and-four style descending from ragtime. By the late Twenties, this style was beginning to give way, albeit reluctantly, to something new. In the first volume of *The Best of Jazz*, I pursued the notion that the really significant changes in jazz history have been rhythmic. For many years, until chordal harmony itself came to be rejected by the *avant-garde*, 'modernism' was always interpreted in terms of harmonic discovery and innovation. Much is made in the history books of Charlie Parker's improvisatory excursions into extended chords such as elevenths and thirteenths, and indeed it was his use of the upper intervals of those chords in the first 'modern jazz' recordings of the mid-Forties that startled so many listeners. But new harmonic practice can soon be assimilated, as witness the veritable spate of clichés based on the flattened fifth and descending minor seventh chords that came in turn to hamstring jazz in the post-Parker period. It was his comparative rhythmic freedom that distinguished Charlie Parker from his predecessors and, during the Bebop years, it was the ability to handle that freedom that separated the men from the boys.

Likewise, in the late Twenties, 'modernism' was in the air. With his recordings from 1926 onwards, Louis Armstrong had opened wide the door on a hitherto unimagined vista of jazz possibilities. At its centre was a rhythmic conception which I have described in detail in earlier chapters. It was not simply that Louis, ahead of all his contemporaries, abandoned the rather

square, even-quavered, one-and-two-and-three-and-four rhythmic
base in favour of the looser, one-and-a-two-and-a-three-and-a-four
rhythm of twelve-eight time. It was the totally free and un-
contrived way in which he moved on, across, through and behind
the regular, four-to-a-bar pulse which gave to his playing the
sustained momentum which came to be known as 'swing'. It took
some time for his example to be followed. I made the point in the
earlier volume that almost all the 'classic' recordings which I
discussed in that book showed some degree of rhythmic schizophrenia. But by the end of the Twenties, Louis Armstrong's
influence had permeated the whole range of jazz instruments and
had inspired a new generation of musicians who wanted to 'swing'
as he did.

In *Jazz Masters of the Thirties* Rex Stewart gave his essay on
Jimmy Harrison the heading 'Father of Swing Trombone'. After
describing Harrison's impact on the New York scene in the mid-
Twenties, he concluded that 'History, inadvertently and unwittingly, bypassed Jimmy Harrison'. To give history its due, it
has done its best with rather flimsy evidence. At the time when
he was alleged to have exerted his greatest influence, around
1927–8, he could be heard on record only in fragmentary solos
with the bands of Charlie Johnson and Fletcher Henderson—and
some of the Henderson solos have been reassessed in recent years
as the work of another young 'modernist', Benny Morton. Indeed,
in one respect history may be accused of bending the truth in
Jimmy Harrison's favour. Jazz historians have always had a
tendency to outline the development of jazz in terms of Old
Testament lineage—Buddy Bolden begat King Oliver, King
Oliver begat Louis Armstrong and so on. Add to this the risky
assumption that, because an overwhelming majority of jazz innovators have been black, the flow of influence will always be from
black to white, and it is not surprising that many jazz histories
settle for the simple view that Jimmy Harrison begat Jack
Teagarden.

The historical facts certainly do not rule out this possibility.
In his recorded interview for Riverside Records, Coleman Hawkins
describes the occasion at the Roseland Ballroom in New York
when the musicians in Fletcher Henderson's band first heard

Jack Teagarden. Hawkins, ever alert to what was going on in musical circles, had hung around to listen to the band that was alternating with Henderson—in all likelihood it was Billy Lustig's Scranton Sirens, with whom Teagarden played at the Roseland in February 1928. Having heard a solo or two from the young trombonist in the band, Hawkins hurried down to the bandroom, his genuine enthusiasm sharpened by the opportunity for a little mischief-making. One has to hear the story in his own words to savour the malicious glee with which he sought out Jimmy Harrison 'to start kiddin' about it, you know'. Having announced to the room in general that 'there's a boy upstairs that plays an awful lot of trombone', he casually asked Jimmy Harrison if he knew him. Harrison's reply was not only predictable from a man accustomed to the Hawkins style of comradely baiting, it also throws light on the way that trombonists were responding to the Armstrong influence.

'Oh no, how am I goin' to know him. I don't know anybody— what's he play? He's a trombone player, ain't he? He can play like the rest of the trombones, that's all. I don't see no trombones. Trombone's a brass instrument, it should have a sound just like a trumpet. I don't want to hear no trombones sound like trombones. I can't see it.'

'But Jimmy,' said Hawkins, 'he don't sound like those trombones, he plays up high. He sounds a whole lot like trumpets to me.'

The upshot clearly satisfied Hawk's sense of theatre. 'I'll never forget it, Jimmy and Jack became the tightest of friends.'

The tight friendship that developed between Jimmy Harrison and Jack Teagarden during the latter's first year in New York clearly provided a historic basis for the assumption that the established star of the famous Henderson Orchestra influenced and gave formative guidance to the newcomer. But it happens that there are recordings by both musicians in that period which tell a different story. Confusion over the identity of trombone soloists with Henderson make one wary of laying down the law. But two recordings over which there seems little doubt—the version of 'King Porter Stomp' recorded in February 1928 and 'Come on Baby' from December of that year—give us a good idea of his style at the time of the Teagarden friendship. In 'King Porter Stomp', he starts in the upper register, playing three anticipated crotchets in the typical Armstrong manner. But the timing is slightly wrong. The notes do not hang in the air as Armstrong's would, and the two notes leading into the first full bar of the chorus are rushed, with a jerky effect. Later on, at the half-way mark in the solo, there is a phrase of five notes played in a sharply tongued, even-quaver manner that could have come straight from a Miff Mole solo. These and other solos from the period of 1928–9 show a certain indecision in style and rhythmic sense which hardly conforms to the legendary image of a grand master ahead of his time. The musician and musicologist, Gunther Schuller, has pointed out, in his book, *Early Jazz*, that in this period both Benny Morton and Claude Jones, temporary colleagues of Harrison's in the Henderson band, recorded solos which were, in his view, superior to Harrison's. And in Luis Russell's recordings made early in 1928, J. C. Higginbotham was demonstrating a formidably agile style, full of lip-trills and ascents into the upper register, which compares well with contemporary examples of Harrison's work.

But we must not dismiss out of hand the testimony of those musicians on the spot who have, like Rex Stewart, asserted that Jimmy Harrison held regal sway in New York while other trombonists stood back to listen and learn. When Don Redman, who had supplied the bulk of Fletcher Henderson's arrangements, left the organization late in 1927, the band moved into what would nowadays be described as a crisis of identity. In the Riverside interview, Coleman Hawkins recalled how Henderson started exchanging arrangements with other bands, to the extent that his own orchestra began to sound like them. Retrospectively, Hawkins disapproved of this—he thought that the band should have carried on 'stomping' as it did under Redman's guidance. Certainly, there is on record plenty of evidence of a passing infatuation with the cool, harmonically contrived music of the white New Yorkers— Nichols and Mole, Frank Trumbauer and, of course, Paul Whiteman—which may have inhibited Harrison's playing. But we must also remember that Jimmy Harrison had been around in New York since 1923 and so had Rex Stewart. It may well be that the period of Jimmy Harrison's pre-eminence should be pre-dated to around 1924–5 when he and trumpeter June Clark, freshly arrived in New York, constituted what Rex Stewart described as a 'red-hot team'. A couple of titles recorded by their band in 1925 —'Santa Claus Blues' and 'Keep Your Temper', made under the name of the Gulf Coast Seven—are enormously impressive. June Clark (in much later life to become road manager and court minstrel for boxer Sugar Ray Robinson) had grasped many of Louis Armstrong's precepts, and Harrison, though rhythmically somewhat stilted, played long solo passages with a drive, range and agility that was, to say the least, unusual for that time. If he seems to have been less far ahead of the field three years later, it would not be the first or last instance in jazz history of an in-strumental pioneer being overtaken by ertswhile 'pupils'.

But how does Jack Teagarden's early performance stand in all this? The earliest readily available recording on which Teagarden was extensively featured is a piece called 'Makin' Friends', recorded by Eddie Condon and his Feetwarmers in October 1928 In this, Teagarden has an opening verse in a minor key which he plays with open trombone. The first thing that one notices, apart from the tone with its burnished matt surface, is the ease with which he handles every rhythmic problem. Coincidentally, the solo begins with the same launching phrase based on anticipated crotchets or quarter notes over which Jimmy Harrison had tripped in his 'King Porter Stomp' solo a few months earlier. Jack Tea-garden's timing is perfect, as is the way he balances notes played on and across the beat in the bluesy phrase that follows. Stretching across the ninth, tenth and eleventh bars is a legato phrase made up of six minims or half-notes which would have thrown quite a few players of that period off balance, especially if they had any leaning towards the old style of eight-to-a-bar phrasing. Tea-garden plays it with great assurance, placing the second note well ahead of the beat, the fourth slightly less so, and prefacing the tied fifth and sixth notes with a 'turn' comprising a couple of anticipatory grace-notes (a Teagarden trade-mark) which serves to avoid dull symmetry. There's a typical Teagarden vocal in which the lazy relaxation of his trombone style is reflected in a Texan drawl in which the harder consonants are replaced by their softer alternatives—f becoming v, t becoming d and s melting into an over-ripe z. The second chorus is a wordless one in which, once again, Jack shows complete rhythmic assurance. In the ensuing trombone choruses, he uses a technique which was, and remains to this day, his exclusive speciality. By removing the bell section of the trombone and covering the exposed piping with an ordinary glass tumbler, he produces a nasal, muted sound with a melancholy quality heightened by the fact that, with the limited range of notes that can be played in tune by this method, it works most effectively in a minor key. Some years later, in the film, *Birth of the Blues*, Jack Teagarden introduced the technique as a novelty effect in the song, 'The Waiter and the Porter and the Upstairs Maid', which he sang with Mary Martin and Bing Crosby. But in pieces such as 'Makin' Friends', 'Tailspin Blues' (with the Mound City Blue Blowers) and the riveting 'St James Infirmary' with Louis Armstrong's first All Star band in 1947, the music which he produced in this unorthodox way was anything but novelty stuff.

Indeed, the final choruses in 'Makin' Friends' combine with other solos of the period played in the normal way to build a formidable case for asserting that, in the significant area of rhythmic fluency and freedom, Jack Teagarden was ahead of all other trombonists, Jimmy Harrison included. In September 1929, he played two choruses on a tune called 'Never had a Reason to Believe in You' with the Mound City Blue Blowers which reveal a man whose style, at the age of twenty-two, was completely matured. In his hands, the trombone was no longer the rather clumsy heavyweight in the jazz instrumental family, but a sensitive and articulate voice capable of the subtlest nuances. The secret of his fluency was an astonishing lip control which established him from the first recordings as a trombone virtuoso, quite apart from his creative talent. The impression, especially in his high-register playing, that the trombone slide had become redundant gave rise to a legend that as a small boy he had devised alternative slide positions near to his face because his arms were too short to push the slide into the lower positions. Like most legends, it contains no more than a grain of truth. There are no alternative positions which will obtain the lower notes in the trombone register, so he would have had to stretch for them or devise some way of extending his reach. Up among the high notes, it is possible to minimize the movement of the slide with alternative positions. But having once stood alongside Jack Teagarden on a bandstand (at the Nice Jazz Festival in 1948) and marvelled at the leisurely way in which his huge, square right hand seemed to wave languidly an inch or two in front of his face while the notes tumbled out, I fancy that it was the finely controlled 'lipping' of additional ornamental grace-notes and turns that made it appear that he was getting by with the minimum of mechanical assistance. The proof of his technical virtuosity lies in the fact that, whereas it is the trombone, with its large mouthpiece, which is on paper the more cumbersome instrument, it was some fifteen years or so before modern trumpet players became adept at using the sort of fast triplet 'lipped' ornamentation which abounds in Teagarden's early solos.

It is difficult to understand the reluctance, in some areas of jazz commentary, to give Teagarden full credit for lugging the trombone into the field of untrammelled rhythmic freedom which came to be called 'swing'. Much early writing on jazz had an understandable (and in most instances justified) bias towards black performers as the true originators, leading to an assumption that Teagarden's style must have derived from Jimmy Harrison simply because of the colour of his skin. There is no excuse for us today to make such easy assumptions. We know that, in his youth, Jack Teagarden had plenty of opportunity to listen to the blues in its basic, rural form and also to the 'gospel' music of black Holy Roller meetings where the preacher would incite the singers to fervour in a manner strongly reminiscent of Teagarden's early blues style. And though the legend that he used to carry a favourite Louis Armstrong record around in his trombone case may test our credulity (I speak as one who had difficulty in keeping his old 78s intact in their *shelves*), there is no doubt that he eagerly absorbed the recordings by Louis and also by Bessie Smith during the Twenties. There is no reason to doubt that he arrived in New York with a style strongly influenced by these and other black artists and sounding, to Coleman Hawkins, 'a whole lot like trumpets'.

A more serious reason for equivocation about Jack Teagarden's role in jazz history may be that his subsequent career, for all the elegant and delightful music that it produced, did not fulfil the early promise. It can be summed up in a few sentences. After the first few years in New York, during which he recorded for practically every bandleader and session organizer who could get his hands on him, he graduated, via the bands of Ben Pollack and Mal Hallett, to the exalted ranks of the Paul Whiteman Orchestra. While under tight contract to Whiteman, he had to turn down the offer to lead a team of fine jazz players stranded by the break-up of Ben Pollack's Band. The job went to Bing Crosby's younger brother Bob who, though little more than a moderate singer himself, succeeded in attracting commercial success to a band with a strong jazz policy. Teagarden's own efforts to enter the big-band field after his stint with Whiteman led to a series of financial disasters. He lacked both the business sense and the strong autocratic streak which brought success to erstwhile colleagues such as Benny Goodman and Tommy Dorsey. Between 1947 and 1951, he restored and burnished his international reputation as a member of Louis Armstrong's All Stars, before returning to lead his own small groups with a predominantly Dixieland style and repertoire. He was on tour with his band in 1964, when he died suddenly, at the age of fifty-nine.

Taking recorded samples from this fluctuating career, one is reminded of one of Duke Ellington's sage remarks *apropos* the cornetist, Ray Nance, of whom someone had said that he played within a relatively narrow technical and expressive range. Duke's reply was (and I quote from memory): 'In all the years that he has been in our band, there has never been a night on which Ray did not play *something* of exquisite beauty.' Likewise, it is hard to find a single Teagarden record which he did not enhance with his beautiful, curiously blunted tone, his marvellously fluent and controlled articulation, his perfect rhythmic poise and the sheer elegance of his musical thought. There was a phase, in the mid-Thirties, when he reacted so far from the passionate and vibrant manner of his first recordings that his sound, especially with the much favoured straight mute, acquired a rather flat and distant quality, as though he were performing inside a cardboard box.

But it was a passing phase and may have been to some extent attributable to studio acoustics.

What one does find missing, after the first exciting year or two, is the spirit of adventure. The mutual admiration between Jack Teagarden and Jimmy Harrison had, by the end of 1930, produced some curious results. In his finest recordings, made with a studio band called the Chocolate Dandies in December, 1930, Jimmy Harrison sounds, in the piece 'Dee Blues' especially, much nearer to Jack Teagarden than before. The phrasing is less four-square and symmetrical, sweeping phrases are played across the beat and the phrase endings have the sort of rapid, fluttering vibrato that gave Teagarden's early playing such heat and intensity. Important differences remain, largely in the rhythmic area. Though the earlier awkwardness had been ironed out, Jimmy Harrison still tended to play dotted quaver and semiquaver combinations in a somewhat jerky manner, inherited from the 'vo-de-o-do' syncopations of earlier dance music and bequeathed, in turn, to fellow-trombonists Jimmy Archey and Vic Dickenson, in whose styles it remained an idiosyncracy for four or more decades. But in the common adherence to Louis Armstrong's influence (almost every recorded solo by Harrison, and not a few by Teagarden, start with the three ahead-of-the-beat crotchets or quarter notes that had been an Armstrong trade-mark since the mid-Twenties), both Harrison and Teagarden were briefly in the same stylistic stable.

But at the very time that Jimmy Harrison appeared to have absorbed much of Teagarden's rhythmic assurance into his playing, Jack Teagarden himself had already begun to round off the rough edges of his style and settle for a more placid approach, a process that was to continue throughout the Thirties. The symptoms went beyond the smoothing out of the tone referred to earlier. Stock phrases began to appear over some of the more familiar cadences of the blues and popular song. Blues choruses, if not repeated verbatim, took on a repetitive shape, often consisting of minor variations on a familiar structure. There is nothing disreputable about this. Few of the very greatest jazzmen have survived a lifetime of persistent improvisation without accruing a vocabulary of personal clichés with which to peg out, so to speak, the line of invention. Nor is it every jazzman of distinction who has been temperamentally disposed to keep pushing his style outwards in the direction of unexplored areas. If one feels some slight disappointment that Jack Teagarden appeared to draw in his musical horns so early in his recording career, it is because the very first records, revealing jazz trombone as it had never been heard before, aroused such high expectations—and still do when one listens to them again within their historical context.

Perhaps those expectations are in themselves misplaced. One of the choruses over which I am about to enthuse, the opening twelve bars of 'Knockin' a Jug', recurs in Jack Teagarden's contribution to a Red Nichols version of 'Basin Street Blues' made just ten weeks later. We must face the fact that a solo that can be played on record twice within three months might well have been conceived five years earlier on a gig with Peck Kelley's Bad Boys and trotted out a hundred times in the intervening years, and that Jack Teagarden was never, at any stage, the kind of jazz musician who will lay his reputation on the line with continuous creative progress. This gives us all the more reason for supposing that, in the encounter between Jack Teagarden and Jimmy Harrison, it was the former who wrought changes in the style of the latter and not the other way about.

Those who attach overriding importance to the role of improvisation in jazz may feel that, in the past few paragraphs, I have systematically destroyed Jack Teagarden's right to be included in this book at all! But the creation of jazz is a more mysterious process than the mere pouring out of spontaneous ideas. The requirements of 'improvisation' can be satisfied, in jazz terms, if an identical sequence of notes is played with the subtlest alteration in rhythmic emphasis, the slightest change in the use of dynamics or vibrato, the almost imperceptible raising or lowering of the emotional temperature. Likewise, 'originality' in jazz lies not only in the pattern of notes that is produced, but also in the instrumental tone or 'voice' in which it is uttered.

I know no better confirmation of this than in the comparison between the opening twelve bars of 'Knockin' a Jug' and the 'Basin Street Blues' solo with Red Nichols. The notes are identical

for six of the twelve bars and the ensuing bars are very similar in
shape. And yet 'Basin Street Blues' is merely a good solo, 'Knockin'
a Jug' a great one. There is some mystery surrounding the
circumstances of the recording. In his book, *We Called it Music*,
Eddie Condon describes how he pursuaded Tommy Rockwell of
Okeh records to record a mixed group of black and white musicians
featuring both Louis Armstrong and Jack Teagarden. Such
politically daring sessions were not unknown—Jelly Roll Morton
had recorded with the New Orleans Rhythm Kings as early as
1923, and Condon himself had just recorded a similar group for
Victor records. But they were rare enough for Rockwell to have
reservations. However, Eddie Condon's powers of persuasion
are among the most solidly based of jazz legends. According to
him, 'Louis Armstrong came on from Chicago that spring for a
one-night stand at the Savoy Ballroom in Harlem with Luis
Russell's Orchestra. Afterwards an impromptu banquet was
staged in his honour. I looked around the table and shook my
head; I had never seen so many good musicians, white and
coloured, in one place at the same time. "You ought to make a
record while Louis is here," I said to Tommy Rockwell, Armstrong's adviser at the time.' The upshot of this conversation was
that Rockwell put back until the afternoon a session booked for
Armstrong with the Luis Russell band, and 'the group made
"Knockin' a Jug" and "I'm Gonna Stomp Mr Henry Lee" '.

At this point, doubts arise. For one thing, no trace has ever
been found of the second title. For another, the actual recording
of 'Knockin' a Jug' falls well below the Okeh company's standards
at that time. The piano, played by Joe Sullivan, is distant and
lacking in presence, and Kaiser Marshall's drums, using both wire
brushes and sticks on the snare drum rim, dominate the proceedings. All in all, the recording sounds like something taken
down during rehearsal or at a party. In a section on Louis Armstrong's recordings in the Max Jones-John Chilton biography,
Louis, John Chilton confidently puts forward an account that
differs significantly from Condon's. After referring to the scheduled
session with Luis Russell, he goes on, 'All the previous night was
spent celebrating with welcoming musicians, black and white.
Louis, with his fellow revellers still in tow, arrived at the studio

early. The party's warm-up on the impromptu blues, "Knockin'
a Jug", was mercifully recorded for posterity by the enterprising
studio engineer.'

The results favour Chilton's account, yet Eddie Condon was
not a man given to boastful invention. It is probable that the
truth lies between the two, and that the musicians arrived too
late, or having 'knocked the jug' too enthusastically, for the
arranged session to be completed.

Whatever the circumstances, we must be thankful that the
one title emerged to mark the first meeting in a recording studio
of Jack Teagarden and Louis Armstrong, and that their contributions were satisfactorily recorded. To say that between them,
they dominated the performance is not to belittle the other solos.
Eddie Lang had already shown himself in recorded duets with the
New Orleans guitarist, Lonnie Johnson, to be well versed in the
blues, and his twelve-bar chorus here is economical and convincing. Happy Caldwell had come to New York from Chicago
some years earlier and established a reputation which is not
satisfactorily explained by the few recordings which he made. His
tenor solo, phrased in the manner of a trumpet, is attractive but
seems to make rather heavy weather of the technical handling of
the instrument. As I have already observed, Joe Sullivan's chunky
barrel-house piano is almost obliterated by the elephantine soft-
shoe shuffle of Kaiser Marshall's over-recorded brushes. But it is
redolent with 'atmosphere' and contributes to the tastiness of the
filling in a sandwich in which the strongest musical nourishment
lies in the bread.

The opening phrases of Jack Teagarden's introductory solo
would be enough to prove, had he never affirmed it himself, that
the trombonist had listened avidly to the recordings of Bessie
Smith. There is the *gravitas*, the immediate establishment of a
mood that blends melancholy with commanding authority and
proud dignity. The rawness of the phrases is counteracted by an
immense poise and authority of execution, revealed in the perfect
rhythmic timing, effortless articulation and complete tonal
command. No white musicians of that period, and relatively few
since, have so effectively combined a sophisticated technique
with an understanding of the unorthodox characteristics of the

blues. Of these, the most elusive are the so-called 'blue notes', produced when certain notes in the scale, most usually the third, fifth and seventh, are perceptibly flattened. The nearest that conventional European notation can get to these notes is to apply the 'flat' (♭) sign that lowers them by a semitone, turning E to E flat, for instance, in the key of C. But when the notes are played strictly according to such notation, the result is, at best, prim and colourless and, at worst, melodramatic or maudlin.

Much of the imposing character of Teagarden's solo derives from the masterly use of blue notes. The opening statement, for instance, starts with a positive and forthright two-bar phrase, not unfamiliar in the context of the blues, in which, after two introductory notes, the melody descends from an upper key note to the note an octave below by way of the notes of the major chord. This establishes the key of the piece in no uncertain terms. It is answered by a two-bar phrase with the reverse shape that takes the melody back to the upper key note by much the same route, using the third and the fifth as stepping-stones. As described, this is pretty naïve stuff. But reference to any one of Bessie Smith's recordings will show that the distortion of a naïve framework by the subtle bending of notes is the very stuff of the blues. In his second two-bar phrase, Teagarden comes to rest on a note (at the beginning of bar three of the chorus) which should, if it is to match the clarity of the opening phrase, be a straight fifth. Instead, the note starts a fraction below the fifth and drops downwards, giving a vaguely off-pitch effect which defies mathematical analysis but it is indescribably effective, introducing a fleeting element of doubt into the tonality established by the opening phrase.

A point that is often missed about these blue notes is that they are frequently directional, in the sense that the note seems to be straining away from its temporary tonality towards a preferred destination. In the fifth bar of the chorus, Teagarden plays an ascending phrase, from the third to the fifth, in which this upward straining effect is noticeable. On paper the notes would be written as D, E flat, E and F (the piece is in B flat), but by pitching the D noticeably sharp, he throws all the note placings out of true, in the deliberately casual manner of a blues singer. The 'vocalized' effect is enormously expressive, especially in the context of meticulously pitched playing.

One other striking use of instinctively off-pitch playing occurs at the beginning of the second chorus. In contrast to the measured steps with which the first chorus entered, this one is more impassioned and seemingly less articulate, with irregular phrases and long pauses. I say 'seemingly' because in fact the passage is superbly constructed for maximum emotional effect. Here is the urgent exhortation of the preacher leading the choir at the open-air church meetings to which Jack Teagarden used to listen as a boy back home in Texas. It is possible, too, that the notes which stutter so impatiently across the beat were influenced by Bubber Miley's similarly rhetorical muted cornet solo in Duke Ellington's 'Black and Tan Fantasy'. Two notes are involved in the first six bars of the second chorus, the B flat key note and a note of indeterminate pitch that hovers somewhere around the C and D flat. In other words it is neither a perfect second nor a minor third but a tone that approximates one or the other whenever it occurs. The way in which Teagarden builds strongly contrasting phrases out of these two notes underlines his rhythmic mastery. First, a whip-up to the upper note initiates a long phrase over two bars in which he plays crotchet triplets across the basic four beats in the bar on the B flat key note. One expects another whip-up at the end of the phrase, but it comes two bars later, tagged on the end of two further B flats which pick up, after a pause of almost a full bar, where the others left off. Two beats later the two notes alternate briefly, there is a further pause and back they come again at the junction of bars five and six, this time with more rapid and urgent alternation, to lead into a descending phrase which breaks the impasse. It is a fine example of the building up of tension with the simplest of basic materials. Essential to it is the use of the blue notes with all their subtle grades of pitching, giving the effect of a vital message striving for expression. Once the pattern is broken, there is an air of almost jaunty relief surrounding the remainder of the chorus, involving much skipping across the beat and a casually 'lipped' upward glissando—involving lip pressure rather than the crude use of the slide—that was a Teagarden trade-mark.

Since this chapter concerns Jack Teagarden, it is not the place to dwell on Louis Armstrong's solo that ends the piece. But it is beyond my will-power to deny myself the opportunity of pointing to two of its main features. One is the dramatic element which Louis introduced into instrumental jazz and which Duke Ellington, with his great sense of 'theatre' was among the earliest to exploit. The opening of the trumpet solo in the low register, heightened by a temporary cessation of the drumming as Kaiser Marshall juggles with brushes and sticks, is one of the most gripping theatrical entrances in all of jazz, combining an overwhelming presence, a feeling of high expectation and a certain dark foreboding that transcends the customary emotional range of the blues. This would be so much huff and puff without the second element, which is Louis Armstrong's capacity to conceive a solo as one developing unit rather than a succession of 'choruses'. Jack Teagarden's two twelve-bar choruses complement each other splendidly, but each is a self-contained unit capable of standing alone if the other were removed. Armstrong's solo, on the other hand, is indivisible. The veiled menace of the first twelve bars in the low register demands some kind of resolution, the impassioned leap into the upper register for the second twelve bars would sound ludicrously abrupt and melodramatic without the emotional build-up. It is an astonishing *tour de force*.

Jack Teagarden was never to rival Louis Armstrong as a dramatic performer in the grand manner. I have already noted that much of his standing as a great jazz master rests on innumerable exquisite cameos—brief choruses of matchless form and eloquence dropped into the middle of big band or Dixieland performances. Slow ballads apart, it is rare to find a Teagarden record in which he takes the lion's share of the limelight. My second Teagarden masterpiece is a rare exception and I have chosen it for that reason without prejudice to all the other fine examples of his work. It is also another blues, giving us the opportunity to compare it directly with his youthful work on 'Knockin' a Jug'.

'Jack Hits the Road' was recorded in 1940 during a session under the leadership of Bud Freeman. It says something about the pervasive myth of 'Chicago-style' jazz that, of Bud Freeman's

Famous Chicagoans, only Freeman and Dave Tough were actually born in that city. The remainder of the principals came from areas as far flung as Boston, Missouri, Buffalo and Texas. Most of what is generally considered a classic session was devoted to the sort of loosely knit, free-swinging, all-pile-in-together music that matured in New York rather than Chicago and inherited its genes from such diverse sources as the Original Dixieland Jazz Band, King Oliver and Louis Armstrong, the New Orleans Rhythm Kings and a heavy injection of Bix Beiderbecke. Jack Teagarden, with his preference for fluent, upper-register playing as against the trombone's limited harmonic role in the formal New Orleans ensemble, was ideally suited to these faintly anarchic surroundings, and titles such as 'Muskrat Ramble', 'Prince of Wails' and 'Shimme Sha Wabble' contain superb trombone solos.

The blues piece earned its title from a lyric which Jack put together for the occasion. 'I started up to see Bud Freeman, but I lost my way—and I thought for a minute I was on the road for MCA' made oblique reference to his current troubles with his big band and the booking agency that handled it. Apart from a chorus each from Pee Wee Russell and Bud Freeman, the whole track is devoted to the Teagarden trombone and voice. Since the work and place in jazz of Freeman and Russell will be considered more fully in the third volume of this series, when I shall discuss both big bands and small groups, I shall confine my comments here to the three trombone choruses by Jack that are spread through the record.

There are two things which one notices at once, coming to this record after listening to 'Knockin' a Jug'. One is that after Dave Bowman's chunky piano introduction, Jack Teagarden makes a similarly imperious entrance, ascending for his take-off to the same upper B flat key note. It was his favourite opening gambit in the blues, and he always attacked it with gusto. The second remarkable thing is the complete disappearance of the rapid 'shake' which intensified his sustained notes in his early recordings. I have remarked earlier that this characteristic, which he shared with most of the black trombonists of the late Twenties, disappeared quite early from his playing when he seemed to settle for a more placid approach. In his best work, its departure was compensated for by an even greater fullness and control of tone, as exemplified in the wonderfully sustained singing quality of that first high B flat.

We hear in this later performance that Jack Teagarden's conception of the blues had changed very little over the years, in contrast to Louis Armstrong's, whose blues work from the mid-Thirties onwards underwent drastic simplification. Jack's blues choruses were from the start built on a spare, economical framework in which Bessie Smith's influence was always to the fore. Here, in the first chorus, we have the twelve bars divided into broad, sweeping four-bar phrases, with a characteristic intensification of fast, decorative flourishes around the ninth and tenth bars. It is always dangerous to make pronouncements about tone on the strength of recordings, but it always strikes me that on this session, and in this number in particular, his playing regained in full and with interest the warmth and generosity of tone which it had sometimes lacked in the intervening years.

On careful listening, one discovers that the rhythmic modernity and assurance which marked Teagarden's earliest work had blossomed even more fully by 1940. The evidence is in the way in which his solo is draped, so to speak, over the regular four beats in the bar without ever adhering closely to them for support. In 'Knockin' a Jug', the high B flat that virtually launches the opening chorus is played firmly on the first beat of the bar, and we find that in the subsequent phrases, despite frequent across-the-beat excursions, the important notes similarly land on the beat. In 'Jack Hits the Road', the short climb up to B flat reaches it ahead of the beat, giving notice of an independence which is sustained throughout the chorus. Indeed, if some electronic device existed to remove all accompaniment from the record, the result would sound like an out-of-tempo trombone cadenza. The fact that we don't notice the absence of a strict toe-tapping tempo is further evidence of total jazz mastery.

The second chorus is particularly intriguing. Whereas in 'Knockin' a Jug', Teagarden raised the intensity of the second chorus by the impassioned use of blue notes, here he does the opposite, deliberately 'unblueing' the normally flattened seventh note of the scale and playing three repeated phrases based on the arpeggio of a major seventh. Here again, the timing is not what it seems. Each time that seventh is reached, it falls further behind the beat, successively defusing the threat of rhythmic squareness inherent in the notes themselves. In bars five and six there is a prime example of Teagarden's natural instinct for 'elegant variation', an ascending one-bar phrase that is then rearranged rhythmically in the most blithe way. In bar eight the 'blue' flattened seventh receives due recompense for having been shunned earlier on, emerging with a roar to initiate a final four-bar section that is pure, down-home blues.

Of Jack Teagarden's blues singing, opinions have over the years ranged from eulogy—'the only white man who could sing the blues authentically'—to dismissal from the blues purists. My own view is that, as a *jazz* singer, he showed all the qualities of rhythmic assurance, warmth of sound and effortless swing that belonged to his trombone playing, and they were consistently apparent whether he was singing a ballad, a breezy Dixieland standard or one of his stock blues variations. These latter tended to be stereotyped ditties on the 'Mama, Mama, Mama, why do you treat me so?' lines and, as such, neither deserved nor expected to be rated as profound blues singing. But taken in the context of other excursions into the twelve-bar blues idiom by jazz singers —Louis Armstrong, Mildred Bailey, Wingie Manone, Henry Allen, Ella Fitzgerald and others—they come out near the top of the pile. The single chorus here has the added attraction of some probing and sensitive backing from Pee Wee Russell's clarinet.

And finally to the last chorus, which follows the solos by Russell and Bud Freeman. It may be that Louis Armstrong's dramatic entrance in the low register on 'Knockin' a Jug' had lodged in Jack Teagarden's subconscious, for he adopts a very similar ploy for his re-entry. A more obvious precedent is the famous chorus in the New Orleans Rhythm Kings recording of 'Tin Roof Blues' which, since George Brunies recorded it in the early Twenties, has taken its place alongside the Alphonse Picou clarinet chorus in 'High Society' and King Oliver's 'Dippermouth Blues' solo on muted cornet as an instrumental set-piece. But somehow Teagarden invests the first low B flat, approached from the depths by a gruff upward glissando, with a much darker sense of

foreboding, threatening, as did Armstrong's entry, more impassioned and explosive things to come. Compressed into a
single chorus, Teagarden's dénouement comes sooner. After four
bars of intensely sad soliloquy in the bottom register, he makes an
unheralded leap of two octaves to unleash, over bars five and six,
a great cry of anguish of such uncharacteristic volume that it
causes a perceptible tremor of distortion in the recording. What
follows is even more startling. Connoisseurs of Teagarden's work
over the years are familiar with the decorative flurries, full of
rapid turns and triplets and the cadenza-like, across-the-beat
phrasing with which it was punctuated. Here, the same outbreak
of complexity is used for more than decorative purposes. Something is needed to dispel the tension which the sudden impassioned
outcry in bar six has generated. Like a cascade of molten larva
after an eruption, the notes tumble across the ensuing three bars
in a complicated and yet logical pattern that rivals Louis Armstrong's famous introduction to 'West End Blues' for intuitive,
on-the-spot composition. To say that the long phrase is totally
independent from the regular four-to-the-bar pulse is to risk
underrating its musical skill. Any fool can close his ears to the
beat and take off on an out-of-tempo joy ride. The way in which
accomplished jazz performers can float above the beat, seldom if
ever actually alighting on it, and yet remain firmly and audibly in
touch with it, is one of the qualities in the term 'swing' that
defies verbal definition. Throughout, 'Jack Hits the Road' demonstrates the art at its highest, and never more so than in the
magnificent last chorus.

Art Tatum

COUNT BASIE ONCE TOLD, in an interview, of his first encounter with Art Tatum. He recalled (and I reconstruct the quotation from memory): 'We were playing in Toledo, Ohio, and everybody's talking about this young piano player they have there, how great he is. After a while this young fellow comes up and asks if he can play a number. I moved off the piano stool, but stood nearby so that I could move back real quick if necessary. Well, I'm still standing there . . .'

Count Basie is a notoriously modest man, but his dumbstruck reaction to the youthful Tatum's playing is shared by every other contemporary musician. Fats Waller, so legend asserts, once stopped playing when he saw Art Tatum walk into the premises, announcing to the audience, 'I play piano, but God is in the house tonight!' In an autobiographical section in Stanley Dance's book, *The World of Earl Hines*, that other great pianist is more explicit. 'Art . . . didn't know anything but playing the piano, and that's all he wanted to do. He lived with the piano, day and night. Every time he saw one, he was playing. I don't think he really knew how much he could play. He was certainly one of the greatest and most individual pianists I've ever heard in my life. He could do as much with his left hand as most people could do with their right. I never did try to have a jam session with him, because I knew exactly what this man could do. There are many who are sorry that they did!'

Many indeed! Like an iceberg, Art Tatum's professional career presented only a small fraction of itself to be chronicled in terms of engagements, tours and recording sessions. Born and raised in Toledo, he was working steadily in local clubs in 1926 when he was only sixteen years old. Three years later, he procured a contract with a local radio station which lasted two years and helped to establish a reputation already being spread by the word of mouth of such as Count Basie and other travelling musicians. In the early Thirties, he went to New York, having been recommended by the pianist Joe Turner as accompanist for the singer, Adelaide Hall. In 1933, he recorded the first of the piano solos which were to occupy by far the largest space in the catalogue of his work on record. From then on until his death in 1956, he worked mostly as a club pianist—in Chicago, on the West Coast and, briefly in 1938-9, in Britain and Europe. But it was to New York, whether it be on 52nd Street in the Thirties or at Clarke Munroe's Uptown House in the Forties, that Art Tatum belonged for most of his creative life. His highest peak of commercial success came in the World War II years when the Art Tatum Trio with guitarist, Tiny Grimes, and bassist, Slam Stewart, broadcast prolifically on programmes aimed at US Forces the world over. Altogether, his was a relatively unruffled musical career, although even he, forerunner as he was of many of the innovations that Modern Jazz was to bring in the late Forties, felt a cold draught from the obsession of critics, bookers and the jazz public with the rival claims of Revivalism and Bebop. The crowning achievement of his last years was a monumental series of recordings, as soloist and with such distinguished contemporaries as Ben Webster, Benny Carter and Roy Eldridge, made at the instigation of impresario Norman Granz. The project was finished in March 1955. In November of the following year, Art Tatum died.

The cause of his death was uraemia, a kidney disease. The reason why it should have carried him off at the early age of 46 leads us straight to that submerged area of Art Tatum's career to which I referred earlier. After-hours sessions, in which clubs sporting (and paying) no more than a trio could confidently expect to be inundated with star soloists in a gladiatorial frame of mind, are nowadays largely things of the past. It is not simply that musicians, or their union representatives, became wary of the opportunity for exploitation inherent in such profligate distribution of unpaid talent. As musicians have increasingly moved towards 'doing their own thing' in musical surroundings of their own idiosyncratic choosing, the common ground of popular songs, show tunes and blues on which the older players would stage their tests of improvisational skill has been deserted. The 'Lot Vacant' signs began to go up in the early Forties when the young 'modernists', either by accident or design, devised a new musical code that effectively kept the masters of a previous generation off the stand. Before that, in every city where social conditions offered round-the-clock entertainment, epic subterranean battles raged. Whether it was Willie the Lion Smith resisting the challenge of Fats Waller, Louis Armstrong fighting off Jabbo Smith or Louis Metcalf, or Coleman Hawkins battling his way out of an ambush laid by the fierce tenor men of Kansas City, no jazz hero however much he was revered, was immune from the gauntlet.

In this nocturnal jungle, Art Tatum was in his element. The picture we have of his progress through it, built as it necessarily is on hearsay that belongs to legend rather than verifiable history, is a fascinating one. The cornetist Rex Stewart recalled having heard him in Toledo in 1926 or '27 and being amazed that the young virtuoso was humble and insecure, expressing himself not yet ready to 'make it in the big city'. A few years later, with innumerable encounters such as that with Count Basie behind him, the attitude was different. He is alleged to have told bandleader, Don Redman, 'Tell them New York cats to look out. Here comes Tatum! And I mean every living "tub" with the exception of Fats Waller and Willie the Lion.'

Much of the background to Tatum's nocturnal career in New York comes from an interview which pianist, Billy Taylor, gave to jazz writer, Orin Keepnews, printed in the book *The Jazz Makers*. Taylor recalls that Art Tatum 'would usually sit around for quite a while before he'd feel ready to play'—a situation which satisfied club owners who had enticed in other pianists worth hearing and didn't wish to have them put to flight before time. So it might have been seven or eight in the morning before Tatum started. As his fame increased, his procedure became more and more lofty and Olympian. He would visit the clubs with a protégé in tow, like some medieval monarch with a trusted knight at his elbow. In Los Angeles in the mid-Forties, Billy Taylor fulfilled this lieutenant's role. Tatum would seek out the top man in the region. 'He'd know that fellow's best number,' recalls Taylor, 'and he'd ask me to play it, to sort of bait the guy. I wouldn't know what was going on, so I'd play it. Of course, if I (or any of Art's boys) were getting carved, he'd just step in and take over.'

In an appreciative sleeve-note to a posthumous album by the superb stride pianist, Don Lambert, Dick Wellstood allowed himself an anti-Lambert story which illustrates the magisterial attitude which Art Tatum acquired towards his challengers: 'One night, Lambert got all liquored-up in Jersey and headed for Harlem, looking to do battle with Tatum, who was generally acknowledged to be the king. He found Tatum and Marlowe Morris (considered second only to Tatum), sitting in the back room of some bar. Lambert flung himself at the piano, crying, "I've come for you, Tatum!" and things of that nature, and launched into some blistering stride. Tatum heard him out. When it was all over and Lambert stood up, defiant, Tatum said quietly, "Take him, Marlowe." '

There is a danger, in recounting anecdotes such as these, that the newcomer to jazz will receive the romantic notion that all jazz is created in the heady atmosphere of a tournament, a sort of world championship prize-fight set to music. The impresario, Norman Granz, who devised and presented the touring package show, *Jazz at the Philharmonic*, was once reported as summarizing his policy by saying that he provided the best possible working conditions for the great musicians who toured with him—'but when they get out on that stage, I want blood!' One has only to listen to the live recordings of his concerts to realize that some musicians thrive under such competitive, gladiatorial conditions and others do not. 'Cutting contests' have played an important role in jazz history, concentrating the minds and raising the ambitions of those whose role has been to extend the boundaries of instrumental technique. But as a means of judging a musician's creative worth, they are no substitute for considered critical assessment. In refusing to do battle with Art Tatum, Earl Hines was not admitting inferiority. He was simply declining to offer himself for judgement on those terms. One can reel off a list of fine jazz artists—Bix Beiderbecke, Johnny Dodds, Benny Carter, Jack Teagarden, Bobby Hackett, Johnny Hodges, Buck Clayton, Count Basie, Miles Davis—whose talents were not designed to prosper in the atmosphere of a jousting arena.

Having said this, one must go on to confess that 'considered critical appraisal' often did scant justice to Art Tatum during his lifetime. In the Thirties and again in the 'revivalist' Fifties, it was easy to find jazz *aficionados* who did not consider him to be a 'real' jazz performer, as witness the fact that in widely read and authoritative books on jazz by the Americans, Wilder Hobson and Winthrop Sargent, and British writers, Iain Laing and Rex Harris, his name does not even appear in the index. In the majority of commentaries by writers of wider knowledge and vision, you will find praise for his brilliance hedged with a thick outcrop of 'ifs' and 'buts'—for instance, the judgement by Whitney Balliett, jazz critic of the *New Yorker*, that 'if Tatum had played with more musicians of [Jo] Jones's strength, he might in time have pocketed some of his insuperable fireworks and got down to business.'

To understand the yawning gulf between the views of many critics and those of musicians of Art Tatum's generation and since, it is necessary to digress for a moment on the prickly subject of 'technique'. I say 'prickly' because the time is not so very distant when 'technique' was a dirty word in the terminology of jazz. We have to remember that the first generations of jazz writers consisted predominantly of enthusiasts who had little musical training, and indeed declared a bias against schooled or 'conservatoire' music. If many of their idols were self-taught musicians who defied the academic rules of music, then it seemed justifiable that they should be judged on the same terms. Thus we find that much critical writing of the Thirties, Forties and, so far as traditional jazz was concerned, Fifties was expressed in terms of abstractions such as 'feeling', 'sincerity', 'swing' and 'hotness' rather than in analysis of the actual notes or harmonies which were being played.

One must add to this the fact that much of that early criticism had strong sociological, if not political, undertones. In the pages of the now defunct British magazine *Jazz Music*, published in the late Forties, jazz was once lengthily discussed, by pundits on both sides of the Atlantic, as 'the music of the proletariat'. And, generally speaking, there was a tendency to think of jazz as the expression of an underprivileged and oppressed minority which was somehow betrayed by too great an assimilation of established and alien musical practice. In extreme instances, a patent inability to handle an instrument properly and produce the ideas which the player had in mind actually commended that musician to some listeners, who took it as a demonstration of 'sincerity'. In this climate, it is not surprising that Art Tatum, who appeared on the jazz scene with a piano technique unrivalled in all of jazz, was given a reserved reception. Musicians, on the other hand, to whom the acquisition of instrumental skill is of central importance, could have been expected to take a position at the other extreme, applauding a fellow-artist in much the same way that athletes will applaud a colleague who has far out-stripped them.

In reality, the question of technique and its application in jazz is far more complex than these two extreme positions suggest. One can best circumvent profound philosophical discussion on the role of primitivism and sophistication in art by calling in Duke Ellington, whose rare excursions into musicology were often wise and penetrating. An interviewer once asked him to comment on the discrepancy in technical prowess between two of his featured trumpeters. 'Let's be like the businessmen and talk in percentages,' said the Duke. 'Nobody plays a hundred per cent of the instrument. But some guys play ninety per cent of the instrument, and that's great. Another guy will play just ten per cent of the instrument—but on that ten per cent he'll be better than anyone else in the world.' Musicians as diverse as clarinettists Edmund Hall, Pee Wee Russell and Jimmy Guiffre, trumpeters Ray Nance, Max Kaminsky and Miles Davis, pianists Count Basie, Jess Stacy and Thelonious Monk—the reader can make up his own lists—have demonstrated that original, diverse, profound and, in some instances, highly influential jazz can be created with an instrumental technique that falls far short of virtuosity. But fit into these categories the names of Benny Goodman, Barney Bigard and Buddy de Franco, the early Louis Armstrong, Clark Terry and Dizzy Gillespie, Art Tatum, Bud Powell and Oscar

Peterson, and it becomes clear that the converse is also true. Each group has its own special pitfalls—inarticulacy, slow-footedness and poor execution in the first, garrulity, flashiness and dexterity for its own sake in the second—and both share the proneness to repetition, platitude and cliché which is the occupational hazard of every improvising jazzman.

Am I saying, then, that technique is an irrelevance, to be dismissed from our minds when judging the final product? If we are to apply strictly the refined principles of high art, I suppose the answer should be 'yes'. But in reality, for better or worse, jazz has shown itself, in the brief sixty-year span of its overt existence, to be the most human of all the arts. Despite the social elevation of jazz from the brothels and seedy nightspots to the concert platform and the recital room, jazz enthusiasts resolutely continue to refer to their idols in terms which, in matey familiarity, go far beyond the call of democracy and social equality. Europeans, brought up in a tradition which would regard the public reference to Fred Delius, Fats Handel or Hector 'Red' Berlioz as grotesque, have taken naturally and unselfconsciously to the native American habit of applying nicknames, abbreviations and descriptive tags to citizens great and small.

This is not the frivolous point which it may seem. Unlike so-called classical music, jazz is not the distillation of a composer's personality. Taking 'composer' to mean an improvising musician, jazz offers the raw spirit, impurities and all. A jazz fan need go to no biographical dictionary to learn that Ben Webster was emotional, Roy Eldridge aggressive, Pee Wee Russell shy. The personality is not only tightly woven into the music, it is essential to our response to it. It used to be said that Benny Goodman would visit Eddie Condon's club in the Forties especially to hear Pee Wee Russell extricating himself from the labyrinths into which his melodic explorations would sometimes accidentally lead him. By the same token, the listener who did not confess to relishing Art Tatum's technical magic for its own sake would be taking a more clinical attiude to the music than most.

To enjoy and admire Art Tatum as a jazz musician, it is essential not to be overawed by the elaborate genuflexions of critics and musicians alike in recent times. Fats Waller notwithstanding, Tatum was not God, neither was he Superman. As many commentators have remarked, his playing incorporated every facet of jazz piano style that preceded or was contemporary to him, and foreshadowed much that was yet to come. His essays into the boogie-woogie idiom (which he did not despise and eschew as did his idol, Fats Waller) were lightweight and superficial compared to such specialists in the idiom as Albert Ammons and Tatum's somewhat unlikely friend and sidekick, Meade Lux Lewis. His straightforward blues playing, though better than critics have acknowledged in the past, quite often subsided into luxuriant, feather-bedding harmonies that softened the firm and muscular outline of the best blues. And there were times when the thematic content of his solos almost vanished beneath the decorative runs and embellishments, like a Christmas tree groaning invisibly under an excess of tinsel and silver balls. To assert that any criticism of Tatum is *lèse - majesté* is to do injustice to the genuinely startling and astonishing flashes of inventive brilliance in which his work abounds.

The origins of Art Tatum's style—and, indeed, of his *modus vivendi*—lie in Harlem stride piano. 'Fats, man. That's where I come from,' was no casual affirmation of his. As we have seen, he eagerly assimilated the stride pianist's zest for battle, about which he must have heard from the New York musicians who passed through Toledo. He carried to extremes the stride men's propensity for flashy technical devices with which to floor an opponent. The existence in his repertoire of such clear favourites as Dvořák's *Humoresque* and Massenet's *Elegie* carried on the Harlem pianists' tradition of giving stride treatment to chosen items from the classical repertoire. And, although he greatly extended its scope, he based his left-hand work on the 'oom-chah' alternation of bass note and middle register chord cluster from which, according to the most plausible definition, the term 'stride piano' derived. Predictably, as a young modern, he moved away from the ragtime affiliations of the style, preferring to work predominantly on material taken from contemporary Tin Pan Alley. But among his relatively few compositions, there are some which suggest that he could well have contributed as rich a collection of original rags as James P. Johnson and Willie the

Lion Smith, had he been so inclined. There's one piece in particular, with the appropriately raggy title 'Gang o' Notes', that is a dazzling up-dating of the idiom. Recorded as late as 1944, it has all the elements of the old Harlem piano test-pieces—several developing themes, plenty of 'fingerbusting' virtuoso passages and constant variation on the left-hand figures. One cannot help thinking that the corporate body of contemporary pianists must have heaved a sigh of relief that 'Gang o' Notes' did not establish itself as an obligatory test-piece, in the way that James P. Johnson's 'Carolina Shout' did two decades earlier!

There were several elements in Art Tatum's style which derived specifically from Fats Waller rather than from the stride pianists in general. As I observed in the essay on Fats, he himself extended and, in some degree, moved away from standard stride practice. Compare Fats's famous solo blues 'Numb Fumblin'' with the early version of 'St Louis Blues' which Tatum recorded in 1933, and it is not hard to recognize the inspiration for the Tatum habit of clothing a simple melodic or harmonic line in a rippling, billowing mantle of cascading notes. From Fats, too, came the use of 'moving tenths' in the left hand as a variation from the 'oom chah' bass patterns of stride. This device of playing simultaneous notes a tenth apart with little finger and thumb of the left hand, and moving them smoothly upwards or downwards depending on the direction of the harmony, would have appealed to Art Tatum with his advanced harmonic sense. Since only two notes of the chord are specified, there are opportunities for the player to fill out the moving tenths with all sorts of enriching harmonies. Art Tatum took full advantage of them, sometimes modulating out of the original key and back again within the space of a single two-bar movement.

Before looking at specific Art Tatum performances, we should give some attention to the ways in which he digressed from accepted stride practice, and they were innumerable. As I have noted, his playing incorporated, in every phase of his career, all the contemporary piano styles. When he first emerged on record in 1933, the two predominant keyboard models were those of Fats Waller and Earl Hines. There are two characteristics of the latter which can be readily discerned in Tatum. One is the dis-

tinctive 'trumpet style'—the use of octaves in the right hand to
produce a single declamatory melodic line in the manner of a
trumpet player. In his later years Tatum was to develop this in a
characteristic way, often interpolating a short octave passage in a
run of notes at breakneck speed, with startling dynamic effect.
The other Hines characteristic was more extensively used by
Tatum, and has been the cause over the years of much of the
adverse criticism of his style. It is the practice of suspending the
stated rhythm of a piece for several bars, during which a complex
elaboration is played over an implied beat which often does not
declare itself until the regular left-hand rhythm is resumed. Thus,
in their varying ways, Hines and Tatum often seemed to be
challenging themselves to depart ever further and further from the
regular pulse without, on their return to earth, having missed so
much as a fraction of a beat. Response to Art Tatum's regular use
of this device depends largely upon the listener's demands. To
those—and I am not unsympathetic to them—who relish the
exhilarating, roller-coaster momentum of an up-tempo Fats
Waller solo, for example, the constant interruptions in a comparable Tatum piece will sometimes prove frustrating, especially
as Tatum in full, two-handed career was irresistible. Against this,
of course, it can be said that the Tatum pyrotechnics offer their
own exhilaration.

As one would expect from an artist acclaimed as an original,
there are elements in Art Tatum's style which are entirely his
own, offering the analyst no very clear precedent. Most of them
spring from his astonishing keyboard technique, which enabled
him to perform, with apparent ease, feats of dexterity which, were
they to occur to other pianists, would be rejected as an invitation
to disaster, if not suicide. The ability to career at breakneck speed
over the keys led him away from the normal practice of the stride
pianists, which was to break a tune up into strong rhythmic
patterns, pounding out percussive phrases by the fistful. There
were times when he used this conventional stride method, but his
more usual practice was to weave a complex, decorative tapestry
around the theme, which itself was no more than a central thread,
sometimes predominant, sometimes disappearing from view, and
occasionally popping up unexpectedly in the low, left-hand

register or in the middle of a great spray of right-hand embellishment. Slow ballads were no deterrent to this practice. The device
known as 'double time'—superimposing eight beats at medium
tempo over four beats to the bar at slow tempo—had previously
occurred somewhat formally in the music of Jelly Roll Morton
and more loosely, in the improvising of Louis Armstrong and his
disciples. But its use was usually restricted to bravura passages or
'breaks'. With Art Tatum, it was far more central to his improvising
technique. Such was his facility that, in all but the fastest tempos
he could as easily *quadruple* the time—that is, rattle off a fusillade
of sixteenth-notes or semiquavers so that, in effect, he was
fitting four bars at high speed into one bar of the regular tempo.

As well as digital dexterity, this sort of playing called for an
advanced and sophisticated command of harmony. The extra
notes crowded into service must have somewhere to go, and this
meant adding to the basic chords all manner of harmonic detours
and diversions.

Art Tatum's ingenuity in this respect was limitless. The use of
passages based on the whole-tone scale and extended chromatic
harmonies were not unknown to the jazz of the early Thirties.
Bix Beiderbecke's piano solo 'In a Mist', recorded in 1927,
epitomized the fascination which the 'impressionist' European
composers such as Debussy and Ravel held for the young musicians
of his generation and circle. Notwithstanding the protests of the
advocates of New Orleans-style contrapuntal improvisation, the
arrival on the jazz scene of the arranger from the mid-Twenties
onwards made the exploration of so-called 'European' harmonies
inevitable, and the orchestrations of the bands of Paul Whiteman,
Frankie Trumbauer and, ultimately, Fletcher Henderson and
McKinney's Cotton Pickers, were rife with them. What distinguished Art Tatum from other musicians who toyed with these
(for jazz) advanced harmonic notions, was the easy and unselfconscious way in which he incorporated them into his solo
improvisations. Rex Stewart propounds the theory that it was
hearing Art Tatum in Toledo in the late Twenties that inspired
Coleman Hawkins to move away from his Louis Armstrong-
inspired, stomping saxophone style towards the more fluent
method of 'running changes' (pursuing a continuous flow of

changing chords) which I discuss more fully in another chapter. Whether it actually happened in such a sudden, revelatory way or more gradually over the years, it seems more than probable that, in the challenging and competitive atmosphere of the early Thirties, Tatum's formidable combination of harmonic sophistication and speed of execution exerted an influence beyond the boundaries of piano playing.

I have in these essays reiterated to the point of tedium that selecting individual masterpieces is a difficult and invidious task. With Art Tatum, it is manifestly absurd. Art Tatum *was* a masterpiece, compounded of several hundred consistently fine, frequently superlative performances. Many of these were recorded in the later years of his life and are readily available in LP collections for the reader to study and enjoy. I am concerned here, as I have been with the other artists under discussion, with his early impact on the jazz scene of the Thirties, and both my selected subjects come from that period.

'Tiger Rag' was one of four solos recorded on Tatum's very first recording session in March 1933. A listener taking in these pieces for the first time will be struck by their enormous variety. 'Tea for Two' has, for Art Tatum, a curiously dated air, presenting such an anthology of Fats Waller mannerisms—heavy broken tenths in the left hand, skittish punctuations in the treble and characteristic stride figures in the upper register for climactic effect. 'St Louis Blues' is approached altogether more gently, padding along on a lush carpet of moving tenths in the left hand and lavishly decorated, as I have noted earlier, with fulsome cascades of notes. As the title might suggest, Duke Ellington's 'Sophisticated Lady' prompts the most 'modern' interpretation of the four in terms of both harmonic and rhythmic adventurousness.

'Tiger Rag' clearly appealed to Art Tatum as a vehicle for a breathtaking and all-conquering display of fireworks. There is plenty of evidence in his version that he took his cue in this respect from Louis Armstrong, who had already recorded two interpretations of the tune in which tempo and arrangement were designed to support an awe-inspiring exhibition of trumpet bravura. Art Tatum offers first a slyly humorous introduction, its out-of-tempo, impressionist langour giving no hint of the fronta

Louis Armstrong (his manager Joe Glaser is on the left)

Fats Waller at the organ

Billie Holiday

Lester Young

Roy Eldridge

Coleman Hawkins, with singer Thelma Carpenter

Jack Teagarden

Art Tatum

Johnny Dodds.

Jimmy Noone.

Earl Hines.

LUIS RUSSELL'S ORCHESTRA, *early Thirties. Henry Allen, third trumpet from the left, Albert Nicholas, third saxophone from the right, George 'Pops' Foster, bass, Paul Barbarin, drums.*

assault on the senses that is to come. Then suddenly we are off into the opening theme. In the earliest versions by the Original Dixieland Jazz Band, one of which was dissected in *The Best Of Jazz* Volume One, much use was made of 'breaks' in which the clarinettist, Larry Shields, filled in with the sort of virtuoso phrases which the musical press used to call 'hot licks'. When Louis Armstrong adopted the tune, the clarinet breaks were developed into a running clarinet counter-melody over band riffs —a sort of supercharged version of the clarinet's decorative role in the New Orleans ensemble. Art Tatum, setting an even more headlong tempo than Louis, focuses his version on this clarinet part, firing off a succession of eighth-note runs that hurtle over the keyboard with barely a pause for breath. The interlude in the key of F which relieves the opening B flat theme highlights Tatum's two-handed facility. While the right hand continues to scurry hither and thither, the left hand assumes the staccato melody, both hands maintaining such steady momentum that one doesn't notice that the stated four-in-a-bar rhythm has been suspended. The second main theme, in E flat, begins as in the original, with more slashing breaks, and then settles into some romping stride that develops towards the end of the section into declamatory trumpet-style octave phrases.

We have not yet reached the main, trio section of the tune, and already almost all the resources of contemporary jazz piano have been drawn upon and demonstrated with masterly ease. What happens next shows that Art Tatum's much suspected technical virtuosity was no mere luxury to be turned on or switched off at will, but essential to his keen sense of construction. Where other pianists would have taken the arrival of the principal A flat theme as the cue to go stomping off down the final straight, Tatum 'holds that tiger' in a state of suspense. In demonstrating how he played the tune long before the Original Dixieland Band got hold of it, Jelly Roll Morton played a crashing bass discord with his elbow at those explosive points in the tune later assumed by the trombone, going so far as to say that the tune acquired its title when a listener remarked, 'Why, that sounds just like a tiger roaring.' Art Tatum eschewed such crude methods, replacing the tiger's roar with a sustained growl, a rumbling bass tremolo over which the right hand stabs out the riffs of the original. Since these riffs are phrased across the beat and the bass continuo has no noticeable pulse, the listener is left, for most of the chorus, in a state of anticipation. Bigger and better fireworks are to come, we feel, but only in his own good time. The tantalizing effect of this chorus is heightened by a glorious stroke of wit. Coming to the last eight bars of the chorus—that familiar sequence which Fats Waller used, in several of his compositions, as a pretext for a joyous, untrammelled romp—Art Tatum holds out on us once again, replacing the familiar chord sequence with dreamy, impressionist, whole-tone harmonies which echo that incongruous introduction. Were it not that their adverse comments were made retrospectively some years later, one might well think that Art Tatum was deliberately thumbing his nose at those critics who poured such scorn on technique and 'alien' European harmonies.

From this point on, the solo roars off in top gear into three choruses which 'build' in the manner, if not the established style, of the classic stride piano solo. The first consists of a stream of eighth-note runs similar to the opening passages but with greater flow and continuity. For the break, Tatum plays an escalating figure that overflows into the second half of the chorus, continuing upwards almost to the limit of the keyboard and then, with a hop and a skip, turning to descend again, like Fred Astaire dancing on a staircase. Technically, the passage is dazzling, the ascending figures being played in thirds so that, if one did not hear the left hand discreetly marking time throughout, one might justifiably assume that both hands were involved in them. The chorus ends in a riotous tumble of notes that congeal into a thunderous, shuddering chord, anticipating the style of the following thirty-two bars.

As these start, the emphasis is on rhythmic, jabbing chords in the right hand punctuating a series of moving bass figures suggestive of boogie woogie. Here one is strongly reminded of Louis Armstrong's treatment of the tune, in which he would blow repetitive high-note phrases over the bustling rhythm. Once again the break prompts a return to a more pianistic approach, and, behind a few tumultuous bars of stride piano, the shades of Fats Waller and Earl Hines can be discerned, smiling appreciatively but nervously. The trumpet-style ride-out to this chorus is pure Armstrong, and seems to signal the end of the piece. But the climax has yet to come. In the traditional firework display, after the rockets and catherine wheels and squibs have soared, whirled and crackled, it is the massed waterfalls of gold and silver rain which signal the finale and draw the biggest 'ooohs' and 'aaahs' from the audience. And so it is with Art Tatum's 'Tiger Rag'. The notes that cascade down no longer come singly or in thirds but by the splashing fistfuls over a pumping left-hand rhythm. If one remarks that the repetitive nature of the first and third beat chords of this stride bass (involving a sixth note that rings out rather monotonously), reveals in this early Tatum a rare glimpse of immaturity, one might seem to demand a technical miracle. Suffice it to say that the Tatum of later years did indeed bring variety to the traditional stride left hand in a miraculous way. When, with the return of the Louis-esque ride-out figures, the performance gallops to a close, the recording seems to lack only one thing—an incredulous voice saying, 'Phew!!!'

Devotees of Art Tatum who come to these first solo recordings late in the day, having been familiar with his later work, will be struck by the brilliance, even harshness, of the piano sound. No doubt some of this can be attributed to studio acoustics and the fact that accurate tuning does not appear to have been high among record companies' priorities in those days. But it is also clear that, as he developed away from the initial Fats Waller influence, Art Tatum cultivated a touch which became progressively lighter and more muted—so much so that even his last recordings, made in the hi-fi era of the mid-Fifties, sound today strangely distant and tonally subdued.

This change is noticeable when we come to my second Tatum selection, a remake of 'Tea for Two' recorded in April 1939. Already the sound is less brash, the texture more silky. Gone is the suggestion, discernible in the first recordings, of a shy and reflective youngster of relatively slight build trying to play in the manner of a rip-roaring twenty-stone extrovert. The most valuable legacy of Fats Waller remains intact—the ability to swing with an express train momentum. But of the mannerisms, no trace remains. Along with this lighter touch has come a more considered organization of material, the result no doubt of six years' work, mainly as a soloist, in clubs of a more intimate and sophisticated atmosphere than those in which the earlier stride pianists flourished.

Comparison between the 1933 and 1939 versions of 'Tea for Two' illuminate the change dramatically. The early version has a jaunty, Wallerish introduction in tempo, leading straight into three choruses of stride piano with relatively few innovations and refinements other than the wealth of decorative runs and bursts of double tempo in the right hand. The strongest hint of things to come occurs in the twentieth bar of each chorus, when Tatum employs a trick which he was to develop markedly in the later version. This is a brief shift of key, an episode no more than a bar in length in which the melody momentarily sidesteps into an adjacent key, rather as if the piano keyboard had been moved an inch or two to the right by a mechanical device. In the otherwise conventional harmonic surroundings of the early version, this movement is quite unexpected, characteristic of many such stimulating surprises which Art Tatum was to perpetrate upon his listeners before his career was over.

If we now concentrate on the second recording of the tune, we find it furnished with an out-of-tempo introduction and opening chorus, a familiar format nowadays when jazz in a concert hall or recital room ambience is commonplace, but unusual enough in the late Thirties to bring upon Art Tatum's head a further critical accusation, that he was no more than a superior cocktail pianist. The charge, still voiced occasionally today, seems to me to ignore the *quality* of the music in favour of its manner. It can only be refuted by pointing to the spare and muscular frame that lies beneath the decorative surface of Tatum's playing. Even in superior cocktail piano one would expect to hear the lush over-statement, indulgently perfumed harmonies and romantic *kitsch* of 'mood music'. What Tatum builds on the melodically unpromis-ing see-saw movement of the Vincent Youmans song is a sober and firmly-constructed piece of composition in which no concess-ion is made to the flippant sentimentality of the original. The repetitive melody line, a challenge to improvisation if ever I heard one, is tossed between right and left hand, between middle and upper register, with the utmost deftness. On the sparing occasion when extended or substitute chords are used—for example, in bar twelve of the opening chorus—they offer an astringent and bracing dissonance rather than extravagant seduction of the ear. And, as if to impose and sustain a sense of discipline and gravity upon the proceedings, Art Tatum ends each out-of-tempo section —introduction, opening chorus and coda—with the same austere, almost sombre middle-register cadence.

Had the performance consisted simply of that one introduction and chorus, played out of tempo, we would look upon it today as a little gem which raised the song 'Tea for Two' far above its modest station in life. But in Tatum's scheme of things it has a purpose beyond its own excellence. That purpose is to establish a calm and reflective mood from which to launch a couple of choruses which, to use a vulgar phrase for which I can find no expressive alternative, swing like the clappers. It is a device which Erroll Garner was later to borrow and extend with exhilarating effect, and it can only be brought off effectively by a jazz pianist with that total command of time that swing demands. The style of these gloriously propulsive choruses is stride piano, decorated without any loss of momentum with the familiar cascading runs over suspended rhythms. To substantiate my claim that Art Tatum's technical prowess could in itself stir the emotions and uplift the spirit, there is a 'break' spanning bars seven and eight of the first chorus which must surely draw spontaneous applause from any listener who is not crabbed by suspicion of 'technique'. Half-way through an escalating series of eighth-note triplets upon which most improvising pianists would need to lavish their un-divided attention, Tatum nonchalantly picks up the rhythm in the left hand with walking tenths that move in the opposite direction.

The 'break' in the middle of the chorus introduces another aspect of Art Tatum's playing which has attracted adverse criticism. Quoting brief excerpts from the classics or from popular song was not a device (some would say 'vice') originated by Art Tatum, nor did it end with him. In discussing Louis Armstrong's 'Sweethearts on Parade', I pointed to a quotation from 'High Society' which Louis had previously used, in a similar context, in his recording of 'Squeeze Me'. The very same quotation (from the first two bars of Alphonse Picou's traditional clarinet variation) occurs more than once in the solos of Charlie Parker. The new-comer to jazz who is encouraged by my earlier references to Louis Armstrong's version of 'Tiger Rag' to explore that recording will find at least three obvious quotes from sources as varied as 'The Rising of the Lark', the 'National Emblem March' and *Pagliacci*. The latter is used in a manner no less dramatic than in the original, establishing the point that not all such quotations are for humorous effect. One can best justify them by pointing to the conversational aspect of jazz improvisation and drawing a parallel with the often enlivening use of phrases from Shakespeare, Wordsworth, Damon Runyan or Groucho Marx in casual talk. If overdone or inapposite, they are a bore and, I am bound to say, *apropos* Art Tatum's injection here (and elsewhere) of 'The Campbells are coming, hurrah, hurrah', that I would have preferred it if the Campbells had remained where they were.

But the episode is over in a flash and one need not make too much of it either way. Before the chorus is ended there is a further ecstatic 'break' to put censoriousness to flight, occurring in bars twenty-five to twenty-eight. The guitarist, Everett Barksdale, was once reported as saying, 'Art Tatum is absolutely infallible— with a man like that there is no such thing as a mistake.' Those who, like myself, prefer their jazz geniuses to acknowledge some symptoms of human fallibility, will prefer Billy Taylor's recollec-tion that Tatum encouraged him to make deliberate mistakes 'to see how quickly you can recover'. When, in bars twenty-five and -six, Art Tatum plays a left-hand run of ascending triplets, the passage differs from the right-hand runs that precede and follow it in that it is not continuous. There is a hole in the middle of it, suggesting that his fingers may have baulked at the preposterous demands made upon them at a moment's notice. If so, his powers of recovery proved equal to the occasion. Without a fraction of a beat's hesitation the triplets are resumed in bar twenty-six. They are still trumbling up to their conclusion when, out of the sky, a silvery cascade of treble notes come down to meet them. It is a dour listener indeed who does not feel the urge to throw his hat in the air at such a display.

The chorus that follows, the last in the piece, is justly famous among connoisseurs of jazz piano. Just as the deceptively placid opening section of the piece may be said to enlarge upon the sly, impressionistic introduction to 'Tiger Rag', so the device with which Art Tatum brings his performance to a climax may be called the apotheosis of the transitory shift of key to which I drew attention in the 1933 version of 'Tea for Two'. Jazz purists, past masters in the art of having it both ways, have complained that to modulate from a parent key to one a minor third away, only to return by semitone steps to the parent key, is no more than an empty piece of technical sleight of hand. These are the same people who allege that Art Tatum strayed from the true path of jazz towards 'cocktail', 'salon' or even 'concert hall' piano, turning a deaf ear to the fact that this bit of keyboard 'business', pursued in romping two-fisted style without any drop in swing or momentum, is the very stuff of the stride piano tradition. Years later, when the younger pianist, Bud Powell, came to record the 'Tea for Two', he borrowed this device of Tatum's in the same way that Fats Waller inherited tricks of the trade from James P. Johnson. No words on paper can describe the fluent ease with which Tatum negotiates the manoeuvre, carrying the melody with the left hand while at the same time continuing the 'oom-chah' rhythm of stride against bouncing counter-rhythms from the right hand. The change from the naïve, monotonous and sub-servient left hand heard in the climatic chorus of 'Tiger Rag' is miraculous.

Art Tatum is consistently cited in the summaries of jazz history as one of the forerunners of the modern jazz of the mid-Forties. In this respect, there is a startling piece of clairvoyance in the second eight-bar section of 'Tea for Twos'' final chorus. In contrast to the scintillating runs that have characterized most departures from the melody hitherto, Tatum fills bars eleven to sixteen with abrupt, angular and rhythmically diverse, single-note phrases that belong stylistically to the 'bebop era' that was still six or seven years away. In the context of this superb final chorus, which with one vast stretch of the fingers links the eras of James P. Johnson and Charlie Parker, the term 'stride piano' acquires a new meaning.

Johnny Hodges and Benny Carter

IN VOLUME ONE OF *The Best of Jazz*, I compressed discussion of
the two New Orleans clarinettists, Johnny Dodds and Jimmy
Noone, into a single chapter. My reasons were several. Neither
musician had a well-documented background history nor a career
that went through a succession of developing phases. Neither was
the sort of 'character' around whom anecdotes cluster. But between them, they dominated jazz clarinet for roughly a decade,
offering contrasting models—a heavy, mordant blues style from
Dodds, a lighter, decorative style from Noone—from which subsequent clarinettists could, and did, draw at will.

   To a large extent, the same reasons prompt the conjuncture of
Johnny Hodges and Benny Carter in one essay. There will be
some who will bridle at the exclusion of altoist Willie Smith
from my reckoning. It is customary in summaries of jazz history
to speak of a 'triumvirate' of Hodges, Carter and Smith having
dominated jazz alto style throughout the Thirties. But Willie
Smith was a comparative latecomer on the scene, making his
mark with recordings by the Jimmy Lunceford Orchestra which
began to emerge in 1934—by which time both Hodges and Carter
had influenced a whole generation. The same considerations apply
to the iconoclastic Pete Brown whose 'jump' style, influencing the
rhythm 'n' blues music of later times, will be discussed in Volume
Three.

   In the reminiscences of Harlem musicians, Johnny Hodges
makes an appearance around the middle Twenties. Duke Ellington
sets the scene in *Hear me Talkin' to Ya*: 'Small's [Small's Cabaret

Club, later the Paradise] was the place to go, the one spot where
everybody'd drop in. And a lot of musicians from downtown, too.
Jack Teagarden used to bring along his horn, and Benny and
Harry Goodman, Ray Bauduc and a gang of others. Then on
Sundays, Small used to hire a guest band, the best he could get,
and there'd be a regular jamboree . . . all kinds of musicians
worked that job, Johnny Hodges, and guys from Chick Webb's
band and a lot of others. There was always plenty of whisky around
those places and the music would jump and everything else
besides.'

The bandleader and saxophonist, Cecil Scott, remembered
another meeting-place for musicians, the Capitol Palace, a more
relaxed rival to the famous Cotton Club. 'When the other clubs
closed, one by one their band members and patrons would drift
into our spot, and musicians from such places as the Cotton Club,
Club Alabam, Roseland, Paradise Inn, used to vie for the chance
to sit in with us. We usually had a waiting line holding their horns
against one far wall waiting turns. Fellows like Johnny Hodges,
members of Fletcher Henderson's gang, Fats Waller, Earl Hines
and fellows from Charlie Johnson's band, Luis Russell's band—
all these and many others . . . often we would pile out of the club
about dawn, shouting and too excited to go to bed. There was an
iron fence which divided Lenox Avenue at 135th Street and we
would line up along it; it became the regular musicians' hang-out.
We would cluster as thick as thieves discussing music and gossiping
about fellow-players until maybe noon. Then home for an afternoon's sleep and that evening we'd begin the same routine.'

It is significant that these and other reminiscences of the period
in Harlem around 1926–7 should single out the twenty-year-old
Johnny Hodges for special mention. Clearly he had even at that
early stage a quality which made him particularly memorable
among the finest musicians in town, amongst whom were almost
certainly the young Benny Carter and probably Coleman Hawkins,
too. That quality is unlikely to have embraced technical pyrotechnics. In his autobiography, *Music is my Mistress*, Duke
Ellington included an appreciation of Hodges in which he wrote,
'His sultry solos were not done in an attempt to blow more notes
than anyone else. He just wanted to play them in true character,

reaching into his soul for them, and automatically reaching everybody else's soul. An audience's reaction to his first note was as big
and deep as most applause for musicians at the end of their
complete performance.' These words are applicable to the very
first recordings which Johnny Hodges made, from whose gritty
grooves a powerful musical 'presence' emerges.

For a clue to the origins of his charismatic style, to which Duke
Ellington retrospectively applied the fashionable term 'soul', we
have available the saxophonist's own reminiscences in the book,
The World of Duke Ellington, compiled by Stanley Dance. These
go back beyond those of his contemporaries, to his first meeting
with Sidney Bechet. As with most musicians' recollections, there
is a certain conjectural quality about the date. Hodges recalls that
he was thirteen when, through his sister, he was introduced to
Bechet, who was in Boston playing in Jimmy Cooper's *Black and
White Show*. But John Chilton's indispensable *Who's Who in
Jazz* puts Bechet's stint with Cooper around 1923–4, when
Hodges was seventeen or eighteen. The relevant part of the story
is that Johnny Hodges met Bechet when he was a young musician
in Boston and was given encouragement by him. In 1924, he
travelled to New York to play with Bechet in a place variously
known as the Club Bechet or Basha. (The second variation, with
the final 'a' long as in 'day', is how many musicians, including
Johnny Hodges, would pronounce Bechet's name.) 'He had a
second soprano, a straight one, which he gave to me, and he would
teach me different things in the duet form. Then I learned all the
introductions and solos, and if he was late I would take over until
he got there.'

In citing the origins of his own style, Johnny Hodges said, 'I
had taken a liking to his [Sidney Bechet's] playing, and to Louis
Armstrong's, which I heard on the Clarence Williams Blue Five
records, and I just put both of them together, and used a little of
whatever I thought of new.' The fact that the Blue Five records
were issued during 1925 gives some idea of the period over which
the Hodges style was taking shape. During that time, his working
visits to New York were sporadic, and he constantly returned home
to Boston, where he clearly made his own influence felt. In the
final years of the Twenties, a procession of fine alto saxophonists

followed Johnny Hodges from Boston into New York—Charlie Holmes, Howard Johnson, Harry Carney (before he turned to the baritone sax)—and all of them played in the Hodges style. In the Stanley Dance book, Harry Carney recalls the period when he first took up the alto. 'Now I felt the influence of Sidney Bechet and Johnny Hodges. Johnny and I used to live a few doors apart and we'd listen to all the records together . . . Charlie [Holmes] used to sound like Johnny, because that was the accepted alto style in those days and everyone was trying to borrow ideas from Johnny and get his sound.'

Everyone in Boston, that is. In New York, there was another strong influence operating from the mid-Twenties onwards, tending to draw musicians away from the passionate, 'hot', blues-saturated music which Bechet and Armstrong purveyed towards a more reflective, carefully-structured approach. This was the influence of the white musicians, most of them working in such highly respected and commercially successful bands as those of Paul Whiteman, Jean Goldkette, Frank Trumbauer, Red Nichols and Miff Mole. Evidence is all around us of the part which these men played in the formative years of jazz. We shall soon see that the alternative which Benny Carter was to provide to the Hodges style was based on an admiration for Frankie Trumbauer, to whom Lester Young also gave acknowledgement. Though we may find it hard to believe, we must accept the word of Roy Eldridge that one of his earliest idols was Red Nichols. Several musicians who were sooner or later to join Johnny Hodges in the Duke Ellington band made no secret of their indebtedness to the white New Yorkers—trombonist Lawrence Brown to Miff Mole, Harry Carney to the bass saxist, Adrian Rollini, Rex Stewart to Bix Beiderbecke.

In no reminiscence that I have been able to find did Johnny Hodges make any reference to such players as Jimmy Dorsey or Frankie Trumbauer, to whom his fellow-saxophonists were listening with such respect. In a first draft of this chapter, I made the bold assumption that the Bechet influence, so richly endowed with passion and blues feeling, was strong enough to immunize his young protégé against seduction from that quarter. But after listening to all the very early recordings which Hodges made with

Duke Ellington, I have to modify it. It would indeed be surprising, in view of the general impact which the white players had on the New York scene, if the young Bostonian, so eager to take in everything that New York had to offer, had remained totally untouched by what was a prevailing fashion. There are hints, in the 1928–9 solos, of the doodling runs and self-consciously modish and angular phrasing that characterized the work of both Dorsey and Trumbauer. But hints they remained. In the one recording—a piece by Ellington called 'The Dicty Glide'—in which he does play in a strangely stilted, on-the-beat manner strongly reminiscent of Trumbauer, he is harnessed closely to the Duke's melody, the title of which ('dicty' was the equivalent of 'posh' or 'toffee-nosed' in Harlem slang) suggests that the composer was drawing upon musical high fashion.

On the whole, I believe that my first assumption was right. With the possible exception of the shallow upward glissando which was to become such a feature of his romantic playing in later years, the jazz style of Johnny Hodges shed all traces of white influence as it developed into maturity. By the time the Thirties dawned, the Bechet influence had completely reasserted itself, its sandpapery edge and sweeping turbulence smoothed and modified to reflect the young man's more equable temperament. Duke Ellington was an unqualified admirer of Bechet, and had employed him in one of the early manifestations of the Ellington band before Bechet's maverick instincts took him off on his lone trek across Europe. When Johnny Hodges eventually gravitated into the Ellington band, after a short engagement with Chick Webb's band, there was a certain inevitability about the move. I drew attention in Volume One to the links that Ellington's early music had with New Orleans jazz—to the origins of Bubber Miley's 'jungle' growling in the style of King Oliver, and to the close resemblance of pieces such as 'Creole Love Call' and 'Black and Tan Fantasy' to certain themes that Oliver used. When the New Orleans clarinettist, Barney Bigard, joined the band in late 1927, followed within a few months by Johnny Hodges with his Bechet sound, the New Orleans connection was immeasurably strengthened. Bigard was to leave after fifteen years, but Hodges remained, except for a brief four-year 'sabbatical' with a small group of his own in the early Fifties, until the day he died, from a sudden heart attack, in May 1970.

Few musicians in jazz history have led such a settled life, and those that come to mind were mostly Ellingtonians. The sturdy, unruffled temperament that made it possible reflects itself in the music of Johnny Hodges. From the time that his style became fully matured in the mid-Thirties to the day that he died several jazz revolutions later, he saw no reason to change it. He was one of the few musicians from the Swing Era who remained totally impervious to the revolutionary changes wrought by the beboppers in the mid-Forties. Indeed, though vulgarity was no part of his musical make-up, the only external influence to impinge upon his music appears to have been the rhythm'n'blues epidemic in the early Fifties that gave rise to rock'n'roll. With his own small group, his intense but highly controlled and economical blues playing was often harnessed to a fashionable shuffle-rhythm with much rugged riffing and belabouring of the off-beat.

It was in his refusal to soften or decorate the stern simplicity of the blues that Johnny Hodges revealed most consistently the influence of Sidney Bechet. Harry Carney's reference to the 'sound' which other altoists tried to emulate draws attention to an aspect of jazz playing which is sometimes overlooked or at least downgraded in all the discussion about melodic, harmonic and rhythmic development. In his obituary remarks about Johnny Hodges, Duke Ellington wrote: 'Never the world's most animated showman or greatest stage personality, but a tone so beautiful it sometimes brought tears to the eyes—this was Johnny Hodges.'

The notion popular among the *avant-garde* in all branches of music that, to paraphrase Marshall McLuhan, 'the sound is the message' (rather than its organization into melodic lines or harmonic or rhythmic patterns), is not totally original, although they characteristically take it to extremes. In the immediate post-World War II days, when 'modernists' and 'traditionalists' in jazz were at each other's throats, Dizzy Gillespie was once subjected to a so-called 'blindfold test' in which, among others, a recording of a blues by Sidney Bechet was played to him. He identified Bechet, but showed no interest in the performance, simply asserting 'Nothing happens'. Writing about this some time later, I made the point that Dizzy's lack of enthusiasm was understandable. As a musician, he was preoccupied with a whole range of experiments and innovations in the context of which the Bechet solo was, indeed, quite devoid of incident. To the listeners, however, who rated the Bechet performance among the jazz classics, a subjective response to the *sound* of the music was more relevant than the nuts and bolts of musical organization. To them, the starkly simple phrases were given profound and powerful meaning by a range of musical effects—involving the manipulation and variation of tone, articulation and volume—just as complex and mysterious to the layman as Dizzy's theoretical explorations.

This mastery of sound was the most valuable asset that Bechet bequeathed to Johnny Hodges. Adapted to the younger man's quite different personality and temperament, it produced some of the most lordly music heard in jazz. Visitors to an Ellington concert during the touring years of the Fifties and Sixties will have etched in their minds the picture of Johnny Hodges emerging, with a routine show of reluctance, from the front rank of the orchestra to play his set of solo features, taking up a golfer's stance with legs wide apart and raking the auditorium with a huge sound the very authority and perfection of which had about it a touch of disdain. A British critic once noted how the soloist's eyes would sweep from one side of the hall to the other 'as if he were counting the exits' (the probing beam of a searchlight always came into my mind), and this combined with the voluminous swelling tone to complete the image of a man almost arrogantly sure of his command of both his music and his audience. Johnny Hodges was small and square in stature, and when he was not actually playing, his features, with the widely spaced, heavily lidded eyes, long muzzle and spacious upper lip that earned him the youthful nickname 'Rabbit', would assume the weary and detached expression of a minor diplomat enduring a tedious conference and wishing devoutly that he were elsewhere. But behind the alto saxophone he was a giant.

It is no surprise that from the outset Duke Ellington, with his keen ear for the dramatic effect, assigned special roles to Johnny Hodges. In fast numbers his solos had an exultant, strutting quality to be found in the Bechet-Armstrong collaborations which he so much admired. With his every entrance, the music positively jumped for joy. But his very first session with the Duke showed another side to his music. 'The Mooche' is an Ellington classic, bursting with that eerie atmosphere which Ellington always seemed able to evoke in a recording studio as well as on stage. Here Hodges demonstrated an ability to match the sinister 'jungle' growling of Bubber Miley and Tricky Sam Nanton with blues playing that combined the declamatory and exhortatory manner of the street-corner preacher with a quality altogether darker and more menacing. Ellington's music around the start of the Thirties was much affected by black church music, an important aspect of his beloved Harlem, and several compositions—notably 'Echoes of the Jungle' and 'Saturday Night Function'—have a distinctly 'gospel' flavour. The former is a Hodges masterpiece in which he invokes the Bechet spirit to match, and even surpass in sheer 'presence', the mood of heavy foreboding established by the muted and open trumpet of Cootie Williams and the low-register clarinet of Barney Bigard. Later on, Duke Ellington and his collaborator, Billy Strayhorn, were able to draw upon another facet of the versatile Hodges style by featuring him in compositions—'Passion Flower', 'Daydream' and so on—of a lusciously warm and romantic kind.

The reader will gather, from the way in which I linger over these examples of the Hodges mastery, that any one of them would keep me happily employed for the next ten pages or so. But the two Johnny Hodges recordings which I have chosen to bring into sharp focus come from the period at the start of the Forties, when the combination of a fully matured style and relatively advanced recording techniques enable us to appreciate to the full the talent that had set the pace for a decade and a half.

It is symptomatic of the magnetism which he could exert even from the impersonal grooves of a gramophone record that we tend to refer to Ellington's 'Never No Lament' as a Johnny Hodges feature, even though he plays for less than one chorus and shares the solo honours with Cootie Williams, Lawrence Brown and the Duke himself. The composition has an involved history. It was originally conceived as a counter-melody to the tune 'I Let a Song Go Out of My Heart', an Ellington hit of 1938. In *Music is my Mistress*, Duke Ellington recalled: 'In preparing my big song of the season for the Apollo [Theatre], I decided to do a new arrangement with rather a strong counter-melody. Opening day, I soon learned that the audience, as always, wanted to hear the version they had heard on the air. So we took out the new chart after the first show and went back to the old arrangement, and that's the way it stayed. The following year, 1939, the new arrangement was reworked and recorded as 'Never No Lament', which brings us to another later story.'

That story is now part of popular music history. 'Never No Lament' was provided with lyrics by Bob Russell and published as 'Don't Get Around Much any More'. With recordings by, among others, the popular Ink Spots, the song became a hit which surpassed the success of 'I Let a Song Go Out of My Heart'.

As was often the case with Ellington instrumentals-turned-popular-song, the original band version is greatly superior to the song. With the Duke, a three-minute recording was never presented simply as a tune dressed up with an introduction and arrangement, but as a composition of which all the components were of essential value. The piece starts with a statement by the muted brass of the familiar theme—but in a very unfamiliar form. The melody over which the lyricist draped the words 'Missed the Saturday dance' is presented in two chunky, rhythmically-symmetrical phrases, as it might be '*Missed* the Sa-*tur*-day dance', with sinuous answering phrases from the saxophones. Here again is the 'churchy' feeling that pervaded so many of Ellington's pieces. It is intensified in the second eight bars, which do not match the opening, but offer an alternative, if closely related theme, in which Ellington's piano does the haranguing and Lawrence Brown's trombone the response over congregational chords from the band. We are now only forty seconds into the piece, and already an evocative atmosphere has been established, preparing the way for a solo 'voice' in a manner that, for all its simplicity, is worthy of grand opera.

Notwithstanding the title, Johnny Hodges clearly interprets the piece as a lament, taking his cue from the closing phrase in the opening theme which, in contrast to the song version, uses the blues minor third interval (where the words 'any more' occur in the lyric) with a pervasively melancholy effect. Indeed, the Hodges solo is a blues in everything but its actual musical shape. Jazz people use the word 'wailing' to denote a certain passionate intensity and drive, but here Hodges wails in every sense of the word. The F note from which the tune's opening phrases descend (the piece is in D flat) is attacked each time from below in the manner of Bessie Smith and the classic blues singers. The first time, he holds it for its normal length, but the second time it is attacked more violently and prolonged with the characteristic Hodges 'swell', pulsating with vibrato. And from this voluminous note the tune's descending phrase is broken up and extended into a stream of agitated semiquavers or sixteenth-notes in double-time, a touch of pure Bechet. When, at the end of the first eight-bar section, he plays without variation the phrase to which the title words were eventually put, he affirms the blues affiliations of the original piece by hitting almost every note marginally off pitch, a blues subtlety which, through the ages, has been the despair of musicians trained in a classical school that acknowledges no fraction of pitch smaller than a semitone. In the second eight-bar section, the ghost of Sidney Bechet is evoked even more vividly in the opening phrase when, once again, the F provides a vehicle for a swelling wave of sound that breaks in a flurry of scattered notes.

It is neither necessary nor, indeed, possible to spend time dissecting the rest of this Hodges solo. His style of improvisation (or, more strictly, of solo-building, since he often repeated a solo once it had become set) adhered closely to the blues tradition, in which the central structure of the theme remained intact save for some minor variations, while the principal embellishment was confined to the spaces in which, in a classic blues, the accompaniment would fill in. As we shall see in a moment, this contrasts strongly with the approach of those contemporaries of Hodges who would use a theme or 'tune' as a base upon which to build what amounted to a fresh composition. Like Bessie Smith and, later, Big Joe Turner, Johnny Hodges had the power to move the listener mightily with the simplest of melodic variations. Thus, after a middle-eight in which the whole orchestra 'sings the blues' lustily, Johnny Hodges returns to the now familiar theme but,

THE BEST OF JAZZ II

in the third and fourth bar, replaces it with an anguished, contorted phrase in which, amidst much twisting and sliding among the notes, his alto-saxophone tone is attenuated to approach that of the soprano sax. In these final eight bars, blues all the way, we can see clearly why Hodges was regarded with such awe by contemporary saxophonists whose speed of execution and complexity of thought equalled and, in some cases, surpassed his. They may have been able to dazzle and astonish by their agility and ingenuity. He could cast a spell with one note. As 'Never No Lament' continues on its stately way, with respectively fierce and mournful contributions from Cootie Williams and Lawrence Brown, it is the Hodges chorus that stays in the mind, a jewel in the superbly contrived setting.

In the later years of his life, Johnny Hodges was rarely featured by Duke Ellington in up-tempo numbers, probably because the technical advances in jazz and the extended concert-hall format called for more complex and energetic displays than he was able—or willing—to provide. But from time to time, usually in informal, small-group sessions, we would be reminded of the joyful and exhilarating side of his playing. In the late Thirties, the agent and impresario, Irving Mills, who then handled Duke Ellington's affairs, instigated a series of recording sessions in which star Ellington soloists were featured as the leaders of small groups from within the band, invariably with the Duke himself at the piano. Known nowadays as 'the Ellington small groups', these sessions, led by Barney Bigard, Rex Stewart and Johnny Hodges successively, inevitably exuded an Ellingtonian flavour, with the Duke providing both compositions and arrangements. Of them all, it was the Hodges sessions which reflected most strongly the distinctive musical taste and background of the temporary leader. Many fine blues pieces later featured in the Ellington band's repertoire—'Wanderlust', 'Jeep's Blues', 'Things Ain't What they used to Be'—had their origins in these sessions, as did the romantic pieces with which Billy Strayhorn brought out the lusher, more sophisticated side of Hodges. But in amongst the slower numbers were up-tempo pieces—'The Jeep is Jumpin'', 'Good Queen Bess', 'Squatty Roo'—which bear an unmistakable Hodges stamp ('Jeep' was another sobriquet bestowed upon

Johnny Hodges at a time when the band broke out in a rash of nicknames derived from the 'Popeye' comic strip).

'Squatty Roo', a reference to the composer's shortness of stature (originally, and still often, misspelt as 'Squaty Roo'), is a favourite of mine for several reasons. It was recorded during the short time in which the Ellington band enjoyed the services of the brilliant young bassist, Jimmy Blanton. Condensed into a mere two-and-a-half years with Ellington before he died at twenty-one of tuberculosis, Blanton's recorded work had a mighty impact upon jazz history. As I will come to in the chapter on Lester Young, the Count Basie rhythm-section of the mid-Thirties radically changed the role of piano, guitar, bass and drums in jazz accompaniment, achieving with a crafty distribution of effort and responsibility greater flexibility and swing than the previous 'all hands to the pump' approach could achieve. In the process, the fine bassist, Walter Page, was relieved of the necessity to pound up and down the arpeggios of the basic chords as his predecessors had done. Harmony and drive were provided in a more subtle way, with the bass helping to define the harmonic progress with a 'walking' movement up and down the scale rather than giving strict attention to every note in the chord. Page was a tower of strength within the Basie section, but it required a player of more precision and agility to take full advantage of the freedom which his new style offered. The man for the occasion was Jimmy Blanton, through whose virtuoso example the double-bass achieved a considerable measure of the creative capacity enjoyed by the front-line instruments. It is indicative of the numbing effect which the sudden exposure to genius can have on slumbering senses that Blanton's arrival on the Ellington scene was greeted, by the leading American music magazine, with the words: BULLISH BOWING ENDANGERS DUKE'S REPUTATION!

The bringing together of Jimmy Blanton's buoyant, thrusting bass playing and the already sparkling and ebullient Hodges alto results in three minutes of sheer joy. One beneficial result of the pragmatic approach to recording that existed in the Ellington camp was that tunes originally conceived in conventional AABA thirty-two-bar form often assumed different and more interesting shapes through parts being curtailed or lopped off to fit the three-minute format. (The original version of 'Cottontail' is a classic example of this 'made-to-measure' approach.) 'Squatty Roo' is a happy, skipping theme based, as have been innumerable compositions in every era of jazz, on the harmonies of George Gershwin's 'I Got Rhythm'. The record opens straightaway with the two opening A sections. But instead of proceeding to the B middle-eight and the final A chorus, we go straight into a full alto solo, starting again at the top. This is followed by what would in any conventional performance be the final 'out' chorus, a reprise of the theme with the alto taking the middle-eight. But since it happens prematurely, there's time for a further alto solo which, after the middle-eight, yields to a final eight bars of ensemble which is then repeated sotto voce for 'one more time'. Set out in alphabetical form, this emerges as AA/AABA (solo)/AABA (ensemble with solo middle-eight)/AAB (solo) AA.

This choppy format, sustained in interest by Jimmy Blanton's ceaselessly inventive bass lines, suits Johnny Hodges admirably. He was never the most long-winded of jazz players, sounding most at ease when popping up for short bursts of joyful, dancing activity rather than piling chorus upon chorus. By comparison with such contemporaries as Benny Carter, Coleman Hawkins and Lester Young, his approach to improvisation may be said to be naïve. No long lines of finely wrought and elegantly balanced melody emerge, no tangled and devious harmonic routes are explored, no startlingly fresh alterations are made to the conventional rhythmic structure of the piece. And yet the whole performance springs along with an abandon which is irresistible.

Popping, dancing, springing—I find that in trying to define the virtues of 'Squatty Roo' I have without thinking used words that go straight to the heart of the matter. For the origins of this side to the Hodges musical personality we should perhaps look to Louis Armstrong of the Blue Five days rather than to Sidney Bechet. The most important lesson that the twenty-five-year-old Armstrong taught to the jazz world at large was how to endow a performance with that rhythmic momentum that came to be called swing. Even in his earliest days, when he was still striving to find a role for the alto saxophone in fast tempos that did not involve decorative doodling more appropriate to the clarinet,

Johnny Hodges swung with that particular buoyancy of Armstrong's that came from applying such seeming irrelevancies as
vibrato, articulation and variation in pitch to the service of
rhythmic uplift. Since, as I have explained, there are few, if any,
melodic or harmonic ramifications on which to dwell here, let us
pick out just some of the ingredients, whether borrowed or new,
which go towards achieving this highly infectious swing.

The first thing that must be established is that Johnny Hodges
in fast tempos played in a manner not dissimilar from that of
Coleman Hawkins. Though he lacked the heavy attack and
machine-gun delivery of Hawkins, he played his long phrases in a
string of uneven quavers or eighth-notes, normally stressing the
first, third, fifth and seventh quavers in a bar and sometimes
articulating those in between so lightly that the effect was of
'DOOdle-DOOdle-DOOdle-DOOdle'. Rhythmic variety would
then be introduced when the emphasis was applied in varied
strengths, sometimes switching from the strong to the weak
quavers in the way that a drummer will create a shifting rhythm.

From the outset of his first chorus in 'Squatty Roo', this
drumming effect is very much in evidence, the phrases skipping
along with frequent shifts of emphasis. In the seventh and eighth
bars, for instance, the rhythmic pattern can be roughly described
in the onomatopaeic method above as 'dooDLE-dooDLE-
DOOdle-doodle-DOOdle-doo-WAH'. Of course, this is a crude
exposition, there being many more shades of accent than I can
put on paper. But it gives an idea of the frequent skipping changes
in step which give a Hodges solo its continuous lift. He was less
relentless in pursuing this rhythmic pattern than Coleman Hawkins. For instance, at the start of the second eight bars of the first
solo, the flow of quavers is interrupted by a sustained, singing
high note from which a long phrase full of variety descends in a
series of blithe, skipping steps.

As one would expect from a player so steeped in the blues,
there is in a Hodges up-tempo romp a more generous use of those
slurred, distorted and otherwise maltreated tones appertaining to
the blues than one finds in contemporaries such as Benny Carter
or Coleman Hawkins. In bars twenty-five and twenty-six of the
first solo chorus, for example, he utters a repetitive call very

reminiscent of the whoo-hooing train-whistle sounds made by blues harmonica players. And in the third full chorus, when Hodges, Blanton and the discreet brushes of Sonny Greer have it all to themselves again, the first sixteen bars are pure blues. That Johnny Hodges was a master in this idiom may seem surprising and, in some cases, unsettling to those romantics who believe the blues to be the exclusive cultural property of one social and geographical area of black America.

Boston, Massachusetts, is about as far from the Deep South as one can get without crossing a border, and the environment into which Johnny Hodges was born could aptly be described as respectable middle class, with good educational opportunities especially in the field of music. Yet he embraced the blues with manifestly more enthusiasm, conviction and understanding than, say, Coleman Hawkins from Missouri, Don Redman from West Virginia and Buster Bailey from Memphis, all of whom were born and bred within earshot of the migratory route of the Southern blues. When all of these musicians, including Hodges, were finding their feet in New York, the city was enjoying a blues boom, especially in the recording studios. As members of Fletcher Henderson's Orchestra, Hawkins, Redman and Bailey were in the thick of it, providing backings for many of the so-called 'classic' blues singers including Bessie Smith. If receptiveness to the raw spirit of the blues were a matter simply of proximity to the source, one would expect them to be infected more, not less, deeply than Johnny Hodges, who was outside their circle. But when it comes to the instrumental interpretation of the blues, we are dealing with music, not sociology. Geography and environment affect a musician only to the extent that they decide whom he hears and with whom he plays and discusses music in his formative years. In one respect, environment may have had a part to play in the direction that Johnny Hodges took, in that by commuting regularly to Boston, he did not become associated with the rather standoffish and contemptuous attitude of the New Yorkers to the powerful but relatively rough music coming into the city from the West—New Orleans, Chicago and the South. While their fastidiousness led them to keep at arms' length the music of Bechet, the blues and the 'soul' or 'gutbucket' extremity of the

New York musical spectrum, Johnny Hodges devoured it all without inhibition, harnessing it to a polished and highly disciplined musicianship. There was, as I have said, a certain inevitability about his gravitation towards the Duke Ellington band. With its extraordinary blend of naïvety and sophistication, of lush saxophones and savagely growling brass, of ancient blues themes and modern concert works, of dark, brooding harmonies and joyful abandon, it was his spiritual home.

Nothing could illustrate the importance of personality and temperament in a musician's development better than the juxtaposition of Johnny Hodges and Benny Carter. A native of New York, born less than a year after Hodges, Benny Carter undoubtedly shared many of the former's youthful experiences and influences. True, he never worked alongside Sidney Bechet and, since he was away from New York for a year or two in the mid-Twenties, it is quite possible that he never heard him in the flesh at that time. That he was not deaf in his youth to the earthier aspects of New York music is shown by the fact that, when he initially chose the trumpet as his instrument, it was the growl-specialist Bubber Miley who was his inspiration. A diligent researcher into his recorded works over the years could come up with plenty of examples of impressive blues solos (the clarinet part in 'Dee Blues' by the Chocolate Dandies, mentioned in the chapter on Jack Teagarden, is particularly convincing). But the same researcher would be forced to the conclusion that, although Carter has always cited Hodges among his early influences, the blues that so permeated the Hodges style have not been an integral part of Carter's music. His ambitions—and the contribution which he made to jazz in the pursuit of them—lay in a different direction from those of Johnny Hodges.

Some light is thrown on them by the other names often mentioned by Carter as his chief sources of inspiration. Coleman Hawkins, Don Redman, Frankie Trumbauer each made an important contribution to his musical make-up. With Hawkins, a colleague on many recordings over the years, Benny Carter shared an intense musical curiosity, an eagerness to explore all that orthodox musical teaching had to offer while at the same time showing deep interest in the eccentricities of which jazz is com-

pounded. Less aggressive than Hawkins, he nonetheless assimilated much of the tenor star's gritty drive and momentous swing,
sufficient to turn aside the charges of effeteness and dandyism
which his elegantly turned solos might otherwise invoke. To the
strong tone inherited from Hodges he added a hard cutting edge
comparable to Hawkins's tenor sound, resulting in a solo voice
that could sometimes be as declamatory as that of the trumpet and
an incisive ensemble sound that has been the model for lead alto
players ever since.

Much of the orthodox strength in Benny Carter's playing will
have derived from Don Redman, the man whose section playing
and arrangements did much to give a style to the Fletcher Henderson Orchestra in the Twenties. Clearly, Redman was a powerful
influence on Carter the ambitious professional, who dogged the
older man's steps from the outset with almost uncanny success.
Don Redman arrived in New York in 1923 with a Pittsburg band
called Billy Paige's Broadway Syncopators. When he left a year
later to join Fletcher Henderson, it was Benny Carter who went
back to Pittsburg with Paige. A few years later, Redman left
Henderson to become musical director of McKinney's Cottonpickers. Shortly afterward, the Fletcher Henderson discography
begins to list Benny Carter as alto-sax soloist and arranger. At the
same time, Carter assumed from Redman the leadership of the
ad hoc studio bands which Redman had founded and which
recorded under the name of the Chocolate Dandies. The pattern
now so well established that it seems almost platitudinous to add
that when Don Redman left McKinney's Cottonpickers, it was
Benny Carter who took over the band's musical directorship,
only to leave a year later to start his own band, as Redman had
done before him. Just as Don Redman's trade-mark as arranger
with Henderson had been the 'choir' of clarinets working as a
section, so Benny Carter was later to specialize in passages written
for the saxophones, drawing from the standard team of two altos
and two tenors a remarkably rich texture which was then adapted
to the fluent lines and bursts of double-tempo of a characteristic
Benny Carter solo.

The fourth candidate among Benny Carter's influences, Frankie
Trumbauer, represents the sharpest point of divergence between

the Carter and the Hodges approaches. If Johnny Hodges ever flirted with Trumbauer, it was only for the briefest of periods, after which Bechet and the blues reasserted their hold. Consequently, a Hodges solo would first and foremost create a mood, an atmosphere, using the simplest of musical materials and relying on nuances of tone, pitch and volume to provide the depth. Trumbauer's stock-in-trade was phrase-making—the spinning of a melodic line that aimed for elegance, poise, balanced design and neat construction, with the occasional odd interval or convoluted phrase thrown in to startle and divert. To my ears, his solos were often glaringly contrived and always totally without the swing and buoyance that good jazz demands. But his playing in general, and his solo in 'Singin' the Blues' (cited in Volume One as a Bix Beiderbecke classic) were greatly admired by contemporary musicians of every background.

Its effect upon Benny Carter was to sharpen his already acute sense of musical construction. The writer, Rex Harris, whose book *Jazz* for Pelican Books epitomized the 'purist' approach of the early Fifties, summed up Carter's mature style in a series of apt phrases—'tremendous talent', 'powers of invention, technique, tone, all are of the highest order', 'a demonstration of beauty', 'beautiful, refined, delicate'. The fact that I have had to extract those phrases, in the manner of a theatrical publicist, from a passage that denied Benny Carter the right to be regarded as a jazz musician at all, demonstrates the deep suspicion with which overt musicianship was, and sometimes still is, regarded by the protagonists of 'pure' jazz. By the time Benny Carter's alto style had fully matured, around the mid-Thirties, a curious thing had happened. The conjuncture of the attack, incisiveness and swing that came from other sources, and the penchant for felicitous phrase-making that derived from Frankie Trumbauer had resulted in music that came much closer in style to that of Trumbauer's erstwhile colleague, Bix Beiderbecke.

In pursuit of this idea, I asked Bruce Turner, the distinguished alto saxophonist with my own band and an ardent devotee of Benny Carter, to play me the Bix Beiderbecke solos in 'Singin' the Blues' and 'Way Down Yonder in New Orleans' in the Carter style. They sounded uncannily like original Benny Carter solos.

In detail, the resemblances are striking. Both Carter and Beiderbecke showed an adherence to strict underlying rules of construction in building their solos. In this respect one could say that a player such as Coleman Hawkins, charging along whither his theme took him and piling sub-clause upon sub-clause, improvised in a 'prose' style, while Carter and Beiderbecke observed the metric rules of formal poetry, setting phrase against phrase and line against line. In discussing Bix Beiderbecke's solo in 'Singin' the Blues', I drew attention to the way in which its opening was subdivided into two phrases or 'lines' of one bar each, followed by an answering line of two bars which, in turn, is matched by a long, irregular phrase covering the next four bars. Any Benny Carter solo between 1934 and 1944 (and to a lesser extent after the arrival of bebop) can be shown to rest on a similarly formal pattern.

And there is a further likeness. Despite evidence in their solos of advanced harmonic mastery, both Beiderbecke and Carter leaned heavily upon the simple diatonic scale. In layman's language this means that, transposed into the key of C, a solo by either musician will be full of phrases that can be played entirely on the white notes of the piano keyboard, without recourse to the extraneous sharps and flats that give chromatic harmonies their particular complexity. If we think of a simple progression from dominant to tonic, or from G seventh to C, and express it by playing the cadence F, D, B, G, C (or, alternatively, D, lower G, B, D, C), we have phrases which might well occur in a Beiderbecke or Carter solo. Compared with the progression D, D flat, C that Coleman Hawkins liked to use, or with the flattened or 'bent' thirds, fifths and sevenths of the blues scale favoured by Johnny Hodges, these cadences have a fresh, open, even innocent quality that has prompted, in each instance, the response, 'Very beautiful, but is it *jazz*?' If one believes, as I do, that jazz is a many-splendor'd music that can match the Mozartian, Wagnerian, Schoenbergian and other schools of European music, then the answer will be 'yes' and we can proceed with a clear conscience to look in detail at two Benny Carter fragments.

Fragments, alas, they must be, because although Benny Carter in the Thirties made a strong contribution, as arranger, altoist, trumpeter and/or clarinettist, to all of his recordings, he produced on alto no solo performance comparable to the Hawkins 'Body and Soul' or the Hodges 'Squatty Roo'. When it came to stretching out on a ballad he seemed to prefer the trumpet, on which he was a formidable but derivative performer. Readers eager to hear his best work on trumpet should track down 'Once upon a Time' by the Chocolate Dandies in 1933, when he played very much in the majestic Armstrong vein, and 'More than you Know' by his own orchestra in 1939, by which time he had acquired a lusher style that hints, if ever so slightly, at an admiration for Harry James. On clarinet he played good solos with a strong, fruity tone, but in a manner that was much less distinctive than his alto-saxophone style. His claim to recognition as a jazz giant, as distinct from a superb all-round musician, rests on innumerable alto solos from the late Twenties onwards that bore his unmistakable stamp and established him alongside Johnny Hodges as a leading jazz voice on the instrument.

Between 1935 and 1938, Benny Carter followed the example of Coleman Hawkins, Dickie Wells and many other American jazz stars and moved to Europe, occupying for a short time the curious role of staff arranger to Henry Hall's BBC Dance Orchestra. During this time he made recordings with both British and Continental musicians, often meeting up in the studio with his old friend and colleague in the Henderson band, Coleman Hawkins. One of their collaborations, 'Crazy Rhythm', recorded in 1937 under the heading of Coleman Hawkins and his All Star Jam Band, features in these pages as a Coleman Hawkins masterpiece. It also contains a chorus by Benny Carter which is often cited by musicians and commentators as one of his best and most characteristic.

Before we consider the Carter solo, it is worth taking note of the opening ensemble chorus which has all the hallmarks—the richly textured voicing, the biting attack and the full-bodied, chesty tone—of a Benny Carter saxophone section with himself in the lead. True, this is no more than a hastily sketched out 'head' arrangement with none of the complex phrasing and bursts of double-time that are found in a full Carter saxophone outing. Nevertheless, it has the distinctive sound, almost as elusive in its composition as some of Duke Ellington's voicings, by which a Benny Carter arrangement can instantly be identified.

In the discussion of this record in my essay on Coleman Hawkins, I noted that André Ekyan, as well as Alix Combelle, shows the influence of Hawkins in his solo. There is certainly little of either Carter or Hodges in the bustling, rather untidy phrasing. It may be invidious and unfair to highlight the skill of the Americans by picking out the faults of the Europeans, but comparisons certainly do clamour for attention. The haphazard nature of Ekyan's chorus, whose jumble of ideas sound garrulous rather than fluent, highlights the supreme orderliness and lucidity of Benny Carter's solo. Jazz books—and these volumes are no exception—bristle with diverse and often complex definitions of the jazz quality known as 'swing'. There are, indeed, different ways of achieving that particular characteristic of sustained rhythmic momentum required by the term. But one essential is common to all of them, and that is perfect time. To a musician, this means placing every note, even the most transitory and insignificant, in exactly the right place in relation to the regular four beats to the bar. This does not necessarily mean 'keeping time' in the sense of neither speeding up nor slowing down. There are plenty of examples in jazz of solos and ensembles which continue to swing even though there is noticeable accelerating or slowing down of the tempo. In these instances, as the basic beat changes, the notes continue to relate to it with microscopic accuracy. A common cause of bad time and consequent lack of swing is poor execution—the failure of the fingers or tongue to articulate accurately the ideas fed to them. The solos of Ekyan and Combelle both falter occasionally in this respect, the latter especially making heavy weather of some over-ambitious flights of fancy.

There is a touch of insolence about the effortless style with which Benny Carter takes over the baton from a huffing and puffing Combelle. It is surprising that, among all the efforts that have been made by jazz historians to attribute influences to Lester Young, no one to my knowledge has mentioned the name of Benny Carter. It must be said that Lester Young himself never mentioned him either, suggesting that, from the common inspiration of Frankie Trumbauer, both musicians arrived independently at a very similar rhythmic style. In the comparisons between Young and Coleman Hawkins, much is made of the contrast between the latter's system of unevenly stressed eighth-notes— the DOOdle-DOOdle effect as I have described it—and the flatter, more flowing pattern of even eighth-notes that Lester Young employed. Exactly the same point can be made to distinguish Benny Carter from Johnny Hodges, whom I have placed in this context in the Hawkins school. If I hesitate to put Lester Young in the Carter school it is because we have no evidence of his playing prior to 1936 and therefore cannot judge who preceded whom. But it is certainly worth putting on the record the fact that the even-quaver rhythmic style with which Lester Young and the guitarist, Charlie Christian, paved the way for the rhythms of modern jazz was used by Benny Carter from his earliest days.

The opening of Benny Carter's solo, with its lead up to an isolated 'balancing' note on the first beat of the bar, is very similar to Lester Young's entrance in 'Lady Be Good'. But thereafter, the moods of the solo are different, with Carter's frank preference for explicit, finely balanced lines of melody contrasting with Lester's oblique, veiled approach. At the end of bar one, we have a characteristic Carter trade-mark, a phrase that starts with a note, usually near the bottom of the solo's range, which is leaned on heavily to give it special emphasis, a signal that it is going to play an important part in some ingenious musical pattern. Sure enough, the elegant opening phrase, looped across the beat, returns to the same note, completing a languid four-bar motif which is then balanced, in the next four bars, by one similar in shape but more intricate. A demonstration of beauty indeed, breathtakingly designed and executed. But this is only the start. A linking phrase across bars seven and eight initiates a burst of melody, uttered with that sharp-edged, trumpet-like attack that makes the heart sing. From its joyful opening notes to the more fluent phrases with which they are developed and resolved, the structure is impeccable and the poise complete.

The middle-eight produces further delights—a long, looping, continuous phrase spread over six bars, perfectly shaped, and outlining an idea which, taken up again at the end of bar seven, itself becomes the opening gambit in a further chain of pure melody that sees the solo out. In other words, the whole half-chorus, from the start of the middle-eight onwards, represents a continuous line of spontaneous composition, logically and lucidly expressed without one extraneous note. Much of the elation which the solo inspires derives from that predilection for diatonic lines which have such a Bixian flavour. Indeed, the bursts of melody in bars nine and ten and again in bars twenty-five to twenty-nine, have something of the triumphant, militant sound of Bix in full cry. The very end of Benny Carter's chorus throws new light on the premature entrance by Coleman Hawkins which I have put down to a 'straining at the leash'. Eagerness to enter the fray is certainly there, but there is also the necessity to fill up the final thirty-second bar of Carter's solo, since that meticulous man, having concluded and rounded off his whole musical scheme in bar thirty-one, disdains to fudge the design with the sort of mumbling, semi-audible soliloquy with which many soloists cover their retreat from the microphone.

A chance to hear Benny Carter in a more extended vein arises from a fine session under the revived name of the Chocolate Dandies which was recorded for the American jazz label Commodore in 1940. With limited ensemble work, no piano and only three soloists—Carter, Coleman Hawkins and Roy Eldridge—to be accommodated, each player has plenty of space in the up-tempo numbers. Benny Carter is well represented on both 'I Can't Believe that You're in Love with Me' and 'Smack' and if I choose the latter for special consideration, it is because with two opening choruses and a final middle-eight, Carter is here the principal soloist.

'Smack' (presumably a reference to the nickname of the three principals' erstwhile bandleader, Fletcher Henderson) is not really a composition at all, but a thirty-two-bar chord sequence in conventional AABA form over which the soloists improvise freely from the start. Benny Carter opens the proceedings with eight bars which may or may not have constituted a sketchy theme and which are not repeated. They are very characteristic of Carter, building a symmetrical pattern of four two-bar phrases, a regular feature of which is a descent to one of those stressed low-register notes on the second beat of the first bar. In fact, this downward leap, quite a familiar device in Carter solos of the period, is elevated here to the status of a motif that recurs throughout the solo, sometimes thrown on to another beat, sometimes interjected, with surprise effect, against the directional tide of the melody. In some ways, Benny Carter is less fluent and more daring here than in the previous example, perhaps challenged by the pushing and explosive personalities of his front-line colleagues to take risks. The result is a solo of a more devious structure than before. For instance, the phrase at the end of the first eight bars by which he emerges from the opening pattern is, for him, curiously convoluted, both rhythmically and melodically.

In the second eight bars a more typically elegant line is established, flowing into a middle-eight in which the downward-leaping motif is exploited in a sly and humorous way. The listener will notice, as this solo unfolds, that Benny Carter's style has lost some of its erstwhile innocence. Where a solo would once spin blithely along pursuing a seemingly inexorable melodic course, this one constantly turns aside to give playful chase to a melodic or rhythmic idea, often chivvying the beat in the manner of Coleman Hawkins and, in one extreme instance near the end of the solo, of his fellow-altoist, Pete Brown. There were occasions, before and after Benny Carter's exposure to the new ideas of bebop, when the phrase-making seemed to me to verge upon indulgence, a clever idea being driven to the point of self-parody. But here the balance between ingenuity and intuition sounds to me to be just right, and the ardour of his companions seems to have kindled in his playing an even greater warmth than usual. Indeed, when he bursts in at the end of the single chorus by Coleman Hawkins with a beautifully constructed middle-eight, there is no detectable drop in temperature.

Throughout this essay I have spoken of Benny Carter in the past tense, being concerned primarily with his impact on the jazz scene in the Thirties and, indeed, of its impact upon him. Happily, at the time of writing he is still alive and active, a worthy elder statesman of jazz who has, by example and by active encouragement, assisted and inspired succeeding generations of musicians. In contrast to Johnny Hodges, he took account in his playing of the work of the bebop innovators, adapting both their rhythmic and harmonic ideas to his own style. Whether or not these changes have met with the approval of his earliest devotees, they have never undermined the exquisite poise and elegance of his music without which, over more than fifty years, jazz would have been inestimably the poorer.

Dickie Wells

OF ALL THE INSTRUMENTS in the jazz fold, the trombone seems to
have experienced the greatest difficulty in living down its past.
Whatever crudities and indiscretions the trumpet and clarinet may
have committed in the music's early days, they could point
respectively to a proud tradition of leadership and a schooled
Creole background as the foundation of their jazz role. The piano
derived respectability not only from ragtime, with its quasi-
classical aura, but also from the sombre dignity of the blues. And
as for the saxophone, its past was so negligible in jazz terms that
when the generation headed by Coleman Hawkins, Johnny Hodges
and Benny Carter took it in hand in the late Twenties, they
virtually started with a clean slate, Bechet's example excepted.

The trombone, however, had played a vital role in the earliest
manifestations of jazz. In the New Orleans bands it assumed the
function which it had performed in the military bands from which
jazz in part derived, supplying ripe bass harmonies and a high
degree of rhythmic emphasis. In the hands of a master such as
Edward 'Kid' Ory, who enhanced the bands of Louis Armstrong,
Jelly Roll Morton and King Oliver in the Twenties, it was in its
element, compensating for its lack of agility with the versatile
mixture of sustained, staccato and sliding notes which its relatively
primitive construction makes possible. Except in the blues, where
it could wail and moan with the best of them, the role it played
was supportive. And it was open to limitless abuse in the interests
of showmanship or comedy, reinforcing its image as the amiable
hobbledehoy of the band, cheerfully shouldering the heavy work

and ready at a moment's notice to entertain with a little crude clowning.

It is not an image likely to have commended itself to those young musicians in the mid-Twenties who, in the wake of Louis Armstrong, were beginning to think of jazz less as a band or ensemble music and more as a vehicle for individual solo expression. We have already seen how Jimmy Harrison, when a star soloist with Fletcher Henderson's Orchestra, spoke with some contempt of trombones which sounded like trombones. Just as Miff Mole had done before them, Harrison and Jack Teagarden set about stifling or distorting some of the basic characteristics of the instrument. 'Trombones should sound like trumpets' was Jimmy Harrison's dictum, and in view of the results which he and Teagarden achieved we can hardly assert that he was misguided. By the late Twenties, a rich crop of trombonists had emerged, many of whom followed Harrison and Teagarden in their Armstrong-derived style. By contrast with Kid Ory and his contemporaries, their playing was marked by crisp, clean articulation, extensive use of the high register, rapid trumpet-like vibrato at the end of notes or phrases and an aversion to using the slide to produce glissandi or sliding notes. When the trombone underwent another crisis of identity in the mid-Forties, finding itself once again left behind in the stampede towards greater speed and agility, it was on what one might call the anti-trombone tradition of Harrison and Teagarden that J. J. Johnson and his bebop followers built. In traditional jazz, which has enjoyed a revival from the Forties on, the influence of Jack Teagarden prevailed in what is loosely called the Chicagoan or Dixieland style centred around Eddie Condon, with players such as Lou McGarity and Cutty Cutshall following his path. In contrast, those who sought to revive the fundamental New Orleans-style leap-frogged back beyond the innovations of Harrison and Teagarden to the 'tailgate' model of Kid Ory and his predecessors.

Of course, we are once again in the realms of over-simplification. But allowing for the many borderline cases and the fact that some 'revivalists' used the tailgate style in ensemble and played their solos in a post-Harrison manner, it remains true to say that in the mainstream development of jazz, the practice of playing the trombone as if it were a trumpet in a lower register has prevailed from the early Thirties to the present day.

There have, however, been important exceptions. Among the young trombonists in the late Twenties who responded to the Armstrong inspiration, there were some who were not ashamed, at the same time, to exploit the trombone's own distinct characteristics. One was the splendid J. C. Higginbotham, whose brazen tone and whooping agility was one of the major attractions of Luis Russell's band in the Thirties and who deserves to share with Jack Teagarden and Jimmy Harrison the credit for promoting the trombone to a solo role in jazz. Higginbotham's influence could be heard in the Thirties in the work of Ellington's Lawrence Brown and Chick Webb's Sandy Williams, and it surfaced again during the modern jazz era of the late Forties when Bill Harris, in Woody Herman's band, went against the fashionable staccato grain and fashioned a style whose contrasting gruff low register and grieving upper reaches recalled the Higginbotham of twenty years earlier.

But the greatest, and the most idiosyncratic, of the 'independents' who combined the new thinking with a readiness on occasion to sound like a trombone, was Dickie Wells. Though born in Tennessee and educated musically in Louisville, Kentucky, where his family moved when he was two years old, Wells was established on the New York scene by 1926, when as a seventeen-year-old he started to work with first Lloyd Scott and then his brother, Cecil Scott. I have remarked in the chapter on Jack Teagarden that the mid-Twenties was probably the period when Jimmy Harrison wielded his greatest influence and in the early records which Dickie Wells made with the Scott brothers, there is plenty of evidence, notably in the use of stabbing notes in the upper register, that Wells came under his spell. But there are signs of his own independent style, too, involving, in slow blues especially, some slipping and sliding in a manner more reminiscent of Charlie Green, Harrison's predecessor in the Fletcher Henderson band. This earthiness, together with a strain of humour that sometimes seemed to parody the awkward and ungainly characteristics of the trombone, remained with him throughout his life.

After his earliest recordings with Lloyd and Cecil Scott, the next substantial collection of his work appeared in 1933 when, as a member of Benny Carter's band, he took part in some sessions under the leadership of the Irish-born bassist, composer and critic, Patrick 'Spike' Hughes. As a musician, Hughes had played in the Jack Hylton Orchestra and had also made many recordings in London with his own relatively small groups. Under the pseudonym 'Mike', he wrote regular jazz criticism for the London *Melody Maker*, the weekly paper to which John Hammond also contributed from America. Hammond had a considerable influence on Spike Hughes's viewpoint, leading him to become the first British jazz journalist to try to wean the record-buying public away from the polite sophistication of Red Nichols and Miff Mole towards then lesser known black artists. When Hughes visited New York in 1933, with the opportunity to record some of his own compositions with American musicians, it was John Hammond who took him round and made the necessary introductions. As a result, the recording session was set up with the Benny Carter band providing the basic unit, to which tenor saxists Coleman Hawkins and Chu Berry, and trumpeter Henry 'Red' Allen, were added.

With so much solo talent literally at his command, a composer would have needed unusual resources of ineptitude to avoid memorable results. Spike Hughes was at his best at the slower 'foxtrot' tempos, and romantic pieces such as 'Arabesque', 'Donegal Cradle Song' and 'Sweet Sorrow Blues', redolent with an intriguing blend of Ellingtonian and Hibernian influences, are deservedly cherished today as something more than just adequate vehicles for inspired soloists. The fast numbers suffer from the squared-off jerkiness which marked the British brand of 'hot' arrangement in the early Thirties, but even then there is little sign that the players were at all inhibited, and when classic sessions are recalled today, those by Spike Hughes and his All-American Orchestra will always find a place among them.

In one respect, the Spike Hughes sessions are underrated today. Of the fourteen pieces recorded, all except one ('Donegal Cradle Song') contain a solo by Dickie Wells. Canvass the jazz experts for their views and they will all agree that the performances are typical of Dickie Wells at his best—adventurous, swinging, full of surprise and wit. What you will find missing, if I may venture a guess founded on almost all the established jazz histories, is a due sense of astonishment (a charge to which the British writer, Raymond Horricks, and the French critic, André Hodeir, are honourable exceptions). As often in these instances, we have to perform some mental gymnastics in order to appreciate the startling newness of Dickie Wells's style. In his previous recordings with Lloyd and Cecil Scott, his playing already showed great promise but was still somewhat gawky and immature. The last of these was made in November 1929. In the three and a half years that then elapsed before the Hughes sessions, the jazz trombone enjoyed something of a heyday. From the mutually beneficial association with Jack Teagarden, Jimmy Harrison emerged as a truly modern player in the 1930 recordings by the Chocolate Dandies. In his wake came a string of fine players, of whom Benny Morton and Claude Jones were the most impressive. But with the followers of Louis Armstrong and Coleman Hawkins performing astonishing feats of daring on trumpet and saxophone, even the best of the trombonists were often overshadowed. Jack Teagarden, as I noted in a previous chapter, quite soon settled down into a lifelong style that inclined more towards poise, elegance and relaxed warmth than reckless fervour. And only the ebullient J. C. Higginbotham, short on subtlety but full of glorious vitality, approached the adventurousness of the trumpet and saxophone men.

And then, out of the blue, came the Spike Hughes sessions, with twenty-three-year-old Dickie Wells producing a string of solos which, for range of mood, bursting eagerness and impudent (and occasionally ill-fated) daring, remind one of Louis Armstrong's playing in the later years of the Hot Five sessions. With so much talent erupting all around him, it is perhaps understandable that even Spike Hughes himself seemed not to grasp fully the unprecedented brilliance of his trombonist's contribution. In the second volume of his autobiography, entitled *Second Movement*, he referred retrospectively to 'the admirable and unusual trombone player, Dickie Wells', apt words in themselves but hardly sufficient to describe the finest jazz trombone playing yet committed to wax.

In addition to the compositions by the leader himself, there were among these recordings a couple of 'standards'—'Bugle Call Rag' and 'Someone Stole Gabriel's Horn'—which Hughes arranged, and versions of 'How Come you Do me Like you Do' and 'Sweet Sue' which were played without formal arrangement in jam-session style. The Dickie Wells solo on 'Sweet Sue' is most often picked out for special mention, and it is indeed remarkable. Preceding him there has been a characteristically urgent and across-the-beat statement of the tune by Henry Allen, a hustling and bustling Coleman Hawkins solo and a chorus by Wayman Carver on flute which is more notable for its very existence in 1933 than for its content. Dickie Wells starts with one of his familiar devices—a solitary steadying note in the bar before the chorus proper—and then launches into the solo with some Armstrong-like repeated phrases in punching rhythmic style. It is at the end of the first eight-bar section that he first airs his reckless spirit of adventure with a long phrase that ascends across the beat with a staggering gait, skids upwards to grab at a top D and slide back off it, regains its balance and resumes the rhythmic riffing through the second eight-bar section. It sounds for all the world like a man in a hurry who suddenly hits an unseen patch of ice and flails around to keep upright, startling the onlookers. The next patch of ice occurs in the middle-eight, when Dickie Wells decides to attempt some daring figure-skating based on that first involuntary skid, and all but comes a cropper in the process. First he suggests the slithering phrase from B to D and back in the lower register, then repeats it an octave up but doesn't quite reach the D, a lapse in intonation which is compounded when, going for the same figure again in the low register, he finds that it will land him on the wrong note and, in making a last minute change in direction, lands on the C badly off-centre. The whole brief escapade seems to unnerve him, and the rhythmic phrase that he uses to get out of the middle-eight has a noticeable air of desperation about it.

'Sweet Sue' reveals the only sign of impulsive immaturity in the entire set. Not that the other solos are less adventurous. 'Air in D flat' is full of leaps and pirouettes, this time sure footed and elegantly constructed. In contrast, 'Sweet Sorrow Blues' evokes a deep blues lament, echoing strongly Kid Ory's stark solo on King Oliver's 'Black Snake Blues' from 1927. Here is a trombone sounding like a trombone and proud of it, using all the broad glissando effects that the slide mechanism permits. A notable aspect of the 'Sweet Sorrow' solo is that, in singing the blues so unashamedly, Dickie Wells abandoned the exaggerated vibrato which elsewhere gave his sustained notes such intensity. The French writer, André Hodeir, in a study of Dickie Wells in his book, *Jazz: Its Evolution and Essence*, described this effect as 'terminal vibrato', a phrase which, unhappily overtaken by medical jargon, brings involuntarily to mind the instruction of Miles Davis's first teacher: 'Play without any vibrato—you're gonna get old anyway and start shakin'.' In fact 'vibrato' is not a strictly accurate term to describe the effect which Dickie Wells and some of his predecessors achieved. They did not simply apply the rapid but minute variation in pitch with which vibrato endows a note with a throbbing pulse. With them, the principal note actually alternates rapidly with notes one or two intervals above, through the application of varied lip pressure. In its gentler manifestation, this effect, in modern musical parlance, is aptly described as a 'lip trill', while in its more exaggerated form it becomes a 'shake'.

Dickie Wells was not the first or only jazzman to use it. It appears often in Louis Armstrong's early playing and became ubiquitous in his later years. Jack Teagarden began by using it in moderation, as we have seen, but soon abandoned it. It can be heard, in a sort of fluttering, asthmatic variation, in Jimmy Harrison's solos with the Chocolate Dandies, and it was from the start central to Benny Morton's style. But no one used it with as much gusto as Dickie Wells. In the ferocious 'Bugle Call Rag', it becomes an essential feature of a solo that consists of little more than three sustained notes. Playing in B flat, he starts on a middle F, stretching it taut with a series of rhythmic tugs over five bars and only relieving the tension with a short, rippling shake at the end of the fifth bar. Then from bars seven to nine he unleashes a train whistle's mournful 'whooooeeeee' an octave up, descending in bar ten to the key note B flat and shaking it for two bars until its teeth rattle. It's an amazingly audacious solo—three notes spread over twelve bars of a sixteen-bar chorus and yet imparting a great feeling of heat and urgency through the judicious use of the shake.

Two more solos from the Spike Hughes sessions demand a special mention. One is in a dreamy, ruminative theme called 'Pastoral'. If the implications of the title impinged upon Dickie Wells, he decided to ignore them, going through several startling changes of mood in his short sixteen-bar solo. Following a blithe, sunny half-chorus from Benny Carter on alto, he starts with broad, upward sweeping phrases in the Louis Armstrong grand manner, but conveying a sense of increasingly un-pastoral disturbance and agitation with the intensified use of the shake. A searing 'blue note' on the flattened seventh brings him out of the middle-eight into a last eight-bar section that starts with matching two-bar phrases in a very different manner. The voice is now gruff, the notes abrupt, the phrasing terse, with the second two-bar phrase ending on the second beat of the bar, unexpectedly but extremely effectively. We are now far removed from pastoral serenity and deep in blues country, a fact driven home by the harsh and furious flurry of notes with which the chorus ends. It is hard to think of a more powerful or moving trombone passage from that (or indeed any) period, and it serves to make the rest of the piece, including the lush rhapsodizing of Coleman Hawkins, sound faintly ridiculous, as if a scene from *King Lear* had been interpolated in some romantic Ruritanian operetta.

Of the other noteworthy solo, Spike Hughes wrote '[Dickie Wells's] playing (John Hammond still swears) was spoilt for life by his ingenious and thoroughly musical contributions to the abstruse "Arabesque".' We are left to guess exactly what Hammond meant, but there is, in the way that Wells slithers nonchalantly over the complex background harmonies, a foreshadowing of the droll, quasi-conversational passages which were to become an overworked mannerism in later years. Here it is extremely effective, complementing the abstract nature of the composition with unusual intervals and notes deliberately indeterminate in pitch. The re-entry, after the middle-eight by the saxophone section, must have aroused pure joy in the heart of the composer, so unexpected is the direction from which it comes wafting in. Once again, the style belonged exclusively to the trombone—neither the trumpet nor the keyed instruments could achieve the same subtle gradations of pitch without a consequent loss of tone.

Had Dickie Wells made no more records after that, he would have qualified as a jazz giant, with 'Pastoral' eligible as a masterpiece. But there were greater things to come. In 1937, the trombonist was a member of Teddy Hill's band when it made a trip to France. While in Paris, some sessions were organized by the Hot Club of France, under the active leadership of Hugues Panassié, in which Dickie Wells led some small groups of French and American musicians in informal recordings. Dickie Wells's playing, in line-ups ranging from the somewhat eccentric conjunction of three trumpets and a trombone to more conventional instrumentation, is consistently superb, especially in the several blues pieces. As often when it comes to making a choice, I have gone for two particular favourites of mine, while admitting certain pangs at the necessary exclusion of the fine all-brass arrangement (by Roy Eldridge) of 'Between the Devil and the Deep Blue Sea' and the beautifully relaxed blues 'Hangin' around Boudon'.

Both the last-named were recorded at the same session, on 7 July 1937. In the trumpet section which recorded 'Between the Devil and the Deep Blue Sea', 'I Got Rhythm' and 'Bugle Call Rag' were Bill Dillard and Shad Collins, colleagues of Wells's in the Teddy Hill Band, and Bill Coleman, who was already in Paris working with Willie Lewis's Band. Bassist Dick Fulbright and drummer Bill Beason from the Hill Band were joined by the Belgian-born guitarist, Django Reinhardt, then a revered pillar of the French jazz scene. After the four-brass arrangements had been recorded, Dillard and Collins stood down, leaving Dickie Wells and Bill Coleman to polish off three more unrehearsed sides. The two musicians were no strangers to each other, their paths having crossed in the bands of both Lloyd and Cecil Scott in the late Twenties, and subsequently with Benny Carter and probably Luis Russell, too.

Bill Coleman, like every other trumpet player of his generation, came under the spell of Louis Armstrong in his formative years. It is thanks to the vast scope of Armstrong's style, with its many different facets, that his many disciples did not all sound exactly alike. The Louis Armstrong whom Bill Coleman worshipped was the fleet-footed, mercurial virtuoso of the latter-day Hot Fives, when the newly formed partnership with Earl Hines was spurring Louis into electrifying performances. One record in particular, called 'Fireworks', made a deep impression on Bill Coleman and was clearly influential in the forming of his own agile and sparkling style. For greater mobility he avoided the heavy, declamatory aspects of the trumpet sound, cultivating a light, clear tone to which a fast, rippling shake, sparsely used, gave additional sparkle. His animated and joyous playing was just the thing to bring out the swashbuckler in Dickie Wells, and it is perhaps no coincidence that the tune which produced their most exciting playing on the Paris session was 'Sweet Sue', the scene, four years earlier, of one of his most hair-raising escapades.

The first thing that one notices about this performance is that the convention that a statement of the tune should precede the improvised variations is waived. Perhaps Dickie Wells was encouraged by the scant attention that Henry 'Red' Allen gave to the detail of the original melody in the Spike Hughes version. Anyway, the listener, after a brief reminder of the opening notes, is called on to carry the rest of the original theme in his head and, by way of reward, is granted a rare insight into the jazz art of spontaneous variation. Seemingly untroubled by Django Reinhardt's rather hearty conception of rhythmic guitar playing (not his strong point), Dickie Wells sets about building a finely constructed trombone chorus upon the opening five notes of the song. His tone is now rounded and consistent, and much more sparing use is made of the shake so that some sustained notes have barely noticeable vibrato. There is also total rhythmic assurance, with that natural and unforced movement between on-the-beat and across-the-beat phrases that defies musical notation and yet is the essence of swing.

Dickie Wells makes three separate appearances during the performance, twice in full thirty-two-bar solos and once in a series of eight-bar exchanges with Bill Coleman. Apart from general observations, I will pick out just one salient point in each of these appearances. In the opening chorus, in which the song's repetitive phrases are replaced by a developing line of melody, there is a moment of inventive brilliance at the point when the tune moves into its middle-eight. In the original melody, the second eight-bar section, as the first, ends decisively, and boringly, on the words 'It's you Sweet Sue'. There is then ample space for the singer to take a breath and launch afresh into the equally repetitive middle-eight with the words 'No one else it seems Ever shares my dreams'. Altogether, it represents the sort of dreary symmetry which jazz musicians were created to transform into music. What Dickie Wells does is play, where the words 'sweet Sue' would come, a rhythmic six-note phrase in the upper register which is completed by the actual five notes that accompany 'No one else it seems'. In other words, for the first time since the opening notes of the chorus, he reverts briefly to the notes of the original song, but uses them to end a phrase of his own rather than to start the middle-eight as the composers intended. The resulting passage stretches from bar fourteen to bar eighteen of the tune, thereby straddling the 'natural break' at the end of bar sixteen at which every popular song of this hackneyed construction stops repeating itself, heaves a prolonged sigh of relief and then trots off towards the brief respite of the middle-eight.

Bill Coleman's first trumpet solo that follows is perhaps rather less tidily constructed than his partner's, nevertheless it has a fine lithe and eager shape to it, with phrases that crackle and leap like flames. When Dickie Wells returns, the tension and excitement has been raised by several notches, and he responds with a high declamatory entry in trumpet style which would have gladdened Jimmy Harrison's heart. But as so often in his solos, he seems to be overtaken by the urge to follow one passage with another contrasting one which contradicts it. Thus the opening four bars of the solo produce a clear, positive line of melody which is then followed, in the corresponding section from bars nine to twelve, by an almost derisive descending phrase in which awkward intervals, including a sudden drop of an octave, are made even harder on the ear by a deliberately casual pitching of the notes. Here again is the trombonist taking full advantage of the instrument's unique qualities, this time the capacity for self-mockery. Dignity is soon restored, but the playful mood is not so easily

banished, and returns at the start of the middle-eight in an outbreak of stammering and chuckling effected by the use of rapid
tongueing to punctuate a downward glissando.

Clearly Dickie Wells is now in a devilish mood which, in turn,
strikes a joyful chord in Bill Coleman. Early in his solo there is a
glorious moment when he soars upwards like a lark in a burst of
joie de vivre, and the rest of the solo literally crackles with energy.
This so excites his partner that he can't wait until the end of the
chorus before elbowing in with his first contribution to the eight-
bar exchanges. A riff is thrown at Coleman who barely has time
to respond before Dickie Wells is back, interrupting him with a
challenging whoop. Now it's time for Bill Coleman to cock a
snook, which he does with an insolent quotation from 'The Girl I
Left Behind Me'. In the middle-eight, the slippery high-register
phrase that almost dropped him on his backside in the Spike
Hughes version of the tune presents itself to Dickie Wells again,
but this time he is confident enough to repeat it three times with
a sort of 'Look at me, I'm flying!' exhilaration, the fluttering
effect heightened by more rapid tongueing. After a response from
Bill Coleman, the record ends, as so many spontaneous performances do, with some somewhat indecisive riffing, but by then
the listener is already silently applauding one of the most scintillating conversation pieces in all of jazz.

The second Dickie Wells masterpiece from the Paris sessions
was recorded five days later on 12 July, and once again sounds as
if it was put down as an afterthought when the more exacting
stuff was safely in the can. Here Dickie Wells plays seven choruses
of the blues backed by a trio of Sam Allen on piano, Roger
Chaput on guitar and Bill Beason, drums. The art of a continuous
blues performance such as this is to build the successive choruses
with logic and mounting intensity, one on top of the other so that
in the end an impressive and awesome edifice is erected. If 'Dickie
Wells Blues' is not one of the very greatest recordings in this
genre it is because, to fall back on contemporary jargon, Dickie
Wells 'peaks' too soon. Over five choruses his performance completes a perfect elliptical shape, rising to a high emotional climax
in the third chorus and then gently subsiding to the mood of the
opening. But there are two more choruses to go after that and

full of good things as they are in themselves, they have no new ideas to add to the overall structure and consequently give one a slight feeling of anticlimax.

Nevertheless, the record provides one of the finest available examples of extended blues playing. The opening chorus establishes that, like Jack Teagarden, Dickie Wells was well versed in the history as well as the structural format of the blues. The chorus is based, like the chorus of any classic Bessie Smith performance, on a 'vocal' line stated in bars one to three, repeated in bars five to seven and resolved in bars nine to eleven. The only structural difference between Wells's instrumental approach and a Bessie Smith blues lies in the fact that Wells himself, rather than a separate accompanist, fills in between the principal two-bar phrases. As the choruses unfold, we find that Dickie Wells is uncommonly strict in adhering to this basic scheme of things. Thus when he plays the 'vocal' lines (those over which words would be sung in a vocal performance) he uses simple, stately phrases, adhering closely to the beat and eschewing any decorative variation. In the intervening spaces, on the other hand, we find more elaborate, rhythmically daring passages, reminding one of the way in which the youthful Louis Armstrong would literally dance attendance on the great ladies of the blues.

It is on this strong but flexible structure that the whole performance is built. But unlike a blues singer, who has the changing pattern of words to sustain interest, an instrumentalist cannot simply repeat the same basic phrases with minimal variation for chorus after chorus. Much of the strength of this Dickie Wells performance derives from the variety and quality of the successive themes ('opening gambits', one might say). To my ears, chorus one is melancholy, chorus two defiant, chorus four anguished, chorus five ineffably wistful. I have left chorus three out because it merits separate discussion, being the climax of the whole piece. As is appropriate to what is in effect the keystone of the piece, it differs in shape from the other choruses. Here, there is no alternating pattern of statement and elaboration. The impassioned opening phrase, ending on an explosive fifth in the upper register, is not self-contained but a question, if you like, which demands an equally weighty reply. In this respect, the chorus is strikingly similar to Jack Teagarden's second chorus in 'Knockin' a Jug', with the same sense of urgency. The stretching of the principal 'vocal' line over bars one to four and again over bars five to eight, and the consequent elimination of any contrasting 'fill-in' phrases, gives this climactic chorus enormous strength and power, and serves to lift 'Dickie Wells Blues' to the exalted realms of great blues performances.

After he returned to the United States from Paris, Dickie Wells joined Count Basie's Orchestra for a six-year spell which was to produce many more outstandingly inventive and varied solos. His output of distinguished work between the Spike Hughes sessions and the mid-Forties was rivalled by only a handful of the very greatest artists. But when a decline came—the combination perhaps of hard living, creative exhaustion and the disturbing effects of the advent of bebop—it was as though that great contribution had never been made. Seldom, if ever, has an artist of acknowledged stature been so scorned and derided by the critical fraternity. Seeing how the stories of others who flagged in the race—Billie Holiday, Lester Young—have been told with deep sadness and understanding, one is left with the unattractive thought that Dickie Wells's chief offence has been to remain alive and, until a few years ago, working. Listening to his work in the Fifties and Sixties with Buck Clayton and others, one is bound to regret the absence of the great creative energy and confidence that he showed in the records I have discussed, and to note with sadness how the occasional bursts of passion or drollery in the earlier years had changed to apparent cynicism and self-parody. But musicians are not, like boxers or matinée idols, customarily afforded the opportunity to announce retirement as soon as either will or muscles begin to sag. Dickie Wells played on, adding plenty of entertaining and highly personal performances to the treasury of incomparably great ones.

A 'flower of jazz' is John Hammond's verdict on him in his recently published autobiography. Let it stand.

Lester Young

IN THE MYTHOLOGY OF ART, an innovative genius is popularly supposed to be rejected by the critical establishment, mocked by fellow-artists and scorned by the public, with starvation in a garret as the preferred corollary. Indeed, one need not be a die-hard reactionary to suspect that, sometimes, new and experimental work is prematurely acknowledged as fine art solely because it fulfils the above requirements.

Jazz in its early days offered fruitful ground for revolutionary change. In Volume One of *The Best of Jazz* I was able to propose, without incurring the charge of eccentricity or iconoclasm, that Louis Armstrong overturned, almost single-handedly, the rhythmic foundations of the music, that Earl Hines demolished the accepted notions of jazz piano playing, that Fletcher Henderson with his arranger, Don Redman, introduced an entirely new way of organizing a big orchestra, and that Bix Beiderbecke defied, Canute-like, the on-coming tide of Armstrong's influence and offered the world a less spectacular but strikingly different alternative. If we add the evidence in these pages that the constant alteration and revision that Coleman Hawkins applied to his already highly original style amounted to a one-man cultural revolution, we have enough turbulent activity to have kept the first Jazz Age in a constant state of upheaval.

When we look at the stories that surround these great events in jazz history, a sense of excitement is there in plenty, but there is a notable absence of the reactionary suspicion and hostility that we would today expect such startling change to inspire. Musicians and audiences apparently embraced each innovation eagerly, and jazz criticism, still in its infancy, toddled along behind. Thus I was able to quote the musician, Tommy Brookins, as saying, 'Opposite the young Louis, who was already prodigious, [King] Oliver's style appeared to date a little and it was frequent to hear musicians talk among themselves of "the old style".' Likewise, it took just one note from Bix Beiderbecke's cornet to persuade Eddie Condon that Bix was not the 'clam digger' that he took him to be on sight. Approval for each dramatic departure seemed to be virtually instantaneous. If the British and European writers, epitomized in the late Twenties by the newly born London *Melody Maker*, were a trifle cautious about leading black musicians, it was the alleged 'crudeness' of their work rather than its musical precocity and sophistication that was the cause.

When we come to the story of Lester Young's emergence in the mid-Thirties, we move a large step closer to the stereotyped response to change that I have outlined above. Within the Count Basie band of 1936, his controversial style was matched against that of a more conventional tenorist, Herschel Evans. The rivalry between the two men, leavened by a grudging mutual respect, is part of jazz legend. Evans, a passionate admirer of Coleman Hawkins, insisted—no doubt with a certain seasoning of malice— that Lester's light, airy sound, innocent of the sand-papery overtones of Hawkins and his followers, was more appropriate to the alto saxophone. The taunt drew from Lester Young the famous response, quoted by Billie Holiday, 'There's things going on up there, man'—tapping his forehead—'Some of you guys are all belly!'

In an erudite jazz publication in London in 1946, ten years after the first Lester Young recordings appeared on the market, a critic wrote: 'Of all the elements in the Count Basie band, Lester Young's freakish and imaginatively sterile tenor saxophone style has been the most over-praised.' (Today the writer is recognized as one of the most distinguished, perceptive and eclectic jazz commentators in the world, whose reputation is well able to withstand a few disinterred indiscretions. So if I decline to name him, it is only because justice would demand a litany of similar youthful misjudgements on my own part, and they would occupy a whole chapter.) We should understand the context in which this and similar judgements were made. The flow of new recordings from America had been constipated by the exigencies of war, so that the writer was reflecting, at a seemingly late stage, a view that some American critics had already expressed several years earlier.

Furthermore, the revulsion from the commercial excesses of the Swing Era—which, even as the British critic was writing, was being reflected in the stampede of musicians towards the twin escape routes of New Orleans Revivalism and small-group Bebop —led to much valuable stuff being summarily tipped out with the bath water. Thus his assessment of the Basie band's arrival on the scene as 'the final disastrous event in the development of swing music' was in tune with an anti-Swing trend that also involved some critical denunciations of Duke Ellington's orchestra of the very early Forties, a period now widely acknowledged as an Ellingtonian golden era.

The reactions of musicians on the spot are naturally faster than those of critics removed from the centre of the action, and it was much earlier in his career that Lester Young met the stiffest opposition from other players. It was in 1934, when he was playing in Count Basie's band in Kansas City, that he received a call from Fletcher Henderson, whose star saxophonist, Coleman Hawkins, had just left for Europe. According to Lester, he had already sat in with the Henderson Orchestra—presumably during one of that band's visits to Kansas City—and, in the temporary absence of Hawkins, had been able to show that he could handle all the saxophone and clarinet parts in Hawk's book.

Any euphoric expectations which Lester Young might have entertained after that episode were rudely shattered when he arrived in Detroit to join Henderson for a trial period. In view of my earlier comments on the reaction of critics to Lester Young, it is paradoxical that the one man in Fletcher Henderson's entourage who *did* appreciate the newcomer was critic and *ex officio* musical adviser, John Hammond. 'I thought he was the greatest tenor I'd heard in my life. He was so different. There was a terrific scene. The guys in the band all wanted Chu Berry to replace Hawkins because Chu had a sound like Hawkins. They complained that Lester's sound was "like an alto". Buster Bailey, Russell Procope and John Kirby outshouted me that day.' Despite the immediate opposition, Lester stayed with Henderson for several miserable months. In addition to the hostile whisperings of the musicians, he was subjected to attempted brainwashing by Fletcher Henderson's wife, Leora. The recollection of it in an interview twenty-three years later (with François Postif, published in the book *Jazz Panorama*) aroused in him uncharacteristic aggression. 'That bitch, she was Fletcher's wife, she took me down to the basement and played one of the old wind-up record-players, and she'd say, "Lester, can't you play like this?" Coleman Hawkins records. But I mean, can't you hear this? Can't you get with that? You dig? I split! Every morning that bitch would wake me up at nine o'clock to teach me to play like Coleman Hawkins. And she played trumpet herself . . . circus trumpet! I'm gone!'

And gone he was, back by a devious route to Count Basie's Kansas City Band. Two years later, Hammond picked up a broadcast from Kansas City on his car radio in the small hours of the morning. It featured Count Basie's Orchestra with Lester in one of the two tenor-saxophone chairs. Hammond's subsequent championing of Basie's band gave him a second and more success-ful chance to promote the career of Lester Young.

Careful scrutiny of all the criticism of Lester Young from musicians and commentators that was expressed between 1934 and 1946 reveals in him one fundamental flaw. He was not Coleman Hawkins. And in case anyone should think that British critics were straggling behind their American counterparts by the mid-Forties, it is worth noting that an annual jazz award organized by the American *Esquire Magazine*, and judged by a panel of from sixteen to eighteen professional jazz critics, overlooked Lester Young entirely in the years 1944 and 1946, and could only find room for him in the Silver Award category in 1945. Each year, the top Golden Award went to Coleman Hawkins. At the same time, in an article in the same magazine entitled 'Jazz Greats: Musicians and Bands', one Paul Edouard Miller omitted Lester entirely from a list of no less than sixteen all-time saxophone 'greats', at the same time scraping the barrel for such comparative lightweights as Babe Russin, Joe Garland and Prince Robinson.

Creatively, Lester Young's most fruitful and consistent period spanned a mere eight years between his first recordings in 1936 and his induction into the US Army in 1944. Throughout that time, it took a tenor-saxophone player of almost perverse individuality and persistence not to be Coleman Hawkins. Of all the tenor players who had come to the fore since Hawkins lugged the instrument into the jazz fold in the mid-Twenties, only Bud Freeman comes to mind as a player offering an alternative to the heavy-toned, chesty and romantic Hawkins model. Even so, study of Bud's playing in the early Thirties reveals a hustling, rough-edged sound nearer to Hawkins than Young. The often-made assumption that Bud influenced Lester—rejected by Lester himself in the aforementioned interview with the splendidly dismissive and original expletive 'ladedehumptedorebebop!'—seems to me to have been based on the lighter sound which Bud acquired in the late Thirties, long after Lester's style had been formed. During those eight years when he was battling his way into the jazz history books against the Hawkins tide, Lester Young fought without the ego-boosting support, such as both Hawkins and Armstrong enjoyed, of a 'school' of admirers and imitators. He was not entirely isolated. Within his own coterie of Kansas City musicians, several of them colleagues in Count Basie's band, he found staunch admiration and friendship. And there was the added compensation that the audiences in the dance halls across the country latched on to his 'new' style very much more quickly than did some critics and fellow musicians. Some recordings of on-location broadcasts by the Basie band in the late Thirties enable us to hear the clamorous response which his free-wheeling solos received. Perhaps for this reason, he never shared the jaundiced and somewhat contemptuous view of the paying customer that Coleman Hawkins so often expressed. He once told a somewhat surprised interviewer that he enjoyed playing for dancers because of the rhythmic feed-back that he received from the floor.

It was from musicians outside his own circle that he felt the chilliest draught. The article which Rex Stewart wrote in *Downbeat* in 1966 (and which was reproduced in the compilation *Jazz in the Thirties*) threw light on the prevailing atmosphere in the late Thirties. In the chapter on Coleman Hawkins, I have already quoted Rex's description of the return of Hawkins to New York after his sojourn in Europe and his appearance at Pussy Johnson's 'after-hours' club. Continuing the narrative, Rex wrote: 'Hawk fell in later than usual—it was about 3 a.m.—and as luck would have it, Lady Day was singing, which rarely happened uptown those days (1939). Of course, Lester accompanied her. Bean [Coleman Hawkins] strode in, unpacked his axe and joined them, to everyone's surprise. Then, when Billie Holiday finished, she announced that it had been a pleasure to have had the world's greatest tenor saxophonist backing her up—Lester Young!' The story continues in predictable fashion with Hawkins imperiously routing Lester Young. When the article first appeared, it prompted Billie Holiday to write an angry letter to the magazine refuting it and claiming that Lester had been the victor. The outcome is irrelevant to us now. What is significant is Billie's defensive reaction on behalf of her friend and colleague, and the way in which the resentment which the devotees of Hawkins felt at the challenge from Lester Young seemed to survive the twenty-seven years between the event and Rex's published recollection of it. In more recent times, during the rapid progress of jazz through first modern and then *avant-garde* phases, we have become accustomed to the spectacle of new sounds being angrily—and, if the truth were known, fearfully—repudiated by musicians and *aficionados* of an older school. It is a measure of the total originality of Lester's whole approach to his instrument that, before him, such a thing had never happened in jazz.

If we look beyond the scope of this volume to the fourteen years between Lester Young's discharge from the army and his untimely death in 1959, we are confronted with a terrible irony. For at the very time that swarms of young musicians were homing in on Lester's style and establishing it as the basis of modern tenor-saxophone development, his own playing went into dramatic decline. Whether because of trauma inflicted on his sensitive nature during his army stint or, more simply and probably, through sheer creative exhaustion, the once smooth-flowing and effortless stream of invention became progressively clogged up with a compound of lassitude, eccentricity and technical debility. The irony is brought into sharp focus by the story, probably apocryphal, of a young disciple who, outraged by a lacklustre and uninspired performance by the master, confronted him on the bandstand with the anguished cry, 'You're not you—I'M you!'

At this point, we should pause to look into the origins—so far as we can deduce them—and the nature of Lester Young's once-controversial style. The first thing to say about it is that, unlike the styles of so many other jazz innovators which we are able to trace through their formative, exploratory years, the Lester Young sound burst upon us fully fledged with his very first recording and thenceforward changed only to modify and, eventually, deteriorate. Sound was the principal, though not the only, new ingredient. Let's think for a moment in terms of singing. As most readers may well have discovered for themselves through experiments in the bath, the difference between the tenor, the baritone and the bass voice (or, in the upper range, soprano, mezzo-soprano and contralto) is one of sound production as much as range. Indeed, the actual difference in range of pitch between the tenor and bass voice is rather less than the sound suggests. The bathroom experiment to which I referred often begins with the urge to sound like the late Paul Robeson. 'Oold mahn roover,' we intone, opening the mouth wide but shaping it into closed 'oo' and 'aw' sounds to achieve the resonant, booming effect. Instantly the bath becomes the rolling Mississippi as you and me we sweat and strain, neighbours all achin' and wracked with pain. When we switch to a Mario Lanza tenor, stretching the mouth into a permanent smile with piercing 'ee' and 'ah' vowels and bringing the sound up into the throat, the scene changes miraculously to the sun-speckled waters of Venice—but because our natural tuneless drone is neither bass-baritone nor tenor, the notes are exactly the same, restricted to a very unspectacular middle range. If you doubt me, get out that favourite Paul Robeson record and sing along with it, but in Mario Lanza fashion, all thin vowels and throaty constriction. You will find the pitch is not as low as you thought.

This light-hearted excursion into bathroom opera has a direct bearing on the Lester Young-Coleman Hawkins discussion. The sound which Coleman Hawkins produced from the tenor saxophone using, according to him, a hard reed and open 'lay' (the gap between reed surface and mouthpiece) was a rich chest tone in which impurities such as the sound of breath passing over the reed and the actual buzzing of the reed as it vibrated gave added weight to the note. Further enrichment was provided by a wide and quite heavy vibrato, which saxophonists achieve by a throbbing movement of lips and jaw around the mouthpiece. The choice of this deeply expressive sound—often referred to as a 'vocal sound' because of its similarity to the rough edge and heavy vibrato of the human voice in general and black singers of African origin in particular—was not peculiar either to Coleman Hawkins or to the tenor saxophone. It came naturally to jazzmen playing music closely allied to such folk sources as the blues and black church music. The feeling of high emotional intensity which it conveys— in the trumpet playing of Louis Armstrong, the soprano saxophone of Sidney Bechet, the clarinet of Johnny Dodds and Pee Wee Russell, the trombone of Jimmy Harrison and Dickie Wells—was largely responsible for the application of the word 'hot' to the music which these men and their contemporaries and imitators produced.

To explain why Coleman Hawkins dominated the tenor-saxophone field for over a decade we must look at the character of the instrument itself. The saxophone is not, *pace* Adolphe Sax, the most successful of musical instruments in its pristine state. Despite the claim of its inventor that it would bridge the gap between brass and woodwind, it was spurned by the symphony orchestra and found only a limited role to play in military bands. Even its apparent apotheosis in the ranks of the early dance bands was less of a triumph than it seemed. For the instrument became, in the Twenties, the symbol of everything that was oily, sickly and sentimental about popular music. In the London humorous magazine, *Punch*, decadent dance music was symbolized in cartoons by a limp and languid figure with slicked, patent-leather hair and ankle-length coat-tails, exhaling superciliously into a saxophone. Within the saxophone family itself, judged by its own aspirations, the soprano and alto instruments had at the outset a certain plaintive clarity which is attractive, while there was more masculine character in the gruffness of baritone and bass. But I fancy that Adolphe Sax might himself have conceded, in an unguarded moment, that the tenor saxophone was a flop. The flabby, rubbery sounds, evoking the image of someone trying to juggle pancakes, that can be heard on dance-band recordings made before (and for sometime after) Coleman Hawkins took the instrument in hand, provide evidence of its recalcitrance. Indeed, when we listen to some of the early recordings which he himself made with Fletcher Henderson's band, we may be excused for wondering what manic urge drove him to persevere in such an unpromising task. But persevere he did, and the means by which he gave the tenor saxophone a commanding jazz voice have already been explored. After such massive effort and achievement, it is little wonder that, for years, other tenor-saxophone players were content to base their own explorations on the Hawkins method, as if no other feasible way of playing the instrument existed.

Apart from acknowledging the influence that Louis Armstrong had on all the musicians in Fletcher Henderson's band during his brief engagement with it, Coleman Hawkins never offered any suggestion as to external influences on his style. Lester Young was more obliging. To the consternation of some jazz pundits who have exaggerated the ethnic origins of jazz to the point of a sort of cultural *apartheid*, Lester always pointed to two white musicians as his chief influences. 'I had a decision to make between Frankie Trumbauer and Jimmy Dorsey [Lester was playing alto saxophone at the time], you dig, and I wasn't sure which way I wanted to go. I'd buy me all those records and I'd play one by Jimmy and one by Trumbauer, you dig? I didn't know nothing about Hawk then, and they were the only ones telling a story I liked to hear. I had both of them made ... Did you ever hear Trumbauer play "Singin' the Blues"? That tricked me right then and that's where I went.'

Significantly, Frank Trumbauer played the now obsolete C-melody saxophone on 'Singin' the Blues', an instrument pitched between the E flat alto saxophone and the B flat tenor. So when, at some undetermined point in his career, Lester Young switched to the tenor saxophone, it was easy for him to carry over the Trumbauer influence, such as it was, on to the lower instrument. I say 'such as it was' because, by the time we hear Lester on record, it is hard to find any vestige of Trumbauer except in the lightness of his sound compared with that of Coleman Hawkins. Where Trumbauer's notes are rhythmically flat and lifeless, Lester's, though comparably light on vibrato, have a springy resilience. One note of his—and we shall see that he quite often started a solo with an isolated note as if to balance himself for the flight of fancy ahead—would swing more than a whole phrase of Trumbauer's. Likewise there is no resemblance between Trumbauer's sinuous, rubber-necked and rather contrived phraseology and Lester's free-flying, effortless inventions. Some commentators have called on the paucity of stylistic links between Trumbauer and Lester Young to back the suggestion that the latter simply dredged up Trumbauer's name to satisfy an inquisitive interviewer. But it would not be the first time in artistic history that a small fragment from a predecessor's work has sown in the mind of a fellow-artist the seed of a fully-fledged style.

Referring back to the analogy of the bathroom vocalist, we can understand why Herschel Evans and the musicians in Fletcher Henderson's band thought that Lester's tone sounded like an alto. They would have been equally fair had they alleged that Hawkins made the instrument sound more like a baritone. 'Some of you guys are all belly!' was an apt riposte from Lester, too— the sound to which the Hawkins school aspired did seem to originate not far north of the pelvic region. If the contrast between Lester and the Hawkins 'establishment' rested only in the matter of tone production, then it would hardly warrant the space it occupies in the jazz history books. But from tone production, other aspects of style spring. One consequence of the light, airy sound that Lester Young adopted was that it made him more fleet of foot.

The word that recurs in critical analyses of the Coleman Hawkins style is 'heavy', and it is a word that can be taken literally. Hawk himself had the power and the imaginative resources to overcome the sheer weight of his delivery. His imitators—and through the Thirties they were legion, in Britain and Europe as well as in the United States—often gave the impression, to borrow one British musician's evocative phrase, that they were trying to tow the *Queen Mary* through a sea of Mars Bars. The dichotomy between agility and emotional weight had occurred in jazz years before Lester Young's emergence. In the late Twenties, the trumpeter, Jabbo Smith, challenged Louis Armstrong's supremacy with a style that sacrificed some of Armstrong's richness of tone and vibrato in favour of range and speed. He failed not because his style was too different from Armstrong's, but because it was too close. Encouraged, if not coerced, by a record company to try and match the popular records by Louis Armstrong's Hot Five, he missed the mark artistically (and commercially, too, though perhaps for other reasons) because in his efforts to surpass the *method* of Armstrong's playing he lost its spirit.

At no time in his career did Lester flirt with the Hawkins method. Central to the Hawkins style, especially in heated, up-tempo work, was the technique that musicians used to call 'running changes'. This means basing an improvisation on the changing harmonies that underlie a tune. Consisting of funda-mental chords and 'linking' chords—secondary chords used to pass conveniently and elegantly from one fundamental chord to another—these harmonies often present the improviser with a complex challenge. Take a simple progression—C, C diminished, G seventh—in which the C diminished is the linking chord. This might well occur in the space of two bars at breakneck speed. To 'run the changes' impressively the player will fashion a melodic line which makes explicit use of the arpeggios of the three chords, giving the impression of a terrier snapping at the heels of the harmonies as they twist and turn. Coleman Hawkins, as we have seen, was a master at this, often choosing tunes with complex progressions or using his keenly acquired knowledge of harmony to make simple progressions more challenging by adding or sub-stituting chords.

It is a mistake to think that Lester Young set out consciously to alter this approach to improvisation. Some rather facile judgements delivered in hindsight after the advent of Bebop suggested that Lester was influential in laying the theoreretical foundations of the new style. If the hindsight is focused a little more intently, the interesting fact that emerges is that Lester's most direct influence on post-1945 (still anachronistically referred to as Modern) jazz, through the countless young tenor saxo-phonists who adopted his sound and method of phrase-building, was essentially conservative. Players such as Wardell Gray, Allan Eager, Stan Getz (in his early days), Herbie Steward and Zoot Sims were notably less adventurous, harmonically and rhythmically, than the young altoists and trumpeters who followed Charlie Parker and Dizzy Gillespie.

As regards the raw materials on which he thrived, Lester Young may be said to have been more deeply committed to the tenets of the Swing Era than Coleman Hawkins. While Hawkins was constantly chasing new harmonic patterns on which to sharpen his improvisational wits, Lester appeared to be content with the simplest of harmonies. Indeed, it may have been his upbringing in the environment of Kansas City jazz, with its great emphasis on the blues and on the building of massive rhythmic skyscrapers on the simplest of themes, that, in his formative years, pushed Lester into exploring new paths of invention. There is little future in running changes if those changes resolutely refuse to budge!

So far, our analysis of Lester Young has been somewhat negative. He did not play with a huge, positive sound like Coleman Hawkins. He did not base his improvisations as closely as Hawkins did on the details of moving harmonies. Nor on the other hand did he radically change or extend conventional theory. It has to be said that Lester's own character and personality contributed to this negative impression. One of the many idiosyncratic, short-hand phrases of which his conversation was compounded was 'No eyes'—a simplified reversal of the sentiment in the song-title 'I Only have Eyes for You'. We know of a great many things for which Lester had 'no eyes', among them honking one-note tenor players, drummers who 'dropped bombs'— broke up the rhythm with explosive accents—pianists who intruded on the soloist and so on. But on the positive side, Lester was even less inclined than his predecessors and contemporaries to put his musical ideas into words.

Fortunately, there has been no shortage of commentators ready to analyse Lester's style. Sometimes there has been a tendency to commit, in reverse, the injustice inflicted upon Lester in his early years—in other words, to suggest that, by being different from Coleman Hawkins, Lester Young was *ipso facto* better than him. If our discussions about jazz performances up to now have revealed anything, it is that the intrinsic merit in a jazz musician's work lies not in the materials that he uses, but in the use he makes of them. In the first book in this series, for example, I looked at the work of three contrasting trumpet players, Louis Armstrong, Bix Beiderbecke and Henry 'Red' Allen. We saw how, in 'Potato Head Blues', Louis took the theme and virtually redesigned it, filling it out with rhythmic, harmonic and emotional dimensions that it never possessed before. In 'Singin' the Blues', Bix did something different, building on the harmonies of the tune an entirely new melody, quite different in shape from the original. And I noted that, in 'Panama' and elsewhere, Henry Allen's method was to super-impose on the theme bursts of impressionistic sound that bore the same relationship to the 'tune' as an abstract painting has to the model or still-life that inspired it. If we deduce from this that Bix tended to improvise 'melodically' while the others did not, it does not mean that their melodies were somehow imperfect, nor indeed that they performed the almost impossible task of stringing notes together in sequence without producing a coherent melodic line at all! Least of all does it mean that any one of these jazzmen pursued his own method to the exclusion of the others. It is a matter of emphasis.

In this context, the best way to distinguish between the Coleman Hawkins method and that of Lester Young is to say that, in basing his improvisations on the harmonies of, say, a popular ballad, Hawkins in fact was creating an elaborate cadenza around a tune or melody line which was implied rather than stated. Thus a Hawkins solo is rarely, if ever, as simple in structure as the tune on which it is based. Lester Young was not given to elaboration on these lines. What he preferred to do was to create his own tune, offering in his solo an alternative, if you like, to the nominal theme. Two extreme examples of this method come to mind.

In the Count Basie recording of 'Jive at Five' made in 1938, Lester's way of improvising on the frail, sparse theme is to create another frail theme, no less sparse than the original, and develop that through the thirty-two-bar solo. And in the 1945 version with his own quartet of 'These Foolish Things', he discards Jack

Strachey's tune altogether, jumping—or, in his characteristically diffident way, sidling—in at the deep end with a spontaneously composed melody line of his own.

The beauty and the challenge of this type of solo-building is that it offers the soloist greater freedom from the restrictions of the popular song format. Leaving aside distinguished exceptions which will spring to every reader's mind, the great majority of popular songs written between the Twenties and the Fifties have come in a standard thirty-two-bar length. Some of them, such as I Can't Give you Anything but Love' or 'Pennies from Heaven', are divided into two sixteen-bar halves, sharing an opening four-bar phrase which progresses, in each half respectively, towards an imperfect cadence or half-way mark and a perfect cadence or conclusion. The significant thing about this format in our present context is that it involves repetition, the tune going back to the beginning at the start of the second half. Even more repetition is involved in the other standard formula, represented in tunes such as George Gershwin's 'I Got Rhythm', Fats Waller's 'Honeysuckle Rose' and, with slight variation, Irving Berlin's 'Easter Parade'. Here the tune is divided into four eight-bar sections in the pattern AABA, the B section being known, in a triumph of expediency over geometric accuracy, as the 'middle-eight'. (The variation in 'Easter Parade' and many similar tunes is that there is an imperfect cadence—a musical comma, if you like—between the first two A sections.)

In the 1930s, jazz musicians, increasingly absorbed more with the solo development of a theme than with the structure of the theme itself, often borrowed tunes from Tin Pan Alley or lazily superimposed a set of 'riffs' or repeated phrases on the framework of a standard popular song (Chu Berry's 'Christopher Columbus' is one of perhaps several hundred similar 'compositions' based on 'I Got Rhythm'). The short-winded repetitiveness of these themes presented a challenge to the jazz improviser, whatever his method. Louis Armstrong revealed himself a master at reshaping the tunesmith's repetitive phrases with melodic and rhythmic variation so that they grew into a magnificent edifice that dwarfed the original. Following this Armstrong line, Coleman Hawkins added his own extension of it, which was to build on the equally repetitive harmonies of the tune an inexhaustible flow of varying patterns and embellishments that seem to jostle and fall over each other in their eagerness to pursue each new notion to its conclusion.

It might be thought that in opting for the simplest harmonic framework of popular ditty and the blues ('The blues? Great big eyes!' was how he reacted to a question about the latter) and improvising his own melody over it, Lester Young had gone for the soft option. No 'tune' to enhance and ennoble in the Armstrong manner, no complex harmonic changes to follow and resolve *à la* Hawkins—what could be simpler or less fraught with responsibility, you might ask? Indeed, the Swing Era, geared at its lowest commercial level to the whipping-up of spurious excitement, abounded in solos no less empty and inane than the themes on which they were built. We've all seen those Hollywood 'shorts' featuring big bands in which, inevitably, a trumpet player jumps to his feet, shoulders hunched and brow corrugated with distended veins, to rip off a solo for which the aptest description can be found in *Macbeth*, 'A tale told by an idiot, full of sound and fury, signifying nothing'. Subsequently, the rock'n'roll experience, in which grievous harm has been inflicted by one-note tenor men and three-cliché guitarists upon the noble structure of the blues, has provided added proof that there is nothing easy about improvising on a simple framework, unless it be the production of dire music.

To focus upon Lester Young's mastery we can go straight to one of his very first recorded solos. The session, in Chicago on 9 October 1936, represented a sort of consolation prize to John Hammond for having lost the Count Basie Orchestra to a rival recording company, due to a misunderstanding on Basie's part. But what a prize! Here was a small contingent from the band comprising Lester Young on tenor, Carl 'Tatti' Smith on trumpet and the incomparable rhythm trio of Count Basie, bassist Walter Page, and drummer Jo Jones. For good measure, the rotund Jimmy Rushing (yet to achieve immortality in Tin Pan Alley as the subject of the Gene de Paul-Don Raye novelty song 'Mister Five by Five') was on hand to sing the blues. History has given John Hammond the laugh over his zealous competitor, since these four small-group recordings, originally issued for obvious reasons under the name Jones-Smith Incorporated, gave Lester Young room to stretch out more spectacularly than on the band recordings that followed. The two wholly instrumental titles, 'Lady Be Good', and 'Shoe Shine Boy' (first listed as 'Shoe Shine Swing') are classics, and my choice of the former for close analysis rests on nothing more substantial than old acquaintance.

'Lady Be Good' (pedants please note that I deliberately employ the common jazz musicians' usage, well aware that Gershwin's song is 'Oh, Lady Be Good!' from the 1924 show *Lady, Be Good*) is just the sort of simple tune, in AABA form, that attracts musicians bent upon informal improvisation. With no more than four basic chords and fewer melodic twists, it presents the improviser with what amounts to a bare canvas. The melody gives a Louis Armstrong scope on which to build and expand, the harmonies can be enriched and augmented to provide a Coleman Hawkins or an Art Tatum ample scope for 'running changes'. But, as I have already noted, Lester Young eschewed both these basic methods of improvisation, choosing to construct a line of melody the shape of which was quite independent of the original.

At this point, we must establish the point that Lester's style imposed a heavy responsibility upon the rhythm section, and we may well wonder what would have happened had not a benign Providence brought him together, early in his career, with Count Basie and his rhythm section colleagues. Whether the perfect match was made in heaven or evolved through rehearsal-room or bandstand discussion is not important. Lester Young's requirements have emerged in interviews over the years. 'The piano should play little fill-ins. Just nice little full chords behind the horn. I don't get in his way, and I let him play, and he shouldn't get in mine. Otherwise, your mind gets twisted ... A bass should play nice, four-beat rhythm that can be heard ... On drumming, I don't go for the bomb. I want a drummer to be straight with the section. He's messing with the rhythm when he drops those bombs.'

Pianists, bassists and drummers may well give a wry smile when reading these instructions. They are all too accustomed to being asked to respond to the quirky requirements of front-line men. But the discipline demanded by Lester Young was absolutely essential to his style. We shall soon see that his solos abound in unexpected melodic turns, the subtlest of harmonic nuances and totally unpredictable rhythmic patterns. To have a pianist and drummer dictating fanciful harmonies or rhythmic ideas of their own would have destroyed all the freedom which Lester derived from the simplicity of the thematic framework. Furthermore, it would have been an impertinence on the grandest scale, rather as if a committee of minor sculptors had appointed itself to direct Michelangelo in the carving of his Moses.

Obviously there will be more to say about the Count Basie rhythm section when I come to discuss the Count Basie Orchestra in the ensuing volume of this series. Suffice it to say that, although the great guitarist, Freddie Greene, had yet to join them when 'Lady Be Good' was recorded, Basie, Page and Jones establish from the outset that comfortably slippered, padding rhythm which for almost half a century has been a Basie trade-mark. Though twelve years had elapsed since Gene Krupa demonstrated on the McKenzie-Condon Chicagoan's version of 'Nobody's Sweetheart' that a bass drum could be recorded without damage to the equipment, the tiny studio in which this session took place was still unable to take the strain, and Jo Jones was confined to snare drum and high-hat cymbal. Walter Page, sometimes padding up and down the scale in what is known as 'walking bass' style, sometimes striding across the arpeggios as the New Orleans bassists had done before him, contrived to exude a feeling of strength and security despite his none-too-accurate pitching. As for Basie himself, it may well have been the superb team-work of Jones and Page that prompted him to pare down his once-fulsome stride piano style so as to give them more air. Be that as it may, the three of them sketch in the outline of 'Lady Be Good' with great economy and enormous swing, rolling out a sumptuous red carpet in preparation for Lester Young's entrance.

The British critic and broadcaster, Benny Green, once a tenor saxophonist himself, has told how, as an eager young musician, he learnt Lester Young's solo in 'Lady Be Good' by heart. He was playing in an unenterprising dance band at the time, and it took time and patience to persuade the leader to abandon the stock arrangements and drop an *ad lib* version of 'Lady Be Good' into the routine. When it happened, Benny rose to his feet and reeled off the famous solo note-for-note, his triumph marred only by the fact that he was one bar adrift from the rest of the band throughout. It is not hard to understand the mishap. By the late Thirties, when the Jones-Smith recordings came into wide circulation, jazz enthusiasts had become, through listening to records by Armstrong and Hawkins and Duke Ellington, well acquainted with an established jazz vernacular. As in everyday human speech, certain conventions had emerged—standard and familiar cadences, asides and turns of phrase—which were used, even by the finest players, to achieve continuity in an improvised solo. As a result, the listener came to expect and, indeed, to anticipate a soloist's moves. In Lester Young's work, from the very outset, such expectations are constantly thwarted. In the solo under discussion, there are innumerable surprises of this kind.

The first occurs within the first couple of bars. Lester starts his solo, in characteristic fashion, with a short, isolated phrase the hub of which is a note firmly placed on the first beat of bar one, followed by a long pause of three beats in which he seems to be balancing himself, like a tightrope walker, before making further progress. As a method of launching a solo, this 'balancing note' that Lester often used corresponds to the three anticipated crotchets which were a characteristic of Louis Armstrong's entrances in the Hot Five days. Of particular importance to the surprise effect of the ensuing phrase are the two introductory notes in the preceding bar, a quaver-crotchet combination that serves no purpose other than to lead up to that arresting opening note. If these subsidiary notes are to recur at all, our expectations are that it will be at the end of bar one, as a similarly insignificant lead-in to a new phrase. In the Count Basie recording of 'Jumpin' at the Woodside', there is a concluding riff in which a similar grouping of notes—in this instance three quavers or eighth-notes—lead into the main elements of the riff and occur, as we expect, at the tail-end of each bar. In Lester Young's solo, the notes *do* recur—but they are delayed until half a beat into the second bar, where they become the much more important opening notes of a long, fluent phrase. Had the phrase begun where we expected—at the end of bar one—its main emphasis would have fallen on the first, third and first beats of the ensuing bars, which are fairly conventional stopping and starting places. Lester's 'misplaced' phrase falls heavily on beats three, one and three, altering the whole balance. It may well have been this thwarting of expectations that threw the youthful Benny Green off course.

The solo is full of such departures from common practice. In the second half of the middle-eight (bars twenty-one to twenty-four of the solo) there is another striking example. The chord sequence here is common to many middle-eights. To those acquainted with the language of the harmony text books it can be described as V7 of V, V7. Translated into the 'Lady Be Good' key of G major, these symbols become A seventh, leading on to D seventh. By the time Lester Young came to record the tune, that particular sequence had been played and recorded thousands of times by jazz improvisers. And yet Lester's handling of the sequence strikes us as peculiar and temporarily unsettling. The reason is that, at the end of the first of the two phrases which cover this section, he lands firmly on a C sharp crotchet at the start of bar twenty-two. There is nothing harmonically startling about this—C sharp is the third degree of the scale of A and is therefore perfectly in place in an A seventh chord. Why, then, does the phrase leave us feeling curiously up in the air? The answer is that the C sharp is the leading note into the chord of D seventh which follows. A more commonplace phrase would have ended on A, leaving the ear complacently receptive to several alternative moves from there. But the C sharp arouses positive espectations. As the poet might have said, when C sharp comes, can D be far behind? The answer in this instance is, yes. For with characteristic perversity, Lester Young inserts a linking A minor chord before the D seventh in bar twenty-three, thereby delaying the moment when the expected D is articulated. Indeed, in the whole of the answering second phrase, the D does not appear at all. Instead, the passage is resolved *rhythmically*, with that C sharp crotchet on the first beat of bar twenty-two answered by an E crotchet on the fourth beat of bar twenty-three. The whole episode concludes with a glorious Lesterism. Having played a tantalizing trick on us, Lester produces from behind his back the long-awaited D, drumming away at it over bars twenty-five and twenty-six as if to savour the joke.

Of course, in attributing conscious designs and motives to improvising soloists, one is exercising commentator's licence. The subtle twists and turns which I have described were the intuitive by-products of Lester Young's style, which in turn owed much to the character and personality of the man himself. Likewise, the introduction of terms such as 'modality' and 'Debussian' into discussion of Lester Young's work—and it happens, friends, it happens—can only serve to spread a smokescreen between the artist and the listener. For musicological insight, I would sooner go to Lester Young's former colleague, the blues singer, Jimmy Rushing, who would often say, 'I listened to Lester a million times—and every time you expect him to go one way, he'll go the other.' Many musicians and promoters who had dealings with Lester, especially in his later years, will testify that this judgement aptly describes the personality of the man who devised a strange, monosyllabic vernacular of his own, discouraged interviewers with oblique and devious answers and, in one phase, feigned homosexual mannerisms in order to keep the world at arm's length.

In music, deviousness and unpredictability can be positive virtues when, as in all of Lester's early work and the best from later years, they stop far short of eccentricity. One rewarding outcome of Lester's reluctance to look the world in the eye was his predilection for those notes in the scale, notably the sixth and the ninth, which introduce a degree of harmonic ambiguity. The construction of a tune such as 'Lady Be Good' presents the improviser with certain problems. In its conventional AABA form, the A sections all end with perfect cadences—in other words, they return to the key or 'home' note of G. We have seen how Benny Carter, for instance, would surmount those awkwardly repetitive cadences by disguising each one in a fresh and elegantly fashioned variation, while Coleman Hawkins would charge through and over them like an express train. To less ingenious players, the key note has often seemed to exert a magnetic pull, preventing the soloist from roaming far afield. In fast tempos, this agoraphobic constraint often seemed to afflict Lester's great rival in the Count Basie band, Herschel Evans. Indeed, there are in existence transcriptions of the Basie band in 'live' action in which Evans, and not Lester Young, takes the principal part in band versions of 'Lady Be Good', and his performance is marred by a too-frequent reiteration of the keynote in predictable places.

Lester Young recoiled instinctively from this constant returning to base, in much the same way that Louis Armstrong's built-in radar would steer him away from the dull symmetry inherent in much popular song construction. Lester's characteristic way was to make heavy use of the sixth note of the scale. In the performance under discussion this note is the E in 'Lady Be Good's' key of G. Added to the G major triad of G, A and D, the E creates a G major sixth which is a legitimate, and indeed, familiar thickening of the tonic chord of G. But in its fourth inversion, starting on the E and rising through G, A and D, the chord becomes identical to the chord of E minor seventh. This ambiguity between the major key and its relative minor was clearly attractive to Lester Young, and the arpeggio appears often in his solos, introducing an extra colour—a minor tint, if you like— into a major key composition. Thus we find that instead of returning to the keynote at the end of the first sixteen bars, as Gershwin did with the words 'Oh lady, be good TO ME', Lester ascends to alight on that neutral sixth note, providing a far less conclusive end to the section.

A very similar purpose is achieved by Lester Young's leaning towards the minor chord—in this instance A minor seventh— based on the second degree of the scale, and containing, incidentally, that much favoured sixth note. I have already mentioned this chord's crucial appearance in bar twenty-three of the solo, where it is inserted to delay the resolution from A seventh to D seventh. Lester uses it also in the fifth bar of almost every A-section of the AABA construction, although Gershwin's melody, on the descending notes D, C, A, D, clearly indicate a straight-forward dominant chord of D seventh. Here again, Lester seems drawn towards the minor tonality, resulting in an oblique, sidelong quality to his solos which gives the most simple and mundane harmonic sequence an air of mystery and complexity.

A further consequence of this obliqueness is that when Lester Young did decide to succumb to the obvious and, indeed, confront it head on, the effect was electrifying. In the first thirty-two-bar chorus of his solo there is, as I have pointed out, a studious reluctance to alight or linger on key note G which plays such a prominent part in Gershwin's simple tune. In the second chorus, by contrast, Lester throws circumlocution to the wind. At the end of bar thirty-two, there's a bold upper-register variation on the 'Three Blind Mice' cadence which leads firmly to the key note. Even here, Lester drops down at once to E and A, delineating the ambiguous G sixth/E minor seventh chord on which the ensuing phrase is built. However, at the start of the second eight-bar section of this chorus, he takes the key note by the scruff of the neck, as if to exorcise it once and for all. For over three bars he dances a rhythmic tarantella around it, throwing it from one beat to another and teasing it with an uncharacteristically exaggerated vibrato. This kind of rhythmic by-play, often used by Lester as a contrast to long, flowing lines, reminds us that his first professional work was as a drummer. Sometimes (but not here) he would literally drum on a note by using alternative fingering—producing a note of identical pitch but different timbre through an alternative combination of the instrument's keys.

As in the second chorus of Lester Young's 'Lady Be Good' solo, the moments when he decided to turn from melodic invention to swinging resolution on one note were always perfectly integrated into his solos, with a positive musical purpose. No doubt they produced a tangible response from the dance floor wherever the Basie band played. Certainly, a decade or so later, they were to arouse the audiences at Norman Granz's Jazz at the Philharmonic concerts to an ecstasy of frenzy. And here's a strange irony. The seeds of the honking, exhibitionistic, one-note tenor-saxophone excesses which were rampant in the frenetic rock'n'roll of the Fifties—and for which Lester Young had positively 'no eyes'—are to be found, not in the extrovert, 'hot' playing of his rivals in the Thirties, but in the style of this shy, withdrawn and allegedly 'cool' musician himself!

Before following 'Lady Be Good' to its conclusion, it might

be instructive to examine Lester Young's historic role as the inspiration for the post-war 'cool school' of jazz. No one who has listened to the performance under discussion will accept that 'cool' in this context implies an absense of warmth. The beautifully constructed lines of melody that Lester produced—and I would draw attention to the passage spanning bars thirty-three to thirty-seven of the solo for special reference—are rich in subtly seductive inflections that tug at the heart-strings. The steady building of rhythmic lift and excitement I have already mentioned. The tone which caused such dissension at the time of Lester's début was, as we have seen, less encrusted with opulent overtones and heavy vibrato than that of Coleman Hawkins and his followers, but did it really digress so dramatically from the norm? In the early Fifties, a British writer, who would no doubt prefer to remain anonymous in this context, launched his broadcasting career with a detailed analysis of a Lester Young solo that turned out to be by the Hawkins-inspired Don Byas. A few years later, the compiler of a double album of Lester Young's work with **Count Basie included the title 'Rockabye Basie' which featured** not Lester, but Buddy Tate, playing in the Herschel Evans style. And as late as 1971, the American writer, Ross Russell, in an otherwise fine essay on Lester in his book, *Jazz Style in Kansas City and the South West*, attributed to Lester Young a passage in the Young classic 'Taxi War Dance' that was again the work of Buddy Tate.

All of this reinforces my view, expressed in the essay on Bix Beiderbecke in *The Best Of Jazz*, Volume One that 'hot' and 'cool' elements coexist in every period of jazz and, indeed, in the style of each individual musician. I did, however, offer one interpretation of the 'hot versus cool' theory which seemed to me to be constructive. In this, I categorized as 'hot' those musicians, from Louis Armstrong to Charlie Parker, John Coltrane and beyond, who 'pushed the boundaries of jazz further and further outwards, the cumulative effect of their key recordings giving the impression of men impelled by demons'. In contrast to this, I cited examples of a contrasting creative direction 'which has led musicians of equal genius to dwell upon, explore, refine and illuminate each new extension of the idiom'. Among these musicians I nominated Bix Beiderbecke, Lester Young and Miles Davis in his early phase. What they seem to me to have in common is a lucidity that derives from the fact that their role was to simplify rather than go out in search of new complexities. While others challenged their melodic inventiveness by harnessing it to ever more complex harmonic progressions, Lester Young set himself the no less challenging task of extracting gold from the most basic harmonic soil. Rhythmically, too, he turned away from the headlong career of his contemporaries towards frenetic speed and four-in-a-bar momentum, opting instead for a conservative, almost old-fashioned, two-in-a-bar pattern from which he extracted hitherto unimagined subtleties. Listen again through 'Lady Be Good' and note how many of the important notes in Lester's phrases are firmly placed on the first and third beats of the bar. In one place, indeed, at the start of his second chorus, this inspires Walter Page to revert to the two-in-a-bar bass of a bygone age! In the light of jazz music's almost obsessive pursuit of all that is 'new' and 'progressive', it is salutary to reflect that the most modern sound to be heard in 1936 was built on a rhythmic foundation that went out of style with Bix and Frankie Trumbauer in the late Twenties.

To appreciate how Lester Young transformed that foundation, we need only pick up the 'Lady Be Good' solo where we left it. After the eight bars of rhythmic exploitation, the G key note is given further special attention in the middle-eight, this time in its capacity as the fifth note of the chord of C with which the section starts. Here again, emphasis is given to rhythmic variation. The G occurs as the leading note of three successive phrases, the first two of which start on the first beat of the bar as if establishing a riff. But the third time, the phrase is brought forward on to the fourth beat of the second bar, a move which Jo Jones anticipates and underlines with a clairvoyance which must have brought a grin to his face. The final eight bars of the solo are pure joy. A five-note phrase is spread across the first bar and into the second in a way that once again defies our expectations, simply because the notes that fall on the emphatic first beat of each bar are the sixth and ninth notes in the scale, both secondary and auxiliary notes to the C major chord on which the phrase is based. The components of the phrase are then juggled about in doodling variations for two bars, and then, in bars five and six, its first three notes are repeated, though differently distributed, to round off another superbly balanced piece of intuitive composition.

I have given this solo more detailed analysis than most because, paradoxically, its basic ingredients are so simple. That a work of genius should emerge, like a conjurer's effects, from a childishly simple tune, five chords and a conservative two-beat rhythm is a mystery that demands some probing. If I have left the reader in an investigative frame of mind, I commend the 1939 recording of 'Taxi War Dance' by Count Basie's band as fruitful ground. Charged with opening the proceedings without any preliminary statement of a theme, Lester Young constructs a solo that suggests a composition of endless ramifications, including shifts from major to minor and other diverting harmonic incidents. It is only when one investigates the backing that it transpires that the whole thirty-two-bar 'theme', excepting its middle-eight, is no more than a vamp on one basic chord. But the reader must be left to work that one out, while I return to other things.

Billie Holiday

THE MOST INTRIGUING AND, dare I say, titillating fact in the life-story of Billie Holiday has nothing to do with drug addiction, sexual proclivities, male exploitation or police harassment. These subjects have all been explored, with varying degrees of reliability, in the semi-fictionalized film-biog, *Lady Sings the Blues*, in the book of sometimes shaky reminiscences by Billie herself and William Dufty—from which the film took its title and some of its facts—and in the excellent and thoroughly researched biography, *Billie's Blues*, written by John Chilton. They will not loom large in this essay for two reasons. One is that in the period I am discussing—that of the emergence of great individual performers in the Thirties—Billie Holiday was in no sense the tortured, embattled drug-addict which the surviving legend depicts, but a plump, cheerful teenager, popular with fellow-musicians because of her robust sense of fun and with a zest for the entertainer's life that involved a steady intake of alcohol and marijuana but nothing more. The second reason is that there is a danger that, in harping on the tragic aspect of her life and death, one can come to persuade oneself that her art arose, and was indivisible, from it. Were this true, then we would have to say that the recordings she made and the performances she gave in the last decade of her life were, artistically, the most valid and successful, and that is palpably and distressingly untrue. Many writers have drawn a parallel between the careers of Billie Holiday and her erstwhile close friend and kindred spirit, Lester Young, and indeed it exists in the sense that both were at their very best in the late Thirties and early Forties, both then showed a gradual decline through inconsistency to virtual incapacity, and both died, within months of each other, in 1959.

But when it comes to the reasons for her frustration and disintegration Billie's case is probably closer to that of Bix Beiderbecke. Bix, as I have established in earlier chapters, suffered not because his artistry languished in the restricting atmosphere of the huge Paul Whiteman Orchestra but, conversely, because he felt that his inability to sight-read fluently and play his part in the trumpet section stood between him and the musical respectability, and popularity, inherent in being a Whiteman 'star'. Billie Holiday, a star-struck youngster dazzled by the success and popularity of such as Louis Armstrong and revelling in the attention of famous Hollywood film stars, never had a best-selling record, never topped the most prestigious of jazz popularity polls, never broke successfully into movies and never rose, except sporadically, above the unspectacular, somewhat clandestine, life of a club singer. Ella Fitzgerald's youthful success with a 'hit' version of the song 'A-Tisket A-Tasket' must have increased Billie's perplexity, removing as it did the easy explanation that racial discrimination lay at the heart of the matter. That it played its part is made very clear through her experiences as featured singer with the all-white Artie Shaw Orchestra, when even the friendship and support of the musicians could not protect her from humiliating treatment from those on the entrepreneurial side. But as anyone listening to the massive output of Billie Holiday recordings from the Thirties can tell, the problem was more deep rooted than that. In a world in which the catchy, the amusing and the ingratiating picked up the top prizes, her style was subtle, oblique, harsh and uncompromising. In other words, she was too good.

To revert to my opening sentence, the biographical fact about Billie Holiday that will arouse a *frisson* of excitement in anyone fascinated by the evolution of jazz is that she made her first recordings in the very same Columbia studios in which, three days earlier, Bessie Smith made her last. Both sessions were organized by John Hammond, the twenty-two-year-old son of a wealthy family who used his money, flair, journalistic outlets and connections in the, then, near-bankrupt Columbia Recording Company to pursue, as he puts it, 'two of my favourite roles— producer and catalyst'. With the discovery of such musicians as Billie Holiday, Teddy Wilson, Lionel Hampton, Count Basie's band and Charlie Christian to his credit, Hammond can claim to have had some influence on the course of jazz history. But even he cannot have realized at the time what a significant and symbolic moment it was in jazz history that he unwittingly engineered. Bessie and Billie did not meet in the studios, their appearances being separated by seventy-two hours. In fact, their paths only crossed once or twice, so far as we know, and then it seems doubtful if they exchanged any words. Yet there is, in the circum- stances of those three days in November 1933, a suggestion of the handing over of keys or the passing of a baton from the old to the new.

In the cherishing of this fancy, it matters little that Billie's first records, with a studio band led by Benny Goodman, were neither the best nor the most representative of her recordings, nor that in belting out two feeble 'novelty' numbers, 'Your Mother's Son-in-Law' and 'Riffin' the Scotch', she came closer to the vaudeville and tent-show era of Bessie Smith than she ever would again. The very appearance of Billie Holiday's name succeeding Bessie's on the Columbia record-label symbolizes the dawn of a new era, the extinction of an old one. In writing about Bessie Smith in the first volume of *The Best of Jazz*, I voiced my doubts as to whether she would have survived artistically through the Thirties even if her speciality, the blues, had not fallen from popular favour in the Depression years. Just as an actor on stage must exaggerate his movements and gestures so as to convey his meaning to the furthest parts of the theatre, so the singers who, like Bessie Smith, spent most of their working life in theatres and marquees, had to develop powerful voices and a weighty delivery. This capacity for voice projection came in handy in the early days of recording, when musical and verbal messages for posterity had to be hurled into the craning 'ear' of a recording apparatus that was distinctly hard of hearing.

Times changed with the invention and perfection of the portable microphone, which could be used not only for radio and recording, but also to amplify 'live' sounds in an auditorium. In discussing Louis Armstrong's development as a singer, we have already seen what changes technology wrought upon his style, which evolved from extrovert and musically unsubtle bawling to something far more smooth and subtle. In the early Thirties, Bing Crosby likewise shed the melodramatic dynamics which were a legacy from Al Jolson and adopted a more intimate style.

It goes without saying that the changes wrought by the development of the microphone did not meet with universal approval. One need not delve very far back into the annals of popular music to recall the adverse reaction to 'crooning' among those nurtured on the tenors and baritones of the musical stage. Likewise there were those around when Billie Holiday made her début to claim that she had no voice—or, to put it more colourfully in a phrase attributed to, among others, the established star Ethel Waters— that she sang 'as if her shoes were too tight'. If one uses the word 'voice' to describe the sort of trained, cultivated sound which academies of music classify as 'singing,' then of course the critics were right. In writing in Volume One about Bessie Smith, I suggested that she should be regarded, not as the culmination of a tradition of blues singing, but as the beginning of a new tradition of jazz singing. The word 'beginning' is important. I shall return to the jazz aspect of her work in relation to Billie's in a moment. But so far as the actual voice is concerned, Bessie Smith's retained, through the self-training necessary to project it unaided across a crowded auditorium, enough of the orthodox contralto to render it a not wholly typical jazz sound.

I must explain this. I have observed before that, since jazz criticism took shape a long time after the music itself had begun, we have the luxury of making our basic definitions in retrospect. Listening to all the music described in this book, for instance, one thing becomes apparent—the great diversity of sounds which the various instruments produce in the hands of the masters. It is not enough simply to say that the musicians were 'unschooled' and therefore produced idiosyncratic sounds, as it were, by default. This would be to class players such as Coleman Hawkins, Benny Carter, Lester Young and Jack Teagarden as 'primitives', which is patently absurd. The truth is that in European music, tradition is enshrined in and, to a large extent, exclusive to, the places of learning. The academies both define and pass on orthodoxy. In American popular music in general and black music in particular —whether we choose to define it as dance music, jazz, entertainment music or whatever—this is not the case. Musicians such as Coleman Hawkins and Benny Carter might have spent some formative years in music school, but what they learned there was theory, harmony, composition and so on. The dominant musical tradition to which they applied this learning was to be found outside—in the dance halls and speakeasies, in the vaudeville theatres and cabarets, on gramophone records and over the radio. And that tradition embraced musical sounds as diverse as human speech itself.

Interviews with jazzmen abound in evidence of the study and practice which went into the production of those sounds—the experimentation with mouthpieces or reeds, the single-minded pursuit of a particular tonal nuance or effect. But the end product was not the sort of standardized, homogenized sound that might emerge from a training-class, but a natural sound compatible with the individual's technical equipment, physical make-up, formative influences and unfettered imagination. While it is unwise to make too much of it, one must also mention the African musical tradition—or, to be more accurate, combination of traditions—which the black musicians received primarily from the predominantly vocal music in black churches, and which they imparted, by example, to their white colleagues. Leaving aside the rhythmic aspects, the most important precept to filter down from African music into jazz is that, in contrast to European music, there are no such things as 'legitimate' or 'illegitimate' sounds. I expect to be told by experts in African musicology that the sundry distortions of tone that exist in African vocal music are as 'legitimate' and as much prescribed by tradition as is the 'pure' tone in European music, but that is hardly the point. The *effect* of the African connection on jazz can easily be gleaned from the many unorthodox musical terms—'growl', 'shake', 'honk', 'smear', 'rasp', 'dirty tone' and so on—that abound in jazz criticism.

The first singer to combine this exploitation of a natural,

personal sound with the other requisites of great jazz performance
—swing, spontaneity, an unerring instinct for phrasing and
construction, emotional honesty and richness—was Louis Armstrong. The second was Billie Holiday. If there are others with a
claim to share the very top drawer with them, they do not spring
readily to mind. Billie Holiday gave the best, and most succinct
insight into the origins of her style in an interview quoted in the
Chilton biography. 'I wanted Louis Armstrong's feeling, and I
wanted the big volume that Bessie Smith got. But I found it
didn't work with me because I didn't have a big voice . . . so
anyway, between the two of them, I sort of got Billie Holiday.'

The Billie Holiday that she got, after the first uncharacteristic
records with Benny Goodman ('Well, I get a big bang out of
"Your Mother's Son-in-Law". It sounds like I'm doing comedy.
My voice sounded so high and funny.'), owed her existence to the
microphone. Bessie Smith's voice was projected in conventional,
if self-taught fashion, from the depths of the diaphragm, swelling
in power as it made its untrammelled ascent. Billie's, on the other
hand, resembled Louis Armstrong's in the way that it seemed to
emerge, somewhat the worse for wear, after battling its way through
a jungle of tangled obstruction in the area of the throat. Playing
a Billie Holiday record at slow speed reveals a striking similarity
to Armstrong, especially in the attractive 'frogginess' in the low
register and in the way that notes in the upper range tend occasionally to split into separate strands, like a fraying rope. Recalling
my comments regarding the jazz musician's asssiduousness in
acquiring his own individual sound, the reader might well ask,
with some scepticism, if I am really suggesting that these vocal
aberrations, in conventional singing terms, which Louis and Billie
shared were actually cultivated by her. The answer is no—but
neither, after the first Benny Goodman recordings, were they
suppressed. That voice, as rich in subtle and evocative nuances
of tone and timbre as it was weak in range and volume, was her
natural instrument, and she let it speak for itself.

Lady Sings the Blues, the title of her autobiography and of the
film loosely based on it, was thought up by a publisher more
concerned with the form of words than with musical accuracy. It
is one of the oddest things about Billie Holiday's career that, not

only in the befogged regions of publishing houses, Hollywood and
the mass media but in some otherwise informed jazz commentaries, she has been frequently classified as a blues singer. It is
not necessary in this instance to embark on any deep investigation
into the fine distinction between a blues singer and a jazz singer.
For surely the prima facie qualifications of a blues singer are that
he or she should actually sing the blues—not just occasionally
but as a staple part of the repertoire. Out of the hundreds of songs
which Billie Holiday recorded, only three blues numbers come
readily to mind. 'Billie's Blues', 'Long Gone Blues' and 'Fine and
Mellow' are all attractive pieces, the last-named being one of
Billie's finest recordings in its original version. On the strength
of these, some have argued that, like some other more consistent
blues performers such as Jimmy Rushing and Joe Turner—and
indeed, Bessie Smith herself—Billie treated popular songs as if
they were blues. But this, if it means anything at all, implies a
declamatory delivery and a liberal use of the flattened 'blue notes',
neither of which were characteristic of her singing. The truth is
that Billie Holiday had a unique singing style which she applied
without discrimination to twelve-bar blues or thirty-two-bar
popular songs alike.

In guessing at the origins of that style (we know she listened to
Bessie Smith and Louis Armstrong but can only make assumptions
about what she actually *got* from either of them), it is tempting
to add the name of Lester Young to those twin influences. Billie
herself gave fuel to this notion when she said, 'I don't think I'm
singing. I feel like I'm playing a horn. I try to improvise like Les
Young, like Louis Armstrong, or someone else I admire. What
comes out is what I feel, I hate straight singing. I have to change a
tune to my own way of doing it. That's all I know.' The deep
platonic friendship that existed for a while between Billie and
Lester has given rise to more than one misconception. Enshrined
in much jazz literature is the assumption that they were drawn
together by a common psychological inability to cope with the
hard realities of life, two souls adrift and clinging to each other
for survival. In reality, their friendship pre-dated both her
capitulation to hard drugs and his decline into alcoholism and
eccentricity. It marked a period when, according to all accounts,

she was presenting a robust, if sometimes pugnacious, face to life's injustices and he was riding high as a star soloist in the gregarious environment of the Count Basie band. The later, unhappier times brought a rift between them which was never completely healed. Likewise, the linking of Billie and Lester stylistically ignores historical fact. Though she vaguely recalled an earlier encounter, it seems probable that they first met in the recording studios in January 1937, when the results show that, though there was an immediate rapport between them, Billie Holiday's style was fully formed and not destined to undergo further drastic change. At that time, Lester Young had been featured on no more than four recordings, made three months earlier and hardly likely to have impinged on her consciousness, even if they had indeed been issued by then.

The safest line to take in respect of Billie Holiday's stylistic origins is to say that she clearly grasped to the full the rhythmic freedom, the independence from the basic beat, which Louis Armstrong had demonstrated so miraculously. In listening as often as she could to the recordings of Bessie Smith, she would have heard, behind the 'big volume' which she could not produce, something much more important. It was the capacity to use phrasing and melodic variation to impart to a song more emotional weight than the original words and melody could possibly sustain. It was this quality in Bessie Smith's performance that induced me, in the first book, to describe her as a supreme jazz singer. Billie inherited it in full and bestowed it on every performance.

Few of the 'standard' songs which singers of Billie Holiday's generation performed were written with more than cheap and superficial sentimentality in mind. It's interesting to dwell for a moment on the way in which they actually came to be performed. After the initial recordings with Benny Goodman, Billie Holiday was brought together by John Hammond with another musician, Teddy Wilson, in whose burgeoning career he had an interest. Hammond had secured for Teddy Wilson a recording contract which enabled the pianist to make regular, informal recordings using what are known in the trade as 'pick-up bands'—*ad hoc* groups of musicians assembled from whoever happened to be currently in town. In his autobiography, *John Hammond on*

Record, the author wrote: 'It astonishes me, as I look back, at how casually we were able to assemble such all-star groups. It wasn't that we didn't know how great they were. We did. It simply was a Golden Age; America was overflowing with a dozen truly superlative performers on every instrument. And yet business wasn't that good. Compared to the kind of money that's around today, they all came for scale.'

The Teddy Wilson bands were indeed repositories of all the greatest names in jazz in the mid-Thirties. But they had, nevertheless, to conform to the rules established for hack performers by the popular music industry. Teddy Wilson described the process in an interview: 'In those days the publishers made the hits. They had what they called number one, number two and number three plugs—the songs they were pushing. We never got into the plug tunes. We had our choice of the rest. That's why many of those songs we recorded you never heard anybody sing besides Billie.' Her interpretations even of these low-grade songs didn't always meet with approval from their publishers and composers. One of the latter is said to have complained, on hearing the playback of a Holiday rendering of one of his brainchildren, 'That's a nice job, but it isn't my tune.'

And here is the irony of the situation. Many of the songs which we regard as 'standards' today owe their honoured place in posterity to the skill with which Billie Holiday—and, in similar circumstances, Louis Armstrong and Fats Waller—performed them. Her versions were not so much interpretations as transformations, which the begetters and the proprietors of the material did not always smile upon at the time. The trombonist Bennie Morton, who often worked with Billie, once recalled, 'I have seen Billie turn the melody line around completely simply because a lot of these tunes sung as written were pretty dull.'

As with other selections for these volumes, I have of necessity been arbitrary in choosing two Billie Holiday masterpieces. Many will have assumed, on seeing her name at the head of the chapter, that her historic 1939 recording of 'Strange Fruit', dramatic and startling for its time as an overt 'protest' song, would find automatic pride of place. I have set it aside not because it is a poor example of her work—quite the contrary—but because, like the blues pieces which I have also eschewed, it is not typical of her. Unlike Nina Simone in a later era, to whom she has sometimes been compared, Billie Holiday's work had no specific political or social message. The sorrow, hurt, disillusionment and bitterness which lay close to the surface of her most light-hearted material may have originated, in part, from her racial circumstances, but the feelings conveyed through her huge recorded repertoire of bitter-sweet love songs are universal.

It is into that repertoire that I have dipped for my two favourites. 'I'll Get By', a song of unusual structure by Fred Ahlert and Roy Turk, had enjoyed a modest success on its publication in 1928 and was destined to a renewed lease of life in 1945 when it struck a chord with war-weary Americans. The Billie Holiday/Teddy Wilson recording was made midway between these two peaks, in 1937, when we must presume that the publishers had it on the stock list in the hopes of a premature revival. Happily for posterity, the principal medium of dissemination for songs in those days was the printed song copy, which was comparatively easy and cheap to store and reproduce. So a successful tune would not suffer the fleeting, butterfly existence of a modern hit song but would survive in the catalogues for many years.

Clearly, the bands of Duke Ellington, Count Basie and Benny Goodman were all in town on 11 May 1937, as star names from each—Johnny Hodges from the first, Lester Young and Buck Clayton from the second, Allan Reuss and Arthur Bernstein from the third—joined Teddy Wilson for this session, together with Buster Bailey and Cozy Cole, two of New York's most prolific session players at that time. Wilson always liked to share out the solo space among his musicians on a session, so it was no doubt the luck of the draw that relegated Lester Young to a subdued and almost inaudible supporting role on this number. Billie Holiday herself appeared on the Teddy Wilson recordings simply as the supplier of 'vocal refrain', as they used to describe it, and as such she occupied the traditional vocalist's position, taking a single chorus after the initial exposition of the tune. As we shall see, on sessions under her own name—Billie Holiday and her Orchestra—she played a fuller part, singing the opening chorus and returning again towards the end. Fortunately, her style, as fiercely concentrated as an oxy-acetylene flame, made its mark equally strikingly in either setting.

After a long, meandering introduction with Buster Bailey's clarinet to the fore, it is Johnny Hodges who takes the opening chorus of 'I'll Get By', delineating a melody that occupies the unusual span of twenty-eight bars—most popular songs of the period being thirty-two bars in length. Like these more conventional tunes, the Ahlert-Turk song is couched in an ABAC format, but the B and C sections are six instead of eight bars in length, a daring and effective innovation for its time. Likewise, there is an attractive absence of symmetry in the A sections. On the face of it, the melody consists of two complementary ascending phrases of four bars each. But the words—'I'll get by, as long as I have you Though there'll be rain'—shift the point of balance, the word 'you' clearly belonging to the first phrase although, logically, one would expect it to be the first note of the second. In the same way, the notes carrying the words 'though there'll be rain' complete the A section, providing an obvious punctuation point in the melody. But resolutely spurning the obvious, the lyric spans this junction without so much as a comma—'and darkness too'. It is a relatively rare and ingenious example of a lyric imposing subtleties on the melody line.

Johnny Hodges states the tune majestically, its ascending lines, spanning a range of ten notes in all, ideally suiting his sweeping style. But a newcomer to the tune, aware of Billie Holiday's restricted range, might well begin to wonder during the alto chorus exactly how she will negotiate it. He could scarcely be prepared for what actually happens. Benny Morton spoke of Billie 'turning the melody line around completely'. Here she stands it on its head. As written, the song, in F major, begins on the lower F and ascends, in its two opening phrases, to an upper limit of A above the octave. Billie Holiday starts her chorus on that upper A, and indeed hinges her whole variation on it, with the result that, instead of soaring aloft, all the phrases droop downwards like the boughs of a weeping willow. Furthermore, apart from two descents to a low G in which her voice falls away to vanishing point, she restricts her range to a mere six notes. In my essay on Bessie Smith in Volume One, I wrote: 'Bessie's way . . . was to restrict the range of a song to no more than five or six notes and to construct her phrases so economically that a change in direction of just one note could have a startling, dramatic or emotive effect.' Billie had absorbed that lesson completely. For a beautiful example, listen to the start of the second half of the chorus, in bar fifteen. This is a reprise of the opening phrase, in which the words 'I'll get by' were harnessed to that one nagging note a third above the upper key note. Second time around, the word 'poverty' returns to the A, but this time the third syllable drops down to the E below. It's a minute variation, made all the more effective by the unexpectedness of the interval. Both the melody and the harmony of the original tune prompt a fall from A to F—in other words, down to the key note—and in subsequent versions of the song, this is indeed what Billie does. But the casual drop to the major seventh, no doubt intuitive rather than contrived, is infinitely more effective, underlining the note of doubt which the words 'Poverty may come to me, that's true' introduce into an otherwise optimistic song.

Had it been harnessed to the original rhythmic structure of the song, Billie's drastic reshaping of the melody may have seemed like a mere evasion of the tune's inherent difficulties. But here she draws upon and, indeed, extends the notions of freedom from the basic beat implanted by Louis Armstrong. As written, the song adheres more than most to a sedate pattern of on-the-beat crotchets and minims (or quarter and half-notes). With a true jazzman's instinct, Johnny Hodges loosens this rigid skeleton with notes that anticipate and stretch across the beat. Billie Holiday cuts loose from it altogether. The very first word of the opening phrase 'I'll get by' is placed ahead of the beat, and the others do no more than hover round it. The second phrase, 'As long as I have you' is delayed by more than two beats, and then doesn't bestir itself needlessly. The art of this exaggeratedly 'laid back' phrasing, distinguishing it from mere affectation, is that the listener should not detect the point at which the performer catches up with the regular metre. The listener who expects Billie to re-orientate herself by clinging, if only for a few bars, to the beat must wait, in this instance, for ever. Like a child striding out to avoid stepping on the lines between paving-stones, she picks her way through the entire vocal chorus without once stepping fairly and squarely on the beat.

The ethereal ghostly effect that this produces is heightened by Teddy Wilson's diligent, almost fastidious, attention to time-keeping. His piano style, which so attracted John Hammond, derived principally from Earl Hines. But the two players are temperamentally different. While Hines at the keyboard has always sounded like some volatile and impetuous wayside explorer, now sauntering, now dashing off in pursuit of a fleeting idea, now tumbling head over heels in an ecstacy of *joie de vivre*, Teddy Wilson gives the impression of a man content to make a more measured progress along ordered paths. His solo following Billie Holiday's vocal is typical. Rhythmically, he has always leaned towards a two-beat feeling, the left hand, when not featuring the moving pattern of tenths which are his trade-mark, providing an oom-chah stride bass with the first and third beats emphasized. It is the somewhat precise timing of the left-hand vamping which, among other things, has attracted to Teddy Wilson such not altogether complimentary critical epithets as 'meticulous', 'elegant', 'impeccable' and 'placid'. To me, his playing is a constant joy, especially in the context of a Billie Holiday recording such as this, when the mind, in something of a turmoil after the vocal unorthodoxy, is instantly reassured by the perfect poise with which the piano takes over. Buck Clayton, of whom more in a moment, falls in with this unruffled mood by taking the per-formance out with a return to the original tune, the only way to end a record which, in three short minutes, has taken 'I'll Get By' to its emotional and structural limits and back.

Most listeners will agree that the Billie Holiday recordings in the late Thirties offered something a little bit extra whenever musicians from Count Basie's band—and especially Lester Young and Buck Clayton—were on hand. Michael Brooks, the producer of a series of Lester Young reissues on CBS called *The Lester Young Story*, put it more vividly in his sleeve note. 'There is no question that the alliance between Buck Clayton, Lester Young and Billie Holiday is one of the great romances in musical history, as if Romeo, Dante and Cleopatra met up in the recording studio, looked, listened and said the hell with Juliet, Beatrice and Antony!' In similar vein, John Hammond recalls, 'The electricity between Jo [Jones], Buck, Billie and Prez was just fantastic.' The occasions when the Basie men were on the sessions must have been somewhat unnerving for Teddy Wilson. Jo Jones, the drummer with Count Basie, has described how he and the other Basieites would try and get Wilson to abandon his rather upright, two-beat style and conform to the more pushing four-four beat which Basie used. He stood his ground, however, and it has to be said that the recordings give no hint of musical schism.

Buck Clayton was audibly in his element on the Billie Holiday sessions. Having worked with him often during the Sixties, when he showed himself to be one of those musicians of whom it can truthfully be said that he continued to improve with age, I formed the impression that he was at his happiest in medium and slow tempos, when he had the time and space to exploit his stinging attack, radiant tone, buoyant and poised swing and lyrical imagination. Louis Armstrong was his inspiration, and in his less flamboyant way, Buck, too, could invest an introductory flourish or modulating cadenza with all the authority of a call to arms.

Two 'takes' of Billie Holiday's recording of 'Back in Your Own Back Yard' have been issued, each starting with just such a commanding fanfare from Buck. My preference is for the first one, taken at a rather more taut and brisk tempo. For all the optimism and reassurance of its words, the tune, by Al Jolson and associates, is rather sad. This is no place to go into the psychology of music, but it is true to say that melodies that consist predominantly of descending phrases strike in the listener a melancholy, or at least wistful, chord. This song abounds in them, its main recurring phrase being a descent from the fifth to the tonic, like the return journey of a five-finger exercise. And there is a minor key middle-eight thrown in for good measure.

Billie Holiday needed little prompting to bring out the poignant side of any tune. The words of the song—'The bird with feathers of blue is waiting for you/Back in your own back yard'—urge us to believe that, for happiness, we need look no further than our own doorstep. The tender sadness with which Billie invests the melody imparts the rather less cosy message that we should make the best of life as it surrounds us, because it's all there is. Her approach here is quite different from the dismantling and re-assembling to which she subjected 'I'll Get By'. This tune, like the other, presents a singer of her limited range with problems. The melody accompanying the line I have written out above, keeps plunging down, in a sort of scooping figure, on the second syllable of 'feathers', again on the second syllable of 'waiting', and a third time with the words 'in your' towards the end of the line. We know from elsewhere that Billie could negotiate these sort of swooping melodic lines if she wished, but on this occasion she did not wish. Picking up on the end of Buck's introduction with a phrase that hangs in the air, she lets the melody float gently earthwards, letting the second syllable of 'waiting' rise as if momentarily caught by an upward breeze. This is the pattern that she uses in each of the corresponding sections occupying the second and last eight bars, avoiding monotony by distributing the syllables differently across the beat each time.

With the middle-eight, we find a perfect example of her way of phrasing like a jazz instrumentalist. For four bars, she places the words right across the beat. Of the words 'you can go to the East, go to the West', not one is placed squarely on the beat, and the ensuing words, 'but someday you'll come', are somehow squeezed into the remaining bars like latecomers on a crowded rush-hour Tube. But then, in striking contrast, 'weary at heart' is rapped out like a drum rhythm bang on the beat. Sing the section over wordlessly and it could come from Louis, Lester, Buck or anybody else's horn.

As for Lester Young's solo, it is hard to think of a more beautiful example of his work. As in the 'Lady Be Good' solo discussed earlier, his improvisation is totally independent from the song's original theme. Building upon the wistful mood of Billie's vocal, he unfolds a continuous line of beautifully constructed melody, starting characteristically with one of his isolated 'balancing notes'. It has sometimes occurred to me that a musician's style is often reflected in his playing stance. Louis Armstrong, for example, adopted a heraldic pose, while Coleman Hawkins in furious action looked like some medieval horseman crouched over the neck of his charger. Lester, on the other hand, with the saxophone held out at a forty-five degree angle from his body, head drooping and one hip thrown out as a counterbalance, resembled nothing so much as one of those angular, counterpoised desk lamps. Matching this image, his solos maintained a languid poise that concealed great rhythmic strength. In his second eight bars in 'Back in Your Own Back Yard,' the notes seem to lean just about as far as they can away from the beat without falling over, and yet a muscular swing is maintained. The middle-eight provides a glorious example of his melodic perversity. He seems about to play the melody as written, but turns the tables on anyone rash enough to whistle along with him by, first of all, leaving out the last note of the 'go to the East' phrase and then, in 'go to the West,' turning the 'West' note down when it should go up. Jo Jones shows his appreciation of this subtle manoeuvre with some telepathic rim-shots. And at the very end of the solo, after so much delayed across-the-beat phrasing, Lester raps out some stirring on-the-beat notes that provide a jaunty contrast. On the whole, the solo radiates a sunny mood that contrasts strongly with the equally beautiful but quite different performance in the slightly slower second 'take'. The change in tempo appears to have affected Lester's spirits inordinately, and his playing has an introspective, almost weary sound that foreshadows the more withdrawn style of his declining years.

There is no need for me to apply further analysis to Billie Holiday's final chorus, which repeats the general pattern of the first while lifting the tension in the most subtle way. It completes a performance which was matched on many other occasions during the same period, especially when Buck, Lester and Jo Jones were on hand. Seldom has such a close and consistent feeling of rapport been conveyed on record. To absorb just part of the eagerness, confidence and creative joy that must have crackled round the studio on that day, and then to reflect on the future that was to overtake both Billie Holiday and Lester Young, is almost too much to bear.

Roy Eldridge

WHEN OUTLINING THE COURSE of jazz history from the Twenties to the Forties, jazz historians tend to talk in terms of trumpet players. King Oliver, they will say, gave way to Louis Armstrong, who was succeeded by Roy Eldridge, who influenced Dizzy Gillespie, who spawned Miles Davis . . . It is not an altogether absurd over-simplification, any more than the tendency, after that point, to transfer the principal role to the saxophone and Charlie Parker, John Coltrane, Ornette Coleman . . . Louis Armstrong so dominated jazz in the period around 1930, making new virtuoso strides with every recording session, that his style permeated virtually every instrument in the jazz band, with the possible exception of the double-bass. It was natural, if not particularly scientific, that observers would have eyes and ears fixed on the trumpet for some time to come, if only to see what could possibly happen next.

What did happen next, in equally simple terms, was that a young trumpeter from Pittsburg called Roy Eldridge listened to Louis Armstrong on record and was not overwhelmed. 'The first time I heard any records by him was in 1927, I think,' he told in an interview reproduced in the book, *The Jazz Makers*, 'but Louis wasn't an influence on me until I saw him in person.' Over the years, critics have heard in Roy Eldridge's heated, impassioned playing the influence of Henry 'Red' Allen and, in the manner of critics, have enshrined that opinion as fact in works of jazz information. In recent times Roy has vehemently rejected any suggestion that Allen influenced him, and I hope it is not being wise after the event to say that, rhythmically and melodically, their two styles are fundamentally different. From his earliest recorded appearance, Henry Allen played in what I have called an 'impressionistic' manner, avoiding specific lines of melody and patterns of rhythm and choosing instead to build his solos out of contrasting splashes of sound, some lazily stretched across the beat, others exploding with sudden vehemence. Roy Eldridge, on the other hand, has always preferred to maintain a constant stream of improvisation that stays in close contact with both the beat and the harmonic structure of the theme. It is not surprising to hear from him that, of all the Louis Armstrong disciples with whose music he came in contact, it was Rex Stewart, with his combination of fieriness and speed, who did influence him in his early days.

But it seems that, when he did begin to play professionally in his mid-teens, he was set on a course that might well have taken him out of the Armstrong sphere of influence altogether. To anyone who ever heard the mature Eldridge either on record or in the flesh, when it has seemed after a chorus or two that steam must soon start spouting from his ears, the notion that he ever admired and emulated Red Nichols will present itself as some kind of far-fetched joke. In the Roy Eldridge that we know, it is not easy to detect even an occasional hint of the cool and calculating 'eastern' style of the white New Yorker. But we have it from his own mouth. 'I liked the nice, clean sound he was getting from the trumpet in those days. I was doing all right playing in that style until I got to St Louis.' He was already touring then as leader of his own juvenile band. 'Every Sunday, five trumpet players came down and tore me apart. I was about sixteen and I was playing smooth. They played with a guttural kind of sound. They were more or less on a Louis Armstrong kick, the way Louis used to play only more guttural. I was playing what would be called cool then and I wasn't familiar with that other style. I couldn't understand how they got around to playing like that— the lip vibrato, trills and the like. Some of the names of those trumpet players in St Louis were Dewey Jackson, Baby James, "Cookie" and "Big Ham".'

Ironically, the St Louis of a few years later would probably have given encouragement to his 'cool' style, since it became the breeding ground of a clear-cut, round-toned and relatively placid style of trumpet playing exemplified in the work of Harold 'Shorty' Baker, Clark Terry and Miles Davis. But it is hard to believe that a man of Roy Eldridge's volatile, emotional and highly competitive temperament would have thrived for long in such incompatibly 'cool' pastures. Other influences were to steer him towards the now familiar hustling style. In a word, saxophones. 'Coleman Hawkins and Benny Carter. They played so much music, Hawkins and Carter, how could you help not like them if you like music? They had, and have, distinctive sounds, voices of their own.'

It seems that, at first, the saxophones and his desire to emulate them led him astray. One of the earliest exercises which he set himself was to learn by heart the Coleman Hawkins tenor-saxophone solo in Fletcher Henderson's 1926 recording of 'The Stampede'. What emerged was a new way of playing the trumpet in jazz. Even men like Louis Armstrong and Jabbo Smith, renowned for their speed and agility, had had to bow to the trumpet's innate short-windedness in matters of phrasing. Roy Eldridge set about forming a style which could rival the continuous flow of long, far-ranging phrases, punctuated only by hastily snatched breaths, which Hawkins could produce. The result was not immediately successful. 'The cats used to listen to me and they'd say, "Well, he's nice but he don't say nothing." Consequently I didn't work. No one played as fast as I did, but the other trumpet players broke it up. I didn't. Also, I was playing fine saxophone on the trumpet. Trying to hold notes longer than they should be held, trying to get a sound that I couldn't and shouldn't get.'

Roy Eldridge's problems will not be unfamiliar to anyone who, having acquired a technique, has first tried to apply it to jazz improvisation. Clearly the vocabulary and the syntax were there, the punctuation and the construction were not. He needed an example to follow, someone to provide a revelatory insight into how to use his formidable technique in a way that, to use the jazzman's vernacular, would 'tell a story'. The example he found was one which he had already encountered and spurned. In 1932 he went to hear Louis Armstrong in person at the Lafayette Theatre in New York, '. . . and he finally upset me. I was a young cat, and I was very fast but I wasn't telling no kind of story. Well, I sat through the first show, and I didn't think that Louis was so extraordinary. But in the second show, he played 'Chinatown'. He started out like a new book, building and building, chorus after chorus, and finally reaching a full climax, ending on his high F. It was a real climax, right, clean, clear. The rhythm was rocking, and he had that sound going along with it. Everybody was standing up, including me. He was building the thing all the time instead of just playing in a straight line. I've been digging him ever since.'

Here, then, was the making of the Eldridge style which, though his period as an acknowledged trumpet king was transitory compared with the reign of Louis before him and Dizzy Gillespie after him, was to have a revolutionary effect on jazz trumpet playing. 'I started to feel that if I could combine speed with melodic development while continuing to build, to tell a story, I could create something musical of my own that the public would like.' The speed was as important as the Louis influence. Through the Thirties, there emerged a whole generation of fine trumpet players offering personal variations on the Louis Armstrong model. In extensive jazz histories more justice is done to Oran 'Hot Lips' Page, Frankie Newton, Buck Clayton, Joe Thomas, Bill Coleman, Bobby Stark, Taft Jordan and Jonah Jones than I have space for here. Though their styles had a common source, they developed such personal 'voices' that each one is instantly recognizable to the *aficionado* who hears them on records. But none of them departed far enough from the Armstrong pattern to suggest an alternative way of handling the trumpet in jazz. Were it not for the grotesqueness of associating the word 'philistine' with any creation of Louis Armstrong's, one could say that, in the mid-Thirties, the jazz world was waiting for a David to overthrow the Goliath that Armstrong's decade-long domination represented. The diminutive Roy Eldridge, ambitious, bursting with a sense of his own ability and scared of no one when it came to a musical fight, had just the temperament to fill the role.

Here it was that the influence of the saxophonists, Coleman

Hawkins in particular, played an essential part. Simply to have reproduced Armstrong's basic style but at breakneck speed would hardly have earned Eldridge a place in jazz history as an innovator. What he did was to force the trumpet itself to change its character. In Louis Armstrong's hands—and indeed the hands of his predecessors stretching back to Buddy Bolden—both trumpet and cornet had assumed the role to which the former had always been assigned in the symphony orchestra and the military band. Clarinets, flutes and piccolos, with their multiplicity of keys, were clearly designed to scamper about over a range of several octaves. The trumpet, initially confined, through the absence of any valve or piston mechanism, to the widely spaced harmonics that are found in the present-day bugle, was there to make commanding, declamatory noises, making up in dignity and martial authority what it lacked in agility. Early players such as King Oliver, Freddy Keppard and, presumably, Buddy Bolden himself, made predominant use of the cornet's open notes— that is to say, the harmonics which can be attained without recourse to the valves simply by raising or lowering the lip pressure. As jazz improvisation became increasingly adventurous, it still came more naturally for the trumpet players to construct their solos on arpeggios than to ignore the instrument's basic system of harmonics and play flowing lines based on the scales. Louis Armstrong's showcase of the mid-Twenties, 'Cornet Chop Suey', was in every sense a classic example of this. The themes themselves, written either by Louis, his wife, Lil Hardin Armstrong, or a collaboration of the two, followed the normal scalar construction of any other ragtime or popular song. But when Louis played his variations and added an introduction and a coda, they were all designed to show off his and the instrument s agility in leaping up and down arpeggios. Later, when he began to apply his talents to popular songs from the Broadway shows, it became a characteristic of his to declaim the melody of the tune in the high register while at the same time linking the notes with descending arpeggios which indicated the underlying harmonies.

    In writing about both Coleman Hawkins and Lester Young here, I have mentioned the system of chorus-building known as 'running changes'. If **Rex** Stewart, in his role of jazz historian, is to be believed, Coleman Hawkins was inspired to pursue this line of musical thought after hearing Art Tatum some time in the late Twenties. This was the aspect of saxophone playing which attracted Roy Eldridge. An unsung jazz hero, trumpeter Cuban Bennett, is the man whom Roy acknowledges as his own inspiration in this direction. 'Cuban Bennett was Benny Carter's first cousin. He was really making his changes in those days. You could call him one of the first of the moderns . . . He played more like a saxophone did. You see, the saxophone then, or some of them, would run changes, would run through all the passing chords and things, and then do a little turn around.' To run changes, it is necessary to get completely away from the arpeggio style of playing in which, for example, the harmony is involved only at those strategic points at which the player will run up or down the key notes of the chord to emphasize it. In running changes, the player will construct a continuous line of notes which are selected intuitively to suggest, rather than state specifically, every minute change in the underlying harmony. In jazz analysis, the two methods are sometimes described as improvising 'vertically' (up and down specific chords) or 'horizontally' (along a continuous line of harmony). If we accept Rex Stewart's theory about Coleman Hawkins, we have here a fascinating line of development. With Fletcher Henderson in the mid-Twenties, Hawkins received the message as to how to swing on tenor saxophone from the example of Louis Armstrong, whose style he largely adopted. Hearing Art Tatum inspired him to change course, in a direction which Roy Eldridge eventually followed. It led Roy temporarily into a dead-end from which he was rescued by hearing—Louis Armstrong.

It is one of the great ironies of jazz history that, in extending the expressive range of the trumpet into the fleeter areas occupied by the keyed instruments, Roy Eldridge sowed the seeds of his own destruction as top man. Soon after his encounter with Louis in 1932, he began to attract the attention of other musicians. He played in a succession of popular bands—with Elmer Snowden, McKinney's Cotton Pickers, Teddy Hill and Fletcher Henderson —as well as leading small groups of his own and appearing on record in 'pick up' or *ad hoc* groups. Though he made impressive, indeed startling, appearances on record with Henderson and small groups led by Joe Marsala, Gene Krupa and Teddy Wilson, it was almost certainly through radio broadcasts that his fame spread. Some of the broadcasts by his own little band from the Three Deuces in Chicago and the Arcadia Ballroom in New York have recently been issued on obscure labels, and they show him more strongly committed to the Armstrong brand of trumpet showmanship than on records, while at the same time exploiting his technical range to the full. It is little wonder that, from the mid-Thirties onwards, he had superseded Louis Armstrong as the exemplar of modern 'hot' trumpet playing. New players and indeed, some formerly committed to the Armstrong style (Buck Clayton with Basie and Taft Jordan with Chick Webb in their fiercer up-tempo moments) began to express themselves in tumbling cascades of notes, at the same time prodding and hustling the beat in the impatient manner that later came to be identified as 'jump' style.

Two men especially presented Eldridge with early competition. One was a New Yorker of great technical facility called Charlie Shavers, six years Roy's junior but capable, as a twenty-year-old with John Kirby's Sextet in 1937, of matching the older man's technical feats. What Shavers lacked, then and in later confrontations with Eldridge in the touring Jazz at the Philharmonic shows, was the passionate intensity which has always underpinned Roy's playing. If Shavers seemed, on many occasions, to be able to match Roy phrase for phrase with greater cleanness of execution, it is because he approached the task in hand with a certain detachment. Comic quotations or passages of mock-sentimentality would often interrupt a Shavers solo in full flood—an inconceivable occurrence with Eldridge, whose notes, phrases and, indeed, actual person often seemed about to disintegrate under the intense emotional pressure.

The other trumpeter who followed Roy Eldridge's lead with even more success in matching the original was a young man called John Birks Gillespie, nicknamed 'Dizzy'. When Roy Eldridge was enjoying his reign as trumpet king at the head of his own little band in 1938–9, Gillespie was occupying his old chair in the brass section of Teddy Hill's Orchestra, whose recordings of 'King Porter Stomp' and 'Blue Rhythm Fantasy' in 1938 show how un-cannily the younger man had assimilated his idol's style. Indeed, it was the chiding of other musicians about his lack of an individual style that spurred Dizzy into making the harmonic and rhythmic experiments which characterized his formative contributions to modern jazz in the mid-Forties.

The arrival of bebop in a burst of publicity, both promotional and adverse, found Roy Eldridge hoist with his own petard. Having wrenched jazz trumpet out of Louis Armstrong's grasp, so to speak, and coerced it into running changes with the headlong speed of a saxophone, he was at the mercy of anyone who came along with an even greater turn of speed and a more complex and advanced set of changes to run. In telling the story, one lapses almost without thinking into the terminology of gladiatorial conflict—'hoist with his own petard', 'wrenched from the grasp', 'at the mercy of' and so on—because, in the circumstances of the mid-Forties, a fight for survival is what it was. The situation is summed up by an often told and probably apocryphal story of a night in 1941 or '42 when Roy, an inveterate sitter-in at after-hours jam sessions, had turned up at Minton's Playhouse, the breeding ground of modern ideas. In an interview with jazz writer Ross Russell, the drummer, Kenny Clarke, recalled the incident:

'Monday night was always a free for all at Minton's. All the young musicians in town would be in the place with their horns, waiting for a chance to get up on the stand and blow. Big name stars used to drop in . . . Charlie Christian, Lester Young and especially Roy Eldridge. Roy was the king. Dizzy Gillespie had started out playing like Roy, but had gotten on the new kick, working out his ideas with Charlie Parker, Thelonious Monk, Nick Fenton and myself. Dizzy could play and his ideas were new, but try as he would, Dizzy could never cut Roy. Roy was just too much. Roy had drive and execution, and he could keep going chorus after chorus. Every time Dizzy tried, Roy gave him a lesson, made him pack. But Dizzy never quit. Then one night, Dizzy came in and started blowing. He got it all together that night. He cut Roy to everyone's satisfaction and that night Roy packed his horn and never came back.' Other even more colourful versions of the story have Roy Eldridge running off the stand in tears.

If the story is hard to swallow as a single, cataclysmic event, it does describe quite accurately the fate which overtook Roy Eldridge in the Forties. The conquest of Roy by Dizzy Gillespie is, indeed, the sort of thing which Louis Armstrong could have suffered at the hands of Roy in the mid-Thirties had he not removed himself *hors de combat* into the securer realms of show-business. We need not pursue the story any further here, other than to observe that the law of the jazz jungle is less savage and unrelenting than such stories as the above suggest. Roy Eldridge did, it is true, suffer a period of collapsing confidence in the late Forties, when all ears were on the 'new' music and it seemed to him that he must either try and conform or be left behind. This kind of bebop-inflicted shell-shock assailed many older musicians at the time, but the aspect of the situation which must have hurt him most was the cold shoulder that he received from the younger men at his beloved after-hours jousting spots. As with some other musicians in the doldrums, it was the impresario, Norman Granz, giving Roy a permanent and honoured place in his *Jazz at the Philharmonic* touring package, who did much to restore his confidence and reputation. No admirer of the young David of the mid-Thirties with his bursting enthusiasm and vitality can fail to find something heart warming in the friendly and often cheerfully erratic bouts which have taken place in the JATP arena in the Fifties and Sixties between Eldridge and Gillespie, two old adversaries reliving past and more acrimonious battles in a spirit of comradeship, in front of audiences that acknowledge each as the master that he is.

But the period with which we are concerned here is the late Thirties when Roy Eldridge was undisputed king. In 1937 his small group, in which his brother Joe played alto saxophone, made a small batch of recordings which set the seal on his ascendancy. Most Eldridge admirers, I imagine, would settle for one of three pieces—'After You've Gone', 'Wabash Stomp' or 'Heckler's Hop' —as an Eldridge masterpiece. The first-named makes fascinating comparison with Louis Armstrong's version of the same piece in 1929. Louis takes it at a stately tempo compared to which Roy's is positively headlong. The contrast between their two styles is underlined in the mid-chorus break, corresponding to the line 'You'll miss the dearest pal you've ever had' in the lyric. Eldridge has not, up to this point, diverged to any degree from the Armstrong manner, except in the overall feeling of impatience in his approach. Indeed, in the way that he follows the opening phrase ('After you've gone') with a little downward phrase to indicate the harmony, in case the accompaniment should overlook or understate it, he reproduces a familiar Armstrong trait. But when it comes to the break, he replaces Armstrong's sparse rhythmic phrases with a cascade of quavers or eighth-notes phrased, in Coleman Hawkins fashion, in pairs (DOOdle-DOOdle-DOOdle) with the first quaver in each pair heavily outweighing the second. After a vocal chorus by Gladys Palmer in which Turner Layton's melody receives rather more attentive treatment than Henry Creamer's lyrics, it is all Eldridge in two choruses that show clearly the lesson in chorus-building which he learnt from Louis. Once again, it is in the breaks, between and in the middle of choruses, that Roy Eldridge departs most drastically from the Armstrong pattern. The break that links the two choruses is absolutely astonishing, approached by a sustained note which Louis would probably have carried over the whole four-bar section in majestic fashion, but which Roy subsequently breaks up into a rapid, shifting, drumming rhythm by the combined use of fast tongueing and alternative or 'fake' fingering. The whole performance is a show-stopping *tour de force* in which each successive break involves more reckless feats of daring than the last.

Despite this formidable display, my own choice for the supreme masterpiece from this batch is 'Heckler's Hop'. In this original composition by Roy Eldridge, the Armstrong style is almost entirely superceded, except in the way in which Roy's own choruses build to a climax. The theme itself, a series of bustling riffs relieved by a 'standard' middle-eight, belongs to the saxophone rather than the trumpet. Harmonically, it offers no more challenge than most Swing Era riff themes, changing its basic chords every two bars and resembling, in this instance, other old swing vehicles such as Count Basie's 'Doggin' Around', Teddy McCrae's 'Broadway' and Charlie Shavers's 'Undecided'. Indeed, when Roy Eldridge bows out for a while after the opening chorus, the alto and piano contributions by Scoops Carry and Teddy Cole are pretty commonplace. Then Roy Eldridge makes his entry. The feeling that one gets from the first bar of his solo is not an unusual one to the jazz connoisseur. From the undistinguished and sometimes turgid surroundings of the Fletcher Henderson and Paul Whiteman bands respectively, Louis Armstrong and Bix Beiderbecke would often leap into clear and unequivocal solo statements that announced, in the opening notes, that the serious business of swinging was about to begin. And the rhythm section would respond eagerly as if a burden had been lifted from its shoulders. In drummer Zutty Singleton, Roy had rhythmic support well equipped to rise to the occasion. Erstwhile associate, close friend and running mate to Louis Armstrong in the heady days in Chicago of the late Twenties, Zutty's driving power could always be felt even when recording conditions obscured the detail. He was raised in New Orleans, and to the end of his days advertised the fact through a drum kit in which all kinds of accoutrements— woodblocks, ratchet, cow-bells—clustered behind a massive bass drum. In these modern times when a solo such as Roy's would inevitably have been pushed along by a riding top cymbal, it is interesting to note that Zutty stays on the snare drum throughout, emphasizing the off-beat with the tightest of press rolls and highlighting the climactic moments with swatting rim shots.

Roy Eldridge's solo starts in a way strikingly similar to the Coleman Hawkins 'Crazy Rhythm' solo discussed earlier, with a nagging riff that seems to rally the band behind him. In the interview quoted above, he says of the saxophone players whom he admired and emulated, 'They might play six bars, and in the seventh would start going into the release [the cadence concluding each eight-bar section] and then the eighth would be all set up for the second eight.' The start of the 'Heckler's Hop' solo exemplifies this. The four bars of riffing lead, in bars five and six, to a natural conclusion. Had Roy cut out after the first note of bar seven and left the rhythm section to vamp through two bars, the result would have been typical of any number of swing solos. Bar nine would then have started all over again with a different set of rhythmically stimulating figures, probably ending as conclusively at the start of bar fifteen. Roy's way, learnt from such master saxists as Hawkins and Carter who were adept at composing on their feet, is to pause momentarily on the first beat of bar seven before scurrying off on a new phrase that spans the release and carries over into the second eight-bar section without paying heed to the 'natural break' at the end of bar eight. In this bridging phrase, the flow of quavers is broken up by a rhythmic device that harks back to Louis Armstrong's 'Weather Bird' *tour de force* and, at the same time, anticipates Charlie Parker and Dizzy Gillespie. In it, the emphasis is suddenly shifted from the notes that fall on the beat to those between it, while the usually strong notes are articulated so softly that they are really only suggested or 'ghosted'.

In the second eight bars, the phrases flow blithely, sounding in bars twelve and thirteen much nearer to Gillespie than Armstrong. Once again, the bridge from this section into the middle-eight is crossed effortlessly, this time by starting the first long phrase of the section a bar early, in bar sixteen. It is interesting to note that this phrase would make perfect sense if it were deferred, to start in bar seventeen. But then it would end conventionally in the fourth bar of the middle-eight, with the second phrase starting in the fifth bar after a breath taken bang in the middle of the section. By bringing the whole thing forward so that the phrases start and end in unexpected places, just as Lester Young did in 'Lady Be Good', Roy Eldridge was showing himself well versed in a practice that has often been listed among the 'innovations' of the boppers.

As always in these analyses I have to stress that niceties which take me a laborious paragraph to describe occur intuitively in an improvised solo. To make too much of them is to risk subduing the *frissons* of surprise and pleasure which they can evoke. So I will focus on just two more key points in the solo. The first occurs at the junction of the two choruses. It is to be expected that a man who learned a crucial lesson in chorus-building from hearing Louis Armstrong play 'Chinatown, My Chinatown' would at some stage in a red-hot solo ascend into the upper register. Roy does so in characteristic fashion. Over the last two bars of the first chorus he holds a top C, oscillating the note with a lip trill or shake as Louis Armstrong so often did. But whereas Louis Armstrong's notes thus sustained would float and shimmer, Roy's positively quiver with excitement as if straining at the leash. From this launching-pad he starts the second chorus with a series of short phrases stabbing at top C, then from some preparatory high F's unleashes an A with a pulverizing force that must have come straight up from the soles of his feet. Many commentators have observed over the years that there have been occasions when Roy Eldridge has generated so much high-pressure emotional intensity that he has seemed on the verge of exploding. Sometimes, especially in later years, the courageously assaulted high notes have come out as little more than a quivering hiss of steam. But in 'Heckler's Hop' everything was going Roy's way, and the top A, encouraged by some intensified thwacking of the off-beat by Zutty Singleton, squeals defiantly. It is not in any sense a display of exhibitionistic fireworks, as some contemporary critics with a suspicion of technical agility were wont to suggest. The phrase which Roy Eldridge plays is in itself constructive, raising the tension of the second chorus in much the same way that Louis Armstrong would do. The fact that it carries him way above the normal range of the trumpet gives added excitement.

To have reached such an explosive climax half-way through a chorus would present any soloist with the problem of sustaining the tension and excitement. Other trumpeters with similar technical endowments—and indeed, Roy Eldridge himself with Jazz at the Philharmonic in later years—might have succumbed to the temptation to continue belabouring the upper register, inevitably invoking the law of diminishing returns. On this occasion, fully in charge of both the instrument and himself, Roy resumes the running quavers with sustained invention. Careering again over the junction between the first and second eight-bar sections, he starts the latter with a favourite device of his, a chromatic run of quaver or eighth-note triplets from the third up to the fifth and back. It is a phrase that was to become an Eldridge trade-mark (it occurs twice, stratospherically, in 'After You've Gone') and a much abused cliché among his imitators.

In this instance, Roy shows at once the total control he has over events. In the second and fourth bars of the second eight-bar section, the flow of quavers is interrupted by two relatively long, stressed notes, the first started ahead of the beat, the second right on it. The phrase is perfectly balanced not only rhythmically but harmonically also, the notes in question being 'passing notes' (i.e. the flattened seventh *en route* to the sub-dominant chord and the flattened sixth leading back to the tonic) promoted above their station in life. The shifting of emphasis from the strong to the weak notes in a melody line became, like the stressing of weak beats, common practice among the boppers.

The hints of things to come to be found in the playing of Roy Eldridge and other giants of the Swing Era must not be exaggerated. Too much ink has been spilled in vain by jazz historians trying to trace a clear evolutionary line from Buddy Bolden to the present day. The point that should emerge from these passing observations is that, as most of its still-active founders such as Dizzy Gillespie now insist, bebop was not some sort of revolutionary manifesto, a point by point refutation of, and departure from, everything that had gone before. From the moment when, in the Twenties, Louis Armstrong demonstrated the possibilities inherent in extended solo improvisation, the use of more complex harmonies, greater rhythmic variation, new ways of starting, developing and finishing a solo, different approaches to tone production and so on were inevitable. They began to emerge at all kinds of random points during the Thirties. The idea, unfortunately embedded in many jazz histories, that the boppers invented a new music out of disgust and boredom with all that preceded them does not bear a second's investigation. Indeed, the reverse is true. They were inspired and stimulated by players such as Coleman Hawkins, Art Tatum, Lester Young and Roy Eldridge, just as those musicians acknowledged the influence of *their* predecessors.

If I seem to have turned aside from 'Heckler's Hop' rather abruptly at the point at which Roy Eldridge's two choruses end, it is because, alas, the tenor-saxophone solo which follows demonstrates that it was not *every* saxophonist who had something to teach him in terms of speed and fluency! Luckily, Roy's contribution establishes such momentum that we have hardly finished boggling at its audacity before he is back again with a reprise of the theme, a climactic coda and a casually pipped top A that seems to challenge all-comers with a defiant 'Follow that!'

Bibliography

Albertson, Chris. *Bessie*. Barrie & Jenkins, 1972

Armstrong, Louis. *Satchmo: My Life in New Orleans*. Peter Davies, 1955

Balliett, Whitney. *The Sound of Surprise*. William Kimber, 1960

Bechet, Sidney. *Treat It Gentle*. Cassell, 1960

Blesh, Rudi. *Shining Trumpets*. Da Capo Press, 1945

Blesh, Rudi, and Harriet Janis. *They All Played Ragtime*. Alfred Knopf, 1950

Brunn, H. O. *The Story of the Original Dixieland Jazz Band*. Sidgwick & Jackson, 1961

Chilton, John. *Who's Who in Jazz*. Chilton Book Co., 1970

——. *Billie's Blues*. Quartet Books, 1975

Condon, Eddie. *We Called it Music*. Peter Davies, 1948

Dance, Stanley. *The World of Duke Ellington*. Macmillan, 1970

___. *The World of Earl Hines*. Scribner, NY. 1977

Ellington, Duke. *Music is My Mistress*. W. H. Allen, 1974

Feather, Leonard. *The Encyclopedia of Jazz*. Horizon Press

Foster, Pops, as told to Tom Stoddard. *Pops Foster: The Autobiography of a New Orleans Jazzman*. University of California Press, 1971

Freeman, Bud. *You Don't Look Like a Musician*. Balamp Publishing, 1974

Hammond, John. *John Hammond on Record*. Ridge Press, 1977

Handy, W. C. *Father of the Blues*. Sidgwick & Jackson, 1957

Harris, Rex. *Jazz*. Pelican Books, 1952

Harvey, Eddie. *Teach Yourself Jazz Piano*. English University Press, 1974

Hentoff, Nat and Nat Shapiro. *Hear Me Talkin' To Ya*. Peter Davies, 1955

——. *The Jazz Makers*. Peter Davies, 1958

Hodeir, André. *Jazz: Its Evolution and Essence*. Secker and Warburg, 1956

Holiday, Billie. *Lady Sings the Blues*. Barrie Books, 1958

Hughes, Spike. *Second Movement*. Museum Press, 1951

Jones, Max and John Chilton. *Louis: The Louis Armstrong Story 1900-1971*. Studio Vista, 1971

Kirkeby, Ed. *Ain't Misbehavin'*. Peter Davies, 1966

Lambert, Constant. *Music Ho!* Faber and Faber, 1934

Lomax, Alan. *Mister Jelly Roll*. Cassell, 1952

Mezzrow, Milton 'Mezz', and Bernard Wolfe. *Really the Blues*. Secker & Warburg, 1946

Oliver, Paul. *The Story of the Blues*. Barrie/Cresset, 1972

Rust, Brian. *Jazz Records 1897 to 1942 A–Z*. Storyville Publications & Co.

Schuller, Gunther. *Early Jazz: Its Roots and Musical Development*. Oxford University Press, 1968

Smith, Jay D. and Len Gutteridge. *Jack Teagarden*. Cassell, 1960

Smith, Willie 'The Lion', with George Hoefer. *Music On My Mind*. McGibbon and Kee, 1965

Stewart, Rex. *Jazz Masters of the 30's*. Macmillan, 1972

Sudhalter, Richard and Philip Evans. *Bix: Man and Legend*. Quartet Books, 1974

Vance, Joel. *Fats Waller: His Life and Times*. Robson Books, 1979

Waller, Maurice and Anthony Calabrese. *Fats Waller*. Cassell, 1977

Williams, Martin. *Jazz Panorama*. The Cromwell-Collier Press. 1958